ISBN 978-0-282-58955-4
PIBN 10858083

English
Français
Deutsche
Italiano
Español
Português

www.forgottenbooks.com

Mythology Photography **Fiction**
Fishing Christianity **Art** Cooking
Essays Buddhism Freemasonry
Medicine **Biology** Music **Ancient**
Egypt Evolution Carpentry Physics
Dance Geology **Mathematics** Fitness
Shakespeare **Folklore** Yoga Marketing
Confidence Immortality Biographies
Poetry **Psychology** Witchcraft
Electronics Chemistry History **Law**
Accounting **Philosophy** Anthropology
Alchemy Drama Quantum Mechanics
Atheism Sexual Health **Ancient History**
Entrepreneurship Languages Sport
Paleontology Needlework Islam
Metaphysics Investment Archaeology
Parenting Statistics Criminology
Motivational

A STATISTICAL ACCOUNT OF BENGAL.

VOL. XIX.

MURRAY AND GIBB, EDINBURGH,
PRINTERS TO HER MAJESTY'S STATIONERY OFFICE.

A STATISTICAL ACCOUNT OF BENGAL.

BY W. W. HUNTER, B.A., LL.D.,

DIRECTOR-GENERAL OF STATISTICS TO THE GOVERNMENT OF INDIA;

ONE OF THE COUNCIL OF THE ROYAL ASIATIC SOCIETY; HONORARY OR FOREIGN MEMBER OF THE
ROYAL INSTITUTE OF NETHERLANDS INDIA AT THE HAGUE, OF THE INSTITUTO VASCO
DA GAMA OF PORTUGUESE INDIA, OF THE DUTCH SOCIETY IN JAVA, AND OF
THE ETHNOLOGICAL SOCIETY, LONDON; HONORARY FELLOW OF
THE CALCUTTA UNIVERSITY; ORDINARY FELLOW OF
THE ROYAL GEOGRAPHICAL SOCIETY, ETC.

VOLUME XIX.

DISTRICT OF PURI AND THE ORISSA TRIBUTARY STATES.

TRÜBNER & CO., LONDON 1877.

PREFACE

TO VOLUME XIX. OF

THE STATISTICAL ACCOUNT OF BENGAL.

———◆———

THIS Volume treats of the British District of Purí and the nineteen Tributary States of Orissa ; thus completing the Orissa Division, and concluding the Statistical Account of Bengal. Purí District exhibits a. more varied aspect than either Cuttack or Balasor. The sea-board consists of a belt of sandy ridges, forming, towards the Madras frontier, the long bare spit of land which divides the great Chilká lake from the ocean. Behind this belt lies a rich intervening region of villages and rice fields, interspersed with inundated tracts. The background rises in stony undulations and isolated cliffs to meet the hill ranges of the Tributary States. In this broken country is situated the Government Estate of Khurdhá, which, both in its physical aspect and administrative requirements, exhibits the transition from the peaceful, thickly - peopled Delta, to the wild jungles and mountain passes of the interior. The District is rich in historical remains, from the primitive rock-hewn caves of Buddhism, — the earliest relics of Indian architecture, — to the mediæval Sun Temple at Kanárak, and the world-renowned shrine in Purí town itself, the seat of Lord Jagannáth.

The Tributary States occupy a succession of ranges rolling upwards to the plateau of Central India. The monotony of their wooded glens and towering peaks is only interrupted by the valleys of the Mahánadí, the Bráhmaní, and Baitaraní, here, as in the plains, the three great rivers of Orissa. Hid away in these natural fastnesses, the aboriginal tribes continue to enjoy the freedom which they love, under the nominal rule of hereditary Hindu chiefs. The Paramount British Power rarely interferes; but it is promptly felt wherever anarchy or outrage has to be repressed, or commerce encouraged. The natural difficulties of communication have, so far, shut off the mineral resources of this region from the approach of European capital.

The total area dealt with in this Volume amounts to 18,690 square miles, containing in 1872 a population of 2,052,983 souls.

W. W. H.

TABLE OF CONTENTS:

DISTRICT OF PURI AND THE ORISSA TRIBUTARY STATES.

———

DISTRICT OF PURI.

DISTRICT OF PURI—*continued.*

The People—*continued.*

THE ORISSA TRIBUTARY STATES.

APPENDIX.

I shall be grateful for any corrections or suggestions which occur to the reader. They may be addressed to me, at the India Office, Westminster.

W. W. H.

DISTRICT OF PURI

AND

THE ORISSA TRIBUTARY STATES.

STATISTICAL ACCOUNT

OF THE

DISTRICT OF PURI.[1]

———•———

PURI forms the southern District of the Orissa Commissionership or Division. It is situated between 19° 27′ 40″ and
20° 26′ 20″ north latitude, and between 85° 0′ 26″ and 86° 28′ 0″
east longitude. It contains a total area, as returned by the Surveyor-
General in January 1876, of 2472·37 square miles; and a population,
as ascertained by the Census of 1872, of 769,674 souls. The principal town, which is also the administrative headquarters of the
District, is Purí or Jagannáth, situated on the shore of the Bay of
Bengal, in 19° 48′ 17″ north latitude, and 85° 51′ 39″ east longitude.

[1] This Statistical Account has been mainly compiled from my work on Orissa
(2 vols. London 1872; Smith, Elder, and Co.), supplemented by the following
other materials :—(1) Annual Administration Reports of the Government of
Bengal from 1871-72 to 1874-75; (2) Bengal Census Report for 1872, with
subsequent District Compilation by Mr. C. F. Magrath, C.S. ; (3) Report on
the Food-Grain Supply of Bengal, by Mr. A. P. MacDonnell, C.S. (Calcutta
1876); (4) Report on the Land Tenures of Purí, by Bábu Nandakisor Das,
dated 21st October 1875; (5) Report by the Collector on the Rates of Rent,
dated 24th September 1872; (6) Report of the Commissioners appointed to
inquire into the Famine in Bengal and Orissa in 1866; (7) *The Statistical Reporter*
(Calcutta); (8) Report of the Inspector-General of Police for 1872; (9) Report
of the Inspector-General of Jails for 1872, with special Jail Statistics for the years
1857-58, 1860-61, and 1870; (10) Annual Report of the Director of Public Instruction for 1872-73, with special Statistics compiled for the years 1856-57, 1860-61,
and 1870-71 ; (11) Postal Statistics for 1861-62, 1865-66, and 1870-71, furnished
by the Director-General of Post Offices ; (12) Report on the Charitable Dispensaries of Bengal for 1871 and 1872; (13) Report of the Meteorological Department
for 1873.

BOUNDARIES.—Purí District is bounded on the north by the Tributary States of Bánkí and Athgarh; on the east and north-east by the District of Cuttack; on the south-east and south by the Bay of Bengal; and on the west by the Madras District of Ganjám, and by the Tributary State of Ranpur. The greatest length of Purí District, from Nandlá, on the south-east of the Chilká lake, to the mouth of the Káloí river beyond Márichpur, is ninety miles.

GENERAL DESCRIPTION OF THE DISTRICT.—A belt of sandy ridges, the home of the black antelope, stretches along the entire sea-shore of Purí, varying from four miles to a few hundred yards in width. The District generally may be divided into three tracts : west, middle, and east. The western extends from the right bank of the Dayá across the stone country of Dándimál and Khurdhá, till it rises into the hills of the Tributary States. The middle is the delta, watered by the Bhárgaví branch of the Mahánadí, and comprising the richest and most populous *parganás* of the District. The eastern portion runs from the left bank of the Kusbhadrá to the boundary of Cuttack. It is less thickly peopled, and in the extreme east loses itself in the jungles around the mouths of the Deví river.

The western division contains the only mountains that are to be found in the District. A low range, beginning in Dompárá and running south-east in an irregular line towards the Chilká lake, forms a watershed between Purí District and the valley of the Mahánadí. Almost all the peaks sufficiently important to have names are within the Subdivision of Khurdhá. Most of them are covered with dense jungle. They are too steep for carriages; but, except where the bare rock is exposed towards the summit, they are accessible to ponies. On the north of the Chilká, they are bold and very varied in shape. They throw out spurs and promontories into the lake, forming island - studded bays, with fertile valleys running far inland between their ridges. The middle and eastern divisions consist entirely of alluvial plains. They form the south-western part of the Mahánadí delta, and are watered by a network of channels, through which the most southerly branch of that river, the Koyákhái, finds its way into the sea.

RIVER SYSTEM.—The following scheme briefly exhibits the river system of Purí District :—

Koyákhái
{
Kusbhadrá
{
Práchí
Kusbhadrá
}
Kusbhadrá
}
Bay of Ben-gal.
{
Bhárgaví
Nún
Dayá
}
Bhárgaví
Dayá
}
Chilká lake.
Bhárgaví
{
Bhárgaví

All these rivers are navigable by large boats during the rainy season. None of them is deep enough for boats of 100 *maunds*, or say four tons burden, throughout the whole year. Only one of them, the Kusbhadrá, enters the sea. It follows a very winding course, and is of little value for navigation. Its bed has silted up, and its floods devastate the surrounding country. The three rivers most important to the people of Purí are the Bhárgaví, the Dayá, and the Nún. These all enter the Chilká lake after running widely diverse courses. In the rainy season they come down in tremendous floods, which burst the banks and carry everything before them. In the dry weather, they die away till nothing is left but a series of long shallow pools in the midst of vast expanses of sand. Their banks are generally abrupt, and in many parts are artificially raised and protected by strong dykes. The total length of Government embankments in Purí District amounted in 1866 to 316¾ miles, with forty-three sluices, maintained at an annual cost of £7, 16s. per mile. The following table shows the capacity of the principal rivers in the rainy season, and the number of breaches which they made in their embankments in 1866 :—

PURI RIVERS AT A SECTION HALF-WAY BETWEEN CUTTACK CITY AND THE SEA.

Names of Rivers.	Fall per Mile at Point of Section.	Mean Depth of Section.	Calculated Velocity by Etelwyn's Formula.	Calculated Discharge per Second.	Number of Breaches made in 1866.
	Feet.	Feet.	Feet.	Cubic Feet.	
Kusbhadrá, . . .	1·70	10·64	5·40	9,855	} 8
Práchí, ...	1·70	10·43	5·40	9,580	
Bhárgaví, . . .	1·45	15·42	6·00	59,220	8
Dayá, ...	1·70	16·78	6·80	33,100	36*
	A. vi·64	Av. 13·31	Av. 5·90	111,755	52

* Including the smaller tributaries.

DISTRIBUTION OF THE WATER SUPPLY.—From a reference to the map, it will be seen, therefore, that of the 111,755 cubic feet per second poured down upon Purí, the Kusbhadrá, with its branch the Práchí, obtains only 19,435 cubic feet with which to water the eastern part of the District. Of the remaining 92,320 cubic feet, about two-thirds is carried off by the Bhárgaví, and after watering the middle part of the District, finds its way, by a most tortuous course for many miles almost parallel to the sea, into the Chilká lake. On its way it forms a series of marshes and backwaters; one of which, the Sar lake, to the north-east of Purí town, is four miles long from east to west, and two miles broad from north to south. It has no outlet to the sea, and is separated from it by desolate sandy ridges. It is utilized neither for navigation nor to any extent for fisheries. The sandy desert that divides it from the Bay is destitute of population; and on the north, a few miserable hovels at wide intervals dot its shores. Its waters, however, are used for irrigation when the rainfall proves deficient. The Dayá spreads its 33,000 cubic feet of water per second over the south-western part of Purí. It also receives a few small tributaries from the watershed which separates the District from the upper valley of the Mahánadí. During the rainy season, boats of twenty tons burden carry on a traffic between Cuttack and the Chilká lake by means of its main stream. Towards the Chilká, it divides into many channels, and the Fiscal Divisions (*parganás*) in the lower part of its course are annually devastated by resistless floods. Full details will be found of one of these calamities in a later section of this Statistical Account. The following brief remarks may, however, be fitly made here. The total cost to Government of inundations in Purí District amounted, for construction of embankments, etc., and remission of revenue alone, to £79,963 in fifteen years, equivalent to a charge of ten per cent. on the total land revenue of the District. In addition to this large sum, it is shown that the single flood of 1866 destroyed standing crops to the value of £643,683 in Purí District alone, notwithstanding that 10,620 acres of fertile land are permanently left untilled for fear of inundation. The truth is, that the Mahánadí, in time of flood, pours double the quantity of water into the Purí rivers that their channels are capable of carrying to the sea. The result is, that the surplus overflows in spite of embankments and protective works. The whole District lives in readiness for such calamities; and the deaths by drowning reported to the police, during the three years ending in 1870, averaged only 117 per annum. These figures, however, by no means represent the total loss of life from this cause. The excessive floods also depreciate the productive powers of the soil; and in the localities most subject to inundations, the rents are brought down to one-fifth of the rates obtained for the same quality of land in parts of the District protected from the violence of the rivers. Of the twenty-four Fiscal Divisions (*pargan̄ás*) of the District, twelve are still so completely at the mercy of the rivers that more than fifty per cent. of their area was flooded in 1866. In Sayyidábád and Domárkhand, two *pargan̄ás* of which less than twenty-five per cent. is liable to inundations, the average rate of rent for two-crop land is Rs. 1. 10. 8 or 3s. 4d. per acre. In Chaubiskud and Sirái, two *pargan̄ás* of which more than fifty per cent. is liable to inundations, the average rate for the same quality of land is 14 *án̄ás* or 1s. 9d. In Domárkhand the average rate of winter rice land is Rs. 2. 6. 4 or 4s. 9½d.; in Chaubiskud and Sirái, it is R. 0. 11. 6 or 1s. 5¼d. If, instead of the average rent, the highest rates were taken in these *pargan̄ás*, the difference becomes still greater.

PORTS AND HARBOURS.—PURÍ PORT is nothing but an unprotected roadstead. It is open, for import and export trade, from the middle of September to the middle of March. During the other six months of the year, the surf does not allow of ships being laden or unladen. It is, therefore, at a disadvantage as compared with the Balasor and Cuttack ports. The vessels that frequent Purí consist chiefly of country brigs, and occasionally a barque with an English master. They lie at a distance of about half a mile from the shore, in good weather. All goods are landed through the surf in *masulá* boats, and are received into a customs shed erected a few years ago. The trade consists almost entirely of shipments of rice to the Madras coast, and occasionally to the Mauritius. The Purí minor ports (such as Máchhgáon) are of very little importance, their trade being so insignificant that no establishment is kept up at them; but, in the event of any ships calling there, the Collector of Purí deputes one of his establishment from headquarters to look after the landing or shipment of the cargo. The following table exhibits the sea-borne trade of Purí (including minor ports) for the year 1866-67, and for each of the seven years from 1868-69 to 1874-75:—

IMPORTS AND EXPORTS OF PURI HARBOUR.

Year.	Number of Vessels entered.	Tonnage.	Value of Imports.	Value of Exports.	Total Value of Trade.
			£	£	£
1866-67,*	...	12,719	114,811	*nil.*	114,811
1868-69,	10	4,140	3,937	8,352	12,289
1869-70,	37	6,576	483	2,252	2,735
1870-71,	21	5,426	229	2,239	2,468
1871-72,	33	4,553	735	1,885	2,620
1872-73,	31	5,316	749	1,955	2,704
1873-74,	33	10,371	352	3,150	3,502
1874-75,	32	10,553	544	5,522	6,066

Horsburgh's Sailing Directions give the following instructions for making Purí roadstead :—'The Jagannáth pagodas are three large circular buildings surrounded by several smaller ones. They are of conical form. The westernmost pagoda is the largest, and the easternmost the smallest of the three. They are nearly all in one bearing, W. by N. When brought to bear N.W., they begin to appear separated. When N.N.W., they are perceived to be distinct buildings. Lat. 19° 48′ 21″ N., long. 85° 54′ E.' The latitude and longitude as corrected by the Surveyor-General of India are, lat. 19° 48′ 17″ N., long. 85° 51′ 39″ E.

MACHHGAON.—The only other port in Purí District worthy of mention is Máchhgáon, near the mouth of the Deví river, on the borders of Cuttack. A considerable export rice trade is conducted ; but the silting up of the channel renders the approach perilous to sea-going ships, and involves heavy expenses for lading and unlading by means of cargo-boats. The value of the trade is included in the foregoing table. The mouth of the Chilká lake was once an excellent harbour, and would still be so but for its constant silting up. It is at present wholly impracticable.

THE CHILKA LAKE.— The only lakes of any importance in Purí District are the Sar and the Chilká. The former has been briefly described above as a backwater of the Bhárgaví river. The latter is a shallow inland sea situated in the extreme south-east corner of Orissa. A long strip of land, which for miles consists of nothing but a sandy ridge little more than two hundred yards wide, separates

* This was the year of the great Orissa famine. The imports consisted solely of rice for the relief of the starving population.

it from the ocean; and the roaring of the exterior unseen surf can be heard far across the lake. On the west, it is walled in by lofty mountains, in some places descending perpendicularly upon the margin, and in others thrusting out gigantic arms and promontories of rock into the water. On the south, it is bounded by the hilly watershed which forms the natural frontier between Orissa and Madras. To the northward, it loses itself in endless shallows, sedgy banks, and islands just peeping above the surface, formed year by year from the silt which the great rivers bring down. A single narrow mouth, cut through the sandy ridge, connects it with the sea. Through this, the tide comes rushing and storming against the outward currents; at certain seasons throwing itself up in pyramidal billows topped with spray, and looking like a boiling torrent, in which no boat could live.

Thus hemmed in between the mountains and the sea, the Chilká spreads itself out into a pear-shaped expanse of water forty-four miles long, of which the northern half has a mean breadth of twenty miles, while the southern half tapers into an irregularly curved point, barely averaging five miles wide. Its smallest area is returned at 344 square miles in the dry weather, extending to about 450 during the rainy season. Its average depth is from three to five feet, and scarcely anywhere exceeds six feet. The bed of the lake is a very few feet below the level of sea high-water, although in some parts slightly below low-water mark. The distant inner portions of the lake keep about two feet higher than the exterior ocean, at all stages of the tide. The neck which joins it to the sea is only a few hundred yards broad; so that the narrow tidal stream which rushes through it is speedily lost in the wide interior expanse, and produces a difference never greater than four feet between high and low water, and at times barely eighteen inches, while the tide outside rises and falls five feet. It suffices, however, to keep the lake distinctly salt during the dry months from December to June. But once the rains have set in, and the rivers come pouring down upon its northern extremity, the sea-water is gradually driven out, and the Chilká passes through various stages of brackishness into a fresh-water lake.

This changeable inland sea forms one of a series of lacustrine formations down the western shores of the Bay of Bengal. The strong monsoon and violent currents, which sweep from the south during eight months of the year, have thrown up ridges of sand, in some places rising into lofty yellow cliffs along the coast. A per-

petual war goes on between the rivers and the sea—the former
struggling to find vent for their columns of water and silt, the latter
repelling them with its sand-laden currents. Where the river has
the complete mastery, it sweeps out to the ocean, scouring for itself
a channel through the sand. When the forces are so equal as
materially to counteract each other, a stagnation takes place, the sea
depositing a bar outside the river mouth, while the river pushes out
its delta to right and left inside. But when the river comes down
languid or too widely diffused, the victory is with the sea. The
sand-laden tides and currents of the Bay throw up a beach across
the mouth, which chokes the river and causes the formation of a
lake behind it.

The Chilká lake may be regarded as a gulf of the original Bay
of Bengal, lying between two promontories, and only partially filled
up. On the south, a bold, barren spur of hills runs down to the Bay
of Bengal. On the north, the land-making rivers have pushed out
their rounded mouths and flat deltas into the ocean. Nor has the
sea been idle, but, meeting and overmastering the languid river
discharge that enters the Chilká, it has joined the two promontories
with a bar of sand, and thus formed a lake. At this moment both
agencies are busily at work. The delicate process of land-making
from the river silt at the north-east end of the lake is slowly but
steadily going on, while the bar-building sea visibly plies its trade
across its mouth. I find, from old documents, that a century ago
the neck of land was only half a mile to a mile broad, in places
where it is now two. On the other hand, the opening in the bar
was a mile wide in 1780, and had to be crossed in large boats.
Forty years later this opening was described as choked up. Shortly
before 1825 an artificial mouth had to be cut; and although this also
rapidly began to silt up, it remained, as late as 1837, more than
three times the breadth that it is now. The villagers allege
that it still grows narrower every year. Indeed, so steady a worker
is the ocean, that the difficulty in maintaining an outlet from the
Chilká forms one of the chief obstacles to utilizing the lake as an
escapement for the floods that desolate the delta. Engineers report
that although it would be easy and cheap to cut a channel, it would
be very costly and difficult to keep it open; and that each successive
mouth would speedily choke up and share the fate of its predecessor.

The scenery of the Chilká is very varied, and in parts exceedingly
picturesque. In the south and west, hill ranges bound its 'shores.

In this part, its surface is dotted with a number of small rocky islands, described by Mr. Stirling in vol. xv. of the *Asiatic Researches* as 'huge rounded blocks of a highly indurated porphyritic granite, containing large crystals of felspar, tossed and piled on each other in the wildest confusion, and exhibiting every symptom of violent convulsion and disturbance. Some of the masses are arranged in the form of fortresses with huge round bastions, and others present the appearance of the ruins of some grand ancient edifice.' Proceeding northwards, the lake expands into a majestic sheet of water. Halfway across is Nalbana, literally the Reed Forest, an island about five miles in circumference, scarcely anywhere rising more than a few inches above the level of water. This island is altogether uninhabited, but is regularly visited by parties of thatchers from the mainland, who cut the reeds and high grasses, with which it is completely covered. On the eastern side of the lake lie the islands of Párikud, which have silted up behind, and are now partially joined to the narrow ridge of land which separates the Chilká from the sea. At some places, they emerge almost imperceptibly from the water; at others, they spread out into well-raised rice fields. Their north-western extremity slopes gracefully down to the lake, like an English park, dotted with fine trees and backed by noble masses of foliage. Salt-making is largely carried on in Párikud, by a process described in a subsequent section of this Statistical Account (*vide* pp. 151-152). Beyond the northern end of Párikud, the lake gradually shallows until it becomes solid ground. At this point the Purí rivers empty themselves into the lake, and the process of land-making, described above, is here going on steadily. The northern shores of the Chilká comprise the *parganás* of Sirái and Chaubiskud, and it is these tracts which have to bear the greatest suffering in times of general inundation.

UTILIZATION OF THE WATER SUPPLY.—Artificial irrigation is used in a few *parganás* for the rice cultivation. The difficulty, however, is to keep the rivers from flooding the crops, rather than in leading it on to the fields. Salt is extensively manufactured from the brackish water of the Chilká lake, by the process of solar evaporation. Fishing is largely carried on along the sea coast, and in the rivers. The Bengal Census Report returns the number of Hindu fishing and boating castes in Purí District at 30,073 souls, or 4·0 per cent. of the Hindus, who form 96·1 per cent. of the total population of the District. The foregoing figures only represent the professional

Hindu fishermen; practically, all the labouring and cultivating castes fish when opportunity offers. No important fishing towns have grown up in Purí, and the fish caught are consumed by the local population. The right of fishing is vested by Government in the landholders, and is included in the general Settlement for the land revenue of their estates. The total sum paid into the treasury under this head amounts to about £157 a year.

FORESTS.—There are no revenue-paying forests; but the jungles in the hilly part of the District yield honey, bees-wax, *tasar* silk, the dye called *gundi*, and various medicinal drugs. Tribes of Savars, Kandhs, and Baurís live by trading in jungle products. The timber trees of the District comprise *sál*, *sísu*, ebony (*kendu*), jack-wood, mango, *piásál*, *kurmá*, and all the common varieties. Bamboo is plentiful. The rattan-cane abounds. The palms include the cocoa-nut, palmyra, and date. Oil is manufactured from the cocoa-nut and *pulang* among trees, and from rape and mustard among seeds.

FERÆ NATURÆ.—In the open part of the country, the larger wild beasts have been nearly exterminated. Of the following list, several are now becoming rare :—Tigers, leopards, bison, buffalo, wild cows, hyenas, bears, wild pigs, wild dogs, antelopes, *sambhar*-deer, hog-deer, and *kurangas* (small deer). Crocodiles swarm in the lower parts of the rivers. The sum spent in keeping down tigers and leopards does not exceed £5 a year. The number of deaths from wild beasts and snakes formally reported to the police amounted to 93 in 1869. Snakes are very numerous. Among pythons, are the *ajagar* and *ahiráj*. Among deadly snakes, are the black cobra (*keutá*), the *tampa*, the *gokhurá*, and the spotted slow-killing *borá*. Among water-snakes, are the *dhemná* and *dhanrá*, etc. *Nág* is the generic name for a variety of serpents. Among smaller wild beasts, are jackals, foxes, hares, monkeys of many species, porcupines, and squirrels in immense numbers. Among land birds, are the pea-fowl, jungle-fowl, partridge, golden plover, ortolan, dove, green pigeon (*párá*), owl, vulture, eagle, hawk, kite, crow, and jay, besides the ordinary kinds of smaller tree-birds. On the Chilká lake are found the flamingo, wild goose, Bráhmaní duck, wild duck of various sorts, teal (*bálihán*s), snipe, *pánikud*, crane, and *gaganbhel*. Of paddy birds, the five following are most common—the *kantiyábag*, the *dhalá*, the *rám*, the *kuji*, and the *tár*.

Of fishes there is an endless variety. Among salt-water fish, the most important are the *khaingá*, *dáhángiri*, *ilsá*, or, as it is usually called by Europeans, *hilsa ;* the *khuránti, chandí, bhekti, patá, jhuranga, kantábalangí, phirki, kokali,* and *sahália.* Among fresh-water fish, are the *rohi, bhákur, gágar saul, käu, tori, bami, karandi, ratá, bália, guáchopi,* and *chitál.* There are also turtles, tortoises, crabs, prawns, and oysters. There is no trade in wild-beast skins, nor are the *feræ naturæ,* with the exception of the fisheries, made to contribute in any way to the wealth of the District. The oysters are large and coarse, but palatable when cooked, and not unpleasant even in their raw state, after the eye has become accustomed to their size and colour. No attempt has been made to improve the oyster-beds, or to turn them into a subject of commerce.

POPULATION.—A Census roughly taken by the police, in 1854, returned the population of Puri District at 700,000 souls. In 1866, after the famine, the houses were counted by the police; and after allowing five inhabitants to each, the population was estimated at 528,712. In 1869 the houses were again counted by the police, and returned at 108,199, which would give a population, calculating at the rate of five inmates to each house, of 540,995. A general Census of the District was taken by authority of Government between the 19th and 26th January 1872, the results of which disclosed a total population of 769,674 persons, dwelling in 3175 villages, and inhabiting 143,920 houses; average density of the population, 311 per square mile; average number of inhabitants per village, 242; average number of persons per house, 5·3. An account of the method adopted in carrying out the enumeration will be found in my Statistical Account of Cuttack District (vol. xviii. pp. 61-63). The following table (p. 28), exhibiting the area, population, etc. of each police circle (*tháná*) in Puri District, is reproduced *verbatim* from the General Census Report of Bengal.

POPULATION CLASSIFIED ACCORDING TO SEX, RELIGION, AND AGE.—The total population of Puri District consisted, in January 1872, of 769,674 souls; namely, 389,449 males, and 380,225 females. The proportion of males in the total population was 50·6 per cent., and the average density of the population, 311 persons to the square mile. Classifying the population according to religion and age, the Census gives the following results :—Hindus—under twelve years of age, males 132,792, and females 118,394; total, 251,186 : above twelve years, males 241,434, and females 247,016; total, 488,450.

[*Sentence continued on page* 29.

ABSTRACT OF POPULATION, ETC. OF EACH POLICE CIRCLE (THANA) IN PURI DISTRICT, 1872.

SUBDIVISION.	Tháná.	Area in Square Miles.	Number of Villages, Mausás, or Townships.	Number of Houses.	Total Population.	Averages calculated by the Census Officers.				
						Persons per Square Mile.	Villages, Mausás, or Townships per Square Mile.	Persons per Village, Mausá, or Township.	Houses per Square Mile.	Persons per House.
HEADQUARTERS SUBDIVISION,	Puri,	398	588	34,468	172,207	432	1·49	293	86	5·0
	Gop,	337	600	20,219	96,096	285	1·79	160	60	4·7
	Pipplí,	325	819	38,427	204,375	629	2·52	249	118	5·3
	Labbá,*	470	119	2,878	16,073	34	0·25	135	6	5·6
	Subdivisional Total,	1,530	2,126	95,992	488,751	319	1·38	229	62	5·0
KHURDHA SUB-DIVISION,	Khurdhá,	583	627	34,632	204,272	350	1·07	325	59	5·9
	Tánghí,	109	164	5,517	33,416	306	1·50	203	50	6·0
	Bánpur,	251	258	7,779	43,235	172	1·02	167	31	5·5
	Subdivisional Total,	943	1,049	47,928	280,923	298	1·11	267	51	5·7
	District Total,	2,473	3,175	143,920	769,674	311	1·28	242	58	5·3

* The Chilká lake is comprised in this *tháná*, and occupies 313 square miles of its area, exclusive of 31 square miles beyond the Bengal boundary.

Sentence continued from page 27.]

Total of Hindus of all ages, males 374,226, and females 365,410; grand total, 739,636, or 96·1 per cent. of the District population; proportion of males in total Hindus, 50·6 per cent. Muhammadans —under twelve years of age, males 2333, and females 1921; total, 4254: above twelve years, males 3606, and females 3726; total, 7332. Total of Muhammadans of all ages, males 5939, and females 5647; grand total, 11,586, or 1·5 per cent. of the District population; proportion of males in total Musalmáns, 51·3 per cent. Buddhists—under twelve years of age, *nil:* above twelve years, males 5, and females 3; total, 8. Christians—under twelve years of age, males 106, and females 143; total, 249: above twelve years, males 164, and females 163; total, 327. Total Christians of all ages, males 270, and females 306; grand total, 576, or ·1 per cent. of the District population; proportion of males in total Christians, 46·9 per cent. Other denominations not separately classified in the Census Report, consisting principally of aboriginal tribes, and peoples still professing their primitive forms of faith—under twelve years of age, males 3398, and females 3285; total, 6683: above twelve years, males 5616, and females 5577; total, 11,193. Total 'others' of all ages, males 9014, and females 8862; grand total, 17,876, or 2·3 per cent. of the District population; proportion of males in total 'others,' 50·4 per cent. Population of all denominations—under twelve years of age, males 138,629, and females 123,743; total, 262,372: above twelve years, males 250,820, and females 256,482; total, 507,302. Total population of all ages, males 389,449, and females 380,225; grand total, 769,674; proportion of males in total District population, 50·6 per cent.

The percentage of children not exceeding twelve years of age in the population of different religions is returned in the Census Report as follows:—Hindus, male children 18·0, and female children 16·0 per cent.; proportion of children of both sexes, 34·0 per cent. of the Hindu population. Muhammadans, male children 20·1, and female children 16·6 per cent.; proportion of children of both sexes, 36·7 per cent. of the Muhammadan population; Christians, male children 18·4, and female children 24·8 per cent.; proportion of children of both sexes, 43·2 per cent. of the Christian population. Other denominations, male children 19·0, and female children 18·4 per cent.; proportion of children of both sexes, 37·4 per cent. of the total 'other' population. Population of all denominations, male children 18·0, and female children 16·1 per cent.; proportion of children of both sexes, 34·1 per cent. of the total District population. Here, as elsewhere throughout Bengal, the small proportion of girls to boys, and the excessive proportion of females above twelve years of age to males of the same class among both Hindus and Muhammadans, is attributable to the fact that natives consider girls have attained womanhood at an earlier age than boys reach manhood. The proportion of the sexes of all ages—50·6 males, and 49·4 females —is probably correct.

INFIRMITIES.—The number and proportions of insanes and of persons afflicted with certain infirmities in Purí District are thus returned in the Census Report :—Insanes—males 121, and females 19 ; total, 140, or ·0182 per cent. of the District population. Idiots —males 53, and females 9; total, 62, or ·0081 per cent. of the population. Deaf and dumb—males 121, and females 15; total, 136, or ·0177 per cent. of the population. Blind—males 353, and females 183 ; total, 536, or ·0696 per cent. of the population. Lepers—males 239, and females 17 ; total, 256, or ·0333 per cent. of the population. The total number of male infirms amounts to 887, or ·2277 per cent. of the total male population ; number of female infirms, 243, or ·0639 per cent. of the total female population. The total number of infirms of both sexes is 1130, or ·1468 per cent. of the total District population.

I omit the returns of the population according to occupation, as they do not stand the test of statistical criticism.

ETHNICAL DIVISION OF THE PEOPLE.—The native population is nominally divided according to the ancient fourfold classification of Bráhmans, Kshattriyas, Vaisyas, and Súdras. In reality, it is divided into the Bráhmans, or priests ; the Kshattriyas, or royal and military class ; and the Súdras, who comprise the residue of the population. In order, however, to maintain some show of keeping up the ancient fourfold division, several classes are admitted to hold a position halfway between the Súdras and the Kshattriyas. The most important of these are the Karans, who correspond to the Káyasths or writer caste of Bengal. The bulk of the population of the District consists of Uriyá-speaking castes, but many little colonies from other parts of India have settled in the District. There is a considerable sprinkling of Bengalís among the official and landed classes. This element is steadily on the increase. It has already purchased many valuable estates, and monopolized almost all the offices of trust in the administration. Some of the richest Bengalí landholders are absentees. They live in Calcutta, and seldom or never visit their estates. But a large number of Bengalís among the official classes and smaller proprietors have gradually settled down in Purí District, and consider themselves naturalized in it. Behar and the Districts of the North-West Provinces have sent many families of the Lálá Káyet (Káyasth) caste. They are pleaders in the courts, or petty officials, such as head-constables and clerks. A number of Telingás have come from the south, and established themselves along the coast, on the shores of the Chilká, and around the mouths of rivers. Almost the whole boat traffic of the District is in their hands. The Kumtís are immigrants from the adjoining District of Ganjám. Most of them reside in Purí town, and live by wholesale and retail trade. They do not intermarry or eat with people of the District, although many of them settle permanently in it. The trading classes contain families who have come from Bhojpur, Bundelkhand, and other parts of North - Western India. The Márwárís have also effected settlements. They are the leading cloth merchants, and buy up the surplus crops of the year for exportation. A scattered Marhattá population survives from the time when the country was in the hands of their race. They live chiefly by trade, or enjoy little grants of land, and form a very respectable, although not a numerous class. The Musalmáns, who also represent a once dominant race in Orissa, exhibit no such powers of adapting themselves to their altered circumstances. They are generally poor, proud, and discontented. They contain representatives of Afghán and Pathán families from beyond the confines of Northern India; but, as a rule, they are the descendants of the common soldiery, camp-followers, and low-caste Hindu converts. The only two Musalmán landholders of any importance are—the Málud family, on the Chilká lake; and the Marichpur house, in the extreme north-east of the District. The Muhammadan religion never made any progress among the native population. There are also two hill tribes, the Kandhs and the Savars or Saurás. They live in leaf huts in the recesses of the forests, and earn a precarious livelihood by bringing jungle products, firewood, and bamboòs to the markets in the plains. They cultivate cotton in small quantities, and various kinds of peas and pulse, such as *múg, arhar, bút,* and *chiná.* A further account of these people, and of the other aboriginal races, who are thinly represented in Purí District, will be found in the Statistical Account of the Tributary

States. There are no predatory castes, properly so called, in the District. A gipsy-like class, the Kelás, wander about begging from village to village, singing and dancing for the amusement of the peasantry. They are skilful bird-catchers, and trade on the humanity of the Hindus by offering to release their prey for a trifle. They speak a curious patois of Uriyá and Bengalí, mixed with the hill language.

The Census Report ethnically divides the population as follows :— Europeans, 8; Eurasians, 16; aboriginal tribes, 16,437; semi-Hinduized aborigines, 88,831 ; Hindu castes and people of Hindu origin, 652,796; Muhammadans, 11,586; total, 769,674. I take the following details from Mr. C. F. Magrath's separate District Census Compilation for Purí. The list of Hindu castes will be reproduced on a subsequent page, but arranged in a different order, showing as far as possible the rank which they hold in local public esteem :—

NAME OF NATIONALITY, TRIBE, OR CASTE.	Number.	NAME OF NATIONALITY, TRIBE, OR CASTE.	Number.
I.—NON-ASIATICS.		*Semi-Hinduized Aborigines —continued.*	
English, . . .	8	Kaorá, ...	46
		Bágdí, ...	7
II.—MIXED RACES.		Nat, ...	11
Eurasian, . . .	16	Baheliyá, . . .	20
		Bhuiyá, ...	12
		Dom, ...	2,113
III.— ASIATICS.		Chámár, . . .	2,355
1. *Aboriginal Tribes.*		Mihtar, ...	6,749
Gond, ...	2	Shiuli, ...	1,246
Kandh, ...	1,644	Yadiká, ...	62
Savar, ...	14,074	Pariah, ...	8
Saurí, ...	105		
Taála, ...	288		
Sáont, ...	323	Total, .	88,831
Kol, ...	1		
		3. *Hindus.*	
Total, .	16,437	(i.) SUPERIOR CASTES.	
		Bráhman, . . .	76,045
2. *Semi-Hinduized Aborigines.*		Ganak, . . .	3,604
		Mastán, . . .	6,931
Baurí, ...	56,113	Rájput, . . .	2,655
Kandárá, . . .	14,441	Bhanjá, . . .	291
Pán, . . .	5,242	Khandáit, . . .	7,768
Baghwá, . . .	16	Mahánáik, . . .	79
Ghusuriá, . . .	390	Total, .	97,373

Name of Nationality, Tribe, or Caste.	Number.	Name of Nationality, Tribe, or Caste.	Number.
(ii.) Intermediate Castes.		**(vii.) Castes chiefly engaged in Personal Service.**	
Káyasth,—			
(1) Bengalí, . .	1,061		
(2) Karan, . . .	29,203	Dhobá, ...	12,247
(3) Others, . .	133	Hajjám or Nápit, . .	17,867
Mahanti, . . .	42	Kahár, ...	1
Baidyá, . . .	9	Lodhá, ...	130
Bhát, ...	108		
Shagirdpeshá, . .	4,066	Total, .	30,245
Total, .	34,622		
(iii.) Trading Castes.		**(viii.) Artisan Castes.**	
Agarwálá and Márwárí, .	17		
Bais Baniyá, . . .	8,668	Kámár, etc. (blacksmith),	5,785
Kumtí, ...	1,466	Kánsárí (brazier), . .	4,774
		Rosora (pewterer), .	58
Total, .	10,151	Sonár (goldsmith), . .	5,990
		Sikalgir (cutter), . .	7
(iv.) Pastoral Castes.		Barhái (carpenter), . .	9,875
		Chitrakár (painter), .	247
Goálá (Ahír), . .	17	Pathariá (stone-cutter), .	245
Goálá (Gaur), . .	43,210	Kachorá (glass-maker), .	1,879
		Sankhárí (shell-cutter), .	270
Total, .	43,227	Kumbhar (potter), . .	9,666
		Darzí (tailor), . .	233
(v.) Castes engaged in preparing Cooked Food.		Sunrí (distiller), . .	1,976
		Telí (oilman), . .	31,973
Madak, ...	1	Thuriá (oilman), . .	4,866
Gánrár, . . .	22,403		
		Total, .	77,844
Total, .	22,404		
(vi.) Agricultural Castes.		**(ix.) Weaver Castes.**	
Chásá, ...	130,436	Tántí, ...	14,154
Golá, ...	5,256	Pátuá, ...	4,723
Or, ...	87,282	Matibansí, . . .	779
Páik, ...	34,082	Hangsí, . . .	260
Ráju, ...	99	Derá, ...	12
Sud, ...	3,880	Rangí, . . .	340
Beljwár, . . .	9	Tulábhiná, . . .	388
Kapásiá, . . .	441		
Rául, ...	75	Total, .	20,656
Támbulí, . . .	1,002		
Agurí, ...	6		
Málí, ...	11,669	**(x.) Labouring Castes.**	
Sadgop, . . .	9		
Koerí, . . .	11	Beldár, ...	1
Kurmí, ...	45	Nuniyá, . . .	80
Total, .	274,302	Total, .	81

Name of Nationality, Tribe, or Caste.	Number.	Name of Nationality, Tribe, or Caste.	Number.
(xi.) Castes occupied in selling Fish and Vegetables. *None.*	...	(xv.) Persons of Unknown or Unspecified Castes,	988
(xii.) Boating and Fishing Castes.		Grand Total of Hindus,	643,915
Keut, ...	27,188	4. *Persons of Hindu Origin not recognising Caste.*	
Naliyá, ...	1,701		
Tior, ...	907		
Gokhá, ...	262	Vaishnav, . . .	6,770
Ujiyá, ...	15	Sanyási, . . .	576
		Jugí, . . .	967
Total, .	30,073	Nánaksháhí, . . .	8
		Buddhists, . . .	8
(xiii.) Dancer, Musician, Beggar, and Vagabond Castes.		Native Christians, . .	552
Kasbí, ...	306	Total, .	8,881
Chokár, ...	287		
Kheltá, ...	634		
Kahaliyá, ...	9	5. *Muhammadans.*	
Adhvaríá, ...	72		
		Mughul, . . .	256
Total, .	1,308	Pathán, . . .	5,764
		Sayyid, . . .	680
(xiv.) Persons enumerated by Nationality only.		Shaikh, . . .	4,591
Marhattá, . . .	93	Fakír, . . .	295
Sikh, ...	1		
Telingá, . . .	547	Total, .	11,586
Total, .	641	Grand Total, .	769,674

HINDU CASTES.—The following is a list of 100 Hindu castes met with in Purí District, arranged as far as possible according to the order in which they take rank in local public esteem, and showing their occupation, numbers, etc. The figures indicating the number of each caste are quoted from Mr. C. F. Magrath's District Census Compilation; the other information comes from a return specially furnished by the Collector :—

HIGH CASTES.—The following 13 rank highest :—(1) Bráhman. —The Bráhmans are divided into two great classes—the Vaidik and the Laukik. The former are said to be immigrants from Bengal or Kanauj, and date their oldest settlements in Purí from about the twelfth century. The legend runs that they had been settled for some hundreds of years at Jájpur, the ancient capital of Orissa; and that the Rájá Anang Bhím Deo, the rebuilder of the Temple of Jagannáth, founded four hundred and fifty colonies of them in Purí District between 1175 and 1202 A.D. They are called the southern line of Orissa Bráhmans, already referred to in the Statistical Account of Balasor. They are subdivided into two classes—the Kulins and the Srotríyas. The former are so highly esteemed, that a Srotríya Bráhman will give a large dower in order to get his daughter married to one of them. But the Kulin who thus intermarries with a Srotríya loses somewhat of his position among his own people. The pure Kulin rarely stoops below the Srotríyas, the class immediately next him, for a wife. The Laukik Bráhmans are supposed to represent the original Aryan settlements in the District. They now work with their hands, and are excellent husbandmen; while the two upper classes of imported Bráhmans would lose caste by holding a plough.

The local subdivisions of the Bráhmans are innumerable. The most general in Purí District is that which divides the Vaidik Bráhmans into—(a) learned men (*Bhatta-misra* and *Sámanta*); (b) ordinary Vaidik Bráhmans; (c) a class between the two (*Madhyam*). But the best classification I have been able to obtain is one which separates them into three great classes and eighteen families. The first class is the Kulin Bráhmans, and includes three families—the *Bachhas, Nandá,* and *Gautríya.* These live on lands granted by former Rájás, or by teaching private students, or as spiritual guides, or, more seldom, as temple priests. They are few in number, for the most part in middle circumstances, often very poor, but always greatly esteemed. The second class is the Srotríya, and includes nine families—the *Bhatta-misra, Upádhyáya, Misra, Rath, Otá, Tiári, Dás, Páti,* and *Sátpasti.* Of these, some live on lands granted to them by former Rájás, some by teaching private students, some on presents from rich men, some as pilgrim guides, and many as domestic chaplains, spiritual guides, and priests of the temple. They are numerous, some of them rich, but many poor, and are esteemed a little less than the Kulins. The third class is the Laukik Bráhmans, who are subdivided into six families—the *Pandá, Senápati, Párhi, Bastiá, Páni,* and *Sáhu.* These live as husbandmen holding their own ploughs, as traders, vegetable dealers, rice merchants, and lenders of rice or money on interest to the cultivators, and as pilgrim guides. They are numerous, some of them rich, but most of them in middle circumstances, like the better class of husbandmen. They are less esteemed than either of the other two classes, but are generally highly respected as well-born, well-to-do men. The Census Report returns the Bráhmans under two classes —namely, Bráhmans proper, who number 76,045 souls; and Mastání or cultivating Bráhmans (presumably the Laukik Bráhmans mentioned above), who number 6931.

(2) Kshattriya.—The Kshattriyas rank next to the Bráhmans. Strictly speaking, there is not a single Kshattriya of pure descent in Orissa ; but the petty Rájás claim this pedigree, and in the case of the Mahárájá of Khurdhá the claim is admitted by the Bráhman genealogists. The Rájás confer on their chief Kshattriya servants honorific titles, such as *Báhanpati, Pátjosi,* etc. The Kshattriyas are divided into three great classes, with seven subdivisions. The first class is the so-called Kshattriya proper, and includes the three following families—*Deva, Lál,* and *Ráya.* They are Rájás, landed proprietors, or holders of dependent tenures, and some of them lend money and rice on interest. They are few in number, generally rich, and much esteemed. The second class is the Khandáits, consisting of two subdivisions—the *Bhanjá* and *Harichandan.* They hold dependent tenures or occupy lands, and claim for themselves the rank of Kshattriya, but are generally regarded as Súdras, and, indeed, rank below the Karans in popular estimation. They are few in number, some of them rich, but many poor. The *Bhanjá* family of the Khandáits are great huntsmen, but also cultivate lands ; and some of them make high pretensions to pure Kshattriya descent,—pretensions which are not admitted by the Bráhman genealogists. The third of the Kshattriya classes is the Rájput, subdivided into *Sinh* and *Chanda.* These are generally employed as *jamádárs,* doorkeepers, and messengers, or are petty landholders. They are not a numerous class, and are held in fair estimation. The Census Report does not return the Kshattriyas at all in its list of Orissa castes, but puts down the Khandáits proper at 7768, the Mahánáiks (a branch of the Khandáits) at 79, the Bhanjá Khandáits at 291, and the Rájputs at 2655.

(3) Karan.—The Karans are admitted to hold a position midway between the Súdras and the Bráhmans, and themselves claim to belong to the great Vaisya or trading caste of ancient India. They are divided into three classes—the *Patnáik, Dás,* and *Mahanti.* Many of them are landholders, or lend money and rice on interest ; but a large proportion are clerks, accountants, and petty officials. They are

generally in good circumstances, and some of them are highly esteemed as rich men. The Census Report returns the number of Karans proper at 29,023, of Mahanti Karans at 42, and other Karans 133. (4) The Káyasths, the Bengalí counterpart of the Orissa Karans, number 1061 in Purí District. The Collector mentions three other castes—namely, (5) Das, (6) Sahu, and (6a) Prushti—as claiming to belong to the ancient Vaisya caste, who are admitted to hold a rank superior to any of the Súdra castes. These castes are not returned separately in the Census Report; but the Collector states that they are few in number, in middling circumstances, and somewhat less esteemed than the Karans. (7) Ganak or Jyautishik, astrologers and fortune-tellers. They claim to be fallen Bráhmans, and wear the sacred thread. Number in Purí District in 1872, 3604. (8) Bhát; heralds and genealogists, also beggars. These too claim to be lapsed Bráhmans, but their right to the rank is not recognised, although they wear the sacred thread; 108 in number. (9) Baidyá; physicians, also landholders and petty officials; 9 in number. (10) Shagird-peshá; a mixed caste, said to be the offspring of low-caste women by Bráhman, Karan, or Bhát fathers; 4066 in number. (11) Agarwálá or Márwárí; traders and merchants, who lay claim to the status of the ancient Vaisyás; 17 in number. (12) Bais-baniyá; merchants and traders; 8668 in number. (13) Kumtí; a caste of Madras traders; 1466 in number.

RESPECTABLE SUDRA CASTES.—Next in point of rank come the following 28 respectable Súdra castes :—(14) Páníkendu; village accountants; not mentioned in the Census Report, but returned as a separate caste by the Collector, who states that they are few in number, and generally in poor circumstances. (15) Bhandárí or Nápit; barbers; 17,867 in number. (16) Kámár; blacksmiths; 5785 in number. (17) Kumbhar; potters; 9666 in number. (17) Kánsárí and Thatárí; braziers and coppersmiths; 4774 in number. (18) Sundárá, and (19) Daitá; pilgrim guides; not mentioned in the Census Report, but returned as separate castes by the Collector, who states that they are few in number and generally in middling circumstances. (20) Sadgop; the highest of the cultivating castes; 9 in number. (21) Támbulí; growers and sellers of betel leaf, also traders and money-lenders; 1002 in number. (22) Málí; gardeners, flower sellers, etc.; 11,669 in number. (23) Telí or Tilí; oil pressers and sellers; also grain merchants and traders; 31,973 in number. (24) Thuriá; oil sellers and petty traders; 4866 in number. (25)

Patrá ; cloth dealers ; not mentioned in the Census Report, but returned as a separate caste by the Collector, who states that they are numerous, some being rich and some in poor circumstances. (26) Páik; cultivators; also messengers and village watchmen; 34,082 in number. (27) Chásá; the generic name for the cultivating caste; 130,436 in number. The other agricultural castes are nearly all subdivisions of Chásás, and rank together nearly equally. They are—(28) Golá; 5256 in number. (29) Or; 87,282 in number. (30) Ráju ; 99 in number. (31) Súd ; 3880 in number. (32) Beljwár; 9 in number. (33) Kapasiá; 441 in number. (34) Rául; 75 in number. (35) Agurí; 6 in number. (36) Koerí; 11 in number. (37) Kurmí; 45 in number. (38) Gaur; the Orissa cow-keeping and pastoral caste, corresponding to the Goálás of Bengal ; they are also palanquin-bearers ; 43,210 in number. (39) Goálá ; cow-herds and milkmen from Bengal ; 17 in number. (40) Muduli ; pilgrim guides ; not mentioned in the Census Report, but returned as a separate caste by the Collector, who states that they are few in number, some being rich and some poor. (41) Guriá ; makers and sellers of sweetmeats ; not mentioned in the Census Report, but returned as a separate caste by the Collector, who states that they are few in number, some being rich and some poor.

INTERMEDIATE SUDRA CASTES.—The following 17 castes hold a position above the lowest :—(42) Gánrar; preparers and sellers of parched grain and other cooked vegetable food ; 22,403 in number. (43) Rosorá ; workers in lead and tin ; 58 in number. (44) Sikalgir ; cutlers and arms-polishers ; 7 in number. (45) Barhái; carpenters ; 9875 in number. (46) Chitrakár ; painters ; 247 in number. (47) Pathariá; stone-cutters ; 245 in number. (48) Kachorá ; glass makers ; 1879 in number. (49) Sankhárí; shell cutters ; 270 in number. (50) Kharárá; workers in brass; not mentioned in the Census Report, but returned as a separate caste by the Collector, who states that they are numerous in the District, some being rich and some poor. (51) Vaishnav; not a caste, but a religious sect of Hindus, who profess the doctrines inculcated by the Vishnuvite reformer Chaitanya in the sixteenth century. All classes belong to this sect, which, in theory at least, rejects caste and asserts the religious equality of all men in the sight of God ; 6770 in number. An account of Chaitanya and his teachings will be found at pp. 50-52. of this Statistical Account. (52) Sanyásí; a class of Sivaití religious ascetics and mendicants ; 576 in number. (53) Jugi ; another sect of

Sivaití ascetics and mendicants; 967 in number. (54) Nánaksháhí; followers of Nának Sháh, the founder of the Sikh religion; 8 in number. (55) Madák; confectioners; 1 in number. (56) Dasiputra; domestic servants, peons, etc.; not mentioned in the Census Report, but returned as a separate caste by the Collector, who states that they are few in number and poor. (57) Kitivansa; village school teachers; not mentioned in the Census Report, but returned as a separate caste by the Collector, who states that they are few in number and poor. (58) Golá; petty traders; not mentioned in the Census Report, but returned as a separate caste by the Collector, who states that they are numerous in the District, some being rich or in well-off circumstances, and others poor.

LOW CASTES.—The following 22 are low castes :—(59) Dhobá; washermen; 12,247 in number. (60) Lodhá; domestic servants; 130 in number. (61) Darzí; tailors; 233 in number. (62) Sunrí; wine sellers and distillers; 1976 in number. (63) Kahár; up country caste of palanquin-bearers; 1 in number. (64) Sonár; goldsmiths and jewellers; 5990 in number. (65) Málikatá; makers of wooden beads; not mentioned in the Census Report, but returned as a separate caste by the Collector, who describes them as few in number and very poor. (66) Tulábhíná; cotton carders; 388 in number. (67) Beldár; labourers; 1 in number. (68) Nuniyá; salt workers; 80 in number. (69) Chunárí; lime burners; not mentioned in the Census Report, but returned by the Collector, who states that they are few in number and very poor. (70) Tántí; weavers; 14,154 in number. (71) Patuá; weavers; 4723 in number. (72) Matibansi; weavers; 779 in number. (73) Hánsí; weavers; 260 in number. (74) Rangní; weavers; 340 in number. (75) Derá; weavers; 12 in number. (76) Keut; fishermen; 27,188 in number. (77) Naliyá; fishermen; 1701 in number. (78) Tior; fishermen; 907 in number. (79) Gokhá; fishermen; 262 in number. (80) Ujiyá; fishermen; 15 in number.

THE VERY LOWEST CASTES OF HINDUS are the following. Except where otherwise mentioned, they are employed principally as agricultural or as ordinary day-labourers :—(81) Baurí; 56,113 in number. (82) Kandárá; village watchmen, fishermen, labourers, and cultivators; 14,441 in number. (83) Pán; musicians, and collectors of jungle produce, labourers, etc.; 5242 in number. (84) Baghwá; 16 in number. (85) Ghusuriá; swine-herds; 390 in number. (86) Káorá; swine-herds; 46 in number. (87) Bágdí;

cultivators, labourers, etc.; 7 in number. (88) Nat; 11 in number. (89) Baheliyá; 20 in number. (90) Bhuiyá; 12 in number. (91) Dom; makers of bamboo mats, etc.; 2113 in number. (92) Chámár; shoemakers, leather dealers, and skinners; 2355 in number. (93) Mihtar; sweepers; 6749 in number. (94) Shiuli; 1246 in number. (95) Yadiká; 62 in number. (96) Kheltá; bird-catchers, jugglers, beggars, thieves, etc.; 634 in number. (97) Kasbí; prostitutes; 306 in number. (98) Chokar; offspring of prostitutes; 287 in number. (99) Kahaliyá, 9; and (100) Ad-havariá, 72 in number; two vagabond castes.

RELIGIOUS DIVISION OF THE PEOPLE.—The Hindu population of Purí District consists of 374,226 males, and 365,410 females; total, 739,636, or 96·1 per cent. of the total population. As Purí forms one of the religious centres of Vishnuvite Hindus throughout India, a separate account of their forms of religion, particularly in relation to the great shrine of Jagannáth, is given below. The Muhammadan population of Purí consists of 5939 males, and 5647 females; total, 11,586, or 1·5 per cent. of the total population. The Musalmáns are scattered all over the District, and are princi-pally employed in agriculture and as messengers. As a rule they are poor and ignorant. The religion of Islám makes no progress whatever in the District. The Buddhist community consists only of 8 persons. The Christian population consists of 270 males, and 306 females; total, 576, or ·1 per cent. of the total District popula-tion. Deducting 24 for the European and Eurasian residents, there remains a balance of 552 as representing the total native Christian population. The Christian community is mainly composed of a flourishing colony at Pippli, under the care of the Baptist Mission.

THE SHRINE OF JAGANNATH.—The following paragraphs, descrip-tive of the shrine of Jagannáth at Purí, are condensed from my *Orissa* (vol. i. chapters 3 and 4), to which I must refer the reader for a further and more detailed disquisition on the position occupied by this worship among the religions of India :—

For two thousand years, Orissa has been the Holy Land of the Hindus. The Province is divided into four great regions of pilgrimage. From the moment the pilgrim passes the Baitaraní river, on the high road forty miles north-east of Cuttack, he treads on holy ground. Behind him lies the secular world, with its cares for the things of this life; before him is the promised land, which he has been taught to regard as a place of preparation for heaven. On the bank of the river rises shrine after shrine to Siva, the All - Destroyer. On leaving the stream, he enters Jájpur, literally, the City of Sacrifice, the headquarters of the region of pilgrimage (Vijayí or Párvatí *kshetra*) sacred to Párvatí, the wife of Siva. To the south-east is the region of pilgrimage sacred to the sun (Hara *kshetra*), now rarely visited, with its match-·less ruins looking down in desolate beauty across the Bay of Bengal. To the south-west is the region of pilgrimage dedicated to Siva (Arka or Padma *kshetra*), with its city of temples, which once clustered, according to native tradition, to the number of seven thousand around the sacred lake. Beyond this, nearly due south, is the region of pilgrimage beloved of Vishnu, known to every hamlet throughout India as the abode of Jagannáth, the Lord of the World (Vishnu or Puríshottama *kshetra*).

As the outlying position of Orissa long saved it from conquest, and from that dilapidation of ancient Hindu shrines and rites which marks the Muhammadan line of march through India, so Purí, built upon its extreme south-eastern shore, and protected on the one side by the surf and on the other by swamps and inundations, is the corner of Orissa which has been most left to itself. On these inhospitable sands Hindu religion and Hindu superstition have stood at bay for eighteen centuries against the world. Here is the national temple, whither the people flock to worship from every Province of India. Here is the Swarga-dwára, the Gate of Heaven, whither thousands of pilgrims come to die, lulled to their last sleep by the roar of the eternal ocean. Twenty generations of devout Hindus have gone through life, haunted with a perpetual yearning to visit these fever-stricken sand-hills. They are Purí, '*the* City' of their religious aspirations on earth; they are Puríshottama, the dwelling of Vishnu, 'the Best of Men;' they are the symbolical Blue Mountain; they are the mystic navel of the earth. A tract sold to pilgrims at the door of the temple states that 'even Siva is unable to comprehend its glory; how feeble, then, the efforts of mortal men!'

This great yearning after Jagannáth is to some extent the outcome of centuries of companionship in suffering between the people and their god. In every disaster of Orissa, Jagannáth has borne his share. In every flight of the people before an invading power, he has been their companion. The priests, indeed, put the claims of their god upon higher ground. 'In the first boundless space,' they say, 'dwelt the Great God, whom men call Náráyan, or Parameswar, or Jagannáth.' But without venturing beyond this world's history, the first indistinct dawn of Orissa tradition discloses Purí as the refuge of an exiled creed. In the uncertain dawn of Indian tradition, the highly spiritual doctrines of Buddha obtained shelter here; and the Golden Tooth of the founder remained for centuries at Purí, then the Jerusalem of the Buddhists, as it has for centuries been of the Hindus.

Jagannáth makes his first historical appearance in the year 318 A.D., when the priests fled with the sacred image and left an empty city to Rakta Bahu and his buccaneers (*vide* Statistical Account of Cuttack District, vol. xviii. p. 182). For a century and a half the image remained buried in the western jungles, till a pious prince drove out the foreigners and brought back the deity. Three times has it been buried in the Chilká lake; and whether the invaders were pirates from the sea, or the devouring cavalry of Afghánistán, the first thing that the people saved was their god.

The true source of Jagannáth's undying hold upon the Hindu race consists in the fact that he is the god of the people. As long as his towers rise upon the Purí sands, so long will there be in India a perpetual and visible protest of the equality of man before God. His apostles penetrate to every hamlet of Hindustán, preaching the sacrament of the Holy Food (*maháprasád*). The poor outcast learns that there is a city on the far eastern shore, in which high and low eat together. In his own village, if he accidentally touches the clothes of a man of good caste, he has committed a crime, and his outraged superior has to wash away the pollution before he can partake of food or approach his god. In some parts of the country, the lowest castes are not permitted to build within the towns, and their miserable hovels cluster amid heaps of broken potsherds and dunghills on the outskirts. Throughout the southern part of the continent it used to be a law, that no man of these degraded castes might enter the village before nine in the morning or after four in the evening, lest the slanting rays of the sun should cast his shadow across the path of a Bráhman. But in the presence of the Lord of the World, priest and peasant are equal. The rice that has once been placed before the god can never cease to be pure, or lose its reflected sanctity. In the courts of Jagannáth, and outside the Lion Gate, 100,000 pilgrims every year are joined in the sacrament of eating the holy food. The lowest may demand it from, or give it to, the highest. Its sanctity overleaps all barriers, not only of caste, but of race and hostile faiths;

and a Purí priest will stand the test of receiving the food from a Christian's hand.

The worship of Jagannáth, too, aims at a catholicism which embraces every form of Indian belief, and every Indian conception of the Deity. Nothing is too high, and nothing is too low, to find admission into his temple. The fetishism and bloody rites of the aboriginal races, the mild flower-worship of the Vedas, and every compromise between the two, along with the lofty spiritualities of the great Indian reformers, have here found refuge. The rigid Monotheism of Rámánuja in the twelfth century, the monastic system of Rámánand in the fifteenth, the mystic Quietism of Chaitanya at the beginning of the sixteenth, and the luxurious love-worship of the Vallabháchárís towards its close, mingle within the walls of Jagannáth at this present day. He is Vishnu, under whatever form and by whatever title men call upon his name. Besides thus representing Vishnu in all his manifestations, the priests have superadded the worship of the other members of the Hindu trinity in their various shapes; and the disciple of every Hindu sect can find his beloved rites, and some form of his chosen deity, within the sacred precincts.

LEGENDARY ORIGIN OF THE IDOL.—The very origin of Jagannáth proclaims him not less the god of the Bráhmans, than of the low-caste aboriginal races. The following story of the Divine Log is one of the most popular legends of Orissa, and was taken down from oral tradition upon the spot. It is entitled the 'Dáru Bráhma,' and, like most of the religious legends of the people, is an adaptation from the Puránas:—

. 'For a long time in the golden age, men had been seeking for the god Vishnu throughout the earth. So the good King Indradyumna sent out Bráhmans from his realm of Málwa, to the east and to the west, and to the north and to the south. And those who went to the west, and to the north, and to the south, returned; but he who went to the east returned not. For he had journeyed through the great jungle till he came to the country of the Savars, the old people of Orissa, and there he dwelt in the house of Básu, a fowler of the wilderness; and Básu, seeing the man to be a Bráhman, forced him by threats to marry his daughter, and thus to bring honour to his tribe. This the Bráhman did, and abode in the villages of the ancient people.

'Now Básu was a servant of Jagannáth, the Lord of the World, and daily he went into the jungle to offer fruits and flowers in secret to his god. But one morning, moved by the prayers of his daughter, he took the Bráhman with him, binding his eyes by the way, so that he might behold the lord Jagannáth in his holy place, and yet he should not know the way thither. Then the Bráhman, having received from his wife a bag of mustard seed, dropped it as he went blindfold through the forest, till he reached the shrine, and the old man unbound his eyes. There he beheld lord Jagannáth in the form of a blue stone image, at the foot of the undying fig-tree. Presently the old man left him, and went to gather the daily offering of flowers. Then the Bráhman prayed to the Lord of the World. And as he poured out his heart, a crow that sat rocking herself upon a branch above fell down before the god, and suddenly taking a glorious form soared into the heaven of Vishnu. The Bráhman, seeing how easy the path to eternal bliss appeared to be from this holy spot, climbed into the tree, and would have thrown himself down; but a voice from heaven cried, "Hold, Bráhman! First carry to thy king the good news that thou hast found the Lord of the World."

'At the same moment the fowler came back with his newly gathered fruits and flowers, and spread them out before the image. But, alas! the god came not, according to his wont, to partake of the offering. Only a voice was heard saying, "O faithful servant, I am wearied of thy jungle flowers and fruits, and crave for cooked rice and sweetmeats. No longer shalt thou see me in the form of thy Blue God (*Nil-madhab*). Hereafter I shall be known as Jagannáth, the Lord of the World." Then the fowler sorrowfully led the Bráhman back to his house, but the Blue God appeared no more to that poor man of the ancient people.

'For a long time the fowler kept the Bráhman captive in the wilderness; but at last, moved by the tears of his daughter, he allowed him to depart to tell that the Lord of the World had been found. When the king heard the good news he rejoiced, and set out with his army of 1,300,000 footmen, and a vast company of wood-cutters to hew a road through the great jungle. So they journeyed 800 miles, till they reached the Blue Mountain. Then the king's heart swelled within him, and he cried, "Who is like unto me, whom the Lord of the World has chosen to build his temple, and to teach men in this age of darkness to call on his name?" But the lord Jagannáth was wroth at the king's pride, and a voice was heard from heaven, saying, "O king! thou shalt indeed build my temple, but me thou shalt not behold. When it is finished, then thou shalt seek anew for thy god." At that same moment the blue image vanished from off the earth.

'So the king built the temple, but saw not the god; and when the temple was finished, he found no man on earth holy enough to consecrate it. Therefore King Indradyumna went to heaven, to beg Brahmá to come down and consecrate the temple. But Brahmá had just begun his devotions, and could not be disturbed. Now the devotions of Brahmá last for nine ages of mortal men; and while Indradyumna waited in heaven, many other kings had reigned on earth. The city that he had built around the temple had crumbled into ruins, and the lofty fane itself was buried under the drifting sand of the sea. One day, as the king of the place was riding along the beach, his horse stumbled against the pinnacle of the forgotten shrine. Then his servants, searching to find the cause, dug away the sand, and there was the temple of lord Jagannáth, fair and fresh as at the time of its building.

'So when Brahmá's devotions were over, and he came down with Indradyumna to consecrate the shrine, the king of the place claimed it as the work of his own hands. Therefore Brahmá commanded that witnesses should be heard, and first he called upon the crow. But the crow was busy with her devotions, and cried, "Who art thou that callest me?" "It is I, Brahmá, the master of the Vedas; and dost thou, poor carrion bird, dare to despise my summons?" Then said the ancient crow, "Which Brahmá art thou? I have seen a thousand Brahmás live and die. There was he with a thousand faces, whose existence was as a period of five days to me. Thou wast born but yesterday from the body of Vishnu, and commandest thou me?" Then Brahmá entreated the crow, and she declared it was Indradyumna that had built the temple.

'But for all this, King Indradyumna found not the god. So with austerities and penance he ceased not to call upon Jagannáth, till the Lord of the World appeared to him in a vision, and showed him his image as a block of timber half thrown up from the ocean upon the sand. Then the king, with his army and five thousand male elephants, tried to drag the block with crimson cords to the temple; but he could not, until, chidden for his presumption by lord Jagannáth in a vision, he summoned Básu the fowler to his aid.

'Thereafter the king gathered together all the carpenters in his country, and gave them lands and villages as the price of fashioning the block into an image of lord Jagannáth. But when they put their chisels on the wood, the iron lost its edge; and when they struck them with their mallets, the mallets missed and crushed their hands; till at last the lord Vishnu came down in the form of an aged carpenter, and by signs and wonders declared his power unto the king. Him the king shut up alone in the temple with the block, and swore that no man should enter for twenty-one days, sealing the doors with his own seal. But the queen longed to see the face of the god, that he might redeem her life from barrenness. So she persuaded her husband; and he, opening the door before the end of the promised time, found the three images of Jagannáth and his brother and sister, fashioned from the waist upwards. But Jagannáth and his brother had only stumps for arms, while his sister had none at all, and even so they remain to this day. Then the king prayed to the god; and being asked to choose a blessing, begged that offerings should never cease in all time to come before . the images, and that the temple should ever remain open from daybreak until midnight, for the salvation of mankind.

' " So shall it be," said the vision. " But they are matters which concern me. Ask for thyself." " I ask, then," said the king, " that I may be the last of my race, that none who come after me may say, "I built this temple; I taught men to call on the name of Jagannáth." Thus it fell out that the good King Indradyumna was the last of his line.'

In this legend at least two distinct stories are mixed up. Its latter part probably refers to the exile of Jagannáth during the Yavana occupation of Orissa, A.D. 318 to 473. The pious founder of the Lion dynasty, who expelled the intruders, is still called the second Indradyumna; and the rebuilder of the temple in A.D. 1198 also enjoys this title. The first part of the legend shadows forth the original importation of Vishnu-worship by an Aryan king from the north-west, and its amalgamation with the aboriginal rites existing in Orissa. It is worthy of note, that although a Bráhman figures in this as in all the religious legends of the Hindus, he is not the principal person. An ancient text mentions that Vishnu was specially the god of the kingly and warrior caste, and in this legend it is the king who plays the chief part in introducing his worship.

In the foregoing legend, we find the aboriginal people worshipping a blue stone in the depths of the forest. But the deity has grown tired of the jungle offerings of the primitive people, and longs for the cooked food of the more civilised Aryan race. When the Aryan element at length comes on the scene, the rude blue stone disappears, and gives place to a carved image. At the present hour, in every hamlet of Orissa, this twofold worship co-exists. The common people have their shapeless stone or block, which they adore with simple rites in the open air; while side by side with it is a temple to one of the Aryan gods, with its carved image and elaborate rites. Some shapeless log, or a black stone, or a red-stained trunk of a tree, is still the object of adoration among the masses. Whenever the villagers are questioned about their religious beliefs, the same answer is invariably given—' The common people have no idea of religion but to do right, and to worship the village god.'

In the reply of the crow to Brahmá, is preserved an acknowledgment that the present Aryan system of worship was preceded by religious cycles that have disappeared. The Aryan king might come with his army from the north, but he had to accept as his deity the primitive god of the country. Even after the temple had been built, everything was again at a stand-still, until the fowler of the wilderness, at the present day one of the lowest castes, reappears upon the scene. The poor aboriginal bird-killer, whose blue stone image disappeared before the Bráhmans and their elaborate rites, has for hundreds of years been known by the name of Básu, an epithet from which the god Vishnu derives one of his most august titles, viz. Básu-deva, explained in the Vishnu Purána as meaning 'the god who dwells in all things, and in whom all things dwell.'

The worship of Vishnu was not, however, the first form of the Aryan faith that penetrated these remote jungles of the sea-board. For centuries before and after the birth of Christ, the rock caves of Orissa resounded with the chants of Buddhist monks. But about the fourth century of our era, Buddhism in Orissa began to lose its sharply marked identity, and gradually gave way to other developments of spiritual life, which took the form of Siva-worship. The great city of temples, Bhuvaneswar, dedicated to Siva, dates from the seventh century. This worship incorporated the doctrines of the Aryan conquerors with the rites of the aboriginal races. The doctrines were spiritual, and it kept them in the inner sanctuary for its Aryan priests; its rites were gross and bloody, and it paraded them in the outer courts as a bait to the mixed populace. It fixed its seat in the west of Puri District, where the mountains and forest tracts of Central India slope down on the alluvial plain. There it struck its roots deep in the ignorance and the fears of a people who knew God only by the more terrible manifestations of his power; as a God mighty indeed, but to be dreaded rather than loved.

But side by side with Siva-worship, there can be dimly traced another spiritual form struggling into life. The worship of Vishnu likewise took its doctrines and all its inner mysteries from the ancient Aryan faith, and engrafted upon them rites which appealed to the imaginations and the passions of a tropical race. Both Sivaism and Vishnuvism were attempts to bring the gods down to men. The former plunged boldly into the abyss of superstition, and erected its empire without shame or scruple upon the ignorance and terrors of the people. The worship of Vishnu shrank from such lengths, and tried to create a system wide enough and strong enough for a national religion, by mixing a somewhat less base alloy with the fine gold of Aryan spirituality. It was a religion in all things graceful. Its gods are bright, friendly beings, who walk and converse with men. Its legends breathe an almost Grecian beauty. But pastoral simplicities and an exquisite ritual had no chance against a system like Sivaism, that pandered to the grossest superstitions of the masses. The spiritual element in Vishnu-worship has no doubt always existed among the Aryan settlements throughout India. But its popular conquests have generally been subsequent to those of Sivaism; and this is the case in a very marked manner in Orissa.

In the eleventh century, the Vishnuvite doctrines were gathered into a great religious treatise. The Vishnu Purána, which dates from about 1045 A.D., probably represents, as indeed its name implies, 'ancient' forms of belief that had co-existed with Sivaism and Buddhism for centuries. It derives its system from the Vedas; not, however, in a direct channel, but filtered through the two great epic poems of the Rámáyana and the Mahábhárata. It forms one of eighteen religious treatises, which, under the name of Puránas or Ancient Sayings, are devoted to the mythology and legendary history of the Hindus. These works especially extol the members of the Hindu trinity, now claiming the pre-eminence for Vishnu, and now for Siva; but in their nobler flights always rising to a recognition that both are but manifestations of the one eternal God.

The Vishnu Purána, compiled barely 800 years ago, starts with an intolerance equal to that of the ancient code of Manu. It still declares the priests to have sprung from the mouth, and the low-castes from the feet, of God. Its stately theogony disdains to touch the legends of the people. Its cosmography confines itself to the Aryan world. It declares, indeed, that there is but one God; but this God is the God of the Bráhmans, to whom he gives the earth as an inheritance, and in whose eyes the ancient races are as demons or wild beasts.

Vishnuvism had to preach a far different doctrine before it could become, as it has for ages been, the popular religion of Orissa. These withered sticks of mythology could never blossom forth into a national faith. Sivaism had also its ancient sayings, and it out-rivalled Vishnu-worship by a ritual singularly adapted to terrify and enchain the masses. But about the middle of the twelfth century a great change began to take place. Up to that time, Vishnuvism had been the religion of the upper ranks. Jagannáth, although unknown to the Vedas, had ever been the companion of the ruling race in Orissa. We find him sharing the flights of the priests, and appearing in the dreams of kings. But from the twelfth century a curious movement began. Vishnuvism in its turn began to throw itself upon the people. Sivaism had enlisted their ignorant terrors; Vishnuvism was soon to appeal to the eternal instinct of human liberty and equality. The movement first commenced in Southern India, where Rámánuja about 1150 A.D. preached from city to city the unity of God under the title of Vishnu, the Cause and the Creator of all. The preacher made converts from every class, but it was reserved for his successors formally to enunciate equality of caste before God as an article of the Vishnuvite faith.

And meanwhile, the great temple of Jagannáth, which now stands at Purí, was built. It was a last magnificent assertion of aristocratic devotion. In 1174 A.D., King Anang Bhim Deo ascended the throne of Orissa. He ruled all the country from the Húglí river on the north to the Godávarí on the south, and from the forest country of Sónpur on the west, eastward to the Bay of Bengal; his kingdom comprising an area of over forty thousand square miles. But in the midst of his grandeur he was struck down by a great calamity. He unhappily slew a Bráhman, and the rest of his life became one grand expiation of the guilt. Tradition relates that he built sixty stone temples to the gods; bridged ten broad rivers; dug forty great wells, and encased them with solid masonry; constructed one hundred and fifty-two flights of stairs on the river banks, as landing and bathing places; planted four hundred and fifty colonies of Bráhmans upon lands granted out of the royal demesne; and excavated one million tanks to protect the crops of the husbandmen.

To him appeared lord Jagannáth in a dream, and commanded him to journey to the sands of Purí, and there to call on his name. So the king in the twelfth year of his reign journeyed to Purí, and offered up his prayers. Thereafter he gathered around him his princes and vassals, and all the chief men of his state, and said: 'Hear, O chiefs and princes! It is known to you that the kings of the ancient Lion line ruled over a wide country, and enjoyed a revenue of fifteen hundred thousand measures of gold. But by the grace of lord Jagannáth, the princes of my line have subdued many chiefs and peoples, and enlarged the kingdom, so that my revenues are now three and a half millions of measures of gold. Out of this I have assigned fixed sums for the payment of my generals, for the captains of my horse and of my elephants, for the priests, and for the temples of the gods. Princes and chiefs! touch not these grants, lest ye suffer the penalty which the holy scriptures denounce against those who take back that which has been given. Above all, in the countries under your charge, be merciful to the people. Be just to the husbandmen, and exact no more than the established rates. And now I have gathered together a great treasure. Four millions of measures of gold have I taken from the nations I conquered, and jewels to the value of eight hundred thousand measures of gold besides. What can I do better with this great treasure than build a temple to the lord Jagannáth? Speak freely your minds with regard to the work.'

All the chiefs and princes applauded the king's speech. Gold and jewels to the value of a million and a half measures of gold were set apart for the work, being estimated at half a million sterling in the money of our time. For fourteen years the artificers laboured, and the temple was finished, as it now stands, in 1198 A.D.

VISHNUVITE REFORMATION : CHAITANYA.—At the end of the thirteenth century, according to some authorities,—at the end of the fourteenth, according to others,—the great reformation took place which made Vishnu-worship a national religion of India. Rámánuja's early movement in Southern India had left behind a line of disciples. The first in the inspired descent to illustrate the doctrine in Northern India was Rámánand, who wandered from place to place proclaiming the equality of man before God. One of his disciples, Kabír, carried his master's doctrine throughout Bengal; and a monastery called after his name exists in Purí at the present day. As his master had laboured to gather together all castes of the Hindus in one common faith, so Kabír, seeing that the Hindus were in his time no longer the whole inhabitants of India, tried to build up a religion that would embrace Hindu and Muhammadan alike. The voluminous writings of his sect contain the amplest acknowledgment that the God of the Hindu is also the God of the Musalmán. His universal name is The Inner, whether he may be invoked as the Alí of the Muhammadans, or as the Ráma of the Hindus. 'To Alí and Ráma we owe our life, and should show like tenderness to all who live. What avails it to wash your mouth, to count your beads, to bathe in holy streams, to bow in temples, when, whilst you mutter your prayers or journey on pilgrimage, deceitfulness is in your heart? The Hindu fasts every eleventh day; the Musalmán on the Ramazán. Who formed the remaining months and days, that you should venerate but one? If the Creator dwell in tabernacles, whose dwelling is the universe? The city of the Hindu God is to the east, the city of the Musalmán God is to the west; but explore your own heart, for there is the God both of the Musalmáns and of the Hindus. Behold but One in all things. He to whom the world belongs, He is the father of the worshippers alike of Alí and of Ráma. He is my guide, He is my priest.' The moral code of Kabír is as beautiful as his doctrine. It consists in humanity, in truthfulness, in retirement, and in obedience to the spiritual guide.

The labours of Kabír may be placed between 1380 and 1420 A.D. In 1485 Chaitanya was born. As Rámánand and Kabír were the Vishnuvite reformers of Hindustán and Bengal, so Chaitanya was the prophet of Orissa, and for twelve years laboured to extend the worship of Jagannáth. Signs and wonders attended him through life, and during four centuries he has been worshipped as an incarnation of Vishnu. For thirteen months the holy child lay in the womb. An eclipse ended as he entered the world. On the lonely shores of Purí he was visited by beatific sights and revelations. On one occasion he beheld the host of heaven sporting upon the blue waves, and plunged into the ocean in a religious ecstasy, but was miraculously returned to earth in a fisherman's net. After forty-two years of preaching, he disappeared in A.D. 1527.

Extricating ourselves from the halo of legends which surround and obscure the apostle, we know little of his private life, except that he was the son of a Sylhet Bráhman, settled at Nadiyá, near Calcutta; that in his youth he married the daughter of a celebrated saint; that at twenty-four he forsook the world, and, renouncing the status of a householder, repaired to Orissa, and devoted the rest of his life to the propagation of his faith. But with regard to his doctrines we have the most ample evidence. No caste and no race was beyond the pale of salvation. The followers of Chaitanya belong to every caste, but they acknowledge the rule of the descendants of the six original disciples (Gosáins). The sect is open alike to the married and the unmarried. It has its celibates and wandering mendicants, but its religious teachers are generally married men. They live with their families and dependants in little clusters of houses around a temple of Vishnu, and in this way the adoration of Chaitanya has become a sort of family worship throughout Orissa. In Purí there is a temple specially dedicated to his name, and many little shrines are scattered over the country. But he is generally adored in connection with Vishnu; and of such joint temples there are at present 300 in the town of Purí, and 500 more throughout the District. The worship of Chaitanya extends through all Orissa; and there has been compiled a long list of landed families, who worship him with a daily ritual in household chapels dedicated to his name.

At this moment, Chaitanya is the apostle of the common people. The Bráhmans, unless they happen to enjoy grants of land, in his name, ignore his work. In almost every Bráhman village the communal shrine is dedicated to Siva; but in the villages of the ordinary husbandmen, it is Vishnu who is worshipped, and Chaitanya who is remembered as the great teacher of the popular faith.

VISHNUVITE CORRUPTION.—The death of this reformer marks the beginning of the spiritual decline of Vishnu-worship. The most deplorable of its corruptions at the present day is that which has covered the temple walls with indecent sculptures, and filled their innermost sanctuaries with licentious rites. It is very difficult for a person not a Hindu to pronounce upon the real extent of this evil. None but a Hindu can enter any of the larger temples, and none but a Hindu priest really knows the truth about their inner mysteries. But between Vishnuvism and Love-worship there is but a step, and this step has been formally and publicly taken by a large sect of Vishnuvites.

As early as 1520, a teacher, Vallabha-Swámí, appeared in Northern India, preaching that the liberation of the soul depended not upon the mortification of the body, and that God was to be sought not in nakedness and hunger and solitude, but amid the enjoyments of this life. The special object of his adoration was Vishnu, in his pastoral incarnation as Krishna, leading a glorious Arcadian life in the forest. The legends surround him with all that makes existence beautiful. Shady bowers, lovely women, exquisite viands, and everything that appeals to the luscious sensuousness of a tropical race, are mingled in his worship. His daily ritual consists of eight services, in which his image is delicately bathed, anointed with essences, splendidly attired, and sumptuously fed. His great annual ceremony in Lower Bengal is the Car Festival of Jagannáth, hereafter to be described. It is a religion of luxury and systematic indulgence. The followers of the first Vishnuvite reformers dwelt together in secluded monasteries, or went about scantily clothed, living upon alms. But this sect performs its devotions arrayed in costly apparel, anointed with oil, and perfumed with camphor or sandal-wood oil. It seeks its converts not among weavers, or leather-dressers, or barbers, but among wealthy bankers and merchants, who look upon life as a thing to be enjoyed, and upon pilgrimage as a means of extending their trading enterprises.

In a religion of this sort great abuses are inevitable. It was a revolt against a system which taught that the soul could approach its Maker only by the mortification of the body. It declared that God was present in the cities and marts of men, not less than in the cave of the ascetic. Faith and love were its instruments of salvation, and voluptuous contemplation its approved spiritual state. It delighted to clothe the Deity in a beautiful human form, and mystical amorous poems make a large part of its canonical literature. One of its most valued theological treatises is entitled the Ocean of Love ; and although its nobler professors have always recognised its spiritual character, to the common order of minds it has become simply a religion of pleasure. The loves of Rádhá and Krishna, that exquisite woodland pastoral, has been materialized into a sanction for licentious rites.

In Orissa, among the common people, Jagannáth reigns supreme. Different Fiscal Divisions claim, as a precious hereditary right, the privilege of rendering service to the god. The jungly highlands on the west of the Chilká supply the timber for the Car Festival. The lowlands on the north of the lake annually send thousands of peasants to drag the sacred vehicle. The inhabitants delight to explain the etymology of their towns and villages by referring the names to some incident in the history of the god. The royal line has for centuries performed menial offices before the image; and as the sweeper caste is the lowest in the Hindu commonwealth, so the kings of Orissa have reached the climax of religious humility, in their most cherished title of Hereditary Sweeper to Jagannáth.

ENDOWMENTS: RELIGIOUS OFFERINGS.—The devotion of centuries has long ago made Jagannáth a very wealthy god. The Muhammadans spared so opulent a deity for the revenue that he could be made to yield. All other idols in Orissa they smashed in pieces; and the common saying at this day is, that the noses and ears of the Hindu gods dropped off at the sound of the Musalmán kettle-drum. But Jagannáth was too lucrative a property to be roughly handled; and a native historian informs us that they raised the enormous sum of nine *lákhs* of *sikká* rupees or £100,000 per annum, by licensing his worship. If this statement be correct, the Musalmáns must have taxed the priests as well as the pilgrims; as the total sum realized by the British Government, on its taking charge of the country, averaged only £6619 a year *net*, after deductions had been made for all charges, etc., the average gross collections being £12,574. The Marhattás, being Hindus, encouraged the worship and richly endowed the god. In 1755 they sanctioned a regular payment for the support of the temple, estimated, when we took possession of the country, as equal to a landed estate of £1700 a year. The monasteries connected with the temple also enjoy a revenue, estimated in 1848 to amount to £20,000 per annum. The present rental of the monasteries connected with Jagannáth amounts, so far as can be ascertained, to £27,000 per annum; and at the moderate computation of fifteen years' purchase, represents landed property of the value of nearly half a million sterling.

The English Government has scrupulously respected the patrimony of Jagannáth. On our taking over the country, it was practically decided that all disbursements hitherto made for charitable uses should be continued, on the scale which the orthodox Marhattá Government had established. Among these costly bequests, the superintendence of the temple of Jagannáth was the chief. During the years that preceded their expulsion, the Marhattás had paid from £3000 to £5000 a year from their treasury, to make good the deficit between the receipts and the charges of the establishment. Lord Wellesley expressly enjoined our troops, when they marched to occupy the Province in 1803, to respect the temple and the religious prejudices of the Bráhmans and pilgrims. At the same time, our officers were to make no arrangements that would hamper Government in any subsequent reform of temple abuses. The General communicated these orders to the priests of Jagannáth when he entered the Province; and a deputation of Bráhmans accordingly came into the camp, and placed the temple under his protection without a blow being struck.

The first effect of our occupation was temporarily to suspend the tax on pilgrims, as we found the system under which the Marhattás had levied it to be grossly oppressive. At all fords and passes the unhappy pilgrims had to pay toll. Every governor along the road levied as much as he could extort; and one chief fixed the impost in his district at the enormous rate of Rs. 14. 8. o or £1, 9s. for each foot-passenger. With regard to the temple, we simply engaged to take the place of the late Government. The Marhattás, however, had granted no fixed sum, but had annually made up the difference between the receipts and the expenditure of the temple. For the first four years we followed the same plan, and struggled to thread our way through the endless maze of chicanery in which the temple accounts were involved. Practically, there was a deficit of £3000 a year, which the ruling power had to make good. In 1807 the Government endeavoured to get rid of the minute supervision of idolatrous rites which this system involved. A year later it formally vested the temple superintendence in the Rájá of Khurdhá, the representative of the ancient royal line of Orissa, whom the Marhattás had so grievously oppressed. He received a total allowance of £6000 per annum, on the understanding that the sum was to be wholly spent in the maintenance of the temple.

Meanwhile, Government reimbursed itself by a pilgrim tax similar to that which had been always levied by the native governments, but of a much lighter character. It stationed guards at the two entrances to the town, who classified the pilgrims and levied the rates. The richer sort paid from 12s. to £1 per head, the commonalty paid 4s.; but all religious devotees, carriers of holy water, and *bona fide* inhabitants of Orissa, went free. By exempting merchants and hucksters of every sort, care was taken not to let the tax interfere with trade. All poor pilgrims, who should declare their inability to pay, were also exempted; and practically only two-thirds of the registered number paid. The registered number itself seldom represented one-half the actual total that crept into the city unperceived.

The pilgrim tax thus levied formed an important item in our revenue from Orissa. During the twenty-one years ending 1831, it yielded a net sum of £139,000, or £6619 a year, after deducting £5955 a year from the gross returns for the temple expenses and charges. It was felt, however, that the money thus received was to a certain extent the price of a State sanction to idolatry, and in 1840 the Company removed this stain from its administration. It abolished the pilgrim tax, and made over the entire management of the temple to the Rájás of Khurdhá. The Government, however, scrupulously maintained the pledges on the strength of which the temple had been placed under our protection by the priests; and while utterly withdrawing itself from the management, and refusing thenceforward in any way to recognise the shrine, or to levy a tax upon the devotees, it declined to interfere with its ancient grants. The money allowance had been from time to time reduced, as several functions of the administration—the police, for example, which had formerly been defrayed by the temple—passed under the regular authorities. This annual money allowance was subsequently converted into a grant of land, estimated to be worth about £4000 a year; and all payments from the treasury, and all State inter-ference of whatever sort, have long since ceased.

It is difficult to form anything like an accurate estimate of the present income of Jagannáth. Accepting the computation of the rent-roll of the monasteries connected with the temple at £27,000, and adding £4000 as the present value of the lands granted by the State, we have a total of £31,000. This sum, however, represents but a fraction of his actual income. The offerings of the pilgrims form the great source of his wealth. No one comes empty-handed. The richer pilgrims heap gold and silver and jewels at the feet of the god, or spread before him charters and title-deeds, conveying rich lands in distant Provinces. Every one, from the richest to the poorest, gives beyond his ability; many cripple their fortunes for the rest of their lives in a frenzy of liberality; and hundreds die on the way home, from not having kept enough to support them on the journey. It may be mentioned that Ranjit Sinh bequeathed the

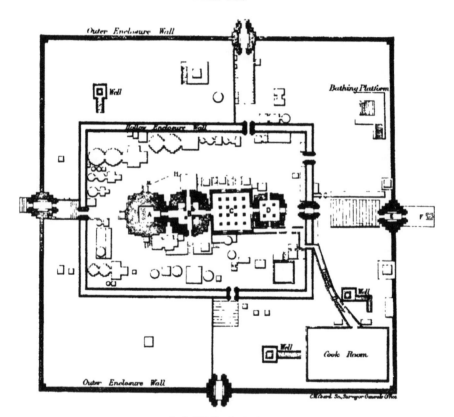

PLAN OF TEMPLE OF JAGANNÁTH
AT PURI

Presented to the Author by Babu Radhika Prasad Mukarji Ass^{tt} Eng^r D.P.W.

Ground Plan

Scale 200 f^t to the Inch

A   TOWERED SANCTUARY CONTAINING IDOLS
B   HALL OF AUDIENCE FOR PILGRIMS
C   PILLARED HALL FOR DANCING GIRLS
D   HALL OF OFFERINGS
E   LION GATE
F   SUN PILLAR

celebrated Koh-i-Nur diamond, which now forms one of the Crown
jewels of England, to Jagannáth. The total annual value of these
offerings can never be known. Some have stated it to me as high as
£70,000. This, I think, is excessive; although it should be remembered that, according to native historians, the Muhammadans managed
to extract £100,000 from the pilgrims before they entered the city at
all. A moderate computation estimated the offerings to the priests at
twice the gross sum which the British officers realized as pilgrim tax;
and now that the tax is withdrawn and the pilgrims enter the city so
much the richer, the oblations cannot fall much short of three times the
amount. This would yield a yearly sum of £37,000, which, added
to the £4000 derived from the temple lands, and to the revenues
of the religious houses valued at £27,000, makes the total income of
Jagannáth not less than £68,000 per annum.

A religious society so ancient and so wealthy, naturally gathers
around it a vast body of retainers. A quarter of a century ago,
there were as many as six thousand male adults as priests, warders
of the temple, and pilgrim guides. The number has probably
increased since then; and, including the monastic establishments,
their servants and hired labourers, along with the vast body of
pilgrim guides who roam through every Province of India, it is
probable that not less than 20,000 men, women, and children, live,
directly or indirectly, by the service of lord Jagannáth.

The immediate attendants on the god are divided into thirty-six
orders and ninety-seven classes. At the head is the Rájá of
Khurdhá, the representative of the ancient royal house of Orissa,
who takes upon himself the lowly office of sweeper to Jagannáth.
Decorators of the idols, strewers of flowers, priests of the wardrobe,
bakers, cooks, guards, musicians, dancing-girls, torch-bearers,
grooms, elephant-keepers, and artisans of every sort, follow.
There are distinct sets of servants to put the god to bed, to dress
him, and to bathe him. A special department keeps up the temple
records, and affords a calm literary asylum to a few learned men.
The baser features of a worship which aims at a sensuous realization
of God, by endowing Him with human passions, appear in a band
of prostitutes who sing before the image.

THE TEMPLE.—The sacred enclosure is nearly in the form of a
square, protected from profane eyes by a massive stone wall 20
feet high, 652 feet long, and 630 broad. Within it, rise about
120 temples, dedicated to the various forms in which the Hindu

mind has imagined its God. In the list are counted no fewer than thirteen temples to Siva, besides several to his queen, the great rivals of Vishnu. The nature-worship of primitive times is represented, even in this most complex development of modern superstition, by a temple to the sun. But the great pagoda is the one dedicated to Jagannáth. Its conical tower rises like an elaborately carved sugar-loaf, 192 feet high, black with time, and surmounted by the mystic wheel and flag of Vishnu. Outside the principal entrance, or Lion Gate, in the square where the pilgrims chiefly throng, is an exquisite monolithic pillar which stood for centuries before the Temple of the Sun, twenty miles up the coast.

The temple of Jagannáth consists, like all the larger shrines in Orissa, of four chambers opening one into the other. The first is the Hall of Offerings (*Bhog-mandir*), where the bulkier oblations are made, only a small quantity of choice food being admitted into the inner shrine. The second is the Pillared Hall (*Nat-mandir*), for the musicians and dancing-girls. The third is the Hall of Audience (*Jagamohan*), in which the pilgrims assemble to gaze upon the god. The fourth is the Sanctuary itself (*Bara deul*), surmounted by its lofty conical tower. Here sits Jagannáth, with his brother Balabhadra and his sister Subhadrá, in jewelled state. The images are rude logs, coarsely fashioned into the form of the human bust from the waist up. On certain festivals the priests fasten golden hands to the short stumps which project from the shoulders of Jagannáth. The want of arms has been already accounted for in the legend of Básu the fowler, but the priests give a more spiritual explanation. The Lord of the World, they say, needs neither hands nor feet to work his purposes among men.

The service of the temple consists partly in a daily round of oblations, and partly in sumptuous ceremonials at stated periods throughout the year. The offerings are simple enough : fruits and flowers, and the various articles of food in use among a primitive people. Rice, pulse, clarified butter, milk, salt, vegetables, ginger, and cocoanuts are offered to the images and eaten by the priests. Four times every day the priests clear the sanctuary, and close the tower gates, while the god is at his meals. At the door stand Vishnuvite ascetics, waving large fans and singing his praises. In the Pillared Hall (*Jagamohan*), a choir of dancing-girls enliven the idol's repast by their airy gyrations, while a few favoured servants attend him in his inner shrine.

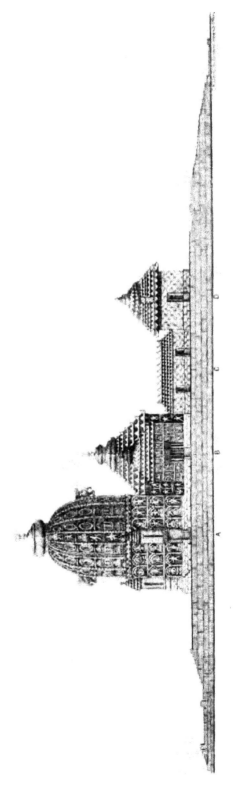

THE TEMPLE OF JAGANNÁTH.

AT PURI.

'Elevation'

A TOWERED SANCTUARY CONTAINING IDOLS.
B HALL OF AUDIENCE FOR PILGRIMS.
C PILLARED HALL FOR DANCING GIRLS.
D HALL OF OFFERINGS.

The offerings are bloodless. No animal yields up his life in the service of Jagannáth. The spilling of blood pollutes the whole edifice, and a set of servants are maintained to hurry away the sacrificial food that may have been thus contaminated. Yet so deeply rooted is the spirit of compromise in this great national temple, that the sacred enclosure also contains a shrine to Bimalá, the 'stainless' queen of the All-Destroyer, who is every year adored with midnight rites and bloody sacrifices.

FESTIVALS.—Twenty-four high festivals enliven the religious year. They consist chiefly of Vishnuvite celebrations, but freely admit the ceremonials of the rival sects. A vein of the old aboriginal rites runs through them all. At the Red-Powder Festival (*Chandan-játrá*), which occurs in the month of Baisákh, and lasts for three weeks, a picturesque boat procession of the gods passes along the sacred lake. Vishnu and Siva enjoy equal honours in the ceremony. The wild age is yearly commemorated in the abduction of the fair nymph by the enamoured god, a primitive form of marriage *per raptionem*, acknowledged by ancient Hindu law. The Aryan advance through India is celebrated on Ráma's birthday, on which the god appears in the dress and arms of the Sanskrit hero who marched through the southern jungles of the peninsula, and slew the cannibal king of Ceylon. At the Bathing Festival (*Snán-játrá*), when the images are brought down in great pomp to one of the artificial lakes, a proboscis is fastened to their noses, so as to give them the look of the elephant god of the aboriginal tribes (Ganesh). The supremacy of Vishnu is declared, however, in the festival of the slaughter of the deadly Cobra-da-Capello (*Káli-damana*), the familiar of Siva and his queen. The indecent rites that have crept into Vishnuvism, and which, according to the spirit of the worshipper, are either high religious mysteries or simple obscenities, are represented by the Birth Festival (*Janam*), in which a priest takes the part of the father, and a dancing-girl that of the mother, of Jagannáth, and the ceremony of his nativity is performed to the life.

THE CAR FESTIVAL (*Rath-játrá*) is the great event of the year. It takes place, according as the Hindu months fall, in June or July, and for weeks beforehand, pilgrims come trooping into Purí by thousands every day. The whole District is in a ferment. The great car is forty-five feet in height. This vast structure is supported on sixteen wheels of seven feet diameter, and is thirty-five feet square. The brother and sister of Jagannáth have separate cars a few feet smaller. When the sacred images are at length brought forth and placed upon their chariots, thousands fall on their knees and bow their foreheads in the dust. The vast multitude shouts with one throat, and, surging backwards and forwards, drags the wheeled edifices down the broad street towards the country-house of lord Jagannáth. Music strikes up before and behind, drums beat, cymbals clash, the priests harangue from the cars, or shout a sort of fescennine medley enlivened with broad allusions and coarse gestures, which are received with roars of laughter by the crowd. And so the dense mass struggles forward by convulsive jerks, tugging and sweating, shouting and jumping, singing, and praying, and swearing. The distance from the temple to the country-house is less than a mile; but the wheels sink deep into the sand, and the journey takes several days. After hours of severe toil and wild excitement in the July tropical sun, a reaction necessarily follows. The zeal of the pilgrims flags before the garden-house is reached; and the cars, deserted by the devotees, are dragged along by the professional pullers with deep-drawn grunts and groans. These men, 4200 in number, are peasants from the neighbouring Fiscal Divisions, who generally manage to live at free quarters in Purí during the festival.

Once arrived at the country-house, the enthusiasm subsides. The pilgrims drop exhausted upon the burning sand of the sacred street, or block up the lanes with their prostrate bodies. When they have slept off their excitement, they rise refreshed and ready for another of the strong religious stimulants of the season. Lord Jagannáth is left to get back to his temple as best he can; and in the quaint words of a writer half a century ago, but for the professional car-pullers, the god 'would infallibly stick' at his country-house.

In a closely-packed, eager throng of a hundred thousand men and women, many of them unaccustomed to exposure or hard labour, and all of them tugging and straining to the utmost under the blazing tropical sun, deaths must occasionally occur. There have, doubtless, been instances of pilgrims throwing themselves under the wheels in a frenzy of religious excitement; but such instances have always been rare, and are now unknown. At one time, several unhappy people were killed or injured every year, but they were almost invariably cases of accidental trampling. The few suicides that did occur were for the most part cases of diseased and miserable objects, who took this means to put themselves out of pain. The official returns now place this beyond doubt. Nothing, indeed, could be more opposed to the spirit of Vishnu-worship than self-immolation. Accidental death within the temple renders the whole place unclean. The ritual suddenly stops, and the polluted offerings are hurried away from the sight of the offended god. According to Chaitanya, the apostle of Jagannáth, the destruction of the least of God's creatures is a sin against the Creator. Self-immolation he would have regarded with horror. The copious religious literature of his sect frequently describes the Car Festival, but makes no mention of self-sacrifice, nor does it contain any passage that could be twisted into a sanction for it. Abul Fazl, the keen Musalmán observer, is equally silent, although from the context it is almost certain that, had he heard of the practice, he would have mentioned it.

It would be well for Jagannáth if these old calumnies were the only charges which his priests had to answer. Lascivious sculptures disfigure his walls, indecent ceremonies disgrace his ritual, and dancing-girls put the modest female worshippers to the blush by their demeanour. But these are not the sole corruptions of the faith. The temple of Jagannáth, that *colluvio religionum*, in which every creed obtained an asylum, and in which every class and sect can find its god, now closes its gates against the low-caste population. It were vain to attempt to trace the history of this gross violation of the spirit of the reformed Vishnuvite faith. Even at the present moment no hard-and-fast line exists between the admitted and the excluded castes; and the priests are said to be much less strict to mark the disqualification of caste in pilgrims from a distance, than among. the non-paying local populace. Speaking generally, only those castes are shut out who retain the flesh-eating and animal-life-destroying propensities and professions of the aboriginal tribes.

A man must be a very pronounced non-Aryan to be excluded. Certain of the low castes, such as the washermen and potters, may enter half-way, and, standing humbly in the court outside the great temple, catch a glimpse of the jewelled god within. But unquestionable non-Aryans, like the neighbouring hill-tribes or forest races, and the landless servile castes of the lowlands, cannot go in at all. The same ban extends to those engaged in occupations either offensive in themselves, or repugnant to Aryan ideas of purity, such as wine-sellers, sweepers, skinners, corpse-bearers, hunters, fishers, and bird-killers. Básu the fowler would now be driven from the doors of the temple dedicated to his own god. Criminals who have been in jail, and women of bad character, except the privileged temple girls, are also excluded—with this difference, however, that a criminal may expiate the defilement of imprisonment by penance and costly purifications ; but a woman once fallen can never more pass the temple gates.

The following list of excluded castes has been drawn up partly from the statements of the Bráhmans, and partly from those of the low castes themselves :—1. Christians ; 2. Muhammadans ; 3. Hill or forest races ; 4. Bauris ; 5. Savars ; 6. Páns ; 7. Háris (except to clean away filth) ; 8. Chámárs ; 9. Doms and Chandáls ; 10. Chiriámárs (bird-killers) ; 11. Sials (wine-sellers) ; 12. Gokhás (fishermen) ; 13. Siulas (fishermen) ; 14. Tiors (fishermen) ; 15. Nuliás (Telingá boatmen) ; 16. Pátrás (low-caste cloth-makers) ; 17. Kandárás (village watchmen) ; 18. Common prostitutes ; 19. Persons who have been in jail, but with right of expiation ; 20. Washermen ; 21. Potters. But these last two may enter the outer court.

THE PILGRIMS OF JAGANNATH. — The name of Jagannáth still draws the faithful from the most distant Provinces of India to the Purí sands. Day and night throughout every month of the year, troops of devotees arrive at Purí ; and for 300 miles along the great Orissa road, every village has its pilgrim encampment. The parties consist of from 20 to 300 persons. At the time of the great festivals, these bands follow so close as to touch each other ; and a continuous train of pilgrims, many miles long, may often be seen on the Purí highroad. They march in orderly procession, each party under its spiritual leader. At least five-sixths, and often nine-tenths, of them are females. Now a straggling band of slender, diminutive women, clothed in white muslin, and limping sadly along, shows a pilgrim company from Lower Bengal ; then a joyous retinue with flowing garments of bright red or blue, trudging stoutly forward, their noses pierced with elaborate rings, their faces freely tattooed, and their hands encumbered with bundles of very dirty cloth, proclaims the stalwart female peasantry of Northern Hindustán. Ninety-five out of a hundred are on foot. Mixed with the throng are devotees of various sorts,—some covered with ashes; some almost naked ; some with matted, yellow-stained hair ; and almost all with their foreheads streaked with red or white, a string of beads round their necks, and a stout staff in their hands. Every now and then, covered waggons drawn by the high-humped bullocks of Upper India, or by the smaller breed of Bengal, according to the nationality of the owner, creak past on their wooden wheels. Those from the

Northern Provinces still bear traces of the licentious Musalmán rule, by being jealously shut up. The Bengalí husband, on the other hand, keeps his women good-tempered, and renders pilgrimage pleasant, by piercing holes in the waggon-hood, through which dark female eyes constantly peep out. Then a lady in coloured trousers, from some village near Dehli, ambles past on a tiny pony, her husband submissively walking by her side, and a female domestic, with a hamper of Ganges water and a bundle of dirty cloth, bringing up the rear. Next a great train of palanquins, carrying a Calcutta banker and his ladies, sweeps past. But the greatest spectacle is a north-country Rájá, with his caravan of elephants, camels, led horses, and swordsmen, looking resigned and very helpless in his sedan of state, followed by all the indescribable confusion, dirt, and noises of Indian royalty.

The great spiritual army that thus marches its hundreds, and sometimes its thousands, of miles, along burning roads, across unbridged rivers, and through pestilent regions of jungle and swamp, is annually recruited with as much tact and regularity as is bestowed on any military force. Attached to the temple is a body of emissaries, called pilgrim guides, numbering about three thousand men, who visit every Province and District of India in search of devotees. Each of the leading priests keeps up a separate set of these men, sending them to the part of the country of which he enjoys the spiritual charge, and claiming the profits of the disciples they bring in. They wander about from village to village within their allotted beats, preaching pilgrimage as the liberation from sin. The arrival of a pilgrim-guide is a memorable event in the still life of an Indian village. He seldom shines in public exhortation, but waits till the men have gone out to the fields, and then makes a round of visits to the women. Skilled in every artifice of persuasion, he works upon the religious fears and the worldly hopes of the female mind; and by the time the unsuspecting husbands come home from their work, every house has its fair apostle of pilgrimage. The elder women, and some of the aged fathers of the hamlet, long to see the face of the merciful god who will remit the sins of a life, and are content to lay their bones within his precincts. Religious motives of a less emphatic sort influence the majority. The hopes of worldly reward for a good deed swell the number. The fashionableness of pilgrimage attracts the frivolous. The young are hooked by the novelty of a journey through strange countries. Poor widows catch at anything to relieve the tedium of their blighted existence; and barren wives long to pick up the child-giving berries of the banyan tree within the sacred enclosure, and to pour out the petition of their souls before the kindly god.

In parties of thirty pilgrims, more than five men are seldom met with, and sometimes not more than three. The proportion may be taken at ten per cent. The first part of the journey is pleasant enough. Change of scene, new countries, new races, new languages, and a world of new customs and sights await the travellers from Upper India. A good part of the distance is now accomplished by railway, and the northern pilgrims can thus get over their first thousand or even fourteen hundred miles, if they chose to travel straight through, in three days. But they generally walk from three to six hundred miles, although within the last two or three years a steamboat service between Calcutta and Orissa has attracted large numbers of pilgrims, which is steadily increasing. Those who keep to the road have spent their strength long before the holy city is reached. The sturdy women of Hindustán brave it out, and sing songs till they drop; but the weaker females of Bengal limp piteously along with bleeding feet in silence, broken only by deep sighs and an occasional sob. The pilgrim-guide tries to keep up their spirits, and insists, with a necessary obduracy, on their doing a full day's journey every day, in order that they may reach in time for the festival. Many a sickly girl dies upon the road; and by the time they reach Purí, the whole party have their feet bound up in rags, plastered with dirt and blood.

But, once within sight of the holy city, the pains and miseries of the journey are forgotten. They hurry across the ancient Mar-hattá bridge with songs and ejaculations, and rushing towards one of the great artificial lakes, plunge beneath its sacred waters in a transport of religious emotion. The dirty bundles of rags now yield their inner treasures of spotless cotton, and the pilgrims, refreshed and robed in clean garments, proceed to the temple. The pilgrim-guide makes over the flock to his priestly employer, and every hour discloses some new idol or solemn spectacle. As they pass the Lion Gate, a man of the sweeper caste strikes them with his broom to purify them of their sins, and forces them to promise, on pain of losing all the benefits of pilgrimage, not to disclose the events of the journey or the secrets of the shrine.

In a few days the excitement subsides. At first nothing can

exceed their liberality to their spiritual guide. But thoughts of the slender provision remaining for the return journey soon begin to cool their munificence, and the ghostly man's attentions slacken in proportion. Before a week is over, money altercations commence, which in process of time resolve themselves into an acrimonious haggling over every shrine; and the last few days of their stay are generally devoted to schemes for getting out of the holy city with as few more payments as possible.

Every day the pilgrims bathe in one of the sacred lakes. These vast artificial sheets of water are embanked with solid masonry, honeycombed by time, and adorned with temples rising from the edge or peeping from beneath masses of rich foliage. At the principal one, 5000 bathers may be seen at once. On the masonry banks, which are formed into one continuous flight of steps all the way round, a good mile in length, there is sometimes not an inch of standing room to be had. Here, as in every spot where the common people congregate, the primitive adoration of local divinities and village gods makes its appearance. In this centre of Vishnu-worship, half-way down the grand flight of steps to the lake, stands a venerable banyan tree, the abode of an ancient sylvan deity, whom the pilgrims propitiate by sticking red flowers into the crevices of the weather-beaten trunk.

Not far off is the garden-house of Jagannáth, whither the three sacred images are drawn during the Car Festival. It stands at the end of a long, broad, sandy avenue, somewhat under a mile in length, which runs direct from it to the temple. It is surrounded by a massive wall about twenty feet high, castellated at the top. The principal gateway looks towards the temple, and is a handsome structure, with a fine pointed roof adorned with lions in the most conventional style of Hindu sculpture. Inside, one catches glimpses of long straight walks, and groves of bright evergreen trees, with an ancient shrine at the end of the vista.

Another place visited by all pilgrims is the *Swarga-dwára*, the Gate of Heaven. The devotee threads his way through the deep-sunk narrow alleys of the town, with their thatched huts of wattle and mud gaily painted with red and yellow gods, till he reaches the shore. There, on the south of the city, he comes on a region of sand-hills, bordered by temples and tombs behind, and with the surf-beaten beach in front. No distinct boundaries mark the limits of the Gate of Heaven. It runs about a quarter of a mile along the coast, or 'as much as may be occupied by a thousand cows.' In the background the lofty tower of Jagannáth rises from the heart of the city; and in the intervening space little monasteries cluster, each in its own hollow between the sandy hills. Sometimes an outlying rood or two of land is reclaimed, with infinite labour, from the sandy slopes, and fenced in by a curious wall made of the red earth pots in which the holy food is served out to the pilgrims. The sacred rice can only be placed in a new vessel, and every evening thousands of the unbroken pots are at the disposal of any one in want of such slender building materials.

Here the pilgrims bathe. At the great festival, as many as 40,000 rush together into the surf; and every evening, silent groups may be seen purifying themselves for their devotions under the slanting rays of the sun. It is a spot sanctified by the funeral rites of generations. The low castes who bury their dead, dig a hasty hole in the sand; and the hillocks are covered with bones and skulls, which have been washed bare by the tropical rains, or dug up by the jackals. Every evening, funeral pyres are lighted here for the incremation of the bodies of the more respectable Hindus who have died in the town.

No trustworthy statistics exist as to the number of pilgrims who visit Jagannáth. But a native gentleman, who has spent his life on the spot, has published as his opinion that the number that daily flocks in and out of the holy city never falls short of 50,000 a year, and sometimes amounts to 300,000. Not a day passes without long trains of footsore travellers arriving at the shrine. At the Car Festival, food is cooked in the temple kitchen for 90,000 devotees; at another festival for 70,000; and on the morning of one of their solemn full moons, 40,000 pilgrims wash away their sins in the surf. The old registers, during the period when the pilgrim tax was levied, notoriously fell below the truth; yet in five out of the ten years between 1820 and 1829, the official return amounted to between one and two hundred thousand. The pilgrims from the south are a mere handful compared with those who come from Bengal and Northern India, yet it has been ascertained that 65,000 find their way to Purí, across the Chilká lake, in two months alone. Along the great north road the stream flows day and night. As many as 20,000 arrive at a favourite halting-place between sunrise and sunset. As many as 9613 were actually counted by the police leaving Purí on a single day, and 19,209 during the last six days in June. This is the number absolutely ascertained to have departed; and probably many more slipped off unperceived. The records of the reverend missionaries in Orissa estimate the number of the pilgrims present at the Car Festival alone, in some years, as high as 145,000.

PILGRIM MORTALITY.—Disease and death make havoc of the pilgrims. During their stay in Purí they are badly lodged and miserably fed. The priests impress on them the impropriety of dressing food within the holy city; and the temple kitchen thus secures the monopoly of cooking for the multitude. The eatables served out chiefly consist of boiled rice. Peas, pulse, clarified butter, sugar, and rice are also made into a variety of confections. The charges seem to be reasonable enough; a mess of rice sufficient for two men costing three halfpence, except during the festivals, when the vast number of customers enables the cooks to raise their prices. Before being offered for sale, it is presented to Jagannáth in the outer hall, but within sight of the image, and thus becomes holy food. When fresh it is not unwholesome, although the pilgrims complain of the cooking being often very bad. But, unfortunately, only a part of it is eaten fresh, as it is too sacred for the least fragment to be thrown away. Large quantities of it are sold in a state dangerous even to a man in robust health, and deadly to the way-worn pilgrims, half of whom reach Purí with some form or other of bowel complaint. 'When examined after twenty-four hours, even in January,' writes Dr. Mouat, late Inspector-General of Jails, 'putrefactive fermentation had begun in all the rice compounds; and after forty-eight hours, the whole was a loathsome mass of putrid matter, utterly unfit for human use. This food forms the chief subsistence of the pilgrims, and the sole subsistence of the beggars who flock in hundreds to the shrines during the festival. It is consumed by some one or other, whatever its state of putrefaction, to the very last morsel.'

But bad food is only one of many predisposing causes to disease which the pilgrims have to encounter. The low level of Purí, and the sandy ridges which check the natural drainage towards the sea, render it a very dirty city. Each house is built on a little mud platform about four feet high. In the centre of the platform is a drain which receives the filth of the household, and discharges it in the form of black, stinking ooze on the street outside. The platform itself becomes gradually soaked with the pestiferous slime. In many houses, indeed, a deep, open cesspool is sunk in the earthen platform; and the wretched inmates eat and sleep around this perennial fountain of death. As a rule, the houses consist simply of two or three cells leading one into the other, without windows or roof ventilation of any sort. In these lairs of disease the pilgrims are massed together in a manner shocking to humanity. The city contains 6363 houses, with a resident population in 1872 of 22,695 souls. But almost every citizen takes in pilgrims, and in 1869 there were not fewer than 5000 lodging-houses in the city. The scenes that formerly took place in these putrid dens baffle description. 'I was shown one apartment,' says Dr. Mouat in the Report above cited, 'in the best pilgrim hotel of the place, in which eighty persons were said to have passed the night. It was 13 feet long, 10 feet 5 inches broad, with side walls 6½ feet in height, and a low pent roof over it. It had but one entrance, and no escape for the effete air. It was dark, dirty, and dismal when empty, and must have been a pest-house during the festival. In this house occurred the first case of cholera in the last outbreak. If this be the normal state of the best lodging-house in the broad main street of Purí, it is not difficult to imagine the condition of the worst, in the narrow, confined, un-drained back-slums of the town.' About the time of the Car Festival, there can be little doubt that as many as 90,000 people were often packed for weeks together in the 5000 lodging-houses of Purí.

At certain seasons of the year this misery is mitigated by sleeping out of doors. In the dry weather, the streets of Purí look like a great encampment, without the tents. The soaking dews are unwholesome enough; but as long as the people can spend the night outside, some check exists to the overcrowding of pilgrims by rapacious lodging-house keepers. How slight this check practically proves, may be judged of from the fact that the official reports before cited are specially selected as referring to the season when people can sleep out of doors with impunity. But the Car Festival, the great ceremony of the year, unfortunately falls at the beginning of the rains. The water pours down for hours in almost solid sheets. Every lane and alley becomes a torrent or a stinking canal, which holds in suspension the accumulated filth heaps of the hot weather. The wretched pilgrims are now penned into the lodging-house cells without mercy. Cholera invariably breaks out. The living and the dying are huddled together, with a leaky roof above, and a miry clay floor under foot, 'the space allotted per head being just as much as they can cover lying down.'

But it is on the return journey that the misery of the pilgrims reaches its climax. The rapacity of the Purí priests and lodging-house keepers has passed into a proverb. A week or ten days finishes the process of plundering, and the stripped and half-starved pilgrims crawl out of the city with their faces towards home. They stagger along under their burdens of holy food, which is wrapped up in dirty cloth, or packed away in heavy baskets and red earthen pots. The men from the Upper Provinces further encumber themselves with a palm-leaf umbrella, and a bundle of canes died red, beneath whose strokes they did penance at the Lion Gate. After the Car Festival, they find every stream flooded. Hundreds of them have not money enough left to pay for being ferried over the network of rivers in the delta. Even those who can pay have often to sit for days in the rain on the bank, before a boat will venture to launch on the ungovernable torrent. At a single river, an English traveller once counted as many as forty corpses, over which the kites and dogs were battling.

The famished, drenched throng toils painfully backward, urged by the knowledge that their slender stock of money will only last a very few weeks, and that, after it is done, nothing remains but to die. The missionaries along the line of march have ascertained that sometimes they travel forty miles a day, dragging their weary limbs along till they drop from sheer fatigue. Hundreds die upon the roadside. Those are most happy whom insensibility overtakes in some English Station. The servants of the municipality pick them up and carry them to the hospital. The wretched pilgrims crowd into the villages and halting-places along the road, blocking up the streets, and creating an artificial famine. The available sleeping places are soon crammed to overflowing, and every night thousands have no shelter from the pouring rain. Miserable groups huddle under trees. Long lines, with their heads on their bundles, lie among the carts and bullocks on the side of the road.

It is impossible to compute, with anything like precision, the number that thus perish on the homeward journey. Personal inquiries among the poorer pilgrims lead to the conclusion that the deaths in the city and by the way seldom fall below one-eighth, and often amount to one-fifth, of each company; and the Sanitary Commissioner for Bengal confirms this estimate. Among the richer devotees, who travel in bullock carts or by palanquin, the losses, so far as can be ascertained, do not exceed the ordinary contingencies of a long journey performed in the most trying season of the Indian year. But, on the other hand, outbreaks of cholera take place, which, although now controlled to some extent by science, spare neither rich nor poor. Indeed, few pilgrims from the distant Provinces of Upper India attend the great Car Festival in mid-summer, except the very fanatical, who first make their arrangements for dying on the road. While the population of Lower Bengal flocks to this ceremonial, the northern devotees content themselves with a cold-weather pilgrimage to the Swinging Festival in March; and even then, the deadly hot season catches them before they regain their native villages. It is impossible to reckon the total number of the poorer sort who travel on foot at less than 84,000. It is equally impossible to reckon their deaths in Purí and on the road at less than one-seventh, or 12,000 a year. Deducting 2000 from these for the ordinary death-rate, we have a net slaughter of 10,000 per annum.

It may well be supposed that the British Government has not looked unmoved on this appalling spectacle. Nothing but a total prohibition of pilgrimage would put a stop to the annual massacre. But such a prohibition would amount to an interdict on one of the most cherished religious privileges, and would be regarded by every Hindu throughout India as a great national wrong.

The subject has come up from time to time for official discussion; and, in 1867, a grand effort was made to enlist the educated classes against so homicidal a practice. Circular letters were sent to every Division of Bengal, and the utmost influence of the higher officials was brought to bear. But the answers which came in from every part of Bengal admitted of no hope. All that remained was to institute a system of sanitary surveillance and quarantine, which should reduce the inevitable loss of life to a minimum.

SANITARY MEASURES.—Such measures are of three kinds,—the first being directed to lessen the number of pilgrims; the second, to mitigate the dangers of the road; and the third, to prevent epidemics in Purí. Anything like a general prohibition of pilgrimage would be an outrage upon the religious feelings of the people. But, in seasons of cholera or of other great calamity in Orissa, it would be possible to check the pilgrim stream, by giving warning in the Government *Gazette,* and through the medium of the vernacular papers. Thousands of devotees would put off the enterprise to another year. It is very difficult, however, to give such warnings before the month in which the pilgrims usually start. But in extreme cases they might be stopped upon the road, and turned back before they entered Orissa. This was done in the famine year 1866, and native public opinion supported the action of Government. But it could not be too distinctly understood, that such an interference is only justifiable under extreme and exceptional circumstances.

The second set of preventive measures can be applied with greater safety, and with more certain results. Thousands of pilgrims every year die upon the journey from exhaustion and want of food. Nor does there seem any possibility of lessening the number of deaths from these causes. But, until very recently, some thousands also died of diseases which, if taken in time, are under the control of medical science. Within the last few years, pilgrim hospitals have been established along the main lines of road, and a medical patrol has been, through the energy and devotion of the Civil Surgeon of Purí, established in the vicinity of the holy city. Great good has been effected by these means; but a heavy drawback to their utility consists in the fact that the devotees will not enter an hospital except at the last extremity, and the surgeons say that the great majority of pilgrim patients are beyond the reach of aid when they are brought in.

There exists, however, another means of decreasing the danger of the road besides medical patrols and pilgrim hospitals. The large towns along the route always contain the seeds of cholera; and, indeed, that disease is seldom wholly absent from any Indian city. The arrival of the pilgrim stream is, year after year, the signal for the ordinary sporadic cases to assume the dimensions of an epidemic. Cuttack, the capital of Orissa, suffered so regularly and so severely from the passage of the pilgrim army, that the doctors, having tried everything else, at last determined to shut the devotees entirely out of the city. The result upon the public health has been marvellous. Police are stationed at the entrance to the town, and warn the pilgrims that they must skirt round the municipal boundaries. A sanitary cordon is thus maintained, and Cuttack is now free from the annual calamity to which it was for centuries subject. This inexpensive quarantine might easily be applied to other municipalities along the pilgrim highway. The devotees suffer no inconvenience; for as soon as the change in their route is known, little hamlets of grain-sellers set up outside the cordon. Indeed, the pilgrims would be the gainers by the change, in so far as they could purchase their food free of octroi or other municipal charges, where such charges exist.

But though much may be done upon the road, more could be done in Purí itself. That city becomes annually a centre from which disease and death radiate throughout the Province; and the united testimony of medical officers proves that the returning bands of devotees from Jagannáth carry cholera stage by stage along the pilgrim highway. Sanitary measures which have been introduced since 1867 have effected a marked improvement in the state of the town. The great difficulty has been to check the overcrowding in the lodging-houses. In 1866 a Bill was introduced into the Bengal Council for the better regulation of such establishments. In 1867 an amended Act was based upon it. The first had been too searching and cumbrous. The second confined itself exclusively to the prevention of overcrowding, and omitted provisions regarding conservancy, infectious diseases, and water supply. In 1868, therefore, the Sanitary Commissioner submitted a new Act, which endeavoured to avoid both extremes. It provides for the appointment of a health officer, to inspect the lodging-houses, and report on them to the magistrate. Under this Act no such house is opened without a licence; and licences are granted only upon a certificate from the surgeon, stating the suitability of the tenement for the purpose, and the number of persons which it can properly accommodate. Except in cases where the lodging-house keepers are persons of known respectability, their establishments continue under the surveillance of the health officer, and penalties are provided for wilful overcrowding, and similar breaches of the licence. Much good has resulted from the operation of this Act.

BUDDHIST ANTIQUITIES.—It has been already mentioned that the earliest religion in Orissa, of which we have any actual historical evidence, is that of Buddhism. Indian literature is altogether silent upon the Buddhists, and gives no clue to their origin, or to the era of their first settlements. But the sacred books of Ceylon relate how, immediately after the obsequies of Buddha in 543 B.C., one of his disciples carried the Sacred Tooth to Purí, where it was worshipped in great pomp by the monarch. The only existent traces of Buddhism, which for ten centuries formed the prevailing religion of Orissa, consist in the cave dwellings and rock habitations of their priests and hermits, and in recently deciphered inscriptions. Their principal settlement was at Khandgirí, nearly half-way between Purí

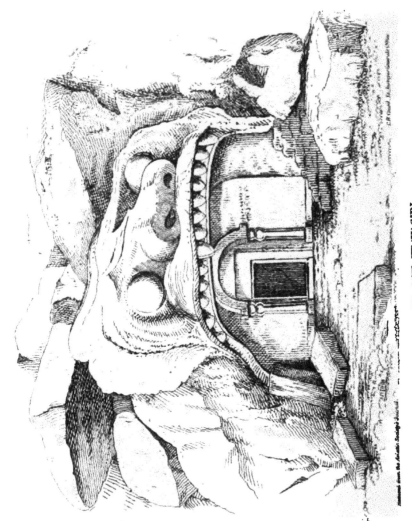

TIGER CAVE, UDAYAGIRI.

(Circ. 300 B.C.)

and Cuttack, and about twelve miles to the west of the present high road. Two sandstone hills, Khandgiri and Udayagiri, rise abruptly out of the jungle, separated by a narrow gorge, one end of which is enclosed by a low ridge that connects the cliffs, while the other extremity is screened by a noble banyan tree, and groves of fruit-bearing mangoes. Massive slabs of laterite once formed a paved path across the ravine, and rose in flights of stairs up either hill. The peaks are a rabbit-warren of caves and temples cut out of the rock. The oldest of them consist of a single cell, scarcely larger than a dog - kennel. Several are shaped into strange distorted resemblances of animals. One has from time immemorial been known as the Snake Cave, another as the Elephant Cave, a third as the Tiger Cave. The last stands out from the rock in the form of a monstrous wild beast's jaw, with nose and eyes above, and the teeth overhanging the entrance to the cell. Others are more elaborate, and contain several chambers supported by pillars, and shaded from the sun by a verandah in front. Sculptures of the Hindu deities are carved in relief upon the walls, or on slabs of chlorite fixed into the sandstone. These figures, however, belong to a comparatively recent date, and with the exception of a few worn and blunted representations of the sacred tree of Buddha, the oldest of them cannot be placed before 600 A.D.

These sandstone hills in Orissa exhibit what are believed to be the very earliest memorials of Buddhistic life. The small single cells cut in the face of inaccessible precipices, utterly destitute of ornament, and crumbling from long exposure to the air, represent the first human dwellings yet discovered in India. The most recent date which, so far as I know, has been assigned to them, is 200 B.C. But Bábu Rajendra Lala Mitra places even the more elaborate of the adjoining chambered monasteries in the third century before Christ. The single - cell caves of Orissa are certainly very much older than anything to be seen in Bombay ; so much older, indeed, as to belong to an entirely different period. They are holes rather than habitations, and do not even exhibit those traces of primitive carpentry architecture which the earliest of the western specimens disclose. Some of them are so old that the face of the rock has fallen down, and left the caves in ruins. The men who, year after year, crouched in these holes, and cramped their limbs within their narrow limits, must have been supported by a great religious earnestness, little known to the Buddhist priests of later times. Such cells, however, soon gave place to more comfortable excavations, shaded by pillared verandahs, and lighted by several doors. These appear to have been intended for the religious meetings of the brotherhood. Some of them are very roomy, and have apartments at either end, probably for the spiritual heads of the community; small, indeed, when compared with the temple chambers, but greatly more commodious than the primitive single cells.

The temples in their turn are succeeded by still more elaborate excavations. Of these, the most important is a two-storied monastery known as the Queen's Palace (Ráni-nur). It consists of two rows of cells, one above the other, shaded by pillared verandahs, with a court-yard cut out of the hill-side. Two stalwart figures, in shirts of mail down to the knees, stand forth from the wall as guards. One of them wears boots half-way up the knee; the other seems to have on greaves, the feet being naked, but the legs encased in armour. Whoever excavated this and the neighbouring monasteries had very much more advanced ideas of comfort than the ancient hermits who cut out the first holes in the rock above. The court-yard opens towards the south, and is lined on the other three sides with rows of chambers. On the right and left appear to be the cooking-room and common dining-hall. The verandahs are commodious, and the rock brackets, which extend from the pillars to support the intervening roof, are finely sculptured. The favourite form of ornamentation in Orissa is one common alike to European and Indian art, the curve of the brackets being skilfully taken advantage of to represent the swelling bosoms and delicately retreating heads of beautiful women. The upper storey contains four large cells, each fourteen feet long by seven broad, and three feet nine inches high. The verandah outside is about sixty feet long by ten broad, and seven in height. Each cell has two doors, and at either end is a rock lion; by no means the conventional monster of the Hindu temples of the twelfth century, but done with some spirit and fidelity, as if the artist had really seen the animal he tried to depict.

Altogether, the Queen's Palace represents a very different phase of Buddhism from that which consigned its votaries to uncomfortable holes in rocks. The great Bombay monastery at Kárli prefers the splendour of its temple to the comfort of its devotees; and its magnificent pillared hall contrasts greatly with the adjoining narrow

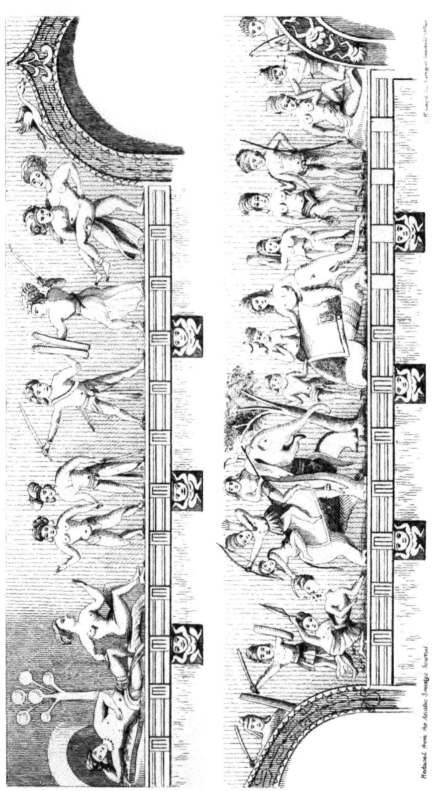

THE ORISSA HELEN.

SCULPTURED FRIEZE OF A ROCK MONASTERY.

N.B. In the Copper Plate, the Figures are more distinct than in the Original.

Reduced from the Asiatic Society's Journal

cells in which the monks passed their lives. But the Queen's Palace in Orissa belongs neither to the period in which the Buddhist missionaries and hermits devoted themselves to meditation in solitary holes of the rock, nor to that other period when the religion had built for itself a stately system of worship, and had gathered its devotees into religious houses. It must have been excavated at a time when the creed had acclimatized itself to the air of royal ante-chambers, and represents fashionable Buddhism not many centuries before its fall.

The upper verandah of the Queen's Palace is adorned with a sculptured•biography of its founder. The first tableau, worn almost level with the rock, seems to represent the sending of presents, which preceded the matrimonial alliances of the ancient dynasties of India. A running figure stands dimly out, apparently carrying a tray of fruit. The second appears to be the arrival of the suitor. It delineates the meeting of the elephants, and a number of confused human forms, one of whom rides on a lion. From the third tableau the biography becomes more distinct. It represents the courtship. The prince is introduced by an old lady to the princess, who sits cross-legged on a high seat, with her eyes averted, and her arms round the neck of one of her maidens below. The fourth is the fight. The prince and princess, each armed with swords and oblong shields, engage in combat. The fifth is the abduction, depicting the princess defeated and carried off in the prince's arms, her sword lost, but her shield still grasped in her hand. The prince holds his sword drawn, and is amply clothed. The princess is scantily draped, and her hair done up in a perpendicular chignon, rising from the top of her head, and a long tress falling over her bosom to her waist. She wears heavy anklets. The sixth is the hunt. A tree forms the centre of the piece, on one side of which the prince and princess are shooting at a bounding antelope; while a led horse stands near, and attendants armed with clubs. The prince draws his bow in the perpendicular fashion of English archers. It is about two-thirds his own height. A lady looks down upon the chase from the tree. A court scene follows, in which the prince sits on a throne on the left, with attendants holding fans on either side. Dancing girls and musicians are grouped in front, and the princess appears on a throne on the extreme right. The eighth and ninth tableaux are effaced. Three scenes of dalliance between the prince and the princess follow, and the series in the upper storey ends in a mysterious running figure with a snake twisted round him. The lower verandah exhibits the sequel. A convent scene discloses the princess retired from the vanities of life, sitting at her cell door in the upper storey of a sculptured monastery, with her ladies, also turned ascetics, sitting at separate doors in the lower one. The remaining tableaux, four in number, represent the prince, princess, and courtiers as hermits, with their hands on their breasts in an attitude of abstraction, freed from human passion, and wrapped in contemplation of the Deity. Throughout, the prince is generally fully dressed, with a cotton garment falling from his girdle, but leaving the leg bare from the knee. The lady wears a head-dress something like the Prince of Wales' feathers, with her hair done up in a towering chignon. A scroll of birds and beasts and leaves runs the whole way along. The battle and hunting scenes are given with much spirit, the animals being very different from the conventional creatures of modern Hindu art.

Higher up the hill, and facing the south, is a smaller monastery or temple, known as the Ganesh cave, from a figure of the elephant-headed god inside, evidently a work of much later date than the original cells. The inside wall of the verandah is adorned with a series of tableaux, that seem to give a different version of the same story which is told on the frieze of the Queen's Palace. In the first scene, a lady watches over her husband, who is sleeping under the sacred Buddhist tree. In the second, a suitor makes advances to the lady, who turns her head away. He has seized one hand, and she seems to be in the act of running from him, with her other hand thrown up, as if crying for help. The third is the battle. The husband and the lover (or perhaps it is the lady and her suitor) fight with swords and oblong shields. In the fourth, the warrior carries off the vanquished princess in his arms. In the fifth, the successful paramour is flying on an elephant, pursued by soldiers in heavy kilts. The prince draws his bow in the perpendicular fashion, as in the previous series, and a soldier has cut off the head of one of the pursuers. The sixth is the home-coming. The elephant kneels under a tree, the riders have dismounted, and the lady hangs down her head, as if in shame or sorrow. The seventh represents the home-life. The lady stands with her hand on the prince's shoulder, while he has one arm round her waist, and in the other hand grasps his bow. The series ends in a scene of dalliance.

The sandstone caves, as a whole, represent ten centuries of

GANESH GARBHA CAVE

human existence (500 B.C. to 500 A.D). They form the relics of three distinct stages through which Buddhism passed,—from the period when its first-missionaries started out on their perilous work, to the time when it had become the religion of queens and kings. The first was the Ascetic Age, and is represented by the single sandstone cells, scarcely bigger than the lair of a wild beast, and almost as inaccessible. The second, or Ceremonial Age, has left its relics in the pillared temples where the brethren were wont to meet, with commodious chambers for the spiritual heads attached to them. The third, or Fashionable Age of Buddhism, achieved its highest, although not its latest effort, in the two-storied Queen's Palace, built at a time when the whole resources of a kingdom were at the disposal of the religious fancies of royalty; and when art, having lost its monastic tone, had learned to turn even a convent's walls into a record of human pomp.

I have mentioned above, the Ceylon story of the transfer of the sacred tooth of Buddha to Purí in 543 B.C. European researches now render it doubtful whether the first missionary efforts of Buddhism must not be placed half a century later. The Ceylon texts relate that the Orissa king worshipped the sacred relic; and that ultimately the Sanskrit emperor became converted to Buddhism by the miracles which the relic worked in his presence.

Orissa Buddhism next emerges into history about three centuries later, or 250 B.C. Since that year, a rocky eminence on the bank of the Dayá river at Dhauli, about a day's journey to the south of the Queen's Monastery, has borne an inscription, long illegible to the Hindus, but which has at last been deciphered by European scholarship. The credit of reading this inscription belongs to Mr. Prinsep, C.S. It consists of eleven edicts promulgated by Asoka, the Buddhist emperor of Northern India, with two others apparently added by the local prince of Orissa. The eleven are almost identical with similar inscriptions published throughout the length and breadth of India.

They start with prohibiting the shedding of animal blood, whether for food or for religious sacrifices; and incidentally give a little picture of the imperial house-keeping. Formerly, they say, in the great dining-hall and temple of the heaven-beloved king, many hundred thousand animals were slain for meat. They proceed to describe an organized system of medical aid throughout the whole kingdom, and in the conquered provinces as far south as Ceylon.

This institution provided advice and drugs for all living creatures; for the brute creation not less than for men. Wells were also to be dug, and trees to be planted along the roads, for the refreshment of travellers and beasts of burden. They then proclaim a public humiliation every fifth year, and enumerate the cardinal virtues of the Buddhistic code,—obedience to parents; charity to all men, especially to the priests; the non-sacrifice of animals, and reverence for the vital principle in man or brute; dutiful service to the spiritual guide, and the propagation of the true creed. The king appoints missionaries to go forth to the utmost ends of the earth, and 'intermingle with all the hundred grades of unbelievers for the establishment of the faith, and for the increase of religion. They shall mix with Bráhmans and beggars, with the poor and the rich.' They shall deliver 'those bound in the fetters of sin' by declaring the truths that procure the 'final emancipation which is beyond understanding.' 'Among the terrible and the powerful shall they be mixed, both here and in foreign countries; in every town, and among all the kindred ties, even of brotherhood and sisterhood,—everywhere!'

The edicts then go on to regulate the household life of the people. They speak of a system of moral surveillance greatly more searching than that of the *censor morum* in the primitive age of Rome. Overseers watched over each stage of the citizen's life, from the cradle to the grave. No circumstance, however private, escaped their scrutiny. A staff of inspectors was appointed for every season,—for behaviour during meals, in domestic relations, in the nursery, in conversation, and on the bed of death. Care was taken, however, that these overseers should not degenerate into spies; and the king solemnly declares that he has instituted the system not for his own gain (through fines or penalties), but for the eternal salvation of his people.

The next tablet consists of a prayer for the spread of the faith, 'and that all unbelievers may be brought to repentance and peace of mind.' But it contains nothing like a hint at religious persecution, and speaks of 'every diversity of opinion' being blended together 'in undistinguishing charity.' The king then contrasts the hunts and feasts and gaming parties of former sovereigns with the more spiritual enjoyments which he has inculcated on his subjects. The world, he says, 'seeks pleasure in many ways—in marriage, in offspring, and in foreign travel; but true happiness is to be found in virtue alone, in kindness to dependants, reverence to spiritual teachers, humanity to animals, almsgiving to the priests.'

Such was the moral code of Buddhistic India, two hundred and fifty years before Christ. The two other Orissa tablets, which are distinct from Asoka's edicts, partake of a political character, and seem to lay down the local laws of the sovereign. They need not be more particularly referred to here. It may be well, however, to make a few remarks with regard to the tolerant light in which Buddhism appears in these Orissa Inscriptions. While, on the one hand, nothing can be more absolute than the declarations of the royal authority which the Orissa Inscriptions contain, so, on the other, nothing can be more respectful than the manner in which they speak of the priestly classes. They specify Bráhmans by name as objects of profound reverence and of liberality. They strongly assert their claims, and place obedience to the religious guide among the cardinal virtues. Although breathing from first to last the spirit of freedom, and contemplating all races and castes as subjects for the operation of their faith, and as equal heirs to the salvation which they believed that faith to bestow, yet they distinctly recognise the teacher as the superior of the taught; and so far from degrading the Bráhmans, they appear to look on them as peculiarly suited for the high office of spiritual leaders.

Nor do the Orissa Inscriptions make any parade of that mono-theism which is popularly regarded as the second distinctive feature of the Buddhistic faith. They proceed from first to last on the assumption that there is but one God. But they do not bring forward this doctrine with any particular prominence. They start from it as an axiom, rather than declare it as a dogma. Indeed, the later inscriptions bear witness to the existence of other religions co-existing with Buddhism; and one of them describes the Orissa monarch who engraved it as a 'worshipper of the sun.' Here, too, as elsewhere, the names of the monarchs bear testimony to the ancient religion, and to the tutelary Sanskrit gods. The prince whose life is recorded in the rock inscription of 50 A.D. wavered between the faiths, at one time publicly declaring himself a Bráh-manist, and at another a Buddhist. The inscriptions scattered throughout Upper India prove that the ancient Hindu triad never wholly lost the veneration of the people, and received some casual acknowledgment even from priests and kings during the Buddhistic era.

The one great feature of Buddhism, as interpreted by the Orissa inscriptions, is its intense humanity. It provides alike for the bodily comfort and for the eternal salvation of all whom it can reach. While the Bráhmanical religion kept its consolations for a single race, and, even within that race, jealously doled out its fragments of spiritual instruction to the different castes, Buddhism cried aloud in tones of earnest remonstrance to the whole Indian world, and covered the rocks with its missionary appeals. Nothing can be more solemn than the commands which it lays upon its followers, to go forth among all races and to all countries, and to preach 'the righteousness which passeth knowledge.' The Orissa Buddhists found themselves far away from the religious centre of their race, and surrounded by forest tribes and aboriginal superstitions. The mention of these primitive races and 'barbarian countries' had, therefore, a peculiar significance. They set up no tests of race or of birth. 'Every righteous man,' says one of the tablets, ' is my true subject.' When a man relieves his fellow from the bondage and misery of sin, he releases himself. Wherever there is religious darkness, there shall the truth be preached, 'both here and in foreign lands, in every town, even to the ends of the barbarian countries; and these, being themselves absorbed in righteousness, shall become ministers of the faith.' But this proselytizing spirit bears no trace of Bráhmanical intolerance. Throughout the whole no glimpse is disclosed of anything like compulsory conversion. Indeed, the edicts repel the very idea of such measures, and declare that the truth can be reached only by an inward process—a process of conviction, and not of force.

But the Buddhism of these inscriptions does not confine itself alone to the spiritual side of man's nature. Its strong humanity labours to increase the sum of physical happiness. It cares for the sick, it digs wells for the thirsty wayfarer, it plants shady resting groves for man and beast. It jealously guards the life of all created beings, organizes a system of medical relief for diseased animals, and in some respects anticipates that higher Christian humanity which protects the dumb creation against the oppression of man.

BHUVANESWAR AND SIVAISM.—The decay of Buddhism in Orissa dates from the expulsion of the Yavanas in 474 A.D., and the accession of the Kesárí or Lion dynasty, which ruled Orissa during forty-three generations, or till 1132 A.D. These kings were Bráhmanical rather than Buddhistic from the commencement: the first began the great Sivaite Bhuvaneswar temple about 500 A.D., which was completed by the fourth of the line in 657 A.D. No evidence exists, however, of any immediate change in the popular faith; Buddhist hermits still prayed among the rocks, and rich devotees continued to honeycomb the sandstone hills with fresh cave-dwellings. But the creed was wearing itself out, and even before the accession of the Kesárí dynasty, Buddha's sacred tooth had been removed from Purí to Ceylon. The ancient Sanskrit gods, who had all along co-existed more or less distinctly with Buddhism, now asserted their supremacy, and came forth arrayed in their new garb as modern Hindu deities. Guided by signs and wonders, the king sought out the image of Jagannáth in the jungles, where it had lain hid during the Yavana occupation, and brought it back to Purí in triumph. In a previous section of this Account has been traced the progress of Vishnu-worship in Orissa, and its culmination in the Jagannáth Festivals of the present day. But, in spite of the temple chronicles, which naturally glorify their own god, it is Siva-worship which, during the decay of Buddhism, first enters upon the scene.

For 150 years Buddhism and Siva-worship struggled for the victory. At the end of that period the contest had practically ceased. The reigning monarch was a worshipper of the All-Destroyer, with Bhuvaneswar, the temple city of Siva, as his capital. Of the 7000 shrines which once clustered around the sacred lake, not more than 500 or 600 now survive; and these are nearly all deserted and more or less in ruins. They exhibit every stage of Orissa art, from the rough conceptions of the sixth century, through the exquisite designs and ungrudging artistic toil of the twelfth, to the hurried and dishonest stucco-like make-beliefs of Hindu architecture at the present day. Exquisite friezes, scrolls, and carvings adorn these long-deserted walls. One of their most ingenious ornamentations is the infinite variety into which the erected hood of the cobra is worked. Sometimes it forms a gloria above a god; sometimes it appears as a canopy, bending over like the Prince of Wales' feathers; and instead of the monastic cord of Gothic architecture, scrolls of snakes distend themselves in graceful convolutions, or twist together in stony knots.

Many of the figures were evidently done from the life. Although intended for Hindu sages and deities, they preserve the Buddhist type, and took as their models Buddhist hermits seated on the ground in an attitude of abstraction. While Sivaism became the religion of royalty on the plains, Buddhism continued to build rock temples on the mountainous western frontier; and the ornaments on the ears, arms, wrists, and breasts of the figures present the counterparts of those which the Sivaite builders of the Royal City carved upon the shrines of the All-Destroyer. Besides devotional pieces, the older sculptures at Bhuvaneswar represent long processions of infantry, cavalry, and elephants. The warriors form models of manly grace, and the ladies frequently exhibit that exquisite type of face which the Grecian artists have left behind them alike in Eastern and Western India. One little group of a nymph, with an upright chignon, and a hero with a cross-handed dagger in his waist-belt, might serve as a model of Helen and Paris, but that the warrior is of a more robust type than the graceful Trojan archer.

In another frieze, knights on heavily caparisoned horses meet in deadly combat. Bowmen and swordsmen march behind on foot, very much as in Norman tapestry pieces of the Crusades; while porters and camp-followers, with led horses, straggle after them, and fresh detachments of swordsmen with oblong shields bring up the rear. In the background, courtiers and aged ministers sit in council, while holy men in an attitude of devotion shed the sanction of religion upon the scene. On most of the temples both sexes have their hair done up in a sort of tower above their heads, but some of the ladies have also a braid falling over the bosom to the waist. In the more modern sculptures, the hair is brushed back, and either falls in a braid as above, or is arranged in a fillet behind. The horizontal chignon projecting from the back of the head does not come into fashion until the twelfth century. There are scarcely any indelicate sculptures, but a great deal of honest love-making, which generally finds expression by the gods and warriors chucking the goddesses under the chin.

The Kesári or Lion line was essentially a Siva-worshipping dynasty. Temples to the All-Destroyer formed the great public works of the six centuries during which it ruled Orissa. Their founder, Yayati Kesari, began the lofty fane at Bhuvaneswar about 500 A.D., two succeeding monarchs laboured on it, and the fourth of the house completed it in 657 A.D. A slab inscription some centuries later recounts how a pious princess reared another 'cloud-reaching temple with four beautiful halls' to the lord Siva, 'who destroys the sins of the worshippers, and gives salvation to those who touch (his image) in his holy place.' Almost the only event by which the Palm-leaf Record relieves its monotonous list of kings of the ninth century, is the erection of the Siva temple in Puri, the city destined so soon to become the centre of the rival worship. The last public act of the dynasty was the building of the beautiful vestibule to the great shrine at Bhuvaneswar, between 1099 and 1104 A.D., or barely thirty years before the extinction of the race.

The religion of royalty everywhere becomes, sooner or later, a religion of luxury. The sixty-three kings of the Lion line not only built temples, but endowed them with noble estates, and covered the country with settlements of priests. Siva-worship, although the creed of the dynasty almost from the first, very slowly became the accepted faith of the people. The aboriginal and semi-aboriginal low castes might be fascinated and appalled by its awe-striking solemnities; but the ruling Aryan race, bred up for centuries in the gentle doctrines of Buddha, required a higher order of attractions. To these latter, therefore, it presented itself not as a brutal and bloody superstition, but as a great catholic religion, wide enough and high enough for the loftiest spiritual flights, and yet glowing with that warmth and colour after which a human soul, chilled by the unrealities of the Buddhistic theism, yearns. To the sage it was the adoration of Mahádeva, the Great God; of Maheswara, the Great Lord; of Bhuvaneswara, the Lord of the Earth; of Brahmes- wara, the Lord of Lords, or the Lord of the First Creative Energy. The higher minds among the Sivaite sects asserted the unity of the Deity as strenuously as the Buddhists ever did. For common natures they organized a ritual, splendid, mysterious, and tragic; at one moment enshrouded in the silence and gloom of the inner- most sanctuary, at another celebrated amid throngs of frenzied devotees, with thousands of hearts beating together in a unison of religious ecstasy. To the lower classes it was indeed a religion of blood; but from gentler natures the god accepted a tray of fruits, or a garland of white scented flowers, with an equally propitious eye. It touched every chord of the human imagination; and men contrasted its tropical passionateness, and its solemnities, which by turns fascinated, appalled, and enchained, with the neutral-tinted doctrines and the barren rites of Buddhism.

But Siva-worship did not depend alone upon its new converts. The local legends and the Palm-leaf Records alike relate how about 500 A.D. the founder of the Lion line imported ten thousand Bráhmans from Oudh, and endowed them with lands around Jájpur on the sacred Baitaraní river. The new-comers professed the royal religion, and were Sivaites to a man; and it is a curious fact that to this day, while the great majority of the population of Orissa are Vishnu-worshippers, the Bráhmans, almost without exception, are Sivaites. The decline of Sivaism as the popular religion of Orissa dates from the fall of the Lion line of kings, and the accession of a new dynasty, which professed Vishnuvism; *vide* the Statistical Account of Cuttack (vol. xviii. pp. 184-185).

SUN-WORSHIP: THE KANARAK TEMPLE.—Sun-worship formed one of the religions into which Buddhism disintegrated,—a religion of the Vishnuvite type, identified with the Vishnuvite dynasty, opposed to the dark rites of the Sivaite kings, and destined, after running a brief, but beautiful course, to give place to the warmer form of Vishnuvism as represented by Jagannáth. Sun-worship is a creed little susceptible of material representation; nevertheless, besides the lovely ruined pile at Kanárak described below, its architectural remains survive in many parts of Orissa. Even in Jájpur, the ancient capital of the Sivaite dynasty, the flight of steps by which the pilgrims descend into the river exhibits a granite bas-relief of the Sun-god seated on his celestial car, and drawn by seven prancing horses. A similar sculpture exists among the almost unknown ruins of Shergarh; and the Sun-god in his golden chariot appears among the divinities which a native artist has figured as the objects of popular adoration in Orissa. Both there and in Bengal, the Bráhmans daily repeat a prayer to the sun after bathing; and the stricter sort of Vishnu-worshippers refrain from animal food on the first day of the week, which bears the name of Sunday alike in England and India (*Rabíbár*). The common people on the plains merely bow to the orb after their morning ablutions; but in the highlands of Mánbhúm, to the north-west of Orissa, the low castes do not break their fast till they catch a clear view of the deity, and in cloudy weather have sometimes to remain a day without food. During the whole harvest month (*Agrahayan*, falling within our November and December), each Sunday brings round weekly solemnities in honour of the bright god. Every village household prepares a tray covered with earth, into which rice seeds are dropped. Little earthenware cups containing pure water are placed upon it; and on Sundays, the family priest goes through a few simple rites, pouring a libation of fresh water upon the tray, and invoking the sun (*Ritu-pújá*). All Bengal celebrates the sun's entry into Capricorn by fairs; and the great gathering at Ságar, at the mouth of the Huglí, takes place on that occasion.

The most exquisite memorial of sun-worship in India is the temple of Kanárak upon the Orissa shore. The temple at Jagannáth has been already described, but it falls far short of this marvellous structure, which rose in honour of the sun fifty years later. Built, according to the most trustworthy records, between 1237 and 1282 A.D., shortly after the triumph of the graceful Vishnuvite creed, it concentrates in itself the accumulated beauties of the four architectural centuries among the Hindus. Notwithstanding the indecent sculptures which disgrace its exterior wall, it forms the climax of Bengal art, and wrung an unwilling tribute even from the Muhammadans. Abul Fazl, the minister of Akbar, speaks of it about the year 1580 in the following terms :—'Near to Jagannáth is the Temple of the Sun, in the erection of which was expended the whole revenue of Orissa for twelve years. No one can behold this immense edifice without being struck with amazement. The wall which surrounds the whole is 150 hands high, and 19 hands thick. In the front of the gate is a pillar of black stone of an octagonal form, 50 yards high. There are nine flights of steps, after ascending which you come to an extensive open space, where you discover a large arch constructed of stone, upon which are carved the sun and stars. Around them is a border, where are represented a variety of worshippers of all tribes, some standing on their heads, some sitting, some prostrated, some laughing, some weeping, some bewildered, some sensible, together with minstrels and a number of strange and wonderful animals, such as never existed but in imagination. There are twenty-eight other temples near to this pagoda, and they are all reported to have performed miracles.'

The great temple alone survives ; and even this seems never to have been completed, as the foundation of the internal pillars on which the heavy dome rested gave way before the outer halls were finished. A perfect jungle of legends soon sprang up, to explain the desertion of so costly and beautiful a shrine. It forms a landmark along the coast which ships still sight on their passage up the Bay ; and inaccuracy in the bearings, or neglect to use the lead, constantly wrecked vessels on the shore. The villagers explained such mishaps by a story of a huge lodestone (*Kumbhar pathar*) on the summit of the tower, which, like Sinbad the Sailor's rock, drew the unhappy ships on the sands ; and they circumstantially relate how a Musalmán crew at length scaled the temple and carried off the fatal magnet. The priests, they say, forthwith abandoned the desecrated shrine,

and migrated with their god to Purí.   Certain it is that the great
shrine at Purí has a little temple to the sun within its all-embracing
walls ; and the exquisite polygonal tower which Abul Fazl mentions
as outside the Kanárak edifice now stands in front of the Lion Gate
of Jagannáth.   The delicate proportions of this monolith may be
judged of from the accompanying plate.   Another, of nearly equal
beauty, although of much more modern workmanship, stands outside a
temple at Kendrapárá, in one of the loneliest parts of the delta.   A
third column of the same type, but dedicated to Vishnu, and formerly
surmounted by his sacred vulture, has survived the iconoclastic
ravages of the Musalmáns at Jájpur; and half a century ago, such
pillars were common throughout Orissa.   They resemble the
Buddhist columns (*láths*) ; and in this, as in its rosaries, monastic
attitudes, and laws of ornamentation, Hinduism, and especially
Vishnu-worship, borrowed its architecture from the ancient mono-
theistic faith.

The Sun Temple at Kanárak now forms a picturesque ruin looking down upon the sea.   It lies nineteen miles north-west of Purí,
and will well repay a visit from any lover of art.   On the 4th
February 1870, I started from Purí about midnight by palanquin,
and reached Kanárak at daybreak.   We found our tents pitched
under three fine old banyan trees fifty yards from the temple, on
the skirt of a grove of cocoa-nuts, palms, and mangoes, from amid
which two ancient shrines peeped out.   A jungle of delicate-leafed
shrubs of the citron tribe lay in front of the dilapidated pile, and
the roar of the sea came faintly over the sandy ridges which lay
between us and the shore.   No traces of the outer wall remain,
the Marhattá officers having carried away the stones as building
materials to Purí ; and of the temple, which in a complete state
would have consisted of four chambers, only a single one, the Hall
of Audience, survives.   Its great doorway, facing the east, is blocked
up by masses of stone, and festooned with creepers.   In front rises
a huge mound of jungle-covered rubbish, the remains of the outer
Hall of Offerings.   Sculptures in high relief, exquisitely cut, but of
an indecent character, cover the exterior walls, and bear witness to
an age when Hindu artists worked from nature.   The nymphs are
beautifully-shaped women, in luscious attitudes ; the elephants move
along at the true elephant trot, and kneel down in the stone exactly
as they did in life.   Some of the latter have, however, the exaggerated ear and conventional mouth of modern Hindu sculpture, and

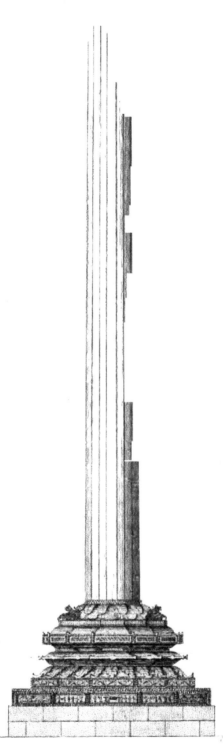

AN ORISSA SUN PILLAR

(now outside the Gate of Jagannath.)

the lions must have been altogether evolved from the artists' inner consciousness. Each of the four doorways, on the north, south, east, and west, has two lintels of chlorite, a bluish slate-like stone, very hard, and exquisitely polished. On these lintels rest two massive beams of iron supporting the wall above. The eastern entrance was, till lately, surmounted, as in other Orissa temples, by a chlorite slab, on which the emblems of the seven days of the week, with the ascending and descending nodes, are carved. The beauty of this elaborate piece proved to it a more fatal enemy than time itself, and tempted English antiquarians to try to remove it by sea to the museum at Calcutta. A grant of public money was obtained; but it sufficed only to drag the massive block a couple of hundred yards, where it now lies, quite apart from the temple, and as far as ever from the shore. The builders of the twelfth century had excavated it in the quarries of the Hill States, and carried it by a land journey, across swamps and unbridged rivers, for a distance of eighty miles.

.I can only describe Kanárak as a ruin; but, lovely as it still is, it presented beauties half a century ago that have now disappeared. Mr. Stirling visited it about 1820, and has left behind him the following tasteful account :—' The skill and labour of the best artists seem to have been reserved for the finely-polished slabs of chlorite which line and decorate the outer faces of the doorways. The whole of the sculpture on these figures, comprising men and animals, foliage and arabesque patterns, is executed with a degree of taste, propriety, and freedom, which would stand a comparison with some of our best specimens of Gothic architectural ornament. The workmanship remains, too, as perfect as if it had just come from the chisel of the sculptor, owing to the extreme hardness and durability of the stone. A triangular niche over each doorway was once filled with a figure cut in alto-relievo, emblematic of the deity of the place, being that of a youth in a sitting posture, holding in each hand a stalk of the true lotus, the expanded flowers of which are turned towards him. Each architrave has, as usual, the Nava-graha, or nine Bráhmanical planets, very finely sculptured in alto-relievo. Five of them are well-proportioned figures of men, with mild and pleasing countenances, crowned with high-pointed caps, and seated cross-legged on the lotus, engaged in religious meditation. One hand bears a vessel of water, and the fingers of the other are counting over the beads of a rosary which hangs suspended. The form of the planet which presides over Thursday (Vrihaspati or Jupiter) is distinguished from the others by a flowing, majestic beard. Friday, or Venus, is a youthful female, with a plump, well-rounded figure. Ketu, the descending node, is a Triton, whose body ends in the tail of a fish or dragon; and Ráhu, or the ascending node, a monster all head and shoulders, with a grinning, grotesque countenance, frizzly hair dressed like a full-blown wig, and one immense canine tooth projecting from the upper jaw. In one hand he holds a hatchet, and in the other a fragment of the moon.'

Among the life-sized pieces, elephants crouch in terror under rampant lions, while mutilated human figures lie crushed beneath the flat, pulpy feet of the elephants. Clubmen, griffins, warriors on prancing horses, colossal figures of grotesque and varied shape, stand about in silent, stony groups. The elephants have the flabby under-lips of nature, and exhibit a uniformity in all the essential points of their anatomy, with a variety in posture and detail, which Hindu art has long forgotten. Two colossal horses guard the southern façade,—one perfect, the other with his neck broken and otherwise shattered. The right-hand stallion has a Roman nose, prominent eyes, nostrils not too open, and in other respects carved from a well-bred model; excepting the jowl, which is bridled in close upon the neck, making the channel too narrow. The legs, too, have a fleshy and conventional look. He is very richly caparisoned with bosses and bands round the face, heavy chain armour on the neck, tasselled necklaces, jewelled bracelets on all four legs, and a tasselled breast-band which keeps the saddle in position. The saddle resembles the mediæval ones of Western chivalry, with a high pommel and well-marked cantle, but has a modern girth, consisting of a single broad band clasped by a buckle outside the fringe of a sumptuous saddle-cloth. The stirrup-irons are round, like those of our own cavalry. A scabbard for a short Roman sword hangs down on the left, a quiver filled with feathered arrows on the right, while a groom adorned with necklaces and breast jewels runs at the horse's head, holding the bridle. The fierce war-stallion has stamped down two of the enemy —not kicking or prancing, but fairly trampling them into the earth. These appear to be Rákshasas or aborigines, from their woolly hair, tiger-like mouths and tusks, and their short curved swords like the national Gurkhá weapon, half bill-hook, half falchion, and equally suited for ripping up a foe or for cutting a path through the jungle.

They wear heavy armlets, but no defensive armour, excepting a round shield made of several plies of metal richly carved, with a boss in the centre, and tassels or tufts of hair hanging down from it. The shields appear to have borne some heraldic device; and the most perfect of them still exhibits two lizards climbing up on either side of the boss, done to the life. Such *quasi*-armorial bearings frequently appear in Orissa. Stirling noticed one at Bhuvaneswar in 1820; and the chiefs of the adjoining Tributary States have each a heraldic device or emblem of signature, handed down in their families from remote generations.

A pyramid-shaped roof rises by terraces of exquisitely carved granite to a lotus-crowned pinnacle. Viewed from below, this lofty expanse of masonry looks as if one could not place a finger on an unsculptured inch. I clambered up to it by means of a vast pile of stones, the ruins of the Towered Sanctuary, to which the existing hall only formed an outer chamber. The roof rises by three tiers, each consisting of a number of receding layers of masonry. It forms, as it were, three lofty flights of steps, covered with elephants, horses, cavalry, and foot-soldiers, in endless processions. Innumerable busts of nymphs stand out from the mass of carving, while images of the four-headed Brahmá look towards the sea, and shed the sanction of religion on the aëriel sculptured world. The favourite musical instruments of the thirteenth century among the Hindus seem to have been the guitar (*sitar*), the little drum (*nágara*), and the cymbals, just as at the present day. The nymphs are rather over life size, with swelling breasts, full throats, and delicately retreating heads. They wear their hair in enormous chignons, projecting horizontally from behind. A head-dress falls in graceful festoons across both temples, ending in a golden boss at either ear, from which hang elaborate earrings. Their necklaces consist of many plies of the *tulsi* bead, and fall in a triangular shape upon the bosom. Each arm has a handsome bracelet just below the shoulder, and a still more elaborate one at the elbow. Their ornaments— ornaments so abundant, however, as to form a sort of clothing— supply their only drapery above the waist, which is encircled by a girdle of many folds. From this, a garment of gauzy muslin falls upon the limbs, but scarcely conceals their delicate curves. The whole is carved in reddish granite, highly polished, and just enough touched by time to give a softness to the profiles which stand out against the blue sky.

If all this ungrudging labour was lavished on merely the Outer Chamber, we may judge of the magnificence of the towered sanctuary, whose ruins now constitute the jungle-covered hill behind. This inner edifice, if it was ever completed, finds no place in Abul Fazl's description, and had probably tumbled down before his day (1580 A.D.). But its size may be inferred from the proportions of other temples belonging to the same order, and a restored elevation of it will be found in Mr. James Fergusson's *History of Architecture* (vol. ii. p. 591, ed. 1867). The enormous pyramidal roof of the still existing Outer Chamber rests on walls sixty feet high, and rises a further sixty-four feet above them. It furnishes an admirable illustration of the Hindu arch as applied to roofing, and consists of layers of masonry each projecting a little beyond the one below it, like inverted stairs, and so converging eventually at the top. Hindu architecture, from its very commencement in Orissa, 500 A.D., seems to have had an unlimited command of iron; but the metal clamps, upon which the builders of the City of Temples in the sixth century so much depended, are here more sparingly used. The architects of the twelfth century trusted to their improved mechanical appliances for lifting enormous weights, and kept the converging layers of the roof in position by the mass of masonry behind. They handled their colossal beams of iron and stone with as much ease and plasticity as modern workmen put up pine-rafters, and fitted in blocks of twenty to thirty tons with absolute precision at a height of eighty feet. The lower part of the roof, however, was supported not only by the superincumbent mass behind, but also by enormous monolithic pillars forty feet high. The sandy ridge, the only foundation which the architect could find so near the shore, yielded under these vast blocks. By degrees the columns sank; and the inner layers of the roof, thus deprived of part of the support on which they depended, came down with a crash. The ruins now lie heaped upon the floor, a gigantic chaos; and the contrast between their unwieldy bulk, and the laborious sculpture which covers almost every square inch outside, forces on the memory Bishop Heber's criticism, that the Indians built like Titans and finished like jewellers.

The pyramidal temple roof forms one of the most typical features of the religious architecture of the Hindus. In the Outer Chambers, the overlapping national arch is manipulated into a gently converging apex; in the Towered Sanctuaries, it takes the shape, so to speak, of a conical dome. In the former, the pyramidal roof requires the internal support of pillars, and sometimes also of colossal rafters of iron. But in the latter, the roof converges more slowly into a cone, and the weight behind sustains the overlapping of each successive tier of masonry. The Hindus never could form a perfect dome till the Muhammadans taught them to turn the arch, but they formed a conical dome almost as plastic and as enduring as the true circular one. Even in the Outer Chamber of the Sun Temple, when the pillars had fallen down, the massive blocks of the roof sufficed by their own weight to sustain their pyramidal converging tiers.

DIVISION OF THE PEOPLE INTO TOWN AND COUNTRY.—The population of the District is entirely rural, and the only town in the whole District containing upwards of five thousand inhabitants is Purí itself, with a resident population of 22,695 souls. Mr. C. F. Magrath's District Compilation for Purí thus classifies the towns and villages:—Headquarters or Purí Subdivision—1372 villages containing less than two hundred inhabitants; 579 with from two to five hundred; 131 with from five hundred to a thousand; 39 with from one to two thousand; 4 with from two to three thousand; and 1 with from twenty to fifty thousand; total, 2126. Khurdhá Subdivision—562 villages with less than two hundred inhabitants; 349 with from two to five hundred; 96 with from five hundred to a thousand; 39 with from one to two thousand; and 3 with from two to three thousand; total, 1049. Total for the whole District—1934 villages with less than two hundred inhabitants; 928 with from two to five hundred; 227 with from five hundred to a thousand; 78 with from one to two thousand; 7 with from two to three thousand; and 1 with from twenty to fifty thousand; grand total, 3175.

PURI TOWN is situated on the coast, in 19° 48′ 17″ north latitude, and 85° 51′ 39″ east longitude, separated from the sea by low sandy ridges. In 1825, according to Stirling, it contained 5741 houses. In 1841 the houses numbered 6620, inhabited by 23,766 persons. In 1868 the number of houses was returned at 6363. In 1869 a careful enumeration showed that the number of houses had fallen to 5789, and the population to 19,875. This decrease is attributed to the famine of 1865-66. The regular Census of 1872 returned the population of Purí town as follows:—Hindus—males 11,848, and females 10,492; total, 22,340. Muhammadans—males 156, and females 61; total, 217. Christians—males 6, and females 8; total, 14. Others—males 67, and females 57; total, 124. Population of all denominations—males 12,077, and females 10,618; grand total, 22,695. This is the ordinary resident population, but during the great festivals of Jagannáth the number is swollen sometimes by as many as a hundred thousand pilgrims. Purí covers an area of 1871 acres, including the whole *Kshetra* or sacred precincts of the town. It is a city of lodging-houses, and is destitute alike of manufacture or commerce on any considerable scale. The streets are mean and narrow, with the exception of the principal avenue, which leads from the temple to the country-house of Jagannáth. The houses consist of wattle covered with clay, raised on platforms of hard mud, about four feet high, and many of them gaily painted with Hindu gods, or with scenes from the Indian epics. The intervening sand-hills between the town and the beach intercept the drainage, and aggravate the diseases to which the overcrowding of the pilgrims gives rise. The sanitary state of the town, and the measures which have been taken for its improvement in this respect, have been described in a previous page. The Government offices lie upon the beach, with the sandy ridge between them and the town. The site is salubrious; but the dwellings of the English residents barely number six thatched cottages, much out of repair. The monsoon blows so fresh and cool from the sea, that in former days the officials from Cuttack used regularly to come to Purí for the hot weather. During the rains it is less healthy. A full account of the temple of Jagannáth, and the various religious festivals held at Purí, has been given in a previous section of this Statistical Account.

MINOR TOWNS.—Besides Purí, the only other towns in the District requiring mention are Pippli, on the Cuttack road, twenty-five miles from Purí; and Bhuvaneswar, situated in 20° 14′ 45″ north latitude, and 85° 52′ 26″ east longitude. The latter, as a place of pilgrimage, has been described in the preceding section of this Account. Both are seats of a considerable trade in rice and cloth. Pippli has a flourishing colony of native Christians.

MATERIAL CONDITION OF THE PEOPLE.—The people are poor, and appear even poorer than they are. They wear inferior clothes to men of the same class in other Districts. The well-to-do settlers from the south are distinguished by their earrings and necklaces of gold. A respectable shopkeeper's house is built principally of wattle and mud. The front verandah is of brick, and the roof of thatch, firmly fixed on a good bamboo or wooden frame. The dwelling of a prosperous merchant or landholder, worth about £100 a year, generally consists of a series of houses built round two courts, which lead one into the other, with the street in front of the outer court, and a garden behind the inner one. The outer court is bordered by the chambers of the male members of the family, and the inner court by the women's apartments, the family storehouses, and the cook-room. The furniture of such a house would consist of a few low bedsteads, a press or two, some wooden stools, a few broken chairs, and perhaps a single striped cotton carpet for the reception-room. The dwellings of the common people consist of sheds or thatched huts built round a single court. The outer apartments are used by the men, and for the cattle. The inner are devoted to the women, to the cook-room, and the storehouse.

The food of a well-to-do shopkeeper comprises the following articles :—Rice, split-peas, vegetables, fish, milk, *ghí* or clarified butter, curds, and occasionally goat's flesh. The family of a husbandman in good circumstances, consisting of six persons, and able to spend Rs. 8 or sixteen shillings a month, would consume the following food per diem :—5 *sers* (10 lb.) of rice, 2 *dnnás* 8 *pies*, or fourpence ; vegetables or split-peas and fish, 6 *pies* or three farthings; and oil and spice, 6 *pies* or three farthings.

There are very few rich families in Purí District. In 1870 the income tax returns estimated the total of the incomes of the District above £50 per annum at £106,500 sterling. The income of the richest landholder was estimated at £8000 a year; and the fourteen largest incomes amounted to £37,154, or an average of £2654 each.

AGRICULTURE.—No well-tested statistics have been obtained ; but the following remarks are taken from a number of returns, which have from time to time been officially submitted to, and accepted by, Government. Purí is strictly a rice-growing tract. Of rice crops, the following are the most important :—(1) The *biáli*, which is sown on high but moist land, in June or July, and reaped in October or November. Its principal varieties are the *sáthiká*, the *kuliá*, and the *aswiná*. (2) The *sárad*, which is sown on middling high land in July, and is reaped in December. A hundred varieties are included under the generic name of *sárad*. Of these, the ten following are the most important :—*Khaiará, kalásur, bánkoi, matará, rangiásiná, nripatibhog, gopálbhog, básubati, bandiri,* and *narsinhbhog.* (3) The *dálua* rice, sown on low wet lands in November or

December, and reaped in April. Its most important varieties are
the *piá* and *kasundá*.

The *sárad*, or winter rice crop, is generally transplanted by the
more diligent husbandmen; and by this process a much larger
return is obtained. If not transplanted, the following are the
operations required for the winter crop :—(1) Ploughing, March or
April; (2) sowing, May or June; (3) weeding, after first rainfall;
(4) harrowing and ploughing, July or August; (5) second weeding,
August; (6) laying (arranging the crop for convenience of cutting), December; (7) reaping, December or January; (8) thresh-
ing, January or February; (9) scalding (a little water is poured
upon the paddy, which is then placed over a fire until the water is
evaporated, for the purpose of loosening the husks); (10) cleaning
or husking. Unhusked rice is called *dhán;* husked rice, *chául;* if
broken in husking, *khud-chául;* boiled rice, *bhát;* if broken, *jáu;*
boiled rice kept in water till it is cold, *pakhál;* rice liquor, *toráni;*
besides sweetmeats, parched rice, miscellaneous preparations, such
as *khai, liá, ukhurá, churá, bhajá-churá, nurumbá, chháchi ukhurá,
muri.* See Statistical Account of Balasor (vol. xviii.). No improvements are known to have taken place in rice cultivation within the
memory of man; nor have any new varieties, adapted either for
the deeper marshes or the drier upland, been introduced.

Of the pulses, the most important are the following :—*Múg* (Pha-
seolus mungo), including three varieties, *kalá, sáuli,* and *dhalá,* sown
in January or February on *sárad* rice lands, and gathered in March
or April; *birhi,* including the varieties called *ná* and *cháitá; harar*
or *arhar,* sown in July, and reaped in December or January; *chaná*
(Cicer arietinum), sown in December or January, and reaped in
February or March; *kolath* (Dolichos biflorus), sown in October
or November, and reaped in February or March; *barguri,* sown
in December, and reaped in January or February.

Of fibres, the most important are jute, hemp, and flax. The two
first are sown in July or August, and cut in September or October;
flax is sown and reaped in the same months, but rather later. Fibre
crops are always put down on high land; that used for jute is a
poor soil of little value; hemp is generally sown on dry fields close
around the homestead.

Of oil seeds, the most important are castor-oil (*gab*), sown on low
wet lands or river banks; *rási* (Sesamum orientale), sown on high
lands; mustard (*sarishá*), and linseed (*tisi,* called in Uriyá *pesu*).

Among miscellaneous crops are tobacco, on low moist lands; cotton, sown early in the cold weather, and reaped in May or June, on *sárad* rice land; sugar-cane, on fine high land, with abundant moisture, or with capabilities of irrigation; turmeric (*haldí*); *báigun* (Solanum melongena), on homestead land; potatoes, red pepper, and *pán* or betel-leaf.

CULTIVATED AREA.—Of the area of the District as returned in 1870, 970 square miles were shown as having been under cultivation in 1840, 54 square miles as cultivable, and 1486 square miles as incapable of cultivation; total, 2504 square miles. The present area (1876) is returned by the Surveyor-General at 2472·37 square miles. The total cultivated area in 1870 was returned at 741,197 acres, or 1158 square miles. This return, with the following classification of lands based upon it, is taken from an official report, but must be accepted rather as a piece of intelligent guesswork than as trustworthy statistics:—Of the 741,197 acres under tillage, 243,230 are enjoyed by the landholders as *jágír*, and pay no revenue to Government; 462,935 pay rent to Government as actually under crops; and 35,032 lie fallow. There are, therefore, according to this estimate, only 462,935 acres of cultivated land that actually pay rent to Government. As each acre would have to yield nearly a rupee of Government rent to make up the total actual land revenue of the District, I am inclined to think that the total return of tillage (741,197 acres) is below the mark, and that 800,000 acres would be a nearer approximation. No trustworthy information exists as to the acreage under cotton and other crops; but it is believed that, of the 462,935 acres under cultivation, 446,014 are under rice; 5267 under cotton; 6029 under pulses; and 5625 under tobacco, sugar-cane, and miscellaneous crops. The total crop of rice is estimated at about five millions of hundredweights; the cotton at about 21,000 hundredweights; and the pulse at about 25,000 hundredweights. It is estimated that about 60,000 hundredweights of rice are annually exported—one-third by sea, and two-thirds by land and the Chilká lake. The above figures must be received with great caution, but they are the best I have to offer.

OUT-TURN OF CROPS.—Four *bharans* of paddy are considered a good yield from an acre of first-class land. Two *bharans* an acre is considered poor. The *bharan* consists of eighty baskets (*gaunis*) of grain; but, unfortunately, the baskets vary in size. Those used for weighing unhusked paddy contain 5 Cuttack *sers*, or between

13 and 14 lbs. avoirdupois. A *bharan* of paddy, therefore, contains 10 Cuttack *maunds*, or about 9 hundredweights. The smaller basket contains only 3¼ Cuttack *sers*, and is used for weighing husked rice. The yield per acre in Purí District is, therefore, from about 16 to 36 hundredweights per acre of unhusked paddy, and from 8 to 16 hundredweights of husked rice. The average from fair land may be put down at 10 hundredweights of rice.

CONDITION OF THE CULTIVATORS.—Land is not yet so scarce in Purí as to cause an excessive subdivision of holdings. A husbandman who holds less than five acres is held to be ill off. Ten acres make him a prosperous peasant. Thirty acres are a large holding, and eighty acres an unusually large one. A husbandman with ten acres is supposed to be as well off as a small retail shopkeeper, or a servant earning about Rs. 8 or 16s. a month. The husbandman dresses worse, but he has more to eat. The cultivators, as a class, are deep in debt to the landholders, who make advances of money and rice to them. A large proportion of them hold at fixed rates, and represent the *thání rayats* of the Settlement papers. Such husbandmen hold their land under leases (*kálipattás*), granted by the Settlement Officers in 1836-37, and remaining in force until the next Settlement in 1897. The number returned as holding at fixed rates is 119,168; and this may be taken as evidence to show that the larger proportion of husbandmen in the District hold at fixed rates. All other husbandmen are tenants at will, except in rare instances where leases have been given. Act x. of 1859, therefore, scarcely applies to Purí District. Rent suits of any sort are rare, and the twelve years' occupancy right is unknown. In 1861-62 there were 464 original suits under Act x. and laws based upon it; in 1862-63, 487; in 1866-67, 545; in 1868-69, 977. In 1866-67 there were also 356 miscellaneous applications; and in 1868-69, 630.

THE DOMESTIC ANIMALS of the District are—cows, oxen, and buffaloes, kept by Gaurs and cultivators; sheep and goats, kept by castes below the Gaurs; pigs, kept by the low-caste Ghusuriás; pigeons, kept, but not eaten, by the respectable classes; fowls and ducks, kept only by Musalmáns and very low castes. A few undersized ponies are kept by the richer classes for riding, but are never used for ploughing or draught. The following prices may be received as an approximation to the current rates :—A cow giving 2 *sers* or about 1½ quarts of milk daily, fetches about Rs. 12. 8. 0 or £1, 5s., but in some parts may be got as low as Rs. 8 or 16s. ; a pair of good plough bullocks, Rs. 30 or £3 sterling; a good cow buffalo, giving 4½ *sers* of milk, Rs. 20 or £2; a pair of draught buffaloes, Rs. 40 or £4; a score of sheep, Rs. 20 or £2; goats about the same price; a score of full-grown pigs, Rs. 100 or £10.

AGRICULTURAL IMPLEMENTS.—Ten acres are locally known as a 'plough' of land, but practically six or seven acres are as much as a good pair of bullocks can manage. The implements required for ten acres are the following:—One plough, value 2s.; two mattocks (*koris*), Rs. 2. 8. o or 5s.; one spade (*kánk*), R. 1 or 2s.; one axe (*kuráli*), 12 *annás* or 1s. 6d.; three choppers for cutting wood (*káturi* and *dá*), 10 *ánnás* or 1s. 3d.; a clod breaker (*mai*), 8 *ánnás* or 1s.; a harrow (*bidá*), 4 *ánnás* or 6d. : total, Rs. 6. 10 or 13s. 3d., which, with Rs. 30 or £3 for the oxen, make Rs. 30. 6. 10 or £3, 13s. 3d. The husbandman would also have to borrow occasionally a pair of oxen for a holding of this size. Few hired labourers are employed, but the Báuris, Savars, and Kandhs are practically labouring classes. The Kandhs cultivate lands in the hills, but only appear in the plains as hired labourers.

WAGES.—Wages are lower in Purí than in either Cuttack or Balasor Districts. On this subject, I extract the following from the Annual Report of the Collector of Purí for 1871-72 :—'The wages of unskilled labour are very low. The main employment is, of course, agricultural; the Baurí, or labourer of the servile class, is comparatively well off who receives as remuneration one *gauní* or basket of paddy of 5 Cuttack *sers* a day, or 6½ Bengal *sers*, as his remuneration. According to the average of prices for cleaned rice, this would be less than 1½ *ánnás* or 2¼d. for every day of service. This is for tolerably permanent employment; for mere occasional jobs the rate is, of course, higher. The most common rate of wages for permanent employment is Rs. 2 or 4s. a month, plus a suit of cold weather and warm weather clothing. The clothes consist of two *khadís* or loin wrappers, of about four yards each, costing 12 *ánnás* or 1s. 6d. a piece; a *gámchá* or wrapper, of some four yards, costing 6 *ánnás* or 9d.; and for the cold weather a *chádar* or cotton sheet, costing R. 1 or 2s. To these may be added an occasional dole of tobacco; and if the employer be a Bráhman, whose food is accessible to any caste, then an occasional meal when the labour of the day has been unusually prolonged. Altogether, this would be in money Rs. 24 or £2, 8s. od. a year, in clothes Rs. 3 or 6s., and in occasional donations Rs. 6 or 12s.; in all, Rs. 33 or £3, 6s. od. a year, or less than Rs. 3 or 6s. a month. On this, the labourer feeds and clothes his family. The Baurís have not always to pay house rent; but those who have to pay, do so at the rate of about 8 *ánnás* a year. For occasional employment, *e.g.* on public works, the rate is higher; it may be quoted at 2 *ánnás* or 3d. to 3 *ánnás* or 4½d. a day. Skilled labour, like that of a carpenter or weaver, fetches about 4 *ánnás* or 6d. a day. The hard time of the year for an ordinary labourer to get over is that before the harvest, viz. August, September, and October, when stocks are low and *mahájans* are calculating the chances of the standing crop. The plentiful time is from November to January, the reaping season. At that time a man can earn from 2 *ánnás* or 3d. to 3 *ánnás* or 4½d. a day, besides a sheaf of straw with some 5 *sers* of grain to carry home on his head; and his wife and children can glean 2 or 3 *sers* of grain over and above.

' In salt manufacture, the rate of remuneration is 2 *ánnás* a *maund* of the out-turn of salt, all at the risk of the labourer. It takes four men to make 400 *maunds* of salt in a fair season of three months. They receive for this Rs. 50 or £5, from which, however, they have to defray charges for their implements, about Rs. 2 or 4s. ; thus, their wages are not more than Rs. 48 or £4, 16s. od. for the three months, or Rs. 4 or 8s. a month. This includes nothing whatever for risk of failure in manufacture through unfavourable weather. Out of these earnings they have to pay high for their food in the unhealthy and out-of-the-way places which are the seat of the salt manufacture. The 400 *maunds* of salt, the out-turn of these four men's labour, will ultimately cost the consumers about Rs. 1600 to Rs. 1700 or £160 to £170, at the usual retail rates of Rs. 4. 4 or 8s. 6d. per *maund*. Of this amount, Rs. 1300 or £130 falls to Government as duty, at Rs. 3. 4 or 6s. 6d. per *maund*; Rs. 100 (£10) or so will represent excise licensee's charges in manufacture, including preventive force and storehouse construction; Rs. 300 (£30) or so will represent remuneration of the distributors, the wholesale and retail vendors. The four labourers who have produced the out-turn by their own labour and at their own risk, receive but Rs. 50 (£5).

' These figures are significant as to the condition of the people. My predecessor, in describing the condition of the District last year, said that the bulk of the people were no better off than they had been a generation ago. It must be admitted that the figures of salt earnings confirm, rather than confute, this opinion. The rate of

2 *ánnás* or 3d. per *maund* of out-turn, equivalent, as we have seen, to Rs. 4 or 8s. a month, is the same now as it was in the time when Government used to manufacture. Thus, people are working at the same rate of wages now, when a rupee fetches only 32 *sers* of rice, which prevailed formerly, when a rupee fetched 64 *sers* of rice. This is not a satisfactory condition of affairs.'

PRICES.—As indicated above, the price of ordinary coarse rice has doubled within the last 30 years. The following tables, compiled from Mr. A. P. MacDonnell's Report on the Food-grain Supply of Bengal, exhibits the average monthly and yearly rates for common rice and pulses, for the four years from 1871 to 1874 inclusive:—

PRICES OF RICE AND PULSES IN PURI DISTRICT FOR EACH MONTH OF THE FOUR YEARS 1871-1874.

MONTH AND YEAR.		PURI SUBDIVISION.				KHURDHA SUBDIVISION.			
		Rice.		Pulses.		Rice.		Pulses.	
		Amount per rupee.	Price per cwt.	Amount per rupee.	Price per cwt.	Amount per rupee.	Price per cwt.	Amount per rupee.	Price per cwt.
		sers.	*s. d.*	*sers.*	*s. d.*	*sers.*	*s. d.*	*sers.*	*s. d.*
JANUARY	1871,	31½	3 6½	18½	6 1	34	3 4	10½	10 11
	1872,	23½	4 9	23½	4 9	27½	4 1	10½	10 11
	1873,	30½	3 8	...	...	42	2 8	10	11 2
	1874,	22	5 1	...	...	26	4 4	9	12 5
Average,		27	4 2	...	...	33	3 5	10	11 2
FEBRUARY	1871,	31	3 7	18½	6 1	29	3 10	9	12 5
	1872,	27½	4 1	18½	6 1	27½	4 1	11	10 2
	1873,	35	3 2	...	...	35½	3 1½	9	12 5
	1874,	23½	4 9	...	...	27½	4 1	10	11 2
Average,		29	3 10	...	...	30	3 9	10	11 2
MARCH	1871,	31½	3 6½	20½	5 5	29	3 10	12	9 4
	1872,	...	...	...	...	29	3 10	10	11 2
	1873,	37	3 0	...	...	35½	3 1½	9	12 5
	1874,	26	4 4	...	...	27½	4 1	10	11 2
Average,		31	3 7	...	...	30	3 9	10	11 2
APRIL	1871,	32	3 6	24	4 8	27½	4 1	13	8 7
	1872,	24½	4 7	...	...	29	3 10	11	10 2
	1873,	40	2 10	...	...	34	3 4	9	12 5
	1874,	28	4 0	...	...	27½	4 1	10	11 2
Average,		31	3 7	...	...	30	3 9	11	10 2
MAY	1871,	33½	3 4	24	4 8	27½	4 1	10½	10 11
	1872,	29	3 10	...	...	27½	4 1	11	10 2
	1873,	35½	3 1½	...	...	34	3 4	9	12 5
	1874,	29	3 10	...	...	27½	4 1	10	11 2
Average,		32	3 6	...	...	29	3 10	10	11 2

PRICES OF RICE AND PULSES IN PURI DISTRICT—*continued*.

MONTH AND YEAR.	PURI SUBDIVISION.				KHURDHA SUBDIVISION.			
	Rice.		Pulses.		Rice.		Pulses.	
	Amount per rupee.	Price per cwt.	Amount per rupee.	Price per cwt.	Amount per rupee.	Price per cwt.	Amount per rupee.	Price per cwt.
	sers.	s. d.	sers.	s. d.	sers.	s. d.	sers.	s. d.
JUNE — 1871,	31½	3 6½	22½	4 11	27½	4 1	13	8 7
1872,	26	4 4	...	...	27½	4 1	11	10 2
1873,	33	3 5	...	...	34	3 4	9	12 5
1874,	26	4 4	...	...	27½	4 1	10	11 2
Average,	29	3 10	...	...	29	3 10	11	10 2
JULY — 1871,	31½	3 6½	24	4 8	27½	4 1	12	9 4
1872,	23½	4 9	...	...	27½	4 1	11	10 2
1873,	34	3 4	...	...	37	3 0	16	7 0
1874,	25	4 6	...	...	27½	4 1	10	11 2
Average,	28	4 0	...	...	30	3 9	12	9 4
AUGUST — 1871,	31½	3 6½	26	4 4	29	3 10	9	12 5
1872,	23½	4 10	...	...	24	4 8	12½	8 11
1873,	36	3 1	...	...	37	3 0	16	7 0
1874,	22	4 11	...	...	27½	4 1	10	11 2
Average,	28	4 0	...	...	29	3 10	12	9 4
SEPTEMBER, 1871,	31½	3 6½	26	4 4	31½	3 6½	10½	10 11
1872,	24½	4 7	...	...	23½	4 9	12½	8 11
1873,	34	3 4	...	...	28½	3 11	14½	7 9
1874,	23½	4 9	...	...	29	3 10	10	11 2
Average,	28	4 0	...	...	28	4 0	12	9 4
OCTOBER — 1871,	...	...	...	...	27½	4 1	12	9 4
1872,	34	3 4	...	...	24	4 8	12½	8 11
1873,	33	3 5	...	...	37	3 0	9	12 5
1874,	23½	4 9	...	...	29	3 10	10	11 2
Average,	30	3 9	...	...	29	3 10	11	10 2
NOVEMBER — 1871,	27½	4 1	27½	4 1	24	4 8	12	9 4
1872,	35	3 2	...	...	42½	2 7½	9	12 5
1873,	31	3 7	...	...	37	3 0	9	12 5
1874,	25½	4 5	...	...	30	3 9	9	12 5
Average,	30	3 9	...	...	33	3 5	10	11 2
DECEMBER — 1871,	23½	4 9	23½	4 9	29	3 10	14½	7 9
1872,	31	3 7	...	...	42	2 8	9	12 5
1873,	24	4 8	...	...	23	4 10	9	12 5
1874,	27½	4 1	...	...	30	3 9	9	12 5
Average,	26	4 4	...	...	31	3 7	10	11 2
Yearly Average 1871,	28	4 0	23	4 10	29	3 10	12	9 4
1872,	27	4 2	...	...	29	3 10	11	10 2
1873,	34	3 4	...	...	35	3 2	11	10 2
1874,	25	4 6	...	...	28	4 0	10	11 2
Average for Four Years	29	3 10	...	...	30	3 9	11	10 2

WEIGHTS AND MEASURES.—The standard land measure of the District is the *mán,* which is as nearly as possible equal to an English acre, being twenty rods square, each rod measuring ten feet five inches and a fraction, called a *jab.* A *jab* is either a barley-corn, or the mark inside the last joint of the thumb. Various smaller local *máns* are current in various parts of the District. The standard of weight in Purí is the Cuttack *ser* of 105 *tolá* weight.

THE REVENUE SETTLEMENT, which practically still continues in force, is that of 1837. It was intended to hold good for thirty years only; and in 1866 a discussion took place with a view to extending the Permanent Settlement to Orissa. But the state of exhaustion in which the famine of that year left the Province, precluded the possibility of doing so, and would have rendered the minute investigations necessary for a re-settlement very distressing to the people. During the early part of 1867, much correspondence passed between the local authorities and the Governments of Bengal and of India on the subject. It was decided that the people should be spared all interference in their then reduced circumstances, and that the Settlement should be renewed at the low rates of 1837. The Government of India, in its letter No. 2405, dated 22d January 1867, proposed to extend the previous Settlement for twenty years. But afterwards it was resolved to grant a thirty years' extension, without any enhancement of the rents (Act x. of 1867). The Settlement of 1837 expired in September 1867, and the current one will therefore run to 1897. On the most moderate computation, the existing land revenue might have been raised by five per cent., or, in round numbers, £2500 a year. Irrespective of interest, therefore, the famine of 1866 has cost £75,000, under the single item of non-enhancement of the rates, in Purí District alone.

LAND TENURES. — The following account of the different varieties of land tenures met with in Purí District is taken from a valuable report on the subject by Bábu Nandakisor Das, dated 21st October 1875. Exigencies of space have compelled me to considerably condense the Report; but I have retained sufficient to afford a clear insight into the nature of the different classes of tenures, and I print it as far as possible in the author's own words :—

'HISTORICAL SKETCH : THE HINDU REVENUE SYSTEM.—Till the conquest of Orissa by the Mughuls in 1578, *i.e.* during the time of the native Hindu kings, property in the soil by a class of persons

answering to the *zamíndárs* of the present day was unknown. No
intermediate tenures or proprietary rights of any kind were allowed
to grow up between the king and the cultivators of the soil; the
ownership was vested in the former alone, and the right of occupancy
in the latter. The Province was then divided into two principal
divisions, civil and military. The lands lying on the eastern and
western frontiers, and some portions of the land in the interior, were
divided amongst a number of military chiefs (called *khandáits* or
bhuiáns), on condition of their protecting the country from foreign
invasion, as also from thieves and *dákáits*, and of furnishing
when required a certain contingent of troops. These chiefs in their
turn distributed the land amongst a vast body of peasant militia,
who tilled the land during peace, and took up arms in time of
war. These men, called *páiks*, were supported by grants of land
which they held of the *jágírdárs*, and each perhaps cultivated
enough to supply the immediate consumption of his own family.
Out of the other portion of the Province which formed the Crown
land, a part was given in *jágír* to the ministers and servants of the
king, and the remainder was divided into several circles, called *bisis*
or *khands*. Each of the circles was managed by one revenue officer,
called *bissoi* or *khandpati*, or *khand-ádhipati*, who had the chief superintendence and direction of affairs, and conducted the police duties
with the aid of an officer called a *khandáit*. There was also an
accountant, called *bhúi-múl*, who superintended more immediately
the collection of revenue, drew up the accounts of produce and cultivation, and kept a register of all the particulars of the fields. Each
of these Fiscal Divisions contained several villages, which formed the
rural unit through which the officers of the State reached the individual husbandmen. The *khandáit* had a body of armed police
under him, whose business it was to watch the persons and property
of the villagers and to enforce the orders of the head-men. There
were, besides, in each village a head-man (*pradhán*) and an accountant (*bhúi*); and as the divisional head and the divisional accountant
were responsible to the king's treasurer for the whole revenue of the
Fiscal Division, so the village head and the village accountant were
responsible to their divisional superiors for the complete revenue of
the village. In like manner, as the divisional officers distributed
the land tax among the various villages in the Fiscal Division, so the
village head and accountant divided the amount due from the
village amongst the individual husbandmen. Both sets of appoint-

ments had a tendency to become hereditary; but both required confirmation, or at least tacit recognition, by the king or his representative. There was, however, a very important peculiarity in the nature of the appointment of the village head-man. While the divisional appointments were purely official, his was more of a representative than of an official character; his position was a matter of usage and unwritten custom; he was the representative of the sovereign amongst his fellow-villagers, and was at the same time the representative of the villagers to the superior officers of State; his nomination rested with the people, and confirmation or recognition with the sovereign.

'THE MUGHUL REVENUE SYSTEM.—This state of things prevailed till the year 1584, when Akbar's general and finance minister, Rájá Todar Mall, after conquering the Province, commenced a Revenue Settlement. He introduced no important change in the financial arrangement of the Hindu Rájás. He retained intact the old division of the Province into military fiefs and Crown lands, which were henceforth called respectively *garhjáts* and *mughulbandí*, contenting himself, in regard to the former, with a verbal allegiance and a nominal tribute. He also respected the provision for the royal household and great officers of the court under the Hindu dynasty, and left 1547 square miles as the undisputed demesne of the Khurdhá Rájás and their dependants. Amongst others, Khurdhá, Ráháng, Sirái, and Chaubiskud in Purí District, aggregating 1342·51 square miles, and being more than half of its present area, were left to the actual heir of the Gajapatí dynasty, Rám Chandra Deo. The remaining portion of the Crown land he managed through the old Hindu officers, only changing the names of Divisions and divisional officers. The *khands* and *bisis* were now called *parganás*, the *khand-ádhipatis* and *bissois* were called *chaudharís*, and the *bhúi-múl* received the appellation of *kánúngo wiláyati.*

'The portion of the *parganá* under the more immediate charge of each of these officials was called a *táluk*, and the managers generally *tálukdárs;* in villages which had a *pradhán*, he was called *mukaddam*, meaning exactly the same thing. The *jágírs* of the great military chiefs were called *kilás;* and for their Hindu title of *bhuián* was substituted 'zamíndár,' an appellation which was originally restricted to the Rájás of Khurdhá, Aul, Sárangarh, and to the Garhját Rájás. The fiscal officers of the *mughulbandí* or revenue-paying tract had no proprietary right in the soil, and were not *zamíndárs* in any sense of the term. During the Hindu period, they were looked upon in no other light than as servants of the State; though from the hereditary character pervading so remarkably all the institutions of the Hindus, it is not unlikely that they possessed some indirect title of property in their offices. The Musalmáns who succeeded them had no leisure or knowledge for the details of administration. What they wanted •was a body of powerful native middle-men, who should relieve them from the trouble of dealing with the people, and who should have both power and local knowledge enough to enforce the revenue demands against the individual villages. In the Hindu fiscal officers they found such a body ready to their hands; but this body, as it became more and more necessary to the foreign rulers of Orissa, also grew more and more independent. It soon lost its homogeneous character as a staff of revenue officers, and split up into a number of different landholders, each with more or less of admitted proprietary right, according as each individual had strength and opportunity for asserting himself; but none possessed anything like a full ownership in the land. This state of things continued till the year 1751, when the Province passed into the hands of the Marhattás.

'MARHATTA PERIOD.—The Marhattás retained the old political division of the Province into military fiefs and royal domain. The former, comprising the hilly country on the western frontier, and extensive marshy woodland tracts along the sea-shore to the east, was parcelled out in divisions, called *kilás*, amongst certain Rájás, servants, chieftains, or *zamíndárs;* and the latter, comprising the plain and open country into which the Mughul Settlement had been introduced, was divided into four *chaklás* or divisions, viz. Cuttack, Bhadrakh, Soro, and Balasor, and into about 150 *pargands.* Each *parganá* was again divided into one, two, three, or more of the following divisions, viz. :—(1) *táluk chaudhari*, (2) *táluk kánúngo wiláyati*, (3) *táluk kánúngo*, (4) *táluk sardár kánúngo*, (5) *táluk mazkuri* or *mukaddami mazkuri.* Unlike the Muhammadans, the Marhattás preferred dealing with the people directly, instead of through a number of middle-men; 32 *ámils* were appointed, each of whom was individually responsible to the estate for the revenue assessed on his division. He was remunerated by grants of land called *nánkár*, which he held rent-free, and by certain other perquisites on account of collection charges. He was assisted by a *sardár kánúngo*, under whom were employed a number of *gumáshtás* or agents in each *pargand.* Each *gumáshtá*, again, had under him two or three *muharrirs* or clerks. These officers assumed the functions which the landholders had performed for the Muhammadans; an annual Settlement of land revenue was made every year, and the amount of it was reported to Government. A large number of superior landholders were set aside; but the hereditary rights of the village heads were respected, and they were allowed *nánkár* lands, which passed under the name of *pitráli.* Owing to the confusion that prevailed in the latter years of their rule, the Marhattá officers became inclined to leave the details of land administration to any person who came forward to engage for the payment of a lump sum. No other class was better qualified to take up this responsibility than the *mukaddams*, and it was thus that they (the *mukaddams*) began to develop into village landholders.

' The Muhammadan emperors had lost much of the sovereign ownership in the soil which the Hindu princes possessed. The *bissois, khandpátís*, and *bhúi-múls*, who, under the designation of *chaudharís* and *kánúngos*, gradually became quasi-proprietors of extensive estates, naturally sought to get rid of the village heads, and began, successfully, to undermine and encroach upon their rights; but with the approach of the Marhattás, the tables were turned. The village heads dealt directly with the treasury officers, and the existence of a superior class of fiscal officers (or, as they had then become, quasi-proprietors) was in a majority of cases ignored. The Muhammadan neglect was the period of aggrandisement for one class, and the Marhattá misrule for another. In one case, the divisional officers grew into divisional landholders, and in the other the village officers developed into village landholders; and after the British conquest of the Province in 1803, claimants belonging to both classes came forward with conflicting titles. It may be safely stated that, during the confusion that prevailed prior to the British acquisition of the Province, there was no class to whom a proprietary right can be said to have been allowed. The State owned the land; while the *kánúngos* (*sadr* and *wiláyati*), the *chaudharís, mukaddams*, and others exercised such rights within their respective limits as they chóse to assume to themselves, without question, so long as the demands made upon them were liquidated. The numerous alienations made by all classes above mentioned is generally considered good proof of ownership, but there is not to be met with anything like an acknowledgment of such a privilege by the Marhattá authorities.

'Those who then or subsequently chose to arrogate to themselves the title of *zamíndár*, were either principal *mukaddams* with a hereditary right of collection, but without any right, title, or interest in the land itself; or fiscal officers, chiefly *chaudharís* and *kánúngos*, in charge of the collections. Some of them, however, the *zamíndár* of Kotdes, for instance, had *zamíndárí sanads*, and were designated as *zamíndárs;* but they had very few of the rights of a *zamíndár* in the present sense of the term.

'The incidents of the quasi-proprietary tenure were—(1) A right of hereditary succession, subject, as stated before, to confirmation or tacit recognition by Government. (2) A right to the profits from the land, consisting of the increase arising out of the annual revision of land tax, on bringing unoccupied lands under cultivation, miscellaneous receipts, transit dues on merchandise, petty alienations of land, commission on collection, and grant of rent - free tenures. (3) Responsibility to Government for the whole of the tax from the land under their management. In case of default the landholder was imprisoned, or his estate was sold, generally by private sale. (4) Power of transferring their rights by gift or otherwise, subject to the formal consent of the ruling power.

'ENGLISH PERIOD AND ORIGIN OF ZAMINDARI RIGHTS.—After the conquest of the Province in 1803, the British officers who first came to undertake the administration were enjoined to make the settlement of the land revenue with the *zamíndárs* or other actual proprietors of the soil, except only when the property in land was disputed, when it was to be made provisionally with the person in possession. But the local officers, not finding a body of landholders with well-defined rights, such as existed in Bengal, proceeded to manufacture *zamíndárs* out of the materials that existed, as far as possible in accordance with the actual facts. But they found themselves lost in a jungle of conflicting, incomplete rights. Engagements were taken from the parties in possession, who had enjoyed the office of collecting the land tax and paying it into the treasury. All such persons, under whatever designation they had discharged this function, became under our system landholders *in capite* from the Company, under the provisions of Regulation xii. of 1805. This was the origin of the Orissa *zamíndárs;* and thus it was that a right which never existed was silently and perhaps unconsciously acquiesced in, and indirectly admitted and confirmed by subsequent legislation. A proprietary body was consolidated out of the tangled growth of quasi-proprietary rights,—a body which included and represented all the various sorts of intermediate holders between the ruling power and the actual husbandmen.

'Having thus selected a number of landholders *in capite*, in accordance with the actual facts, we proceeded to mould them into a homogeneous body by giving the same rights to all. We erected their quasi-hereditary, quasi-transferable office of managing the land and transmitting the land revenue, into a full proprietary tenure. The abstract ownership had always been vested in the ruling power; and this we made over to the landholders, except that we retained the power of raising the land tax. Even this power we placed under severe restrictions, and our present system of thirty years' leases divests us of any means of exercising it except three times in a century. In short, out of inchoate proprietary usages we built up a firmly coherent title. Whatever might have been the former status of the persons now known as *zamíndárs*, their claim to be now considered as *bona fide* proprietors of the land cannot be questioned.

'The several landholders who now pass under the designation of *zamíndárs* are composed of—(1) *Zamíndárs* in the technical sense of the word in the Marhattá revenue system of Orissa (the Kotdes landholders, for instance). (2) Tenure-holders, such as *tálukdárs, chaudharís, bissois, bhúi-múls* or *wiláyati kánúngos, jágírdárs, pradháns* or *mukaddams*, and all others who paid revenue direct to the treasury, or were entitled to separation. (3) Holders of land exceeding 75 acres in extent, which were alleged to have been held rent-free, or on a peppercorn rental, either as *jágír* or *lákhiráj*, but were resumed and assessed with a full or small rental during the general inquiry into the validity of rent-free tenures, whether they were held as *lákhiráj, kháirát, jágír, debottar, pírottar, tanki, kharidá máafi*, or otherwise.

'All these landholders have long since thrown off their distinctive appellation of *tálukdárs, kánúngos, mukaddams*, and *pradháns*, etc., and have readily assumed the generic and more significant title of *zamíndár*. In fact, every *sadr málguzár*, i.e. every person who now pays revenue directly to the treasury, not being a servant of the State, is called a *zamíndár* (meaning proprietor of land), while the distinctive titles of *mukaddams, sarbaráhkárs, pradháns*, etc., have been left to the subordinate tenure-holders or *mufassal málguzárs*. At the present day, the number of estates within

the fiscal limits of Puri District, which pay their revenue direct
to Government, is returned as follows :— Tributary States, 2 ;
permanently settled estates, 1 ; temporarily settled estates, 425 ;
estates held *khás*, or temporarily under Government management,
4 ; estates in which Government is the direct proprietor, 6 :
total, 438.

'TRIBUTARY STATES.—The two Tributary States are Nayagarh
and Ranpur.   Under sections 36, 13, and 14 of Regulation xii. 13
and 14 of 1805, these estates are exempted from the operation of
the general Regulations, and are therefore called Non-Regulation
Tracts ; but they may, at the pleasure of Government, be at any
time brought under the Regulations, this exemption being merely
on grounds of convenience.   The tribute payable by each Rájá is
fixed in perpetuity ; and in return for their tribute they are secured
from foreign enemies, domestic rebellions, and inter-tribal feuds.
The Rájás are the proprietors of the soil, there being no intermediate
proprietor between them and the cultivators.   For further particulars
vide the Statistical Account of the Tributary States (*post.*, pp. 196-198).

'SETTLED ZAMINDARI ESTATES.—The permanently settled estate
of Márichpur and all the temporarily settled estates are alike in
nature.   The only distinctive feature is, that while the revenue payable by the former is fixed in perpetuity, that payable by the others
is liable to adjustment at the expiration of the term of each Settlement ; and that the rights of under-tenants in the latter have been
defined and recorded.   The revenue payable by the permanently
settled estate of Márichpur has been fixed for ever under clause 2,
section 35, Regulation xii. of 1805.   But as regards the temporarily settled estates, after several short summary Settlements,
a Settlement for thirty years was concluded in 1836 ; and, on
the expiration of that term, the Settlement was extended without
enhancement for another term of thirty years, under Act x. (B.C.)
of 1866.   This Settlement is now in force.

'The rights and liabilities of *zamíndárí* tenures are as follow :—
(1) The tenure is absolutely hereditary, sanction of Government to
succession being not now required.   No objection has ever been
made by Government to give full effect to the succession of legal
heirs ; but, on the contrary, such succession has always been fully
recognised by the courts of justice, as well as by the revenue officers.

'(2) It is perfectly transferable by sale, gift, or otherwise, so far as the
State is concerned.   Transfers by *zamíndárs* of the whole or portions

of their *zamíndárís* have always been held by courts of law to be good, provided such transfers are not inconsistent with the national law of the transferor; and the revenue officers have always given effect to such transfers, either in the shape of mutation, or of *batwárá* or partition.

'(3) The amount of revenue payable by each *zamíndár* for his estate has been fixed permanently, or for a certain number of years, according as the estate is permanently or temporarily settled; and the *zamíndár* is not liable to pay anything beyond the stipulated amount of rent during the currency of the Settlement.

'(4) In the *hastobúd* villages, *i.e.* villages in which there is no intermediate tenure-holder between the *zamíndár* and *rayat*, the former is entitled to all the increase of rent arising from whatever cause, except from *tháni* lands and from lands over which a *rayat* has rights of occupancy, if in the latter case the increase is due to the labour or expense of the *rayat*. In the case of villages in which there are intermediate tenures between the *zamíndár* and the cultivators, all such profits go to the tenure-holder, the *zamíndár* being entitled only to the *málikáná* allowed at the time of Settlement.

'(5) The *zamíndárs* cannot as of right demand remission of revenue, in whole or in part, in season of drought, inundation, or other calamity. The insertion of a clause in the *zamíndár's* engagements, to the effect that in seasons of calamity remissions will be given, was after deliberate consideration disallowed, on the ground that it would be productive of endless embarrassment; though at the same time it was said that it was to be understood that, on any great calamity occurring, suitable remissions would be granted.

'(6) If in seasons of calamity the *zamíndárs* are not allowed re-missions, they on their part are not bound by law to grant remissions to their *rayats* and under-tenants, unless there is a provision to that effect in the leases of the cultivators. In the *pattás* granted to the *rayats* of Ráháng, Sirái, and Chaubiskud, and in some other *parganás*, it is almost invariably provided that in seasons of calamity suitable remissions will be made. The allowance made to the *zamíndárs*, to cover risks and collection charges, is in all such cases considered sufficient to protect them against loss, when there is only a partial failure of crop or some other calamity of not very great magnitude.

'(7) The waste land attached to any village belongs to the *zamíndár*; but this is, presumably, subject to the prescriptive right of the villagers to pasturage, roads, and other public rights, though there are no express provisions to this effect to be found in the Settlement proceedings.

'(8) Since the passing of Regulation xii. of 1805, the *zamíndárs* of temporarily settled estates are not allowed to create under-tenures of a permanent nature.

'(9) In several cases in which allowances have been made to *zamíndárs* for the purpose in the Settlement, they are bound to pay for the maintenance of village accountants (*patwáris*) and village watchmen (*chaukídárs*); and where no such provision has been made, they are themselves required to perform the duties of *patwári* (Regulation xii. of 1817).

'(10) They are prohibited from levying any kind of cess, or of receiving any money from their *rayats*, above and beyond the stipulated amount of rent.

'(11) For the recovery of arrears of revenue, they are bound to proceed against their tenants and under-tenants under the law in force for the time being; and they are prohibited from adopting any other means for enforcing payment of the rents due to them.

'(12) The *málikáná* or proprietary share of the rent payable to the *zamíndár*, fixed at the time of Settlement, is not to be altered during the term of the Settlement. Such *málikáná* varies from 30 to 40 per cent. on the gross rental in the case of *hastobúd* villages, and from 7½ to 20 per cent. in the case of villages in which there are intermediate tenures.

'(13) In case of default in the payment of revenue on the date fixed for payment, the estate is liable to be sold by public auction to the highest bidder; and the purchase-money is to be applied to the liquidation of all arrears due upon the latest day of payment from the estate sold, the residue (if any) being then paid to the holder or holders of the estate.

'(14) A *zamíndár* can purchase the rights of a *shikmídár* or subordinate tenure-holder, in a village in his own *zamíndári*, and enjoy both the *shikmí* and *zamíndárí* right; provided, of course, the sub-tenure is not of his own creation since 1805, it having been ruled that no *zamíndár* has power to create such a tenure since the enactment of Regulation xii. of that year.

'(15) Under the laws now in force, the *zamíndárs* cannot be dispossessed of their estates so long as they pay regularly the amount of revenue fixed on their estates, and so long as the Settlement is in force; but if, at the time of the revision of the Settlement, it should appear to the revenue authorities that the continuance or admission of the person who may have engaged for the revenue of the estate, or who may claim to engage, would endanger the public tranquillity, or otherwise be seriously detrimental,—or if, under any other circumstances, they shall consider it inexpedient to take further engagements from him,—they may, under the orders of Government, hold the estate *khás*, or let it in farm for a period not exceeding twelve years (*vide* section · 3, and clause 5, section 7, Regulation vii. of 1822). And in such case the proprietor shall be entitled to *málikáná* at such rate as the Board may consider proper, not being below 5 per cent. on the net amount realized by Government from the lands, and not exceeding 10 per cent. on that amount without the special sanction of Government.

'(16) Under section 90, Act x. of 1872, the *zamíndárs* are bound to give information to the magistrate or police with respect to certain criminal matters.

'·RESUMED LAKHIRAJ TENURES.—These are tenures which were formerly held revenue-free, but which, at the time of the Settlement, were resumed and brought on the District rent-roll, the deeds of grant under which they were held not being considered genuine or valid. The holders were, however, declared entitled to enter into immediate engagements with Government, and a Settlement was accordingly concluded with them. Those dispossessed *lákhirájdárs* who had been in continuous ancient possession, and had held in good faith, were assessed at an amount equal to one-half the gross rental; and in cases where the *lákhirájdár* was himself the cultivator, at one-half of the gross value of the land. Those who had not held their tenure in good faith, but who had been long in possession, were assessed at full rental, and were allowed to retain possession of the land; while the lands of those who had not been in long possession, and whose tenures were not valid, merged into the parent estate, and the Settlement was concluded with the *zamíndár*. The indulgence of assessment at half-rates, however, is not conferred in perpetuity. Government retains the power to impose a full assessment after the expiration of the term of the present Settlement; and the amount to be paid by the *lákhirájdár* is liable to variation whenever the re-settlement of the *parganá* in which the resumed lands are situated shall become necessary.

' Holders of resumed *lákhiráj* tenures exceeding 75 acres in extent were treated in the Settlement as *sadr málguzárs*, and those of tenures of 75 acres or less as dependent *tálukdárs*. With regard to absentee or recusant holders of resumed tenures, the following rules were observed :—(1) In such tenures of 75 acres or upwards, the lands of the absent proprietors were farmed for ten years, and those of recusants for twelve years ; in either case they were entitled to *málikáná*. (2) In respect to tenures of less than 75 acres in extent, a recusant proprietor was allowed the right of re-entry after a period of ten years ; if he did not attend after the issue of notice, he was held to have forfeited all right of re-entry.

'The case of the *lákhirájdárs* of Khurdhá and Pánchgarh was differently dealt with. In consideration of the peculiar condition of the country and the people, and in consequence of the title-deeds of many having been destroyed during the rebellion of 1804, it was not considered desirable to make detailed inquiries into the validity of the tenures. The general character of the compromise at first proposed by the local authorities was a Settlement in perpetuity, on the basis of an assessment at half-rates of the land in cultivation at the time of Settlement, and of that on which the houses of the *minhaddrs* were situated, the same terms being granted alike both to *tanki* (quit-rent tenures described below) and to *lákhiráj* tenures. This proposition was not supported by the Board of Revenue ; and in consideration of the inconvenience and anomaly of allowing permanent arrangements in a temporarily settled District, they suggested that a Settlement might be granted, to all who should accept the compromise, for sixty years, *i.e.* double the usual term of Settlement ; and that the local authorities might be empowered to reduce the proposed demand, if necessary, from 8 to 6 *ánnás* in the rupee. Neither of these propositions met with the approval of the Government of Bengal, and it was ruled that a Settlement might be granted for thirty years at a *jamá* or assessment equal to one-fourth of the rent of the land in cultivation. The correspondence being laid before the Supreme Government, the orders of the local Government were rescinded, and it was directed that the terms to be allowed should be on the basis of an assessment at half-rates, as recommended by the Board of Revenue, with this difference, that the rates only should be fixed in perpetuity, and that the resumed lands should be re-assessed at those rates periodically, at the same time with the re-settlement of all other estates in the two *pargands*. According to these orders, the right to settle at half-rates was conferred in perpetuity, but the actual amount to be paid by the *lákhiráidárs* was liable to variation, whenever the re-settlement of the *párganá* in which the resumed lands are situated became necessary. The *lákhiráj* lands were to be considered open to re-settlement with the other lands of the *párganá*, but the revenue to be assessed upon them was to be calculated always according to the provisions of clause 2, section 8, of Regulation xix. of 1793.

'To these terms, however, the *lákhirájdárs* and *tankidárs* of Khurdhá and Pánchgarh did not agree. In consideration of the deep-rooted prejudices of the people against a measure which they considered would reduce them to the level of the common *rayats*, the Collector proposed to substitute for a detailed Settlement at half-rates the following general quit-rents, viz.:—On *debottar* land, whether *tanki* or *lákhiráj*, Rs. 4. per *bati ;* and on all other *tanki* and *lákhiráj* lands, Rs. 4. 12. o per *bati*. These quit-rents were recommended on the understanding that they were to be fixed on this principle, that in the event of the rents of the *mál* (cultivated) lands of the *párganá* being raised, the quit-rents of the *lákhirájdárs* (which are assessed upon the entire area of the grant, without reference to the extent of cultivation) shall be liable to a proportionate enhancement. But in a subsequent communication, the local authorities gave preference to the arrangement of making the quit-rent perpetual. On the matter being laid before the Government of Bengal, it was decided that the request of the *lákhirájdárs* and *tankidárs* to have their lands assessed at the quit-rent proposed by the Collector, in lieu of the compromise sanctioned by the Supreme Government, should be sanctioned, on the understanding that the principle of a periodical revision of the assessment was to be maintained. Under this arrangement the principle of assessment was, that the *lákhirájdárs* and *tankidárs* will not have to pay at any future Settlement the full assessment on the lands; but the assessment will be subject to revision rateably on the entire *jamá* of the whole of the tenures, in proportion to the modified *jamá* of the *khálsá* lands.

'The rights and liabilities of the resumed *lákhirájdárs* may be summed up as follows :—(1) They are entitled to permanent possession of their lands, whether the land has been assessed with a full or half rental, or in a lump. (2) All lands now paying a half rental may, after the expiration of the term of the present Settlement, be assessed with a full rental. (3) The rent now assessed on the resumed *lákhiráj* lands in Khurdhá and Pánchgarh may in future

Settlements be modified in the same proportion as that of the *khálsá* lands, *i.e.* the future assessments on the *lákhiráj* lands may be raised, to an extent which will bear the same proportion to the present assessment, as the future assessments on *khálsá* lands with reference to cultivation will bear to their present assessment. (4) All *lákhiráj* tenures are hereditary. In the correspondence regarding the *lákhirájdárs* of Khurdhá, the right of transfer by sale, gift, or mortgage was conceded; and doubtless the same right attaches to the holders of resumed *lákhiráj* lands in all parts of the District. All such lands held under grants to individuals may be transferred in any way; but when the grants are for the support of idols or for any public purpose, the trustees have no power to alienate. (5) In default of payment of revenue, the tenure becomes liable to be sold; and the holder of the tenure is entitled to the balance of the purchase-money, after the arrear has been satisfied out of the proceeds. (6) The resumed *lákhirájdárs* have no claim to remission of revenue in seasons of drought, inundation, or other calamity, though in such cases remissions have sometimes been allowed. (7) The *lákhirájdárs* can let their lands to any person and on any terms they choose, unless there is a subordinate holder with right of occupancy or right to hold at fixed rates. (8) In all other respects, such as the procedure for the realization of rent from *rayats*, payments for village officials, etc., their rights and liabilities, are the same as of the *zamíndárs*.

'There are within this District 61,665 acres 2 roods 20 poles of resumed *lákhiráj* lands paying quit-rent. These are to be found in all parts of the District, except in the two Tributary States, the permanently settled estate, and the *jágír;* the number of resumed *lákhiráj* lands assessed with full rental is small.

'SUBORDINATE TENURES: MUKADDAMI.—*Mukaddam,* signifying chief of a village, is a word introduced by the Muhammadans to designate the village officers known as *pradháns* in the time of the Hindu kings. When the country passed into the hands of the Muhammadans, the principal change introduced was a change of names. The *grám* (village) of the Hindus was called *mauzá,* and the chief village officers, the *pradháns,* became *mukaddams.* The Muhammadans lacked much of the local knowledge that was necessary for the close supervision under the Hindu system of management, by means of a large body of public servants; and they necessarily left the details of administration in the hands of the fiscal officers, who engaged for the due payment of revenue.

Thus it was that the village and divisional officers acquired a' fixity of office, which gradually became hereditary, subject only to obtaining a deed of appointment, or rather of confirmation, on succeeding to their inheritance, which was always granted on payment of the customary presents. There are two distinct classes of *mukaddams* in Orissa, viz. the *mazkuri mukaddams*, who pay revenue direct to Government, and who since our first Settlement have been recognised as *zamíndárs* or actual proprietors of the soil ; and subordinate *mukaddams*, who pay through a superior holder. The former are to all intents and purposes *zamíndárs*, and the latter class are the only persons now known as *mukaddams*.

' These *mukaddams* are subdivided into three classes,—the *maurúsí* or hereditary *mukaddam ;* the *khárídá* or purchased *mukaddam ;* and the *záte mukaddam*, appointed by the people of the village as their representative, or appointed by the *zamíndár* to superintend the collections and cultivation of one or more *mauzás*. The incidents of these three classes of *mukaddami* tenure are now exactly the same. In respect to their villages, the holders enjoy the same rights and privileges, and exercise the same functions, as the *zamíndár* does in his *hastobúd* villages. The *zamíndár's* only right in respect of *mukaddami* villages, is to receive the rent fixed at the Settlement as payable to him from the village. The *mukaddams* are proprietors of a share of the rental, and their tenure is hereditary, transferable, and divisible. As regards the last power, however, it is provided that no *zamíndár* or superior tenant shall be required to admit to registration, or give effect to any division or distribution of the rent payable on account of any such tenure ; nor shall any such division or distribution of rent be valid and binding, without the consent, in writing, of the *zamíndár* or superior tenant. The rent payable by the *mukaddam* is fixed for the term of Settlement. In case of default in payment, the tenure is sold by public auction to the highest bidder ; and after paying the amount of arrear, the balance of the purchase-money is made over to the defaulter. All the profits arising out of bringing waste land under cultivation, or from increase in the rental of the cultivated lands, go to the *mukaddam ;* and in every other respect his rights and liabilities are identical with those of the *zamíndár*.

'There is an inferior class of *mukaddami* tenures, which are temporary. I find in the Settlement proceedings of Debiprasád, Hariprasád, and Lakshmiprasád, in *parganá* Kurulo, that three tenures were claimed as hereditary *mukaddami*, but were confirmed as temporary ones, to last only as long as the *zamíndár* of the time should continue in possession of the estate, or until it should be sold for arrears of revenue, when the new proprietor would have power to oust the *mukaddam*. They are in every respect similar to *miádí sarbaráhkárís*, hereafter described, and are not transferable.

'There are altogether 491 *mukaddami* tenures in Purí District, aggregating 474 villages, and covering an area of 115,179 acres, 2 roods, and 15 poles, principally in Kotdes *parganá*.

'In Khurdhá and Pánchgarh, where the revenue system of the Mughuls was never introduced, and which remained in the sole possession of the representatives of the ancient Rájás of Orissa till after the conquest of the Province by the British, not a single *mukaddami* tenure is to be found. Also in *parganás* Lembái, Ráháng, Sirái, and Chaubiskud, which were not separated from the control of the Rájás of Khurdhá till 1168 Amli, all the tenure-holders of this class (except five in Lembái, and one in Ráháng) have retained to this day their original designation of *pradháns*, and in these six exceptional cases the change took place after the conquest.

'PRADHANI TENURES.—*Pradhán* is a Sanskrit word meaning chief or head-man. Besides the tenure-holders now known as *pradháns*, all the *mukaddams*, except those created after the Muhammadan conquest of the Province, were originally *pradháns*, *i.e.* village officials appointed by the villagers, with the approval of the ruling power, to represent them before Government and the superior revenue officers, and to collect from them and pay to the divisional officers the revenue assessed on their villages. I have explained above, how from being mere officials they gradually developed into quasi-proprietors, and were, under the British administration, moulded into a homogeneous body of village proprietors; and also why those of Ráháng, Sirái, Lembái, and Chaubiskud retain their original appellation, while their brethren in the other *parganás* are called *mukaddams*. Besides the *pradháns* originally existing, some have been created by the English Government. The incidents of the *pradhání* tenure as it now stands are the same as those of the *mukaddami*; with the exception that a right of re-entry after recusancy is conceded to the *pradhán* under certain restricted rules, while this privilege is not extended to the *mukaddam*. Purí

District contains 279 *pradháni* tenures, aggregating 278 villages, and covering an area of 82,141½ acres, distributed throughout Chaubiskud, Sirái, Ráháng, and Lembái *parganás*.

'SARBARAHKARI TENURES.—There are three classes of persons in this District known as *sarbaráhkárs*, viz. *sarbaráhkárs* with rights of hereditary succession; *sarbaráhkárs* in temporary possession of their tenures; and *sarbaráhkárs* with no rights, who are mere servants, liable to dismissal at any time at the pleasure of their employers, unless there is a stipulation between them to the contrary.

'The third are called *sarbaráhkárs* merely. All persons who, during the Marhattá Government, and subsequently, engaged with the *zamíndárs* or *tálukdárs* for the collection of revenue in one or more villages comprised within the *zamíndári* or *táluk*, passed under the name of *sarbaráhkár*. Those who had hereditary and uninterrupted possession of their tenures for a period prior to the 14th October 1803 were admitted as *maurúsi* or hereditary *sarbaráhkárs;* those whose rights were not of such old standing, but who were in possession at the time of Settlement, were admitted as *miádí sarbaráhkárs;* and the others were either admitted as *sarbaráhkárs* without any rights, or were dispossessed, the land reverting to the *hastobúd* possession of the *zamíndár*.

'A *sarbaráhkár* is defined as one whose ancestors have been invested long ago with the management of one or more villages as servants of the *zamíndár*, paid by a percentage on the collections, but who has now obtained a hereditary right to continue as manager of such village or villages, independent of the *zamíndár's* permission, to pay a fixed rent for the villages to the *zamíndár*, and to appropriate to himself a certain percentage. Besides these, the old *jágírdárs* of the Khurdhá Rájás, such as Dalláis, Koth-karans, etc., who were dispossessed of their *jágírs*, have been admitted into *sarbaráhkári* engagement for their *jágír* land.

'The incidents of *maurúsi* and *miádí sarbaráhkári* tenures are. the following :—

'(1) The *sarbaráhkárs* have no right in the soil.

'(2) A *sarbaráhkári* tenure, whether *maurúsi* or *miádí*, cannot be alienated or subdivided without the consent of the *zamíndár*. The former, as its name implies, is hereditary; and the latter also can be transmitted to heirs during the time for which the tenure is admitted; which · in almost all cases lasts so long only as the *zamíndár*, under whom the *sarbaráhkár* holds his village, continues in possession of the estate, and it terminates with the sale of the parent estate for arrears of revenue.

'(3) In case of default in payment of rent, the tenure is annulled, and all the rights of the *sarbaráhkárs* revert to the *zamíndár*. In the case of *maurúsí sarbaráhkárs*, this right has rarely, if ever, been exercised by the *zamíndárs*, the tenures being sold by public auction in execution of decree for rent.

'(4) The rent payable by the *sarbaráhkárs* to the *zamíndár* is fixed for the term of the Settlement, or for the term for which the tenure is admitted (according as it is *maurúsí* or *miádí*), and is not liable to enhancement until the expiration of the term.

'(5) *Sarbaráhkárs* cannot claim as of right any remission of rent on account of loss of crop arising from drought, inundation, and other calamity of season; but it is understood that in seasons of great calamity suitable remission will be made.

'(6) All profits arising out of increased or improved cultivation, not being at the expense or agency of a *rayat* having rights of occupancy, and where the land is not included within a *thání* or any subordinate tenure, accrue entirely to the *sarbaráhkárs*, and the *zamíndár* is not entitled to any share in them.

'(7) In the case of *sarbaráhkárí* tenures which at the time of Settlement were found in the possession of several joint *sarbaráhkárs*, one or more of the *sarbaráhkárs* were selected by the Settlement Officer, with the consent of the *zamíndár*, to be recorded as managers of the *sarbaráhkárí*. These managers are called *sadr sarbaráhkárs*, and the others are called *bhayálís*. The *sadr sarbaráhkárs* have the general management of the tenure. They collect rent from the cultivators and other under-holders, and, after paying the *jamá* of the village, distribute the balance amongst themselves and the *bhayálís*, according to the share of each. These recorded *sadr sarbaráhkárs* cannot be ousted, except for default of payment of rent, or for mismanagement.

'A deduction from the gross assets, to the extent of 15 per cent., was allowed generally to the temporary *sarbaráhkárs*. In *sarbaráhkárí* villages, the rent of the resumed lands is paid through the *sarbaráhkárs*, the latter receiving 7½ per cent., and the *zamíndárs* an equal amount of percentage on the total. But there are exceptions to this rule; in some cases, deductions to the extent of 25 per cent. are allowed.

'Purí District contains 198 *maurúsí* and 31 *miádí sarbaráhkárí* tenures, aggregating 197 and 30 villages, and covering an area of 47,438¾ and 16,704 acres respectively.

'*Sarbaráhkárs* of the third class are to be found in the Government estates of Khurdhá and Pánchgarh. These estates, as I have stated above, formed the last remnant of the extensive territory of the ancient Hindu Rájás of Orissa, in which the Mughul institutions were never introduced. When, owing to the rebellious conduct of the *zamíndár* in 1804, these estates were taken under the direct management of the British Government, it was found that there was nobody having proprietary, or even quasi-proprietary, rights in any part of them, and that all those who were concerned in the management were mere servants. No better rights than they had hitherto enjoyed were conceded in their favour by the British Government, but they were allowed to continue to hold the lands under their management on the former footing. They are mere farmers, and may be dismissed at any time for default or bad conduct. These *sarbaráhkárs* are to be found in the Government estates of Khurdhá and Pánchgarh, covering an area of 76 miles in length, and 25 to 5 miles in breadth, and also in two outlying Divisions, Balbhadrapur and Mughulbandí, consisting of villages and portions of villages in *pargands* Ráháng, Chaubiskud, and Siráí. This extensive and valuable estate was settled *rayatwárí*. Every cultivator's rent was fixed, and the rents even of uncultivated lands were fixed in anticipation. Every cultivator received a *pattá* (lease) from the Collector; and the *sarbaráhkárs* with whom the Settlement was concluded are merely collectors of certain fixed rents, receiving, in land and in a share of the rental, about 20 per cent. on the collections. There are two kinds of *sarbaráhkárs* of this class to be found in Khurdhá and Pánchgarh, viz. *sadr* and *mufassal*, the latter being subordinate to the former.

'In those villages in which both kinds of *sarbaráhkárs* exist, each is awarded half of the amount allowed out of the gross rentai for risk, collection charges, etc., in addition to *jágír*, and all profits to be derived from extended cultivation. For all waste lands brought under cultivation, the *sarbaráhkár* cannot demand rent at a higher rate than is fixed on adjoining lands of the same quality; and he is not allowed to participate in the profits derivable from improvements in cultivation.

'The two estates—Khurdhá and Pánchgarh—have been divided into 251 and 74 circles respectively. The former is managed by

581 *sadr sarbaráhkárs* and 204 *mufassal sarbaráhkárs*, and the latter by 121 *sadr sarbaráhkárs*.

'KHARIDA TENURES.—Mr. Stirling, in his Report on Orissa, thus describes the origin of this tenure :—"The word *kharidá* implies simply a thing purchased. Some of these tenures are *mazkurí*; and as such, the holders were directly treated with by Government at the time of Settlement, and are now *zamíndárs*. Many others of these tenures are held subordinate to the *zamíndárs*, to whom is paid a low rate of assessment. There were upwards of eight hundred such estates entered at the first triennial Settlement. It would be vain to attempt a guess at the number of smaller unseparated tenures of this kind existing; but it may be stated generally that almost every village has some *kharidádár* tenants, and that the *hásilat* (assessed) land in nearly every *rakhá* or village account is divided into two classes—*kharidá* and *rayatí*.

' "The possessors of the *kharidá* lands have certainly, I think, a very good title to be considered proprietors of the soil. They bought the actual ground. There is in their deeds no ambiguity of title arising from their purchasing the *zamíndárí*, or *tálukdárí*, or *mukaddamí* of the land. So many *bighás* of *aráji banjar kharij jamá* are clearly stated as the property acquired. The persons who bought land as above, bought it in general free of rent, but sometimes stipulated to pay a light fixed assessment. They were of all classes —Musalmáns, Bengalís, Marhattás, cultivating Bráhmans, etc. The purchases were in general made originally for building on, or to establish a plantation or a village of the sort called *patnás*, to which further portions were afterwards added for purposes of culti-vation, until the acquisitions swelled into estates of vast extent. The ground sold invariably professed to be *banjar kharij jamá*, or long waste, covered with small jungle, unoccupied and unassessed, and ought always to have been soil of a very inferior description, and frequently was so. But great tricks were often played; and the most unauthorized and irregular alienations took place, by the buyers, in connivance with the sellers, obtaining possession of good land liable to, or previously paying, the full assessment. Hence these possessions were often of great value, and occasioned the frequent interference and scrutiny of the provincial officers, or even of the Názim, when the abuse had arisen to a great height. In such cases the land was assessed, or perhaps resumed; but the possessory title of the holder was generally respected, especially if his possession was of long standing. Many of the *patnás* were formed by *sardárs* of the Mughul and Marhattá administrations, relations of the Názim, or by some other favoured individuals. In course of time, these escheated to Government, or were assigned as the perquisites of particular departments, such as *mírsámání, khansámání,* etc., and were then managed through the *pursethí* or head-man elected by the inhabitants. The *kharidjí* tenure was created by the *tálukdárs* and *mukaddams* under them. As long as only a few *bighás* were disposed of, the *tálukdár* or *mukaddam* sold them himself, taking care to get the attestation of the *gumáshtá* of the *sadr kánúngo*, which was requisite to legalize the transaction. When the *mukaddam* sold, the further signature of the *tálukdár*, or *parganá tálukdár*, was requisite. But whenever a large quantity of ground, as a `bátí` or upwards, was alienated, the purchaser deemed it necessary for his security that his title should be acknowledged by the whole of the *chaudharís* and *kánúngos* of the *parganá ;* and hence originated those numerous deeds of sale in the Collector's office and elsewhere, executed jointly by the *parganá zamíndárs.*

' "The most singular, and, in a public point of view, the most perplexing and inconvenient feature of the Orissa *kharidá maháls* is the scattered situation of the lands, and the vast quantity of minute parcels of ground taken from the *rakhá* of an almost incredible number of villages, near and remote, combined together in their formation. The two most striking cases of the kind are *patná* Ghulám Alí, etc., *sadr jamá, sikká* Rs. 900, which stretches with more or less continuity from Purí to Bhadrakh ; and the Bágh Brindában, *sadr jamá, sikká* Rs. 500, which reaches from Balasor to the Subarnarekhá river. Ordinarily, the lands of a *kharidá* estate, paying a *sadr jamá* of Rs. 300 or Rs. 400, will be found to lie in thirty or forty different villages belonging to different *parganás* and *táluks,* comprising for the most part very inferior and unproductive soil, such as would in all probability never have been cultivated under any other tenure." ·

' These tenures were granted by all classes of persons who had anything to do with land, from the largest *tálukdárs* down to the pettiest *mukaddams* and *pradháns ;* and they varied considerably in extent. They were purchased to be held rent-free, or at a *mukarrarí jamá.* The land itself formed the subject of sale, and the transfer was confirmed by the representatives of Government affixing their signatures to the deeds of sale.

'The *mazkurí kharidádárs* (18 in number), including *patnás*, were admitted at the Settlement to the rights and privileges of *sadr mál-guzárs*, and are now called *zamíndárs;* but the *kharidádárs* proper hold their lands at fixed rentals under the *zamíndár*, part of whose *táluk* their lands still form, and through whom their revenue is paid. At first, no distinction was maintained between *kharidádárs* of different classes; and to this point the attention of the authorities was first drawn in 1836, on the occasion of the Settlement of Mallipurá. It was urged that sufficient attention had not been paid to what would seem to be an essential distinction in regard to the respective rights of *kharidádárs*,—to wit, the rights of the parties from whom they severally purchased their lands. These parties could obviously sell only what they possessed; and no one, unless himself a *zamíndár*, could transfer to another person his rights to *málikáná*. After some correspondence on this subject, the *kharidádárs* were divided into two classes: (1) The *kharidádárs* who had purchased their lands from the *zamíndárs*, and were there-fore considered entitled to all the immunities of full proprietorship, including *málikáná* if recusant, received a deduction of 30 per cent. from the assets of their tenure, the difference between that allowance and 35 per cent. going to the *zamíndár*, to compensate him for the trouble and responsibility of collecting the revenue. (2) The *khari-dádárs* who purchased from *mukaddams* and other under-tenants were considered to have no right to *málikáná*. They were merely representatives of the *mukaddams*, and were treated like them, the *zamíndár's málikáná* being fixed on the same scale as that granted in *mukaddamí* villages to *mukaddáms*, viz. 20 per cent. to the *kharidádárs*, and 15 per cent. to the *zamíndár*. The *kharidádárs* of this class forfeit all claims to re-entry by recusancy. It was also ruled that in villages under *mukaddamí* management, *kharidádárs* of the second class should pay their revenue through the *mukaddams*. The *mukaddam* was to be remunerated with 7½, and the *zamíndár* also with 7½ per cent., for rendering themselves responsible for the collection.

'Tenures of the first and second class which have been admitted at a Settlement do not become null and void on the sale of the parent estate for arrears. Tenures created subsequent to the British conquest are vitiated thereby. *Kharidádárs* in *bází asámin maháls*, which had been sold for arrears, were regarded as *kharidádárs* of the second class, and allowed 20 per cent. of the proceeds of the land they held. *Maáfí kharidádárs*, who could not prove that they had actually given value for their tenures, were treated as *kharidádárs* of the first and second class, according as they purchased from *zamíndárs* or *mukaddams;* and otherwise as common *lákhirájdárs*. *Kharidádárs* who had purchased after the conquest were allowed the *málikáná* that would otherwise have been given to the *zamíndár* or *mukaddam* from whom they purchased, and 10 per cent. was given for risks and expenses of collection to the *zamíndár*, or divided between the *zamíndár* and *mukaddam* through whom the *kharidádárs* paid. Recusant *kharidádárs* of the first class were allowed 5 per cent. *málikáná*, and the *zamíndárs* who were placed in possession of their lands, 25 per cent.

'The *kharidá* tenure is now, as to a great extent it was before, hereditary, transferable, and divisible. But as regards its division into shares, it is nevertheless subject to the restrictions contained in section 27, Act x. of 1859. The rent payable by the *kharidádár* to the superior tenure-holder or the *zamíndár* is fixed for the term of Settlement, and all advantages derivable from improved or extended cultivation go to the *kharidádár*. He has, in fact, all the rights of a *zamíndár* or *mukaddam*, according as he is a *kharidádár* of the first or second class. There are altogether 1175 *kharidá* tenures of the first, and 157 of the second class in Purí District, covering an area of 7884½ and 991 acres respectively.

'TANKI TENURES are those which were formerly held revenue-free, either as *lákhiráj* or *jágír*, but were subsequently assessed at a quit-rent. They vary greatly in extent; some consist of entire villages, while others are small, detached patches of ground measuring a few acres altogether. In olden times, every kind of service was remunerated by grants of land; and every kind of donation, charitable or religious, was also given in land. All the military and civil officers of the Hindu Rájás of Orissa were paid in land; and land was assigned for the support of idols, priests, courtiers, members of the royal household, and all others who had any claim to be supported from the public property. Numerous alienations of this nature were made not only by the Rájás, but by their representatives and landholders of all descriptions. When, after the invasion and conquest of the Province by foreign powers, the Rájás found themselves reduced in revenue, they resorted to the practice of gradually levying a quit-rent on most of such tenures lying in the *parganás* which were assigned for their support.

'Some such tenures were also resumed, and the quit-rents in a
few others were altered and raised, by the Mughuls and Marhattás;
but such rent was generally less than that paid for the same
description of *khiráj* or assessed lands in the neighbourhood.
Hence it is that these *tanki* tenures are numerous in Khurdhá
(which, as has already been observed, remained in the possession of
the representatives of the ancient Rájás of Orissa till its conquest
by the English), and in the *parganás* of Ráháng, Lembái, Sirái, and
Chaubiskud, which were ceded to the Marhattás long after they had
taken possession of other parts of the Province. Of those that are
now known as *tanki* tenures, the most numerous belong to the Sásan
Bráhmans in the above-named *parganás*, *i.e.* to Bráhmans imported
from the north by the several Hindu kings, to whom villages were
assigned for furnishing them with a decent livelihood. When,
under the provisions of Regulation vii. of 1822, the *tanki* holdings
were inquired into in the same manner as *lákhiráj*, all grants
which would have been considered valid, and exempted from the
payment of revenue had they been held revenue-free, were also confirmed in perpetuity, subject to the payment of the quit-rent; while
all others were resumed, and were treated as resumed *lákhiráj*,
being assessed at full or half rental, according as the grantees
had or had not been in long possession, in good faith. Such
of the tenures as were paying, as *tanki*, more than what could
have been demanded from them on the basis of Settlement at
half rental, were classed with *kharidádárs* of the first class, and
were, like them, allowed *málikáná* at 30 per cent. The incidents
of these tenures are like those of confirmed or resumed *lákhiráj*
or *kharidá* of the first class, according as the tenure has been
confirmed at the *tanki jamá*, or has been treated as resumed
lákhiráj or *kharidá*.

'None of the *tanki* holders pay revenue direct to Government.
It was ruled that *tanki* tenures which have continued all along
to pay revenue, although only a small revenue, are different in their
nature from *lákhiráj* tenures which have never paid revenue. Such
payment must be held to be proof of their dependence upon the
zamíndári through which they have hitherto paid; and consequently
they must be treated as dependent *tálukdárs*, whether the area
be below or above 75 acres. All *tanki mahals*, therefore, were
treated as dependent tenures, except Haríkrishnapur in *parganá*
Ráháng, which, having been separated and treated as an inde-

pendent *mahál* since the time of the Marhattás, was allowed to remain as such.

'The *tankídárs* pay their revenue to the *zamíndár* of the parent estate, to whom an allowance of 10 per cent. is made for risks and , trouble of collection. Most of the *tankí* villages (notably those owned by the Sasan Bráhmans, within a few miles of the temple of Jagannáth) are held jointly by several shareholders. Each village is held by 40, 50, or 100 or more sharers. They pay their quota of the *jamá* in proportion to the quantity of land in possession of each, without any reference to its quality, and no matter whether it is or is not under cultivation. In these villages, the *tankídárs* select one, two, or more men from amongst themselves, to enter into engagement with the Settlement officers, collect rent, pay the *tankí jamá,* and do all and every kind of business connected with the village; receiving nothing in return for their trouble except the good-will and respect of their brethren, the profits being divided amongst them all rateably according to the interest of each in the tenure. When the *tankídárs* are dissatisfied with their representatives, they add more to their number, or appoint others in their stead. The appointment is reported to the *zamíndár,* with whom the representatives enter into engagements for the due payment of the *tankí jamá.* There are within Purí District 1103 *tankís,* of which the aggregate area is 57,102 acres.

'CULTIVATING TENURES.—The general body of cultivators may be divided into three classes, viz. *tháni, páhí,* and *chandná. Tháni,* a corruption of the word *sthániyá,* or resident, is applied to all *khud-kásht* or resident cultivators, in contradistinction to the non-resident or migratory husbandmen, called *páhí.* This class of tenant cannot be said to have been created at any time by any one in authority. Their rights appear to have been the slow growth of custom. From what has been stated on an earlier page, it will be seen that each village had an official machinery of its own, closely resembling that of the Fiscal Division. The village head-man, *i.e.* the *pradhán,* apportioned amongst the individual husbandmen the rent payable for his village and the land comprised within it; and to each resident husbandman was given as much land as he could cultivate, the residue (if any) being given to the migratory or *páhí* cultivators. The village head was, as has been stated, partly official and partly representative. He was elected to the office by the villagers; and in his turn he was bound to respect their hereditary rights, and he could not dispossess them of their lands so long as they paid rent. They held their lands and paid rent according to hereditary usage. But they could not sell or give away their rights, which amounted to a hereditary right of occupancy, but never grew into a transferable tenure. The *tháni rayat* paid much more than the *páhí*, either in the shape of rent, *rusum*, or *mathut;* but in compensation, he enjoyed many advantages over the other. As a member of the village corporation, the *tháni rayat* paid no house rent or charge for the ground occupied by his homestead. He had the pick of the village lands, leaving only the less favourable sites for the non-resident husbandmen. Even of the declared surplus lands he had always the first choice, paying for them at the cheaper non-resident rates. In the case of rent-free grants situated within his village, the property of priests or others who do not hold the plough themselves, he had generally the preference as under-tenant or metayer. He had, in common with his brother guildsman, the right to use the pasture lands, thatching prairies, and firewood jungles attached to the village. He had an allotment of garden ground and a well-watered plot for his rice nursery, rent-free; above all, he had a hereditary right of occupancy in his fields, and so long as he paid his accustomed share of the village quit-rent, he was safe from dispossession. In short, he had the position of a responsible village burgess, whose homestead and property lay before all men's eyes, who could not run away without permanent loss of status, and whose personal security was therefore of much greater value than that of a non-resident tenant. His credit, accordingly, stood better with the village banker. He could borrow on easy terms, and this alone was well worth the higher rates which he paid for his lands.

'On the other hand, as the *páhí rayats* were lightly assessed, they had none of the privileges enjoyed by the *tháni*. They had no voice in the distribution of land, but had to content themselves with what they could get. The rent-free holders would not trust them with the cultivation of their lands; they could not participate in the enjoyment of the common rights of the village where they did not reside; they had no rent-free homestead lands; their occupancy depended on the pleasure of the village community, who could oust them at any time if any of them required to take possession of their lands; and, worse than all, they had no credit with the village banker or grain dealer, and had to borrow rice or money on condition of paying interest at higher rates.

'When the Province passed into the hands of the British Government, the revenue officers were from the first strictly enjoined to ascertain and record the rights of the cultivators, and to protect them in the possession and enjoyment of those rights. At the commencement of the thirty years' Settlement of 1836, leases were given to the *rayats* in all possible cases, by which the cultivators were preserved in the possession and enjoyment of what rights they had; and as they had clearly no transferable right under native rule, the leases under which they now hold their lands from the British Government have not created any such right in their favour, nor indeed give any additional privileges to it. These leases, and all the Settlement proceedings, merely specify that so long as the cultivator pays his rent, his possession shall not be disturbed.

'The present incidents of the *tháni rayatí* tenure may be briefly stated to be the following :—

'(1) *Tháni rayats* have a right of occupancy; the *zamindár* cannot turn them out of their lands so long as they pay their rent regularly. But if at the end of the year they remain in arrears, they are liable to be ejected; but not otherwise than in execution of a decree or order of the proper court, and not even then if the amount is paid within fifteen days from the date of decree.

'(2) The amount of rent payable by *tháni rayats* is fixed and unalterable during the term of Settlement. This is a condition in the lease granted to them; all profits arising out of improved or extended cultivation belong entirely to them, and the landlord is not entitled to participate.

'(3) The tenure is divisible amongst heirs; but the rent cannot be divided without the consent of the *zamindár* or person entitled.

'(4) The tenure is not transferable. The *rayat* has no right to transfer the whole or any portion of his tenure by sale, gift, or otherwise. The only exceptions to this general rule are the *tháni rayats* on the Government estates of Khurdhá and Pánchgarh, to whom the right of transfer has lately been conceded; the Government, however, as *zamindár*, has reserved the right of re-entry.

'(5) The *rayats* are at liberty to relinquish their lands, provided they give notice of their intention in writing to the person entitled to the rent of the land, or his authorized agent, in or before the

..onth of Chaitra of the year preceding that in which this relinquish-
ment is to have effect, otherwise they must be held responsible for
the rent of the land for the ensuing year.

'(6) In case of flood, drought, or other calamity of season, they
are not entitled to remission unless there is a provision to that effect
in their leases. Such a provision is to be found in almost all leases
granted to the *rayats* in the *parganás* of Ráháng, Sirái, Chaubiskud,
and Lembái.

'(7) In case of sale of the parent estate for arrears of revenue or
otherwise, these tenures are not vitiated thereby.

'Although the transfer of *tháni* tenures is not legal, such transfers
have been frequent of late years, especially in the Ráháng, Sirái,
and Chaubiskud *khás maháls*. The transfers are not, however,
made by regular deeds or sales (*kabálas*, as they are called), but by
a peculiar kind of deed, *samarpan patra*, which is also used for
the transfer of *debottar, pírottar*, and other legally unsaleable lands.
By this deed the land itself is not sold, but only the rights and
interests of the transferor (wharerer they may be) are conveyed to
the transferee.

'PAHI RAYATS.—The *páhí rayats* have been divided into two
classes under Act x. of 1859, viz. those having rights of occupancy,
and those without such rights. Every *rayat* who has cultivated or
held land for a period of twelve years has a right of occupancy in the
land so cultivated or held by him, whether it be held under lease or
not, so long as he pays his rent. The only exception is the *khámár,
níj-jót*, or *sir* land of the proprietor, let by him on lease for a term,
or year by year. The rights of *rayats* having rights of occupancy
are in every respect the same as those of the *tháni rayats*, with the
exception that while the amount of rent payable by the latter is
fixed for the period of Settlement, that payable by the former is
liable to variation at any time on any of the following grounds, viz. :—
It may be enhanced—(1) if the rate of rent paid by such *rayat* is
below the prevailing rate payable by the same class of *rayats* for
land of similar description with similar advantages in the places
adjacent ; (2) if the value of the produce or the productive powers
of the land have been increased otherwise than by the agency or
at the expense of the *rayat;* (3) if the quantity of land held by
the *rayat* has been proved by measurement to be greater than the
quantity for which rent has been previously paid by him (section
17, Act x. of 1859).

'The rent, on the other hand, is liable to abatement,—(1) if the area of the land has been diminished by diluvion or otherwise ; (2) if the value of the produce or the productive powers of the land have been decreased by any cause beyond the power of the *rayat;* (3) if the quantity of land held by the *rayat* has been proved by measurement to be less than the quantity for which rent has been paid by him.

'*Páhí rayats* without right of occupancy are merely tenants-at-will. They cannot remain in possession of their land unless they agree to the terms of their landlord, and the rent payable by them is liable to enhancement at his pleasure.

'CHANDNA OR HOMESTEAD RAYATS.—Under this heading are comprehended the shopkeepers, artisans, unskilled labourers, and others who, having no arable lands, pay rent for homestead land only. *Páhí rayats* also, who, having their proper homestead in one village, have also a house and homestead land in another, where their arable lands are situated, are sometimes called *chandnádárs* of the latter village. *Chandnádárs* who were in possession of their lands at the time of Settlement, and whose holdings have been specified in the Settlement records, are protected by Government order. Those who have been in possession of their holdings for twelve years or more have acquired rights of occupancy under Act x. of 1859 ; and if the land has been acquired under a building lease, enhancement of rent is barred.

'Besides the preceding, there is a fourth class of cultivators, who hold their lands on much more lenient terms than all the rest. They are the relatives of *zamíndárs* of estates in which, according to custom, succession devolves on a single representative of the family. In such cases, the *zamíndár* provides for his relatives by assigning them certain lands subject to a low or *tankí* rent. A sale of the estate for arrears of revenue, however, makes the engagement null and void. These are of the nature of *tháni rayats,* with this difference, that while the *tháni rayats* pay at full rates, and the amount of rent to be paid is fixed for the term of the Settlement, these men are assessed at a quit-rent, but have to pay full rates if the estate changes hands.

'The following table exhibits the total estimated number of cultivators' holdings in each *parganá,* together with the average rental, and the total number of cultivators :—

Name of *Parganá.*	Total estimated Number of Holdings.	Average Rental of each Holding.			Total Number of Cultivators.
		Rs.	*a.*	*p.*	
Kotdes, ...	38,645	4	3	0	18,014
Kot Ráháng, ...	27,567	2	8	0	11,160
Lembái, ...	24,668	2	13	7	14,419
Kálíjori, ...	232	3	15	4	137
Kanmán Tappá, . . .	625	4	15	4	227
Kodhár, ...	2,131	6	14	0	905
Paschim Duái, . . .	2,956	8	7	3	1,847
Atháis, ...	3,595	4	13	4	1,700
Ráháng, ...	52,094	2	1	10	23,608
Antrodh, ...	702	2	15	9	446
Purbá Duái, ...	5,995	2	7	9	1,344
Matkadpatná, . . .	754	3	1	0	315
Sayyidábád, ...	2,760	4	0	0	710
Damárkhand, . . .	2,029	5	12	0	646
Oldhár, ...	4,039	2	6	0	1,492
Bánchás, ...	4,245	2	11	9	2,068
Chaubiskud, . . .	13,480	3	9	5	3,023
Sultánnagar, . . .	568	7	15	6	153
Masrud Mahál, . . .	382	3	15	5	178
Sirái, ...	8,188	5	7	10	4,345
Kurulo, ...	1,772	3	3	8	662
Astrang, ...	438	10	12	1	255
Khurdhá, ...	74,015	2	12	0	40,000
Pánchgarh, ...	7,600	2	12	0	5,000
Bánchás Kathmúl, . . .	609	...			204
Total, . .	280,089	3	1	0	132,858

'LAKHIRAJ OR REVENUE-FREE TENURES.—Lands for which no revenue is paid by their holders are called *lákhiráj*, or more properly *lákhiráj báheli*, meaning confirmed *lákhiráj*, in contradistinction to *lákhiráj baziáftí* or resumed *lákhiráj* lands, described on pp. 111-114. They are of the following descriptions :—

'(1) Lands assigned revenue-free under grants from the Marhattá Rájá of Berár, or from any *zamíndár, tálukdár,* or actual proprietor of land, as endowments of the temple of Jagannáth, or of *maths* in the vicinity of the temple, or for similar purposes.

'(2) All grants for holding land exempt from payment of revenue made previous to October 1791, by whatever authority, and whether by a writing or without a writing; provided that the grantee actually and *bona fide* obtained possession of the land so granted, and held it exempt from the payment of revenue, previously to the date above mentioned, and the land was not subsequently rendered subject to the payment of revenue by proper officers or orders of Government.

'(3) All grants for holding land exempt from the payment of revenue, made subsequently to October 1791, and prior to October 1803, by whatever authority, which had been confirmed or expressly admitted antecedently to the latter date; provided that, by the authority of the existing Government, the grantee actually and *bona fide* obtained possession of the land so granted, and held the same exempt from the payment of revenue previously to October 1803, and the land had not been afterwards rendered subject to the payment of revenue by the officers or the orders of Government.

' (4) Small quantities of land not exceeding 10 *bighás*, held exempt from the payment of revenue under grant made prior to October 1803, and *bona fide* appropriated as endowments for temples or for other religious or charitable purposes, or the proceeds of which were enjoyed by individuals, whether Muhammadan or Hindu, being priests or religious advisers of the great body of cultivators.

' (5) *Bádsháhí* grants made previous to October 1803; provided that the grantee actually and *bona fide* obtained possession of the land so granted previous to that date, and the grant had not been subsequently resumed by the proper officers or the orders of Government.

'(6) All grants made or confirmed by the British Government subsequently to October 1803, and grants held under invalid titles which the Governor-General in Council thought fit not to resume.

'(7) Small plots of ground for village idols and *khusbás* tenures, *i.e.* homestead lands of resident *rayats* and others.

'(8) *Maáfí kharidádárs* of all descriptions. These grants belong to one or other of the following denominations:—(1) *Debottar*, grants for the support of Hindu idols; (2) *bráhmottar*, grants for the support of Bráhmans; (3) *pírottar*, grants for the support of Muhammadan shrines; (4) *kháirát* and *dattá*, grants to individuals other than Bráhmans, and as charitable donations for public purposes; (5) *amrut monohí*, endowments of the temple of Jagannáth; (6) *khusbás*, small tenures of two, three, or five *bighás* of land, principally occupied as homesteads; (7) *maáfí kharidádárs*, described on a previous page; and (8) *madad-másh*, Muhammadan grants for the support of learned or holy men. The rights and immunities of the grantees depend on the nature of the grant; and the same relation exists between them and their tenants, as between the *zamíndárs* and their *rayats*.   There are altogether 14,605 rent-free tenures of all descriptions in Purí (exclusive of *khusbás* lands), covering an area of 91,728½ acres, scattered throughout every part of the District.

'JAGIR OR SERVICE TENURES.—*Jágírs* are of two kinds:—(1) service *jágírs;* (2) *jágírs* granted for services rendered to the State, or on political considerations.   The service tenures include the holdings of *páiks*, *sardár páiks*, *sarbaráhkárs*, village watchmen (*chaukídárs*), village accountants (*patwárís* or *bhúis*), and village servants, such as barbers, washermen, astrologers, etc.   The origin of these tenures may be traced as far back as the earliest Hindu period. I have explained before, how under the Hindu Rájás all public servants, soldiers, policemen, revenue officers, and others were remunerated by grants of land.   The *jágírdárs* were not disturbed in the possession of their lands during the Muhammadan and Marhattá period ; though sometimes they were called upon to pay a·light quit-rental, while in a few cases the small *tankí* levied by the Hindu Rájás was enhanced after the conquest of the Province by the English.

'The *jágírs* of *sardár páiks* and *páiks* were guaranteed to them under section 9, Regulation xii. of 1805, subject of course to the payment of any fixed quit-rental which they had been paying to the former Governments.   Those paying quit-rent are included in *tankí* tenures ; all other service *jágírs* were investigated at the time of Settlement, and such as were considered necessary were confirmed, while others were resumed and annexed to the *khálsá* lands.

'*Jágírs* of all kinds are in no way transferable.   The service *jágír* tenures are not as of right hereditary ; though they are generally allowed to descend from father to son, or to any male member of the family, if he is capable of performing the duties for which the grant is made.   They are granted on condition of service, and may be resumed when the service is not required.   *Jágírs* of *páiks* and *sardár páiks* are protected from resumption by Regulation xiii. of 1805, and so long as that law is in force their *jágírs* cannot be resumed ; but the *páiks* and *sardár páiks* are liable to dismissal for disobedience of orders, neglect of duty, undue violence, or other misconduct.   The *jágírdárs* are allowed all the profits and advantages arising out of the possession of their lands.

'JAGIRS OF VILLAGE OFFICIALS.—(1) *Sarbaráhkári jágír, i.e.* lands granted to *sarbaráhkárs* as remuneration for their service. Of these there are 10,941 acres, 1 rood, 2 poles, granted to 991 *sadr* and *mufassal sarbaráhkárs.* The rights of these officials have been described while treating of the *sarbaráhkári* tenure. Their *jágírs* cannot, without their consent, be resumed or commuted into a money payment, so long as they are in office, and if the term of the Settlement made with them is in force; but on the expiration of the term of Settlement, or when their engagements are cancelled, Government may make any arrangements it deems proper. (2) *Patwári jágír.* There are 420 *patwárís* in Purí, with an allowance of 587½ acres of land, and £461 in money. (3) *Chaukídári* and *khandáití jágír.* There are now altogether 2651 *chaukídárs*, with an allowance of 6037 acres, and 81 *khandáíts* with 1200 acres of land, besides £140 in money. (4) *Tandkárs* or *piyádas;* 90 of these men hold 234½ acres of land for assisting the *sarbaráhkárs* in collecting rents.

'JAGIRS OF VILLAGE SERVANTS. — These are as follow :—(5) Carpenters; 605 men hold 396 acres in return for making agricultural implements for the villagers. (6) Blacksmiths; 569 men hold 366 acres in return for analogous services. (7) Potters; 31 men hold 25 acres on condition of supplying pots for the *zamíndár*, and also to troops on the march. (8) Washermen; 1041 men hold 663½ acres for washing the clothes of the *rayats*, and for doing other work for the *zamíndár*. (9) Astrologers; 375 men hold 133 acres, whose duty it is to consult the stars, and to determine propitious times for agricultural operations, and for marriages and other ceremonies. (10) Barbers; 990 men hold 726 acres, in return for shaving, etc., and for the performance of certain ceremonies at marriages, births, etc. (11) Boatmen; 54 men hold 64½ acres in return for ferrying passengers over rivers. (12) Forest; 1 man holds 2 acres in return for watching the forests at Netábasindhá in Khurdhá. (13) Mehanters; 17 men hold 11 acres for clearing village roads, etc., and for performing other services. (14) Baurís; 13 men hold 5½ acres on condition of performing such labouring work as may be required by the *zamíndár*. (15) Bájadárs; 25 men receive 18 acres for playing the drum at the *zamíndár's kachárí* on festival days. (16) Dancing girls; 4 girls hold 1 acre of land for dancing before the idols on festival days. (17) Gardeners; 3 men hold 29 poles of land on condition of supplying flowers at marriages and other ceremonies. (18) Car-pullers; 2 men hold 9¾ acres, as professional car-pullers of Jagannáth. (19) Gaur; 1 man holds 19 poles on condition of tending the village kine. (20) Madhiá Bráhmans, or lower-class Bráhmans; 2 men hold 2 acres for attending on the priests during the performance of certain ceremonies.

'OTHER JAGIRS.—(21) *Jágír* of Fathí Muhammad; granted by the Commissioners who came to make the first Settlement of the Province, in return for valuable services rendered to our troops at the time of the acquisition of the Province. The *jágír* comprises the *parganás* of Málud, Bájrakot, Andhárí, and Manikpatná, and was granted to Fathí Muhammad and his heirs for ever. (22) *Jágírs* of Dalbeharás, Kat-karans, and other high officers of the Rájá of Khurdhá; there are 138 of such *jágírs*, comprising an area of 1827½ acres. (23) To 499 Daláis or subordinate officers in the native army who could not be otherwise provided for, 2467 acres were granted in *jágír;* and to 28 *páiks* or privates, 240 acres.

'TENURES IN MARICHPUR AND THE JAGIR MAHAL.—The tenures mentioned in the foregoing are exclusive of those in the permanently settled estate of *kilá* Márichpur, and also of those in the *jágír* granted to Fathí Muhammad, as these were not investigated at the time of the Settlement. Their tenures, however, are in every way similar to those in the other *parganás* of the District, both in origin and character.

'The only tenure that is peculiar to the *jágír mahál* is the *shikmí zamíndárí*, of which there are two. The rights and immunities of the *shikmí zamíndárs* are exactly the same as those of the *zamíndárs* in other *parganás;* and they are so called simply because their rent is paid not into the treasury of Government, but into that of the *jágírdár*, who in that respect stands in the same relation to the *shikmí zamíndárs* as Government does to the *zamíndárs* in other parts of the District.

'CREATION OF NEW TENURES.—The sub-letting of lands is not now frequent in Purí District. Sometimes, however, estates or portions of estates are let out on farming leases, called *mustájir* and *ijárá*, for certain terms, generally extending to the end of the present term of Settlement. The *ijárádárs* and *mustájirs* (both of which terms are indiscriminately used to designate one and the same thing) step into the shoes of the lessors, and obtain all their rights and immunities. They become entitled to all the profits arising out of improved and extended cultivation, the lessors being entitled to not more than the sum fixed under their agreement. If the estate, however, is sold for arrears of revenue, the tenure is annulled; and the purchaser of the estate becomes entitled to enter into actual possession of the lands, to the prejudice of the sub-holders, and to exclude them entirely from the possession of all and every part of the estate. The Road Cess returns disclose 100 such *mustájirí* tenures in Purí.

'The following table gives a classified list of the various classes of tenures, together with the number of estates and area of each :—

GENERAL LIST OF LAND TENURES IN PURI DISTRICT.

Names of Tenures.	Total Number of Estates of each Class.	Aggregate Number of *Mausás* comprising or containing the Tenures.	Aggregate Area of the Tenures of each Class.		
			A.	*r.*	*p.*
Permanently settled Non-Regulation Tributary States,. .	2	...	506,240	0	0
Peshkash or permanently settled quit-rent paying estates,. .	1	54	33,983	3	0
Temporarily settled estates held by *zamíndárs,* . . .	430	1,316	484,797	1	11
Temporarily settled estates held *khás* owing to recusancy of proprietor, ...	4	321	135,274	3	25
Government estates, . .	4	1,091	639,553	1	10
Jágír mahals, ...	5	257	88,919	1	17
Mukaddamí (permanent), .	491	474	115,179	2	15
Mukaddamí (temporary), .	3	3	776	2	13
Pradhání, ...	279	278	82,141	2	6
Maurúsi Sarbaráhkárí, .	198	198	47,438	3	14
Miádí Sarbaráhkárí, . .	31	31	16,704	0	2
Khurdhá and Pánchgarh *Sarbaráhkárís,*	511	1,051	627,674	1	10
Kharidá first class, . .	1,175	...	7,884	2	29
Kharidá second class, .	157	...	991	0	35
Resumed *lákhiráj,* . .	...	...	61,665	2	20
Tankí, ...	1,103	...	57,102	2	0
Jágír, ...	10,468	...	23,037	1	15
Confirmed *lákhiráj,* . .	23,391 or 14,605*	...	91,728	2	28

* According as Purí city is reckoned as a single holding, or as 8786 separate holdings.

RATES OF RENT vary greatly in Purí District. The highest rates for rice land nowhere exceed Rs. 4. 11. 0 or 9s. 4½d. per acre. The following tables, submitted to the Government of Bengal by the Collector, in a report dated 24th September 1872, show the highest, lowest, and the mean rates of rent throughout the District generally, for land growing different descriptions of crops, both one and two crop; and also the average rates for ordinary land in different parts of the District :—

RATES OF RENT FOR ONE-CROP LAND.

Class of Crop.	Name of Crop.	Rate per Acre.		
		From	To	Mean.
		R. a. p.	R. a. p.	R. a. p.
Rice, ... {	Sárad rice, . .	1 2 9	4 11 0	2 14 10
	Biáli rice,. . .	0 12 6	2 13 0	1 12 9
	Daluá rice, . .	0 12 6	2 15 0	1 13 9
	Manduá rice, .	0 9 6	1 9 0	1 1 3
Pulses, . . . {	Arhar,. . . .	0 12 6	2 4 0	1 8 3
	Birhi, ...	0 12 6	1 9 0	1 2 9
	Kulthi, . . .	0 6 3	1 2 6	0 12 4
Oil-seeds, . . {	Mustard, . .	0 12 6	2 15 0	1 13 9
	Castor-oil, . .	0 12 6	2 5 0	1 8 9
Miscellaneous, . {	Vegetables, . .	0 12 6	3 2 0	1 15 3
	Cotton, . . .	0 12 6	3 2 0	1 15 3
	Turmeric, . .	0 12 6	1 9 0	1 2 9
High cultivation, {	Pán leaves, . .	9 6 0	15 10 0	12 8 0
	Sugar-cane, . .	3 2 0	6 4 0	4 11 0
	Tobacco, . . .	4 11 0	9 6 0	7 0 6

RATES OF RENT FOR TWO-CROP LAND.

Wet Season Crop.	Dry Season Crop.	Rate per Acre.		
		From	To	Mean.
		R. a. p.	R. a. p.	R. a. p.
Sárad rice . . {	Cotton, ...	1 9 0	4 11 0	3 2 0
	Inferior grain, . .	1 2 9	4 11 0	2 14 10
	Oil-seeds, . . .	1 9 0	4 11 0	3 2 0
Biáli rice, . . {	Cotton, ...	1 9 0	3 2 0	2 5 6
	Inferior grain, . .	0 12 9	3 2 0	1 15 4
	Oil-seeds, . . .	1 2 9	3 2 0	2 2 4
Manduá rice, . {	Cotton, ...	1 2 9	3 2 0	2 2 4
	Inferior grain, . .	0 12 6	2 5 0	1 8 9
	Oil-seeds, . . .	0 12 6	2 5 0	1 8 9

RATES OF RENT TERRITORIALLY DISTRIBUTED.

TRACT.	Rate per *Parganá Mán.*		Rate per English Acre.
	Number of *Dasts* or Hand-breadths in the Local Measuring Rod [the *Mán*=20 Rods Square].	Rate per such *Mán.*	
		Rs. a. p.	Rs. a. p.
1. Kotdesh, in the deltaic upland between the Deví and the Bhárgaví rivers.	Rod of 24 *dasts* or 10 ft. 5 in. long	3 2 0	3 2 0
2. Other *pargands* in the same delta, namely, Bánchás, Bánchás Kathmul, Antrodh, Domárkhand, Kurulo, Kodhár, Astrang, Kanmán, Sayyidábád, Kálijuri, and Ráháng.	Rod of 24 *dasts*,	2 10 0	2 10 0
3. The *pargands* in the immediate vicinity of the Bhárgaví, and somewhat liable to inundation, namely, Masrud - Mahál and Púrbáduái.	Rod of 20 *dasts*,	2 4 0	3 2 10
4. Certain *pargands* having a rather sandy soil, — Oldhár, Mátkadpatná, Atháis, and Kot Ráháng.	Rod of 22 *dasts* or 9 ft. 2 in.	2 0 0	2 6 2½
5. The foreshore of the Chilká with sandy soil, subject to heavy discharge of spill water,—Lembái, Siráí, and Chaubiskud.	Rod of 14 *dasts* or 6 ft. 5 in.	0 12 0	1 14 1½
6. The uplands of Khurdhá and Pánchgarh.	Rod of 14 *dasts* or 7 ft.	0 12 0	1 10 8
7. The seashore isthmus of the Chilká lake, and the similar tract of Márichpur round the mouth of Deví river.	Rod of 12 *dasts* or 6 ft.	0 8 0	1 10 0

MANURE, consisting chiefly of cow-dung, eked out by the black mud from the bottom of tanks and river deposits, is used to a large extent. It is called *khát*, from the Sanskrit *khát*, past participle of *khan*, to dig, meaning either pit refuse or what is dug in. It is measured by bullock-cart loads. Three loads are a fair allowance for an acre, and are valued at from four to eight *ánnás* or from sixpence to a shilling per load. For very high cultivation, a husbandman calculates Rs. 4. 8. o or nine shillings for rent, and about a rupee or two shillings for manure. The refuse of oil seeds and sugar-cane is also used.

IRRIGATION is less sparingly employed. Wells, tanks, rivers, and shallow pools furnish the supply.   The water is raised by means of a mat scoop, swung by two men ; or by the *tendá* apparatus of unglazed earthen pots fixed to weighted bamboo levers; or by the *jantá* apparatus, made of a hollowed trunk of a cocoa-nut palm, with the large end moved up and down the small arc of a circle by means of a heavily-weighted bamboo lever.   Irrigation is seldom used except for the spring rice (*dálua*) and the February pulse crops.   If the water can be raised to the field by means of one lift of the mat scoop, irrigation costs about six *ánnás* or ninepence an acre for rice, and for sugar-cane a little more.   Common wells are made by digging a wide deep hole till the water comes, and then piling short, broad earthenware pipes on the top of each other in the centre, and filling in the earth around.   A double tiled well of this sort, thirty feet deep, costs about Rs. 20 or £2.   In the towns and homesteads, the earthenware pipes are sunk from the top, the centre being hollowed out, and the excavators working downwards as the cylinders sink.   Sometimes the interior of the wells is built round with solid brick.   A double masonry well of this sort, forty-five feet deep, costs about Rs. 400 or £40.

ROTATION OF CROPS.—Land is nowhere left fallow except for sugar-cane.   The following rotation of crops is known, but not very generally practised :—First year, sugar-cane ; second year, a coarse grain, *manduá* (Eleusine corocana); third year, brown peas (Dolichos biflorus); fourth year, cotton ; fifth year, sugar-cane ; and so *de novo*. In rice cultivation, the same sort of crop is taken off the same land year after year.

NATURAL CALAMITIES: BLIGHTS.—Locusts seldom do much damage.   Only one flight is recorded within the past sixteen years, namely, in 1862, when one of the peasants asserted in Court that he lost seven-eighths of his crop.   The general loss to the District was in a much less degree.   Black insects (*kálimakshi*) breed on the wet ground after floods, and occasionally devour the young crops.   Other minute insects (*jhintikás*) attack the young crops when in the milk.

FLOODS do great damage to the crops, especially in the *pargaúás* at the northern end of the Chilká lake.   Every year many square miles of standing crops perish from inundation.   Of the thirty-two years ending in 1866, twenty-four have been years of flood so serious as to require remissions of revenue.   During the last fifteen years of this period, there has only been a single one in which such remissions have not been required. This exceptional year was 1865–66, when the Province was depopulated by drought instead. It must be remembered that, whenever there are floods in Puri District, the shores of the Chilká have to bear the greatest share of the general suffering. I have no separate account of their pecuniary losses; but during the fifteen years above alluded to, the total remissions of Government land rent in Puri District amounted to £41,993, for floods alone. If to this we add £1393 remitted for the famine in 1865–66, we have a total reduction of £43,386, being very nearly equal to a whole year's land revenue of the District. At the same time, the large sum of £35,577 has been expended by Government on embankments and other protective works against inundation. We have, therefore, for the two items of remissions for floods and maintenance of embankments, a bill for £78,963 in fifteen years. This forms an annual charge of ten per cént. on the total land revenue of the District.

But even this does not represent the whole cost of these floods. For, on the one hand, Government has not only to allow remissions of revenue, but it is liable to be called on, as in 1866, for an enormous outlay in charity and relief works; and thousands of acres of the finest lands are left unassessed in consequence of their exposure to inundation. Thus, in seven villages on the north of the Chilká, exceptionally liable to flood, one-fourth of the whole area is excluded from payment on this account. At the present moment, throughout the Fiscal Division of Sirái, 4212 acres are left waste for fear of floods, against 5524 cultivated. In Chaubiskud, the adjoining *parganá*, the proportion is 17,482 left waste, to 23,000 under tillage. Moreover, the part that is cultivated yields only a fraction of what it would but for the floods. The various *parganás* of Puri are classified according to the extent to which they are liable to such calamities. Among them, those on the shore of the Chilká are stated to be entirely within the reach of inundations. By comparing the rent-rate in these regions with that of *parganás* which are comparatively protected, it will be found that the risk of floods diminishes the market value of the same quality of land to nearly one-fifth. Thus, the highest rate for winter rice land in Sirái, on the north of the Chilká, is R. 1. o. o or 2s. an acre; in Domárkhand, one of the best protected *parganás*, it is Rs. 4. 12. o. or 9s. 6d. Again, in Sirái, the lowest rent for the same sort of land is 3 *ánnás* or 4½d. an acre; in Domárkhand it is Rs. 1. 6. o or 2s. 9d. The

average rate for the same land in Sirái is 9⅜ *ánnás* or 1s. 2d. an
acre; in Domárkhand it is Rs. 2. 6. 8 or 4s. 1od.   In addition,
therefore, to the heavy incubus on the public revenue, amounting for
two items alone to ten per cent. on the whole revenue of the
District, the risk of floods on the northern shores of the Chilká
decreases the rent-paying powers of the land to one-fifth of their
natural value.

By the inundation of 1866, out of a total District area then estimated at 2504 square miles, 275 were submerged for from five to
forty-five days.   Throughout this vast area the water was nowhere
less than three feet deep, in whole villages it was ten feet deep, and
over thousands of acres it averaged seven.   The rivers came down
bursting their banks in every direction, and leaving fifty-two wide
breaches behind them as they tore along.   More than 412,000
people were suddenly driven out of house and home, and found
themselves in the middle of a boiling ocean.   When we come to
details, the picture assumes a still more appalling aspect.   In one
part of *parganá* Sirái, on the north of the Chilká, 1200 acres were
under nine feet of water; and the average depth over the entire
7830 acres reported upon in that *parganá* was between seven and
nine feet.   There were, therefore, in one single Fiscal Division of
Purí, more than twelve square miles of solid land suddenly turned
into a sea between seven and nine feet deep; and this sea continued
to cover everything for thirty days.   Thousands of miserable families
floated about in canoes, on bamboo rafts, on trunks of trees, or on
rice stacks, which threatened every moment to dissolve into fragments beneath them.   No lives were lost in the first rush of the
waters; for the unhappy inhabitants of those regions know but too
well, from previous experience, what they have to expect, and live in
a constant state of preparation.   Most of the hamlets have boats
tied to the houses; and for miles, the high thatched roofs are firmly
held down by bamboo stakes, so as to afford a refuge in time of
flood.   Starving colonies might be seen thus perched above the
waters.   Every banyan tree had its rookery of human beings, while
the Bráhmans effected settlements on the roofs of their brick temples,
and looked down in safety as the flood roared past.   The common
danger disarmed all creatures of their natural antipathies.   Snakes
glided up to the roofs, and burrowed harmlessly in the thatch.
Others wriggled up trees, and whenever a canoe or log of wood
passed, slid down into the water and swam towards the ark which

their instinct told them would bear them to dry land. The cattle suffered terribly. Sheep and goats were carried away by herds in the torrent, and in a few days their carcases came to the surface, and floated about covered with crows and scuffling kites. But the most pitiable sight of all was the plough cattle standing in shallow parts up to their necks, and hungrily snuffing the barren waters for food, until they sank exhausted into the slime. Before the flood was over, many a famished family had also sunk beneath the waters.

Such was the flood of 1866; and it must be remembered that, although of unusually long continuance, it was by no means singular as to its extent or its depth. Indeed, we find that in 1855 the inundation was deeper in every one of the *parganás* of the District.

When the waters subsided, the survivors found themselves amid a region of desolated homesteads, fœtid slime, and rotting crops. Close on two million hundredweights of rice had perished in Purí District alone during the thirty days. Its lowest money value was estimated at £643,683; and this vast loss had been sustained notwithstanding that, in this single District, 10,620 acres of fertile land are permanently left untilled for fear of flood.

From time immemorial, the husbandmen have laboured to mitigate this calamity by embankments; and on our annexation of the Province in 1803, the feature that struck the new rulers as the one great fact in the rural economy of Orissa, was this sempiternal struggle between the people and the rivers. At present, were it not for the embankments, two-thirds of Purí District would be at the mercy of the floods. Indeed, notwithstanding the 316 miles of dykes now maintained by Government in Purí District alone, there is not a single one of the twenty-nine *parganás* of the District beyond the reach of inundations.

Floods, however, form only one of the disasters incident to an uncontrolled water supply. Nature has abundantly provided Orissa with rivers and local rainfall; but the water which, if husbanded, would last all through the year, is allowed, in the space of a few weeks, to rush off to the ocean in destructive floods. During the 35 years from 1831-32 to 1866-67, Government had to remit £257,939 of its Orissa rental for droughts alone, or £455,365 for the combined effects of droughts and floods. Inundations are more common, and in general more destructive, than droughts; for, even if the rivers fail, the Province has its own local rainfall of 55 inches a year in reserve.   But a total absence of water produces the climax of misery.

THE FAMINE OF 1866.—The following brief sketch of the great famine of 1866 is compiled from the Report of the Famine Commissioners (folio, 2 vols., Calcutta 1867).   The famine was felt with more intensity in Purí than in either Cuttack or Balasor Districts. The rice crop of 1864 was considerably below an average one, and prices rapidly rose.   Ordinary rice, which in July 1864 was selling at 35 standard *sers* per rupee, or 3s. 2d. a hundredweight, in July 1865 was at 18¾ *sers* per rupee, or 6s. a hundredweight.   The utter failure of the crop of 1865 was due to drought.   The average annual rainfall in Purí is about 55 inches; whereas in 1865 only 36·3 inches fell, of which only 5·2 inches fell in September, and none at all subsequently, at the time when it was most needed.   In October 1865, prices were about two and a half times their ordinary rates.   On the 10th October, the Superintendent of Police reported the prevalence of great distress in the south of the District; and on the 25th of the same month, the Deputy-Collector also brought to notice that a famine was impending.   He stated that in many places the inhabitants were subsisting on fruits and roots, and that rice was selling at famine rates.   Extreme distress was reported about the same time as prevailing in Málud and Párikud, two estates comprising the tract between the Chilká lake and the sea.   Serious distress also appeared in Ráháng *parganá*, in the neighbourhood of Purí town.   The Collector applied early in the season for permission to make inquiries into the losses on the *zamíndárí* estates, which was summarily refused by the Board of Revenue.   A more pressing application to the same effect was made about the end of November, but was again negatived.   The Collector was informed that no remissions were to be granted, and that no hopes of their receiving any aid should be held out to the *zamíndárs*.

On the 25th November the Collector telegraphed that starvation was occurring in Párikud and Málud, that the number of deaths was increasing, and that general destitution prevailed.   Relief works for the employment of the distressed were sanctioned; and on the 29th November a definite scheme for operations on a large scale, in the shape of road-making, was submitted by the Collector, who recommended that wages should be given in food instead of in money, and that grain should be imported and stored for this purpose.   A grant of £4400 was made for works on the Cuttack and Madras road in Purí, and a second of £2500 for the Cuttack and Purí road.   The Government, however, negatived the proposal that wages should be paid in kind.   On this head, the following instructions were sent to the District engineer, under whose superintendence the work was to be carried out :—'It has been suggested that the relief should be given in the shape of wages paid in grain, but it is not desirable that the officers of the Public Works Department should be concerned in any arrangement of this kind.   The ordinary rates of money wages should be paid to all who seek work on those terms ; and any further relief required must be supplemented by committees formed for the purpose, and by such action as the civil authorities can take.'

In January 1866 it became clear that rice in any quantity was not procurable in Purí District; and on the 15th of that month the Collector called attention to the necessity of providing a supply of food for the labourers, which, if neglected, would be 'likely to interfere materially with, if not actually put a stop to, the works.'   He suggested that a sum of £2000 should be advanced, out of the money at the disposal of the Public Works Department, for purchase of rice.   This, however, was disallowed.   In the end of January the Commissioner of the Orissa Division telegraphed as follows regarding the state of affairs:—'Famine relief is at a stand-still. Public Works Department refuse to advance money to Collectors to purchase rice.   Purí must get rice from somewhere.   May I authorize advance for this purpose?'   To this telegram the following reply was despatched :—'Government declines to import rice into Purí. If the market favours importers, rice will find its way to Purí without Government interference, which can only do harm.   All payments for labour employed to relieve the present distress are to be in cash.' The result of this telegram seems to have been to put an end to the discussion regarding the importation of rice, from that time till a period when the state both of the weather and of the people rendered it too late to import it with successful effect.

No further orders were issued on the subject till June.   The Collector did all that he possibly could ; but there can be no doubt that the relief works were rendered to a very great degree inoperative, from want of rice to feed the labourers.   The Commissioner's own statement is to that effect.   He says that the local officers were directed to make arrangements to enable the labourers to procure food ; but it was found impossible to do so, the Collector having neither rice nor agency at his disposal, and finding it impossible to attract shopkeepers. The Executive Engineer stated 'there were great fluctuations in the number employed, and the scarcity of rice was the chief cause.' Another Public Works officer wrote, 'I think the want of grain greatly diminished the efficiency of my works as measures of relief.' The Famine Commissioners express their decided opinion that in the beginning of February the time had come when Government might properly have imported rice into Purí District, and that if grain had been available at the relief works, they might have been immensely extended.

Matters grew rapidly worse in Purí District. In the early part of May an extreme pitch of misery was reached; on the 9th May the Collector, as Secretary to the Famine Relief Committee, made an appeal to public charity through the Calcutta Press. The distress in the town had become such that it was no longer possible to leave it to the unorganized charity of the *mohants*, or heads of the religious houses. A sum of £100 was sent to Purí, partly from a fund which had been set on foot by a mercantile firm, and partly from private subscriptions. With this aid a relief house was opened in the town, at which cooked food was supplied; before the end of the month, 300 paupers were being thus fed daily, and want of funds prevented the Committee from giving relief to a larger number. At the end of May a grant of £1000 was made by Government to the Committee, from the balance of the North-Western Provinces Famine Relief Fund; and an officer was appointed to superintend the relief operations in the rural parts. The Committee resolved to give up a system of out-door money relief which they had first adopted; and accepted the principle that only those really incapable of work should receive gratuitous relief, and that all others should be required to work according to their powers. The daily allowance was fixed at half a *ser* (1 lb.) of rice for each adult, and a quarter of a *ser* ($\frac{1}{2}$ lb.) for each child. Wherever the wages of labour were paid in money, the daily allowance was fixed at $1\frac{1}{2}$ *ánnás* ($2\frac{1}{4}$d.) for men, $1\frac{1}{4}$ *ánnás* ($1\frac{7}{8}$d.) for women, and $\frac{3}{4}$ of an *ánná* (1d.) for children. Sheds capable of accommodating two hundred people were to be erected at each centre, so that when the rains set in the paupers might be employed in mat-making, basket-making, and similar light in-door work. A considerable quantity of rice, too, was procured from Gopálpur.

By this time some little private trade had sprung up with the south; and at the end of May the Collector reported to the Commissioner that during the previous four months nearly a *lákh* of rupees' worth (£10,000) of rice was imported by way of the Chilká lake from Gopálpur, and that he expected further supplies to come down the Mahánadí as soon as it should be open for navigation.

The rice from the south was being brought up from Gopálpur by the Kumtís, a class of Madras merchants settled in Purí; and the supply was dependent on the imports into Gopálpur from the ports still farther south. In the middle of June there was a cessation in the imports, in consequence of the non-arrival of a ship which had been expected at Gopálpur; and on the 16th the Collector reported that rice was scarcely procurable in the District, even for the prisoners, and called on the Commissioner to send him a supply from the rice which had been sent by Government to False Point, in order to avert the impending crisis.

The selling price in Purí was below 6 *sers* of 80 *tolá* weight to the rupee. It was not till the 27th June that the District was eased by the renewal of the supply from the south; the price then fell to 7¼ *sers* for the rupee. By the 17th June, five relief centres had been opened in the interior of the District, exclusive of the Khurdhá Subdivision; by the end of the month six more were established; two were added in July; four in August; and the maximum number, thirteen, was reached in September. Besides these, the Assistant-Collector in charge of Khurdhá was establishing centres in that Subdivision, with funds and rice which were supplied to him by the Purí Committee. By the end of July he had opened nine centres.

In the description of the famine in Cuttack (pp. 148-173 of the Statistical Account of that District), the circumstances are mentioned which compelled the Government to abandon its resolution not to import rice into Orissa. The first quantity of rice imported by Government was 2549 bags, which reached Purí on the 30th June. The Collector then began to make sales of rice to the public in Purí town at the rate of 6 local *sers* of 105 *tolá* weight (=7⅛ standard *sers* of 80 *tolá* weight), that being about the market rate on the 5th and 6th July. £514 worth of rice was sold; and then the Collector raised the price to 5 *sers* for the rupee, which had the effect of stopping the sales for a time. The market price was then 7¼ *sers* of coarse, and 5⅞ *sers* of fine rice for the rupee.

On the 7th of July the steamer *T. A. Gibb* arrived with a cargo of 12,476 bags, and there was every prospect of a full supply of rice with which to carry on operations for some time without stint. The Committee then started a system of selling rice at cheap rates to those who could not afford to buy at the prevailing excessive price, and who yet were not so utterly reduced to pauperism as to have a claim to gratuitous support; the sales were to be made at the rate of 8 *sers* for the rupee. The members of the Committee were authorized to give tickets to deserving persons entitling them to such relief, it being provided that no one person should buy more than three rupees worth at one time. The object of this measure was to reach distressed persons who belonged to other than the ordinary labouring classes.

At the centres in the interior of the District, relief was given in the shape of uncooked rice till the end of July. But, as in other Districts, it was found that the paupers, having no facilities for cooking it, and famishing with hunger, devoured the rice raw, which brought on fatal bowel complaints; and it was also observed that the raw rice was forcibly taken away from the weak by the strong. This led to the distribution of rations of cooked rice.

Unfortunately, the hope that a full supply of imported grain could be thenceforth maintained, proved to be a vain one. Puri harbour is simply an open roadstead, and for many months in the year it is almost impossible for ships to discharge or receive cargo. When the vessel arrived with the grain, the bad weather had set in; and it was with the utmost difficulty that it could be got on shore, at the rate of a few boat-loads a day. Two men were drowned, many boats swamped, and a considerable quantity of the rice lost. At times it was absolutely impossible to go off to the ship at all; and altogether seven weeks passed before the whole of the 12,476 bags were landed. The Assistant-Collector states: 'We went almost as far as manslaughter, in having induced the boatmen to go out in such weather. Two lives were lost, and some men were sent to hospital injured. They behaved very well, never being accustomed to go out at that season; they did all they could. The number of boats when I first came was about seven or eight, and two or three new ones were made. Eventually, we sometimes started with as many as ten after repairs; but that number was soon again reduced to three or four, owing to the damages the boats received.' A brig, which had brought up 1500 bags of rice from Gopálpur on private account, was eventually obliged to leave the port without discharging her cargo.

This period was one of very great distress throughout the District. The quantities of grain which the authorities were able to land at Purí from day to day were so small, that there appeared to be no hope of carrying on the relief operations without a break. On the 20th July the Collector was compelled to restrict his sales at market rates to one rupee's worth to each applicant in the town. Rice was then selling in the market at less than six *sers* for the rupee. In August the miseries of the people were intensified by the disastrous inundation described on a previous page. The dearth of rice rendered it necessary to temporarily stop the sales of rice at market rates to the general public from the 13th August, but the Relief Committee were able to keep their centres in operation. It was found necessary, however, to adopt a still lower rate of sale than that at which they had previously been selling; a second class of selected persons were therefore allowed to buy at the low rate of 16 *sers* for the rupee. The inclemency of the weather had terribly increased the rate of mortality. At the end of August it was resolved to move the paupers out of the town, into a camp on the strip of sand which separates the town from the sea; and sheds were there erected to accommodate 1500 persons.

On the 31st August, another vessel arrived with 7453 bags of rice; and during September, operations were rapidly extended, the shopkeepers being employed as agents for the sale of the Government rice throughout the District. Rice from Gopálpur again began to come into the District on private account. Distress was, however, still at its height. On the 10th September the Committee recorded that the class whom they had hitherto allowed to purchase rice at 16 *sers* for the rupee, had now merged into the pauper population, having sold all that they possessed. They therefore discontinued sales altogether, supplying the destitute gratuitously, and leaving those who could pay to purchase at the Government shops. In October another dearth of the rice stock took place, which compelled the Collector at first to reduce his sales at market rates by only allowing purchasers to take 8 *ánnás'* worth instead of one rupee's worth at a time, and afterwards to put a stop to sales altogether. The Relief Committee, however, had stocks in hand, and were enabled to carry on their operations at all their centres, with the assistance of 15,000 *maunds* of old unhusked rice which was supplied to them by the *mahants* of one of the *maths,* and which they sold at low rates. Further stores of rice were imported in November; and the reopening of Government sales, together with the appearance of the new rice in the market, had a marked effect on prices. Coarse rice, which on the 1st November had been selling at $7\frac{7}{16}$ *sers* per rupee, rapidly fell in price, till on the 23d the rates stood at 21 *sers* for the rupee.

During the latter part of November, the Collector visited the interior of the District, and found the condition of the people much improved; on which the Committee directed the officer in charge of the relief operations to close the centres cautiously, and to centralize the paupers in smaller numbers. It was observed, however, that although the condition of the rural population was fast improving, there was still much distress among the poor but more respectable families in the town of Purí, especially those which depended on widows for support. The system of giving out cotton to be spun by these women in their own houses, the thread being bought by the Committee, was therefore introduced; and in special cases it was determined to give house relief in money. In certain tracts which had suffered more severely than others, it was found necessary to continue gratuitous relief for many months longer. Throughout the famine, orphans and deserted children were collected from wherever they could be found, and sent to the orphanages of the Baptist Mission.

The previous failure of the crop of 1864, the drought of 1865, and the terrible inundations in August 1866, all combined to make the famine more severely felt in Purí than in any other District. In the southern and north-eastern tracts, the scarcity had become a famine some months earlier than either in Cuttack or Balasor; but unfortunately no rice was imported till a month later than to Cuttack. Certainly, private trade was importing something from the south, but not to anything like the extent of adequately supplying the wants of the people in the interior of the District. By June the famine had reached its height, and continued unabated throughout July and August.

Regarding the mortality, the Famine Commissioners state that it is impossible to form any estimate which can be confidently pronounced even to approximate to the truth. They give, however, the following statement, compiled from returns made by the police

in October 1866, which shows a mortality from all causes of not
less than 35·81 per cent. in the year, on a population estimated at
588,841 persons at the beginning of 1866; but they state that it
must not be relied upon as at all exact:—

STATEMENT OF MORTALITY IN THE DISTRICT OF PURI, COMPILED
BY THE POLICE IN OCTOBER 1866.

Names of *Pargands.*	Estimated Number of Inhabitants in 1865.	Number of Deaths in 1866.	Percentage of Deaths to Population.
Málud,	3,329	1,517	25·56
Bájrakot,	3,843	1,896	49·33
Párikud,	10,235	5,802	56·68
Mánikpatná,	6,104	4,477	73·34
Chaubiskud,	28,654	18,927	66·05
Sirái,	11,384	7,418	65·16
Ráháng,	48,182	27,519	57·11
Lembái,	41,896	4,000	9·54
Kot Ráháng,	30,889	3,000	9·71
Paschimduái,	18,326	1,498	8·11
Purbaduái,	13,829	5,434	39·29
Kotdes,	93,424	39,821	42·62
Bánchás,	10,067	4,286	42·57
Atháis,	13,447	5,886	43·77
Antrodh,	20,683	10,020	48·44
Astrang,	2,293	1,548	67·50
Kurulo,	10,920	5,687	52·07
Kodhár,	14,102	7,480	53·04
Marichpur,	7,449	4,227	56·74
Domárkhand,	12,445	6,913	55·54
Oldhár,	8,400	4,104	48·85
Matkadpatná,	1,039	436	41·96
Khurdhá and Pánchgarh,	145,708	29,343	20·13
Rorang,	7,176	4,719	65·76
Town of Puri,	25,017	4,908	19·61
Total,	588,841	210,866	Av. 35·81.

Respecting the foregoing table the Commissioners state as
follows:—'Possibly, some of those who are reckoned among the
dead are really emigrants who may return to their homes. The
Assistant-Collector has told us that in Kákatpur he personally
ascertained that, out of 309 persons, 92 had died, giving a percentage of 29·77. Most of the houses in this village were occupied
by Bráhman families, and the village was well-to-do. That gentleman, therefore, reasonably inferred that in the neighbouring less

prosperous villages, the mortality must have been still greater; and indeed he found this to be the case in two other villages where he made inquiries, of which he could not give us the particulars. As a specimen of the effects of the inundation, where it cut off villages from their supplies, the Assistant-Collector states that one village on the Chilká had been so isolated by the floods, that only two persons remained alive out of the occupants of twenty-eight houses. Doubtless, the inundations very materially raised the percentage of mortality.'

The total quantity of Government grain imported into Purí in 1866 amounted to 47,383 *maunds*, of which 1028 *maunds* were supplied to Government Departments at full cost price, 18,973 *maunds* were sold to the public at the Government shops at the market rates, and 27,382 *maunds* were transferred to the Relief Committee. Out of the last quantity, 16,626 *maunds* were gratuitously distributed, and 5940 were sold at cheap rates to selected individuals. The sum of £10,322 was expended by the Public Works Department in providing work for the distressed. The amount of money expended by the Relief Committee is thus returned:—Grants from the Board of Revenue, £7000; from the Calcutta Relief Committee, £1500; local subscriptions, £1466; total, £9966. The daily average number of persons receiving relief is returned as follows:—July, 2844, of whom 1818 were employed in light labour, and 1026 received gratuitous relief; August, 6599, of whom 4172 were employed in light labour, and 2427 received gratuitous relief; September, 9012, of whom 4853 were employed in light labour, and 4159 received gratuitous relief; October, 10,846, of whom 5082 were employed in light labour, and 5764 received gratuitous relief; November, 10,485, of whom 4632 were employed in light labour, and 5853 received gratuitous relief. The daily average from the 30th June to the 17th November was 7957, of whom 4111 were employed in light labour, and 3846 received gratuitous relief.

ROADS.—The two main lines of road in Purí District are the Calcutta and Madras Trunk Road, and the Pilgrim Road from Cuttack to Purí. I have no return as to the minor roads. The Report of the Purí District Road Fund for 1874-75, published in the *Calcutta Gazette* of the 19th April 1876, shows that the total income for that year, excluding balances, was £977, 14s. 0d.; and the expenditure £1458, 7s. 0d.

MANUFACTURES.—Apart from a little weaving and pottery making, the only manufacture of Purí is salt. In my Statistical Account of Balasor, I have described the process of artificial salt-making by boiling. In Purí, salt is made by solar evaporation, principally in Párikud, and the tract to the north and east of the Chilká lake. The manufacture begins at the commencement of the hot season, in the latter half of March. In the first place, a little canal is dug from the Chilká lake, with sets of broad shallow tanks on either side. These sets of tanks run out at right angles from the canal in rows of four. Each tank is 75 feet square, by from 18 inches to 3 feet deep. On the first day of the manufacture, the brackish water of the lake is admitted by the canal into the first tank of each of the sets of rows. Here it stands for twenty-four hours; and as the depth of this first series of tanks is only 18 inches, evaporation goes on very rapidly. Next morning the brine is transferred from tank No. 1 to tank No. 2 in each of the sets of rows. Tank No. 2 is 24 inches deep; and each successive one deepens by 6 inches till the brine reaches No. 4, which is 3 feet deep. The water stands for a day in each, gradually thickening as it evaporates. On the fourth day it is transferred to tank No. 4; and on the morning of the fifth, some of the brine is ladled from that tank into an adjoining net-work of very shallow pools, each pool being 5 feet square by only 6 inches deep. Here it stands during the intense heat of the day. In the afternoon the manufacture is complete, and the salt is raked out of the network of shallow pools.

The same process goes on, with slight variations, from day to day. Every morning water is let into tank No. 1 of each of the set of rows from the canal; while the brine gradually progresses from one tank to another, in the various stages of evaporation. A constant supply of brine is thus kept up in tank No. 4; and a portion of it is daily ladled into the network of shallow pools; in which the finishing stage of evaporation takes place.

A Párikud salt-field, therefore, consists of a little canal from the Chilká, with 'workings' diverging from the canal at right angles upon either side. Each working is composed of a row of four tanks and a network of shallow pools, and is managed by from three to five men, who are paid by piece work, and earn about 1½ *ánnás* (2¼d.) a day each, or about Rs. 3 (6s.) a month. The out-turn is about fifteen tons the first week; and if the manufacture goes on without interruption for a fortnight, it may amount to as much as eighty tons for the fifteen days. But it is somewhat of a gambling trade. A single shower of rain puts a stop to the whole process, the tanks having to be emptied out, and the work entirely begun afresh.

The total cost of salt made in this way is 4 *ánnás* a *maund*, equal to 8d. a hundredweight or 13s. 4d. a ton. Government, when it kept the manufacture in its own hand, used to allow the workmen 5 *ánnás* a *maund*, equal to 10d. a hundredweight or 16s. 8d. a ton. The duty is Rs. 3. 4. 0 a *maund*, equal to 8s. 10d. a hundredweight or £8, 16s. 8d. a ton, which, added to the cost of manufacture, makes a total of £9, 10s. 0d. a ton. Under the present system, the Government does not itself make salt, but has transferred the trade to licensed manufacturers, charging them with the duty upon the amount actually made, in the same way as the excise is levied from distillers in England. The total amount of salt manufactured in Purí in 1875-76 was 67,170 *maunds ;* but this is not sufficient to meet the local demand, as the quantity of salt sold for consumption in the District amounted to 96,264 *maunds*. The total amount of salt revenue realized was £38,544.

Artificially evaporated salt sells at a slightly higher price than salt made as above; as it is stronger, and goes much farther, the people find it in reality cheaper. Nevertheless, the respectable classes throughout Orissa prefer what is practically the more costly article, made by the pure rays of the sun. They look upon the difference between the two sorts very much as they regard cooked and uncooked rice. All nature's gifts are pure until contaminated by the hand of man. Cooking constitutes such a contamination ; and the priests of Orissa would as soon think of eating rice boiled by a person of inferior caste, as they would of using salt evaporated by the human device of fire.

ROAD TRAFFIC.—Purí District has considerably less trade than either Balasor or Cuttack. Its statistics of sea-borne trade have been given in a former section (p. 22).

Since January 1876, a system of traffic registration has been introduced on the Grand Trunk Road between Calcutta and Madras, the registering station being at Rambhá on the Chilká lake in Ganjám District, just beyond the Purí frontier. The following tables, which have been compiled from the *Statistical Reporter*, show—Table I., the exports into Madras of the two Orissa Districts of Cuttack and Purí for the first six months of 1876, arranged quarter by quarter; Table

II., the imports in these two Districts from Madras for the same period :—

STATISTICS OF ROAD TRAFFIC BETWEEN ORISSA AND MADRAS FOR FIRST HALF-YEAR OF 1876.—TABLE I. EXPORTS FROM ORISSA.

DESCRIPTION OF GOODS.	CUTTACK.			PURI.			GRAND TOTAL.
	January to March.	April to June.	Total.	January to March.	April to June.	Total.	
CLASS I.	*mds.*	*mds.*	*mds.*	*mds.*	*mds.*	*mds.*	*mds.*
Cotton (raw), . . .	26	...	26	...	...	...	26
Cotton twist, . . .	30	14	44	...	...	...	44
Silk (raw), . . .	...	8	8	...	...	...	8
Chemicals and drugs, .	2,288	...	2,288	131	...	131	2,419
Fresh fruits and vegetables,	...	119	119	39	56	95	214
Pulses and gram, . .	2,329	1,602	3,931	172,914	73,391	246,305	250,236
Rice, ...	1,496	324	1,820	59,787	13,311	73,098	74,918
Other cereals, . . .	6	...	6	70	...	70	76
Fibres, manufactures of, .	36	...	36	120	148	268	304
Hides and horns, . .	249	146	395	...	...	...	395
Iron and its manufactures,	451	1,086	1,537	914	170	1,084	2,621
Copper and brass and manufactures, . .	516	392	908	...	...	...	908
Other metals, etc., . .	...	26	26	...	...	...	26
Ghi, ...	...	...	...	75	...	75	75
Oil, ...	285	...	285	...	...	...	285
Oil seeds, . . .	25	140	165	13	...	13	178
Salt, ...	...	...	...	...	70	70	70
Spices, . . .	221	45	266	549	160	709	975
Sugar (unrefined), .	...	...	...	170	280	450	450
Tobacco, . . .	43	...	43	...	30	30	73
Stone, . . .	5	...	5	...	...	...	5
Shell-lac, . . .	36	...	36	...	...	...	36
Opium, . . .	...	...	...	13	...	13	13
Saltpetre, . . .	85	...	85	...	...	...	85
Betel nuts, . . .	5	120	125	732	...	732	857
Miscellaneous, .	4,614	4,070	8,684	761	2,003	2,764	11,448
Total, . .	12,746	8,092	20,838	236,288	89,619	325,907	346,745
CLASS II.	No.	No.	No.	No.	No.	No.	No.
Cattle, ...	...	...	...	8	40	48	48
Hides, . . .	...	96	96	...	96	96	192
Gunny-bags, . . .	...	688	688	...	...	...	688
CLASS III.	Rs.	Rs.	Rs.	Rs.	Rs.	Rs.	Rs.
Cotton (European) manufactures, . . .	1250	...	1250	...	3050	3050	4300
Silk manufactures, . .	...	3000	3000	...	...	...	3000
Miscellaneous (Native) manufactures, .	2158	...	2158	...	...	...	2158
Miscellaneous (European) manufactures, . .	300	200	500	...	...	...	500
Total, . .	3708	3200	6908	...	3050	3050	9958

STATISTICS OF ROAD TRAFFIC BETWEEN ORISSA AND MADRAS FOR FIRST HALF-YEAR OF 1876.—TABLE II. IMPORTS INTO ORISSA.

DESCRIPTION OF GOODS.	CUTTACK.			PURI.			GRAND. TOTAL
	January to March.	April to June.	Total.	January to March.	April to June.	Total.	
CLASS I.	mds.	mds.	mds.	mds.	mds.	mds.	mds.
Cotton (raw),	...	...	...	...	1	1	1
Cotton twist (Native),	24	12	36	...	36	36	72
Cotton twist (European),	...	...	...	4	6	10	10
Chemicals and drugs,	...	...	...	36	...	36	36
Fruits and nuts,	...	...	...	...	12	12	12
Fresh fruits and vegetables,	...	36	36	312	144	456	492
Fuel and firewood,	...	32	32	120	...	120	152
Wheat,	...	...	...	7	24	31	31
Pulses and gram,	1,761	304	2,065	2,431	992	3,423	5,488
Rice,	...	...	...	82	...	82	82
Fibres (manufactures of),	146	...	146	1,004	12	1,016	1,162
Hides,	26	...	26	...	...	...	26
Iron and its manufactures,	...	7	7	62	...	62	69
Copper,	40	...	40	49	26	75	115
Stone,	...	192	192	139	36	175	367
Ghí,	67	108	175	545	157	702	877
Oil,	...	...	...	56	...	56	56
Oil seeds,	...	90	90	509	340	849	939
Salt,	22,953	35,924	58,877	1,337	10,819	12,156	71,033
Spices,	3,425	3,023	6,448	1,297	3,108	4,405	10,853
Sugar (unrefined),	1,265	719	1,984	11,475	7,104	8,579	20,563
Timber,	...	...	...	...	1,600	1,600	1,600
Tobacco,	102	237	339	12	194	206	545
Sandal-wood,	...	...	...	13	...	13	13
Betel-nuts,	12	...	12	...	50	50	62
Miscellaneous,	782	84	866	426	167	593	1,459
Total,	30,603	40,768	71,371	19,916	24,828	44,744	116,115
CLASS II.	No.	No.	No.	No.	No.	No.	No.
Cattle,	...	150	150	68	28	96	246
Timber,	...	...	...	4	...	4	4
Gunny-bags,	...	...	...	...	3,600	3,600	3,600
Bamboos,	...	...	...	1,960	1,110	3,070	3,070
Hides,	...	104	104	...	...	...	104
Miscellaneous,	190	30	220	1,580	146	1,726	1,946
CLASS III.	Rs.	Rs.	Rs.	Rs.	Rs.	Rs.	Rs.
Silk (manufactures of),	...	...	...	1,150	1,000	2,150	2,150
Leather (manufactures of),	...	20	20	...	...	...	20
Wool (manufactures of),	...	...	...	...	427	427	427
Cotton manufactures (European),	2,450	15,280	17,730	8,270	10,840	19,110	36,840
Miscellaneous (Native) goods,	1,710	150,020	151,730	430	220	650	152,380
Total,	4,160	165,320	169,480	9,850	12,487	22,337	191,817

From these tables it appears that the total exports southwards from Orissa in Class I. during the half-year amounted to 346,745 *maunds* or

· 12,684 tons, almost entirely consisting of food-grains; and that Purí furnished no less than 94 per cent. of the total. The imports in the same class amounted to 116,115 *maunds* or 4250 tons, chiefly salt, unrefined sugar, and spices. Of this total, Cuttack received 61 per cent. In Class III. the large amount in the import table under the heading of miscellaneous manufactures was ascertained to be composed of jewellery, etc. imported from Vizagapatam.

For the concluding three months of this period, additional information is given in the *Statistical Reporter*. During that quarter, the total amount of traffic passing the Rambhá station was valued at £74,859; of which £24,050, or nearly one-third, passed southwards into Madras, and £50,809, or more than two-thirds, proceeded northwards. This total includes a few minor despatches to and from remote districts of Bengal and other Provinces, as well as the local trade between Orissa and Ganjám.

ADMINISTRATIVE HISTORY.—The District of Purí was annexed by the British, with the rest of Orissa, in 1803. An account of the occupation will be found in my Statistical Account of Cuttack (vol. xviii.). On the fall of Cuttack Fort, Mr. J. Hunter was deputed to Purí to collect the revenue of that division of the Province, and to superintend the temple. From 1818 to 1828, Purí and Khurdhá were under the charge of the Joint Magistrate and Deputy-Collector of Khurdhá, who, after a time, obtained the rank of Collector. In 1828 Orissa was divided into the Northern, Central, and Southern Divisions, the last of which is nearly identical with the present District of Purí. About the same year, the headquarters were removed from Khurdhá to Purí town. In 1829 the total income of the District was £89,776, and the total civil expenditure £12,357, or one-eighth of the revenue. In 1860-61 the total revenue, deducting transfer accounts, was £126,157, and the expenditure £16,722. In 1870-71 the total civil revenue, after all transfer deductions had been made, amounted to £104,191, and the expenditure to £22,538. During the forty years, therefore, between 1829 and 1870, the revenue has increased by only £14,415, or 16 per cent., while the cost of Government has nearly doubled. Indeed, in the ten years between 1860 and 1870, the revenue had fallen by £21,966, while the expenditure increased by £6,068. The following table gives the details of the revenue and expenditure of the District in 1870-71. The statement has been drawn up by the Collector, and all transfer accounts and inefficient balances have been excluded :—

REVENUE AND EXPENDITURE OF PURI DISTRICT FOR 1870-71.

REVENUE.			
1. Net Land Revenue,	£42,347	2	0
2. *Abkári*,	3,558	17	0
3. Salt,	49,708	19	3
4. Stamps,	3,371	15	11
5. Income Tax,	3,931	2	5
6. Law and Justice (Fines),	394	2	4
7. Registration Fees,	285	13	1
8. Customs Duty,	128	19	1
9. Schooling Fees,	138	17	5
10. Post Office,	325	15	0
Total,	£104,191	3	6

EXPENDITURE.			
1. Salary of Collectorate Gazetted Officers,	£4,219	19	7
2. Salary of Office Establishment,	1,585	11	11
3. Subdivisional Establishment,	175	7	11
4. *Nazir's* Establishment,	108	14	7
5. *Khás Mahál* Establishment and Charges,	479	7	11
6. *Nankár* Allowance of Khurdhá Rájá,	2,480	0	0
7. Maintenance Allowance of Famine Orphans,	745	17	0
8. *Abkári*,	267	2	0
9. Stamps,	2	17	6
10. Salt,	509	16	5
11. Census,	48	19	4
12. Customs,	25	11	11
13. Marine,	60	0	0
14. Income Tax,	394	18	3
14. Post Office,	410	16	0
16. Money Order,	0	6	2
17. Jails,	615	4	3
18. Criminal Court,	353	18	9
19. Registration,	215	4	6
20. Education,	1,283	8	0
21. Dispensaries,	622	6	5
22. Civil Court,	550	1	7
23. Police,	6,171	7	4
24. Compensation for Lands,	206	11	0
25. Pensions,	462	4	0
26. Remittance of Treasure,	61	9	0
27. Travelling of Ministerial and Gazetted Officers,	326	12	0
28. Miscellaneous,	155	6	0
Total,	£22,538	19	4

THE LAND TAX amounted to £44,707 in 1829-30; to £45,973 in 1850-51; and to £47,963 in 1870-71. The subdivision of landed property has rapidly gone on under our rule. In 1828 there were only 194 separate estates, with 670 registered proprietors or co-parceners. In 1850 the number had risen to 272 estates, with 910 registered proprietors. In 1870 the separate estates amounted to 432, and the proprietors to 1191. The effects of this subdivision are visible in the average payments of each proprietor or coparcener. In 1828 the average of the large class of small proprietors who pay below £10 a year of Government rental was £3, 9s. 6d.; in 1850 it had fallen to £2, 12s. 6d.; and in 1870 still further to £1, 10s. 6d. In the next class of proprietors, who pay a yearly rental of between £10 and £100, the average payment of each proprietor in 1828 was £14, 4s.; in 1870 it was £10, 8s. In the large estates paying over £100 a year of Government rental, the average payment of each proprietor was £465 in 1828, and £369 in 1870. Taking the landholding body as a whole, each estate paid on an average £230 of Government rental in 1828, and £111 in 1870. Each proprietor or registered coparcener paid on an average £67 in 1828, and only £40, 5s. od in 1870. The average size of estates has, therefore, diminished by one-half during the last forty years of British rule in Purí.

THE AMOUNT OF PROTECTION given to property and person has greatly increased. In 1828-29 there were only three Courts, revenue and judicial, in the District; in 1850 there were seven; in 1862, nine; and in 1870-71, thirteen. In 1828-29 there was only one covenanted officer in the District. There are now generally three, —namely, (1) a Magistrate and Collector at Purí; (2) a Joint or Assistant-Magistrate and Deputy-Collector, also stationed at Purí; (3) an Assistant-Magistrate and Deputy-Collector in charge of the Subdivision of Khurdhá.

POLICE STATISTICS : THE REGULAR POLICE FORCE consisted at the end of 1872 of the following strengh :—1 European officer or District Superintendent on a salary of Rs. 600 a month or £720 a year; 4 subordinate officers on a salary of upwards of Rs. 100 a month or £120 a year, and 78 officers on less than Rs. 100 a month or £120 a year, maintained at a total cost of Rs. 2130 a month or £2556 a year, equal to an average pay of Rs. 25. 15. 7 a month or £31, 3s. 4d. a year for each subordinate officer; and 345 foot police constables, maintained at a total cost of Rs. 2243 a month or £2691, 12s. od. a year, equal to an average pay of Rs. 6. 8. 0 a month or £7, 16s. 0d. a year for each man. The other expenses connected with the regular police in 1872 were—an average of Rs. 75 a month or £90 a year as travelling expenses for the District Superintendent; Rs. 171. 13. 4 a month or £206, 4s. 0d. a year as pay and travelling allowances for his office establishment; and an average of Rs. 495. 5. 4 a month or £594, 8s. 0d. a year for contingencies and all other expenses. The total cost of the regular police in Puri District in 1872 amounted to Rs. 5718. 14. 8 a month, or £6862, 14s. 0d. for the year; total strength of the force, 428 men of all ranks. The present area of Puri District is 2472 square miles; and the total population, as ascertained by the Census of 1872, is 769,674. According to these figures, there is one policeman to every 5·77 square miles of the District area, and one to every 1798 of the population. The annual cost of the maintenance of the force is equal to Rs. 27. 12. 2 per square mile of the District area, or to 1 *ánná* 6 *pie* or 2¼d. per head of the population.

THE MUNICIPAL POLICE is a small force for the protection of Puri town, which at the end of 1872 consisted of 3 native officers and 80 men, maintained at a total cost of Rs. 471. 12. 0 a month, or £566, 2s. 0d. a year; defrayed by means of rates levied on the householders and shopkeepers carrying on business within municipal limits. The annual cost of the municipal police is equal to 4 *ánnás* or 6d. per head of the population protected by it, there being one policeman to every 273 inhabitants.

THE VILLAGE WATCH OR RURAL POLICE numbered 2527 men in 1872, maintained chiefly by grants of land which they hold rent free, but in some parts by a money allowance from the *zamíndárs*. The estimated total from both these sources in 1872 amounted to £3640, 6s. 0d. As compared with the area and population mentioned above, there is, therefore, one village watchman or *chaukídár* to every ·97 of a square mile of the District area, or one to every 302 of the population; maintained at an estimated cost in money or land of Rs. 14. 6. 5 or £1, 8s. 9½d. per square mile of area, or 9 *pies* or 1½d. per head of the population. Each village watchman has charge of 46 houses on an average, and receives an average pay in money or lands of Rs. 1. 3. 0 a month or £1, 8s. 6d. a year. The following paragraphs respecting the position, etc. of this class of officials, is quoted from a Report on the Land Tenures of the District by Bábu Nandakisor Das :—

'The village watchmen formed a part of the official organization under the Hindu kings of Orissa. They were called *dandwási* or *chhatiás*, and were, like all other officials, supported by assignménts of lands in *jágír*. They were scattered throughout the cultivated plains (known as the Mughulbandí), and were to be found in every village or group of small villages. In the Rajwárá tract, *i.e.* the tableland on the west and the marshes in the east, the watchmen were called *páiks*, who, like their brethren of the plains, were supported by grants of land. No change of any importance seems to have taken place in the position, emoluments, or status of these men during either the Mughul or the Marhattá rule; and the system remained in force till the acquisition of the Province by the British Government. In 1805 a Regulation (No. xiii.) was passed to regulate the police administration of Orissa. It was drawn up on the assumption that police duties were performed by *páiks* and *khandáits*, under the direction and superintendence of *zamíndárs;* and that there was another class of officers, called *dosádh* or village watchmen, who were the private servants of the *zamíndárs*. The *jágírs* of the former were protected from resumption, but the protective clause was not to extend to the latter. How this anomaly came to be introduced has never been satisfactorily explained. The village watchmen have long since thrown off their titles of *páiks* or *dandwásís*, and have assumed the generic term of *chaukídár* or *chaukid*, though in the interior they are still called *dandwásís* and *chhatiás*. There are in this District a superior class of watchmen called *khandáits*. The *chaukídárs* are of the lowest class, Páns and Kandárás, while the *khandáits* are of the Rájput or Khandáit class. The *khandáits* hold larger *jágírs* than the *chaukídárs*, on the understanding that they are to supervise the work of the latter. Both *chaukídárs* and *khandáits* are generally remunerated in land. There are now altogether 2651 *chaukídárs* and 81 *khandáits* in Purí District.

'The *chaukídárs* and *khandáits* receive 6037. 9. o¼ and 1200. 23. 1½ *máns* of land respectively, besides Rs. 1407. 12. 4½ allowance in money, for which deductions are made from the Government land revenue. From each cultivator the *chaukídárs* receive two sheaves of paddy per *mán*, in every part of the District except in Khurdhá and] Pánchgarh, where they are paid by the cultivators in cash. The Khurdhá *rayats* pay Rs. 1379. 7. 6; those of Pánchgarh pay Rs. 142. 6. 6.

'The duties of a *chaukídár* are—(1) To give immediate information to the police of every unnatural, sudden, or suspicious death, and of the offences specified in section 90, Act x. of 1872, within the limits of his jurisdiction, and of all disputes which may lead to riot or serious affray. (2) To arrest all proclaimed offenders and persons guilty of the commission of cognisable offences. (3) To report to the police about the movements of bad characters, and of the arrival of suspicious characters. (4) To present himself periodically at the police station. (5) To supply such information as the Magistrate may require.'

Including the regular District police, the municipal police, and the village watch, the machinery for protecting person and property in Purí District consisted, at the end of 1872, of a total force of 3038 officers and men, equal to one man to every ·81 of a square mile of the District area, or one man to every 253 of the District population. The estimated aggregate cost of maintaining this force, both Government and municipal, and including the value of the rent-free lands held by the *chaukídárs*, amounted in 1872 to Rs. 9224. 4. 0 a month, or a total for the year of £11,069, 2s. 0d.; equal to a charge of Rs. 44. 12. 1 or £4, 9s. 6d. per square mile of the District area, or 2¼ *ánnás* or 3⅜d. per head of the population.

CRIMINAL STATISTICS. — During the year 1872, 966 'cognisable' cases were reported to the police, of which 157 were discovered to be false, and 3 were not inquired into. Convictions were obtained in 354 cases, or 43·92 per cent. of the true cases; in which 1031 persons were tried, of whom 599 or 58 per cent. were convicted. Of 'non-cognisable' cases, 1144 were instituted, in which process issued against 1598 persons, of whom 1002 actually appeared before the Court; of these, 504 or 52·60 per cent. were acquitted, and 475 or 47·40 per cent. were convicted, leaving 23 under trial at the close of the year.

The following details, showing the number of reported cases, with the number of persons tried and convicted for different crimes and offences in 1872, are taken from the Report of the Inspector-General of Police for that year. The cognisable cases were as follow :— Class I. Offences against the State, public tranquillity, safety, and justice—Offences relating to coin, stamps, and Government notes, 3 cases reported, 7 persons tried, and 5 convicted; other offences against public justice, 3 cases, 2 persons tried, and both convicted; rioting or unlawful assembly, 35 cases, 105 persons tried, and 65 convicted; personating public servant or soldier, 1 case, 2 persons tried, and 1 convicted. Class II. Serious offences against the person—Murder, 9 cases, 26 persons tried, and 1 convicted; culpable homicide, 6 cases, 15 persons tried, and 5 convicted; rape, 3 cases, 2 persons tried, and 1 convicted; unnatural offence, 1 case, 2 persons tried and convicted; exposure of infants or concealment of birth, 2 cases, 2 persons tried and convicted; attempt at or abetment of suicide, 11 cases, 6 persons tried, and 3 convicted; grievous hurt, 3 cases, 7 persons tried, and 4 convicted; causing hurt for the purpose of extorting property or confession, 1 case, 2 persons tried and convicted; causing hurt by dangerous weapon, 4 cases, 2 persons tried, and 1 convicted; kidnapping or abduction, 2 cases, 3 persons tried, but none convicted; wrongful confinement and restraint in secret, or for purposes of extortion, 1 case, no arrest; criminal force to public servant or woman, or in attempt to commit theft or wrongfully confine, 1 case, 1 person tried, not convicted. Class III. Serious offences against person and property, or against property only—Robbery, 2 cases, no arrest; serious mischief and cognate offences, 18 cases, 13 persons tried, and 2 convicted; lurking house-trespass and housebreaking with intent to commit an offence, or having made preparation for hurt, 106 cases, 67 persons tried, and 40 convicted. Class IV. Minor offences against the person—Wrongful restraint and confinement, 13 cases, 19 persons tried, and 15 convicted; house-trespass with a view to commit an offence or having made preparation for hurt, 2 cases, 2 persons tried, 1 convicted. Class V. Minor offences against property—Lurking house-trespass or housebreaking, 2 cases, 2 persons tried, none convicted; cattle theft, 6 cases, 11 persons tried, and 8 convicted; ordinary theft, 269 cases, 186 persons tried, and 107 convicted; criminal breach of trust, 22 cases, 18 persons tried, and 4 convicted; receiving stolen property, 19 cases, 44 persons tried, and 25 convicted; criminal or house-trespass, 148 cases, 198 persons tried, and 53 convicted; breaking closed receptacle, 1 case, no arrest. Class VI. Other offences not specified above—Vagrancy and bad character, 1 case, 2 persons tried, and 1 convicted; offences against the excise laws, 13 cases, 16 persons tried, and 13 convicted; offences against the salt and customs laws, 35 cases, 50 persons tried, and 41 convicted; public and local nuisances, 224 cases, 219 persons tried, and 195 convicted. The total number of persons actually tried in 'cognisable' cases was 1031, of whom 599 or 58·09 per cent. were convicted, either summarily by the Magistrate, or at the Sessions Court.

The number of cases instituted, and of persons tried and convicted, in 'non-cognisable' cases during 1872 is returned as follows : —Class I. Offences against the State, public tranquillity and justice —Offences against public justice, 44 cases, 62 persons tried, and 46 convicted ; offences by public servants, 2 cases, 2 persons tried, and both convicted ; false evidence, false complaints and claims, 15 cases, 19 persons tried, and 10 convicted ; offences relating to weighing and measuring, 13 cases, 28 persons tried, and 26 convicted ; rioting, unlawful assembly, and affray, 7 cases, 47 persons tried, and 39 convicted. Class II. Serious offences against the person—Causing miscarriage, 3 cases, 9 persons tried, and 4 convicted.   Class III. Serious offences against property—Extortion, 4 cases, 4 persons tried, and all convicted. Class IV. Minor offences against the person—Hurt, 16 cases, 24 persons tried, and 19 convicted ; using criminal force, 716 cases, 456 persons tried, and 162 convicted.   Class V. Minor offences against property—Cheating, 13 cases, 14 persons tried, and 6 convicted ; criminal misappropriation of property, 10 cases, 35 persons tried, and 14 convicted ; simple mischief, 104 cases, 64 persons tried, and 16 convicted.   Class VI. Other offences not specified above—Offences relating to marriage, 6 cases, 13 persons tried, none convicted ; defamation, 9 cases, 9 persons tried, and 1 convicted ; intimidation and insult, 5 cases, 14 persons tried, none convicted ; public and local nuisances, 20 cases, 22 persons tried, and 17 convicted ; offences under chapters xviii., xx., xxi., and xxii. of the Criminal Procedure Code, 14 cases, 34 persons tried, and 21 convicted ; offences under the Cattle Trespass Act, 56 cases, 50 persons tried, and 13 convicted ; offences under the Post Office Act, 3 cases, 3 persons tried, and 2 convicted ; offences under the Recruiters' Act, 1 case, 2 persons tried, and both convicted ; offences under the Registration Act, 1 case, 3 persons tried, and all convicted ; offences under the Police Act, 1 case, 1 person tried and convicted ; offences under the Puri Lodging-house Act, 55 cases, 56 persons tried, and 38 convicted ; offences under section 163, chap. x. of the Criminal Procedure Code, 6 cases, 6 persons tried, and 6 convicted ; offences under sections 219 and 220, chap. xii. of the Criminal Procedure Code, 7 cases, 12 persons tried, and 10 convicted ; offences under section 270, chap. xv. of the Criminal Procedure Code, 13 cases, 13 persons tried, and all convicted.   The total number of persons actually tried in 'non-cognisable' cases was 1002, of whom 475 or 47·40 per cent. were convicted.

Excluding 157 cases declared to be false by the Magistrate, and 3 not taken up by the police, the total number of 'cognisable' and 'non-cognisable' cases investigated in Purí District in 1872 was 1950; in which 2033 persons were tried, of whom 1074 were convicted, either summarily by the Magistrate or at the Sessions Court; proportion of persons convicted to persons tried, 52·82 per cent., or one person convicted of an offence of some kind or other to every 716 of the District population.

CRIMINAL CLASSES.—Strictly speaking, there are no criminal classes in Purí District,—that is to say, no classes who live by preying on society. Petty thefts, the result of extreme poverty—often, indeed, of the pangs of hunger—form the most common offence. Murders occur very seldom, and are nearly always traced to some complication about women or land. The Bráhmans supply a large proportion of the criminals. But here, as elsewhere, it is the miserably poor and hungry landless castes who fill the jails.

JAIL STATISTICS.—There are two jails in Purí, viz. the District jail at the Civil Station, and a Subdivisional lock-up at Khurdhá. The figures in the following paragraphs, showing the jail population of Purí District for the years 1857-58, 1860-61, and 1870, are compiled from a return specially prepared for me by the Inspector-General of Jails. The figures for 1872 have been taken from the Annual Jail Report for that year. The figures for the two first-named years must be regarded with caution, and taken as only approximately correct. Owing to defects in the original returns, which cannot now be remedied, in some cases prisoners are returned twice over; prisoners transferred to the central jail from the lock-up being returned in both statements without allowance being made for the transfers. Under-trial prisoners at the commencement of the year, who were subsequently convicted, also appear twice, having been returned under both heads. No means now exist of eliminating these discrepancies. Since 1870, an improved form of preparing the returns has been introduced, and the statistics for that year and for 1872 may be accepted as correct.

In 1857-58, the earliest year for which materials are available, the daily average number of prisoners in the Purí jail and Subdivisional lock-up was 86, the total number of civil, criminal, and under-trial prisoners admitted during the year being 439. The discharges were as follow:—Transferred, 25; released, 422; escaped, 1; died, 7: total, 455. In 1860-61 the jail returns show a daily average of 59 prisoners, the total admissions of prisoners of all classes during the year being 258. The discharges were—Transferred, 74; released, 249; escaped, 2; died, 3: total, 328. In 1870 the daily average jail population was 113, the total number of prisoners admitted during the year being 392. The discharges were as follow:—Transferred, 24; released, 388; escaped, 6; died, 4: total, 422. In 1872 the daily average number of prisoners was as follows:—Civil, 0·96; under-trial, 6·27; labouring convicts, 83·26; non-labouring convicts, 1·74: total, 92·23, of whom 4·57 were women. The average daily jail population in 1872 was equal to one male prisoner to every 4442 of the male population, and one female prisoner to every 83,200 of the female population.

In 1857-58 the proportion of prisoners admitted into hospital amounted to 427·17 per cent., and the deaths to 8·13 per cent. of the average jail population; in 1860-61 the admissions into hospital amounted to 332·20 per cent., and the deaths to 5·08 per cent. of the average prison population; in 1870 the admissions into hospital amounted to 112·30 per cent., and the deaths to 3·53 per cent. of the average prison population. In 1872 the death-rate of the Purí jail was 6·52 per cent. of the daily average population, or 1·18 per cent. higher than the death-rate throughout the Bengal jails generally. The Inspector-General of Jails, in his Report for 1872, makes the following remarks regarding the health of the prison:—'It appears from the quinquennial tables that this jail varies very much in point of health, and in three years out of fifteen there were no deaths at all. This year (1872) four deaths out of a total of six arose from bowel complaints, which is perhaps accounted for by the excessive rainfall. The jail grounds were completely swamped at the end of June, and again in October.'

The average cost of maintenance per prisoner in the Purí jail and lock-up, including rations, establishment, hospital charges, contingencies, and all other expenses except the prison police guard, is returned as follows:—In 1857-58 it amounted to Rs. 43. 5. 0 or £4, 6s. 7½d. per prisoner; in 1860-61 to Rs. 37. 4. 1 or £3, 14s. 6½d.; and in 1870 to Rs. 46. 0. 8 or £4, 12s. 1d. per prisoner. The cost of the jail police guard in 1870 amounted to an average of Rs. 16. 8. 6 or £1, 13s. 0¾d., making a gross charge to Government in that year of Rs. 62. 9. 2 or £6, 5s. 1¾d. per prisoner. The Inspector-General of Jails, in his Report for 1872, returns the total cost of the Purí jail and lock-up, including police guard, at £755, os. 9d. Deducting the cost of the prison guard, which is included in the general police budget of the District, the cost of the jail in 1872 amounted to £522, 12s. 5d. Average cost per prisoner in 1872, including prison guard, Rs. 82. 13. 1 or £8, 5s. 7½d.; excluding prison guard, Rs. 59 or £5, 18s. od.

Jail industries have been carried on in Purí for upwards of thirty years. In 1857-58 the receipts arising from the sale of jail manufactures, together with the value of the stock remaining on hand at the end of the year, amounted to £80, 1s. 6¼d., and the charges to £25, 5s. 9½d., showing an excess of receipts over charges, or a profit, of £54, 15s. 8¾d.; average earnings by each prisoner employed in manufactures, Rs. 17. 15. 3 or £1, 15s. 10¾d. In 1860-61 the receipts amounted to £89, 5s. 0¾d., and the charges to £23, 11s. 0½d., leaving a profit of £65, 14s. 0¼d.; average earnings by each prisoner employed in manufacture, Rs. 10. 8. 0 or £1, 1s. od. In 1870 the total credits arising from jail manufactures amounted to £326, 8s. 2d., and the total debits to £285, 16s. 5¼d., leaving an excess of receipts over charges, or a profit, of £40, 11s. 8¾d.; average earnings by each prisoner engaged in manufactures, Rs. 7. 15. 3 or 15s. 10¾d. In 1872 the credits arising from prison industries amounted to £425, 16s. 2d., and the debits to £381, 4s. 5d., leaving a profit of £44, 11s. 9d. Excluding the prisoners employed on jail duties as servants, warders, etc., and the sick and aged, the average daily number of prisoners employed in manufactures in Purí jail in 1872 amounted to 48·05, divided as follows:—Gunny weaving, ·63; gardening, 19·10; cloth weaving, 5·53; brick-making, etc. ·73; bamboo and rattan work, 1·84; oil-pressing, 4·75; string-making, 6·56; flour-grinding, 3·72; bag-sewing, ·09; paper-making, 2·73; baking, ·73; yarn and thread-spinning, ·01; miscellaneous, 1·63.

EDUCATIONAL STATISTICS.—Purí District is more backward in the matter of education than either Cuttack or Balasor, and it is only within the last few years that any progress has been made at all. The following comparative table (pp. 167, 168), compiled from the Annual Reports of the Director of Public Instruction, exhibits the number of Government and aided schools in Purí District for each of the years 1856-57, 1860-61, and 1870-71; together with the number, religion, etc. of the pupils attending them, cost of education to Government, also the amount defrayed by fees or from private sources. During the fifteen years covered by the table, the number
[*Sentence continued on page* 168.

RETURN OF GOVERNMENT AND AIDED SCHOOLS IN PURI DISTRICT FOR THE YEARS 1856-57, 1860-61, AND 1870-71.

CLASSIFICATION OF SCHOOLS.	NUMBER OF SCHOOLS.			NUMBER OF PUPILS.											
				Hindus.			Muhammadans.			Others.			Total.		
	1856-57.	1860-61.	1870-71.	1856-57.	1860-61.	1870-71.	1856-57.	1860-61.	1870-71.	1856-57.	1860-61.	1870-71.	1856-57.	1860-61.	1870-71.
Government English School, ...	1	1	1	88	100	103	1	1	2	...	...	...	89	101	105
Government Vernacular Schools, . . .	...	6	21	...	195	510	...	14	16	...	3	...	...	212	526
Aided English Schools,	...	...	2	...	...	27	...	...	3	...	...	28	...	...	58
Aided Vernacular Schools, . . .	...	4	65	...	109	685	...	3	39	...	...	665	...	112	1389
Aided Girls' School, .	...	...	1	...	...	...	...	...	...	...	...	189	...	...	189
Total, ...	1	11	90	88	404	1325	1	18	60	...	3	882	89	425	2267

RETURN OF GOVERNMENT AND AIDED SCHOOLS IN PURI DISTRICT FOR THE YEARS 1856-57, 1860-61, AND 1870-71—*continued.*

CLASSIFICATION OF SCHOOLS.	RECEIPTS.						EXPENDITURE.		
	From Government.			Fees, Subscriptions, and Donations.					
	1856-57.	1860-61.	1870-71.	1856-57.	1860-61.	1870-71.	1856-57.	1860-61.	1870-71.
	£ s. d.	£ s. d.	£ s. d.	£ s. d.	£ s. d.	£ s. d.	£ s. d.	£ s. d.	£ s. d.
Government English School,	301 1 9	252 17 10	361 11 8	37 10 5	56 6 5	147 1 6	340 3 9	309 4 2	508 13 2
Government Vernacular Schools,	...	111 4 0	360 9 4	...	8 9 0	7 3 0	...	119 13 9	367 13 2
Aided English Schools,	...	...	63 12 0	...	...	96 12 3	...	...	154 12 0
Aided Vernacular Schools,	...	47 6 0	390 10 0	...	54 12 10	313 16 2	...	98 13 9	704 15 3
Aided Girls' School,	...	...	72 0 0	...	...	77 4 0	...	...	149 4 0
Total,	301 1 9	411 7 10	1248 3 0	37 10 5	119 8 3	641 16 11	340 3 9	527 11 8	1558 9 7

Sentence continued from page 165.]

of Government and aided schools increased from 1 in 1856-57 to 90 in 1870-71; and the number of pupils from 89 to 2267 in the same period. The Government grant in aid rose from £301, 1s. 9d. in 1856-57 to £1248, 3s. 0d. in 1870-71; while the amount realized by fees or from private subscriptions increased from £37, 10s. 5d. in 1856-57 to £641, 16s. 11d. in 1870-71. No private schools are returned in the table.

EDUCATIONAL STATISTICS FOR 1872-73.—The scheme for the extension of the grant-in-aid rules to hitherto unaided schools came into operation on the 30th September 1872. Numbers of masters of indigenous village schools applied to be admitted to the benefits of the grant; and the result was, that in six months from the time the reform was introduced, the number of schools brought under the inspection of the Educational Department had increased to 112, attended by 2802 pupils. Notwithstanding the increase in the number of schools, the cost to Government for education in 1872-73 had decreased to £886, 14s. 0d., and the total expenditure to £1446, 18s. 0d. By the 31st March 1875, the number of schools had further increased to 182, and the pupils to 4155. These figures give one school to every 13·6 square miles of the District area, and 4·2 pupils to every thousand of the population. The table on the opposite page, compiled from the Educational Report for 1872-73, exhibits the educational statistics of that year, at the end of which the extended scheme had come fully into operation.

The following paragraphs regarding the various classes of schools in Purí District are quoted from the Report of the Educational Department for 1872-73 :—

'ZILA OR DISTRICT SCHOOL.—This school at the end of the year contained 114 pupils, against 112 at the commencement. Its income from fees and fines was £144, 16s. 0d. in 1872-73, against £148, 4s. 0d. in 1871-72. The decrease is said to be owing to the prevalence of fever last year. The school-house has now been quite completed for school purposes, and is a commodious building. Gymnastics have not yet been introduced into the school. The head-master has undertaken the surveying classes, and has discharged his duty well. Last October three pupils went up for the University matriculation, and two passed. Of the pupils frequenting the school, 37 are Bengalís, 69 Uriyás, 3 Muhammadans, and 5 " others."

EDUCATIONAL STATISTICS OF PURI DISTRICT FOR 1872-73.

Classification of Schools.	Number of Schools.	Number of Pupils.	Receipts.				Expenditure.
			Government Grant. £ s. d.	School Fees. £ s. d.	Subscriptions, etc. £ s. d.	Total. £ s. d.	£ s. d.
Government Higher School,	1	114	219 8 0	144 16 0	...	364 4 0	364 4 0
Aided Middle English School,	1	28	38 4 0	6 18 0	16 10 0	61 12 0	60 0 0
Government Middle Vernacular Schools,	8	196	196 14 0	8 0 0	5 8 0	210 2 0	208 2 0
Government Lower Vernacular Schools,	2	38	12 0 0	1 10 0	4 16 0	18 6 0	78 6 0
Aided Middle Vernacular Schools,	4	120	57 0 0	12 6 0	56 6 0	125 12 0	125 8 0
Unaided Middle Sanskrit School,	1	45	...	...	65 10 0	65 10 0	65 10 0
Aided Lower Vernacular Schools,	3	266	126 0 0	...	135 16 0	261 16 0	261 16 0
Aided Primary Schools,	86	1832	167 16 0	10 6 0	34 8 0	212 10 0	212 12 0
Aided Girls' Schools,	6	163	69 12 0	...	1 8 0	71 0 0	71 0 0
Total,	112	2802	886 14 0	183 16 0	320 2 0	1390 12 0	1446 18 0

'MIDDLE-CLASS SCHOOLS.—During the past year, these schools have been doing somewhat better than in previous years. The only middle-class English school is that at Khurdhá. The pupils are few, but they are well taught. The attendance at the end of the year was 28. The cost of each pupil was £2, 2s. od., of which the State paid £1, 6s. od. The finances of the school are reported to be in a low condition. One pupil from this school did exceedingly well in the minor scholarship examination last October. The building recently erected is a large bungalow, within which the English school, the model vernacular school, and the primary school sit.

'There are thirteen middle-class vernacular schools in the District; of these, 8 are Government schools, 4 aided, and 1 unaided. They are attended by 524 pupils, of whom only 24 are Muhammadans. They cost £470. The average cost of each pupil is about 18s., of which the State paid about 12s. The income from fees in these schools is a little over £20. Of the four schools of this class I have been able to visit, the Khurdhá school is far the best. Although there are other schools in the District in which Sanskrit is taught, the Deputy-Inspector has only furnished returns of the Sanskrit school of the Mahárájá of Balrámpur, known as the Purí Sanskrit school. The Mahárájá endowed the school with £550, invested in Government securities. A schoolroom was erected in 1870; 45 pupils, chiefly Bráhmans, receive instruction in the school, and also free maintenance. It is said that this school was the first attempt made to educate the Purí Bráhmans, and before its establishment there was not a Bráhman in the English school.

'LOWER-CLASS SCHOOLS.—Of these there are three, managed by the missionaries of Pipplí, frequented by 110 boys and 156 girls; and two lower-class schools, supported by Government, attended by 38 pupils only, at Padampur and Aláidihí. The missionary institutions appear to be far the most efficient and important of the kind in Purí. The schools belong to the Orphanage, attached to which is an English school, in which the pupils showed remarkable intelligence. There are also two vernacular schools for boys, one vernacular school for girls, a school of industry, and one English class for girls. The cost of each pupil is 19s., of which the State pays about 8s. Of the pupils attending these schools, 255 are Christians.

'PRIMARY AND GIRLS' SCHOOLS.—Village schools and primary *páthsálás* are numerous, but the people appear jealous of Government interference. They cry out for money, but will not allow the slightest interference in their method of spending it. Of female education little can be said. The orphan girls at the missionary school at Pipplí receive an excellent training ; and as soon as they are old enough, they are married to Christian cultivators at the Missionary Settlements.'

POSTAL STATISTICS.—The following table, showing the number of letters, newspapers, etc. received at and despatched from the Purí Post Offices in each of the years 1861-62, 1865-66, and 1870-71, together with the postal receipts and expenditure for the same years, is compiled from a return furnished to me by the Director-General of Post Offices :—

POSTAL STATISTICS OF PURI DISTRICT FOR THE YEARS
1861-62, 1865-66, AND 1870-71.

	1861-62.		1865-66.		1870-71.	
	Received.	De-spatched.	Received.	De-spatched.	Received.*	De-spatched.
Letters, ...	43,309	29,718	46,051	37,254	48,666	*Materials*
Newspapers, . .	2,479	281	3,022	140	3,644	*not received*
Parcels, ...	1,098	161	705	288	270	*for this*
Books, ...	234	19	251	22	986	*column.*
Total, . . .	47,120	30,179	50,029	37,704	53,566	...
	£ s. d.		£ s. d.		£ s. d.	
Sale of Postage Stamps, . . .	Returns not forthcoming.		88 1 2¼		138 5 0¼	
Cash Collections, .	100 6 9		109 17 5¼		187 10 0	
Total Receipts, . .	100 6 9		197 18 7¾		325 15 0¼†	
Total Expenditure, .	253 3 9		232 0 0		419 2 0	

FISCAL DIVISIONS.—The number of villages or rural communes in Purí District in 1872 was ascertained to be 3175, containing on an average 242 inhabitants each. The number of Fiscal Divisions (*parganás*) has varied at different times. I have two statements of them, which present considerable discrepancies. The first is furnished by the Collector; the second by the Surveyor-General, and may be taken as the more correct. The first shows the number of estates in each *parganá*, the amount of Government land revenue, and the area in acres. The second exhibits each *parganá* divided according to its cultivated and non-cultivated area. I subjoin both

* The figures for this column represent the actuals for only six months, and an estimate for the remaining half of the year.

† Exclusive of £11, 1s. 0d. receipts for sale of stamps for official correspondence. Service stamps were first introduced in 1866.

lists, partly for the value of the different subjects they deal with, and partly to illustrate the discrepancies which such lists show in almost every District. The discrepancies arise from the circumstance that not only is the total area of a District always varying, owing to transfers to other Districts, but the boundaries of the *parganás* themselves are often badly defined. Sometimes, indeed, a *parganá* is so scattered and interspersed with fragments of others, that the Surveyors have had to lump them together, while the Collectorate returns continue as before. Such mistakes creep into the different departments of Government, and are aggravated as time goes on. Thus, I have received five different returns of the area of Purí District, varying from 2080 to 2698 square miles. The present area is, as already stated, 2472 square miles.

The following is the statement of *parganás* as made up in the Collectorate :—

	Number of Estates.	Land Revenue.	Area in Acres.
1. Andhári,	1	*Jágír*	7,959
2. Antrodh,	5	£82	1,873
3. Astrang,	1	151	5,477
4. Atháis,	13	838	33,605
5. Bájrakot,	1	*Jágír*	11,838
6. Bánchás,	36	813	15,922
7. Chaubiskud,	14	2,428	54,658
8. Domárkhand,	16	615	15,869
9. Kálijorí,	4	27	434
10. Kanmán,	2	185	4,699
11. Khurdhá,	1	15,308	595,526
12. Kodhár,	3	434	15,852
13. Kotdes,	30	8,618	129,998
14. Kot Ráháng,	66	2,883	29,445
15. Kurúlo,	8	248	9,602
16. Lembái,	7	3,449	58,854
17. Málud,	1	*Jágír*	10,794
18. Mánikpatná,	1	...	13,563
19. Márichpur,	1	332	33,983
20. Masrud,	2	64	1,739
21. Mátkadpatná,	4	107	6,367
22. Oldhár,	17	523	21,306
23. Pánchgarh,	1	1,547	22,135
24. Párikud Kílá,	1	*Jágír*	44,764
25. Paschim-duái,	94	1,246	12,378
26. Púrbáduái,	43	713	14,340
27. Ráháng,	22	3,006	71,559
28. Sayyidábád,	18	482	12,248
29. Sirái,	9	2,378	43,634
30. Sultánnagar,	3	159	3,178
31. Chilká Lake,	...	...	220,000
Total,	425	£46,636	1,523,599

The Surveyor-General's Return is as follows :—

	Total Area in Square Miles.	Acres.	Cultivated.	Waste.
1. Andhári, ...	12·43	7,959	2,810	5,149
2. Antrodh, ...	53·01	33,926	26,352	7,574
3. Astrang, ...	8·74	5,594	2,728	2,866
4. Atháis, ...	52·01	33,288	11,975	21,313
5. Bájrakot, ...	18·50	11,838	3,520	8,318
6. Bánchás, ...	30·20	19,328	14,294	5,034
7. Chaubiskud, ...	105·46	67,498	20,341	47,157
8. Domárkhand, ...	29·33	18,766	12,356	6,410
9. Kanmán, ...	6·58	4,207	2,024	2,183
10. Khurdhá, ...	929·92	595,150	137,585	457,565
11. Kodhár, ...	27·19	17,404	11,663	5,741
12. Kotdes, ...	181·55	116,194	86,020	30,174
13. Kot Ráháng, ...	55·83	35,728	17,913	17,815
14. Kurúlo, ...	20·01	12,804	7,033	5,771
15. Lembái, ...	89·97	57,579	30,807	26,772
16. Málud, ...	16·86	10,794	2,880	7,914
17. Mánikpatná, ...	21·19	13,563	3,014	10,549
18. Márichpur, ...	53·10	33,983	7,040	26,943
19. Mátkadpatná, ...	10·80	6,914	2,202	4,712
20. Oldhár, ...	41·14	26,330	1,875	24,455
21. Pánchgarh, ...	42·57	27,312	14,424	12,888
22. Párikud, ...	69·94	44,764	18,560	26,204
23. Paschim-duái, ...	25·92	16,588	5,612	10,976
24. Púrbáduái, ...	32·50	20,801	4,283	16,518
25. Ráháng, ...	149·49	95,678	67,480	28,198
26. Sátpárá, ...	8·14	5,211	5,000	211
27. Siráí, ...	67·67	43,307	23,355	19,952
28. Chilká Lake, ...	344·43	220,436	...	...
Total, .	2504·48	1,602,944	543,146	839,362

TEMPERATURE, RAINFALL, ETC.—The average temperature of Purí District, as returned to me by the Civil Surgeon, is 87·3°. The average annual rainfall, as ascertained by a series of observations extending over a period of fifteen years, is 55·55 inches, distributed as follows, according to season :—January to May, 5·88 inches ; June to September, 39·45 inches; October to December, 10·22 inches. The rainfall registered at Purí town in each month of 1873 was as follows :—January and February, *nil ;* March, 1·11 inches ; April, 0·85 inch ; May, 4·19 inches ; June, 2·58 inches ; July, 8·51 inches ; August, 15·81 inches ; September, 9·21 inches ; October, 12·53 inches ; November, 1·19 inches ; and December, 1·74 inches : total, 57·72 inches, or 2·17 in excess of the annual average. At Khurdhá, in the west of the District, the rainfall was as follows :—

January, 0·08 inch; February, *nil;* March, 0·54 inch; April, 0·42 inch; May, 2·39 inches; June, 4·52 inches; July, 13·82 inches; August, 13·75 inches; September, 10·01 inches; October, 3·51 inches; November, 0·41 inch; December, 0·59 inch: total, 50·04 inches.

DISEASES: ENDEMICS.—The prevailing diseases of Puri District are malarial fever in all its varieties; elephantiasis, chiefly of the lower extremities and scrotum; dysentery; and cholera. Fevers, quotidian, tertian, and quartan, are common throughout the whole District; nor, indeed, can it be otherwise, when the mode of life among the people is considered. Many villages stand in the midst of marshes. Square miles of land lie under water during the rains, and the floods sometimes swamp the whole District. The drinking water, especially in the hot season, is charged with organic impurities, and holds in suspension a large quantity of insoluble sediment. The bathing water is generally a fœtid tank. The meagre diet of the people does not enable them to resist the malaria which they breathe. Fatty food is wholly wanting; oil is very sparingly used; and the Civil Surgeon reports that salt is not consumed in sufficient quantities for the requirements of the human frame. Enlargements of the spleen and malarial cachexia follow such fevers; and the withered body, puffy face, and inability to support any strain, physical or mental, bear witness to the generally feeble tone of the inhabitants, and their powerlessness to throw off complaints. Elephantiasis is the most conspicuous endemic. It afflicts men and women alike, and does not spare even children. It is most prevalent in the town of Puri and its environs. In many cases it is associated with a continued fever of three days' duration, attended with inflammation of the lymphatics and the lymphatic glands of the affected extremity. So far as the Civil Surgeon has observed, there is no connection between the fever associated with elephantiasis and ordinary intermittent fever. The local affection often precedes the constitutional disturbance; and the recurrence of the fever is irregular, sometimes once and sometimes twice a month. After each attack, the extremity enlarges by gradual increments. Dysentery chiefly occurs at the beginning and at the end of the rains. It arises from exposure, from insufficient clothing, from bad food, from impure water, and from similar causes, operating on subjects predisposed by malarial dyscrasia.

EPIDEMICS.—Cholera may be added to the list of endemics, as

there is scarcely a month in which it is wholly wanting. Purí city is a hotbed of the disease. It only requires the annually recurring conditions of overcrowding, of filth, of great heat, of dampness, and sudden atmospheric changes, to turn the pilgrim city into a pest-house. But cholera is best considered as an epidemic occurring in February or March, and again in June or July, at the *Dol-Játrá* and the Car Festival. Sometimes it attacks all classes; but the destitute, ill-fed, ill-housed pilgrims generally supply the great proportion of the victims. The richer inhabitants suffer little. Its chief force is concentrated on the town, from whence, however, it often spreads into the District, especially in the villages along the pilgrim high road. It attains its maximum intensity at the Car Festival, rather than at the *Dol-Játrá*. In 1870, the mortality from cholera was ascertained to be 1089 from January to July. The reported cases, however, probably represent but a small proportion of the actual deaths. The only other epidemic of importance is small-pox, which generally makes its appearance in January, February, or March. It has not, however, committed any serious ravages since the famine year, 1866-67. The natives persist in resorting to inoculation, and the epidemic has several times been traced to that practice. They look on vaccination with suspicion, and sparingly adopt it. Until compulsory vaccination is introduced, or at any rate until inoculation is rendered a punishable offence, there is no hope of small-pox being stamped out of the District. Measles and a modified form of small-pox prevailed in Purí city in November and December 1868, but occasioned very little mortality. Epidemic fevers are unknown in the District.

CATTLE DISEASES.—Epizootics in two forms occurred in 1867-68. *Gutí*, or cattle small-pox, appears in its most formidable shape. *Phátud*, or hoof disease, is equally infectious, but less fatal. The first kills in a few days, and from 50 to 80 per cent. of the cattle attacked die. The rate of mortality sometimes rises to 90 per cent. *Phátud* is simply a chronic foot-rot, which wears out the animal by pain and exhaustion. It is often communicated to the mouth by licking, and renders mastication impossible. For further particulars, *vide* Statistical Account of Balasor (vol. xviii.).

FAIRS AND RELIGIOUS GATHERINGS are the great predisposing causes of epidemics. This subject has been fully treated of in my general work on Orissa. The Car Festival annually slays its thousands. It occurs at the most unfavourable and inclement season of the year. Before its close the rains are pretty well advanced, the roads are cut up, the rivers are full, the roadside lodging-houses are close and steamy; and often the sole shelter for travellers is under trees dripping with rain, and charged with malarious influences. The *Dol-Játrá*, in the spring-time, does less mischief. The Panchak Festival, in October or November, often ends in a sharp epidemic of cholera. The whole religious character of the District centres in Purí city, and the rural gatherings are unimportant. So far as can be ascertained, epidemics have never been traced to them.

Puri Pilgrim Hospital and Dispensary, established in 1836, is the principal medical charity of the District. In 1871 the total number of in-door patients receiving treatment at the dispensary amounted to 255, of whom 182 were relieved or recovered, 16 did not improve or ceased to attend, 40 died, and 17 remained in hospital at the close of the year; rate of deaths to patients treated, 15·68 per cent.; daily average number of sick, 14·75. The out-door patients in 1871 were 2583 in number, the average daily attendance being 32·44. In 1872, 308 in-door patients were admitted to the hospital, of whom 220 were cured, 12 did not improve, 69 died, and 7 remained in the hospital at the close of the year; ratio of deaths to patients treated, 22·40; daily average number of sick, 17·44. The out-door patients in 1872 numbered 2451, the average daily attendance being 34·64. Of the deaths in 1872, 23 were due to dysentery, 19 to diarrhœa, 9 to cholera, and 7 to dropsy. The large mortality is attributable to the impoverished and diseased class of patients, mostly pilgrims, resorting to the dispensary for relief. Purí dispensary is entirely maintained by Government, at an expense in 1872 of £233.

Khurdha Branch Dispensary was established in June 1864. In 1871, 129 in-door patients received treatment, of whom 100 were discharged cured, 12 did not improve or ceased to attend, 10 died, and 7 remained in hospital at the close of the year; ratio of deaths to patients treated, 7·75 per cent.; daily average number of sick, 6·07. The out-door patients numbered 1734, the average daily attendance being 20·95. In 1872 the in-door patients numbered 166, of whom 124 were cured or relieved, 10 did not improve, 25 died, and 7 remained in the hospital at the close of the year; ratio of deaths to patients treated, 15·06; average daily number of sick, 6·38. The out-door patients in 1872 numbered 1649, the daily average attendance being 21·91. Cholera prevailed in the Subdivision from April to August and dengue fever in November. Fevers were more than usually severe. The dispensary is maintained out of the funds of the Government estate, with the addition of a few small subscriptions from natives. In 1872 the total income amounted to £79, 8s. 0d., of which £78 was contributed by Government, and £1, 8s. 0d. from private sources.

VITAL STATISTICS.—From the 1st January 1873, a new system for the registration of vital statistics has been introduced. Certain limited areas were selected for the purpose, viz. the town of Purí, with a population of 22,695; and the rural tract of Joharsinh, in Khurdhá Subdivision, with a population of 10,329. The number of deaths within the town area in 1873 was 367, equal to a death-rate of 32·34 per thousand, or 3·92 per cent. above the average town mortality for Bengal generally. In the following year, 1874, a record of births as well as of deaths was effected. The total number of births thus recorded in Purí town in 1874 was 470, equal to a rate of 20·70 per thousand; the deaths numbered 532, equal to a rate of 23·44 per thousand, or 5·07 per cent. below the average town rate throughout Bengal. In the selected rural area of Joharsinh, the number of deaths in 1873 amounted to 126, or 24·38 per thousand, being 1·73 per cent. above the average rural death-rate throughout Bengal. In the following year 378 births and 311 deaths were registered. The death-rate was equal to 30·10 per thousand, or 8·90 per cent. above the rural average for Bengal generally in that year.

INDIGENOUS MEDICINES.—The following are the principal vegetable drugs in the District:—*Pítá-kro*, the bark of Wrightia anti-dysenterica; *indrajab*, seed of Wrightia anti-dysenterica; *bel*, fruit of Ægle Marmelos; *sunt*, the root of Zingiber officinale; *pánmahuri*, aniseed; *sonf*, Anethum; *muthá*, the tuber of Cyperus pertenuis; *bendcher*, the root of Andropogon muricatum; *dhaniyá*, Coriandrum sativum; *methí*, Fenugreek; *amblá*, Emblica officinalis; *báns-lochan*, Tabasheer; *khayer*, catechu; *dhuná*, resin; *kuchilá*, Nux vomica; *chindi-nái*, in Bengalí *ananta-múl*, Hemidesmus; *dálim*, pomegranate. Minerals are not so frequently used as vegetable drugs. *Raskarpur*, the mixed oxide, and *singráf*, the red oxide of mercury, are given in pills, and occasionally smoked in a tobacco pipe. Litharge is made up into an ointment. Gold is a great favourite in the pharmacopœia of the Uriyá practitioners as a stimulant, mixed with musk. The native system of treatment consists chiefly in administering specifics against bile, heat, and excessive humours.

THE KHURDHA SUBDIVISION.

SUBDIVISION OF KHURDHA.—For administrative purposes, the north-west part of Purí is placed under a separate officer, subject to the Collector of the District. The Subdivision is bounded on the south-east by the Chilká lake; on the east by the Dayá river, which, roughly speaking, separates it from Purí District; on the north-east and north by Cuttack District; on the north-west, west, and south-west by the Tributary States of Bánki, Khandpárá, Ranpur, South Gumsar, Athgarh, and Ganjám District in Madras. Khurdhá was the hereditary seat of the last of the Orissa dynasties; and the royal house retained much of its independence until its rebellion against the British Government in 1804. In 1818 Khurdhá became the headquarters of the English District, and continued so till about 1828. It is now under an Assistant-Magistrate. In 1836 it was described by Mr. Wilkinson as extending from within six miles of Cuttack to the pass of Chhatra-garh, seventy-six miles in length, by from five to twenty in breadth. Area in 1872, 943 square miles; population, 280,923 souls.

Along the Dayá river the country is flat and alluvial. But with this exception, Khurdhá is covered with long ranges rising to over 1000 feet high. They run an irregular course from north-east to south-west, breaking up the country into small valleys intersected by petty streams, and well cultivated. The villages are situated on the higher lands, and belted round with picturesque groves of trees. The hills have mostly been stripped of their wood, and bear nothing but a mean scrub jungle. But towards the south, where the ranges run down to the Chilká, they are covered with bamboo and dense jungle. The scenery in some parts, where the hills rise, range after range, towards Central India, is very beautiful.

The most conspicuous mountains in Khurdhá are the Solárí in Bánpur; the Bhelárí, on the south-west boundary; Baithá and Baruní, one mile to the south-west of Khurdhá town. None of them exceed 1800 feet. They are inaccessible to wheeled conveyances, and can with difficulty be ascended by cattle. Solárí is a group of peaks rising one above another from the flat land near the Chilká. The other three are saddle-backed mountains rising into bare, and often inaccessible, precipices. The natural caves in the Barluní and Solárí hills have been hermitages and places of pilgrimage from time immemorial. The Barluní has a few inscriptions. A splendid tank, the work of pre-historic builders, stands on the Solárí hill.

Khurdhá has no navigable rivers, and all are fordable except on occasions of flood. Fifty-five cases of drowning were brought to the notice of the police in 1869.

There are no towns in Khurdhá exclusively occupied by fishermen; though all round the shores of the Chilká, fishing forms the principal occupation, and it is estimated that on the west side of the lake some 5000 or 6000 persons live by it. A natural watershed crosses Khurdhá, and separates the Chilká from the Mahánadí valley. In the western part of the Subdivision the waters run into the Mahánadí by means of its tributary the Kusumí. The north of the Subdivision is drained by the Rann and other small streams. In the east and south, the waters find their way direct into the Chilká lake.

Good building materials abound. A very cellular laterite is easy to quarry, and hardens by exposure. A coarse kind of freestone, veined with spar, is also common; and in many places, lime underlies the laterite. There is a hot spring, the waters of which are impregnated with sulphur, at Garh Atír, in the middle of a highly cultivated valley, where a large fair is held in January, lasting for eight or ten days, and attended by merchants from all parts of the country. There is a small picturesque pass at Sinheswar, on the Ganjám road, and another at Kurárhmal, about five miles south of the Subdivisional town; but the destruction of the bamboos and large trees has greatly spoilt their beauty. The jungle still covers a large part of Khurdhá. Here and there small patches are brought under cultivation, and are assessed at from 5 to 6 *ánnás* or 7½d. to 9d. an acre. With this exception, no revenue is derived from the forests. The timber and bamboos are wastefully destroyed. Trees, such as *sál*, *piásál*, and *sisu*, would grow to a large size and prove of great value, were they not ignorantly cut down.

The wild animals and game found in the Subdivision are the same as those in Purí District. The deaths from snake-bite reported during the year 1869-70 amounted to thirty-three; from wild beasts, seven. Quantities of wild-beast skins are collected from the Khurdhá hunters by traders belonging to other Districts. There is a large flesh-eating population, which mainly depends upon its guns for food.

POPULATION.—The total population of Khurdhá Subdivision consisted, in January 1872, of 280,923 persons, viz. 140,784 males and 140,139 females, spread over an area of 943 square miles, and dwelling in 1049 villages and 47,928 houses. Average density of the population, 298 per square mile; average number of villages, 1'11 per square mile; average number of persons per village, 267; average number of houses per square mile, 51; average number of persons per house, 5'7. Classifying the population according to religion and age, the Census gives the following results :—Hindus —under twelve years of age, males 47,210, and females 43,603; total, 90,813 : above twelve years, males 82,310, and females 85,585; total, 167,895. Total of Hindus of all ages, males 129,520, and females 129,188; grand total, 258,708, or 92'1 per cent. of the Sub-divisional population ; proportion of males in total Hindus, 50'0 per cent. Muhammadans—under twelve years, males 1200, and females 936; total, 2136: above twelve years, males 1725, and females 1833; total, 3558. Total Muhammadans of all ages, males 2925, and females 2769; grand total, 5694, or 2'0 per cent. of the Subdivisional population; proportion of males in total Musalmáns, 51'4 per cent. Christians—under twelve years, males 3, and females *nil;* total, 3 : above twelve years, males 34, and females 5 ; total, 39 : grand total, 42. Other denominations—under twelve years, males 3193, and females 3019; total, 6212 : above 12 years, males 5109, and females 5158; total, 10,267. Total 'others' of all ages, males 8302, and females 8177; grand total, 16,479, or 5'9 per cent. of the Subdivisional population; proportion of males in total 'others,' 50'4 per cent. Population of all denominations—under twelve years, males 51,606, and females 47,558; total, 99,164: above twelve years, males 89,178, and females 92,581; grand total, 181,759. Total Subdivisional population of all ages, males 140,784, and females 140,139; grand total, 280,923.

Mr. C. F. Magrath's separate Census Compilation gives the following details as to the numbers of the various races, tribes, and castes found in the Khurdhá Subdivision. The numbers are included in the general table which has already been given for the District generally (*ante,* pp. 32-34) :—

Name of Nationality, Tribe, or Caste.	Number.	Name of Nationality, Tribe, or Caste.	Number.
I.—NON-ASIATICS.		**(ii.) Intermediate Castes.**	
English, ...	2	Káyasth—	
		(1) Bengalí, . . .	125
		(2) Karan . . .	12,448
II.—MIXED RACES.		(3) Others, . . .	120
Eurasian, . . .	1	Mahanti, . . .	23
		Bhát, ...	72
		Shagirdpeshá, . .	1,716
III.—ASIATICS.		Total, ...	14,504
1. *Aboriginal Tribes.*			
Kandh, ...	1,644	**(iii.) Trading Castes.**	
Savar, ...	13,852		
Saurí, ...	105	Agarwálá and Márwárí, .	2
Taála, ...	288	Bais Baniyá, . . .	1,946
Sáont, ...	322	Kumtí, ...	974
Total, .	16,211	Total, .	2,922
2. *Semi-Hinduized Aborigines.*		**(iv.) Pastoral Castes.**	
		Goálá (Ahír), . .	11
Baurí, ...	11,009	Goálá (Gaur), . .	19,823
Kandárá, . . .	2,138	Total, .	19,834
Pán, ...	2,751		
Baghwa, . . .	16		
Kaorá, ...	46	**(v.) Castes engaged in preparing Cooked Food.**	
Bágdí, ...	7		
Dom, ...	645	Madak, ...	1
Chámár, . . .	165	Gánrár, ...	8,985
Mihtar, . . .	5,310		
Shiuli, . . .	36	Total, .	8,986
Yadiká, . . .	62		
Pariah, . . .	8		
Total, .	22,193	**(vi.) Agricultural Castes.**	
		Chásá, ...	45,635
3. *Hindus.*		Golá, ...	3,237
		Or, ...	31,748
(i.) Superior Castes.		Páik, ...	9,880
		Ráju, ...	98
Bráhman, . . .	21,649	Sud, ...	764
Ganak, . . .	1,026	Beljwár, . . .	9
Mastán, . . .	994	Rául, ...	75
Rájput, . . .	945	Támbulí, . . .	227
Bhanga, . . .	171	Agurí, ...	6
Khandáit, . . .	1,987	Málí, ...	5,809
Mahánáik, . . .	5		
Total, .	26,777	Total, .	97,492

Name of Nationality, Tribe, or Caste.	Number.	Name of Nationality, Tribe, or Caste.	Number.
(vii.) Castes chiefly engaged in Personal Service.		**(xii.) Boating and Fishing Castes.**	
		Keut,	10,681
		Tior,	741
Dhobí,	4,244	Gokhá,	261
Hajjám or Nápit,	6,308		
Kahár,	1	Total,	11,683
Lodhá,	130		
		(xiii.) Dancer, Musician, Beggar, and Vagabond Castes.	
Total,	10,683		
		Kasbí,	101
		Chokár,	125
(viii.) Artisan Castes.		Kheltá,	118
		Kahaliyá,	9
Kámár, etc. (blacksmith),	2,362	Adhvariá,	42
Kánsárí (brazier),	1,432		
Rosora (pewterer),	7	Total,	395
Sonár (goldsmith),	1,248		
Barhái (carpenter),	4,160	**(xiv.) Persons enumerated by Nationality only.**	
Chitrakár (painter),	4		
Pathariá (stone-cutter),	59	Marhattá,	29
Kachorá (glassmaker),	282	Telingá,	170
Sankhárí (shell-cutter),	63		
Kumbhar (potter),	3,765	Total,	199
Darzí (tailor),	67		
Sunri (distiller),	707	**(xv.) Persons of Unknown or Unspecified Castes,**	58
Telí (oilman),	14,425		
Thuriá (oilman),	3,243		
		Grand Total of Hindus,	235,274
Total,	31,824		
		4. *Persons of Hindu Origin not recognising Caste.*	
(ix.) Weaver Castes.			
		Vaishnav,	1,377
Tántí,	6,892	Sanyásí,	79
Pátuá,	2,069	Jogí,	49
Matibangsí,	444	Buddhists,	4
Hangsí,	140	Native Christians,	39
Derá,	8		
Rangí,	59	Total,	1,548
Tulábhiná,	305		
		5. *Muhammadans.*	
Total,	9,917		
		Mughul,	45
		Pathán,	3,318
(x.) Labouring Castes.		Sayyid,	385
None.	...	Shaikh,	1,866
		Fakír,	80
(xi.) Castes occupied in selling Fish and Vegetables.		Total,	5,694
None.	...	**Grand Total,**	280,923

For administrative purposes, Khurdhá is divided into three police stations,—namely, (1) Khurdhá, comprising the station itself and eight outposts, and containing 641 villages and 33,374 houses. The station of Khurdhá is situated in 20° 11' o" north latitude, and 86° 40' 21" east longitude. (2) Tángi, comprising the station and two outposts, and containing 5511 houses. (3) Bánpur, comprising the station and five outposts, and containing 6942 houses.

Fiscally, the Subdivision consists of two great Government estates (*kháds maháls*), namely, Khurdhá and Pánchgarh. The former, Khurdhá, comprises the following Fiscal Divisions, called *kiláds* or forts :—(1) Khurdhá; (2) Dándimál; (3) Tapang; (4) Kuspálá; (5) Kuhurí; (6) Haldiá; (7) Balbhadrapur; (8) Mánikgorá; (9) Bánpur; and (10) Mughulbandí. The first or *Das-Sáld* Settlement for this estate was made in 1819 for £5240. The present assessment, which is for £17,760, will last till 1880. The revenue of the Pánchgarh estate was settled at £1546 in 1837, and this assessment is still current. In both these estates the Settlement is made direct with the cultivators. The following towns in the Subdivision are estimated to contain over 2000 inhabitants:—Bánpur, estimated at about 5000; Darutheng, about 3600; Bolgarh, about 2500 ; and Mánikgorá, about 2000.

HISTORY: THE KHURDHA REBELLIONS.—The two noteworthy political events in the history of Purí District since it passed into our hands, together with the rest of Orissa, in 1803, are the rebellion of the Mahárájá of Khurdhá in 1804, and the rising of the *páiks* or peasant militia in 1817-18. The following account of these insurrections is quoted from Mr. G. Toynbee's Sketch of the History of Orissa from 1803 to 1828 :—

'THE KHURDHA REBELLION OF 1804.—Shortly after our annexation of the Province, the measures of the Commissioners to place the civil administration of the country on a satisfactory footing were interrupted towards the close of 1804 by the events which led to the deposition of the Rájá of Khurdhá, and his confinement in the fort of Cuttack. This prince, although stripped of a considerable slice of his original territory, had been left by the Marhattás in comparative independence within his own *kild.* This, indeed, was more a matter of necessity than of choice. Although the Marhattá cavalry easily overran the open *pargands* of Ráháng, Sirái, and Chaubiskud, they could not penetrate into the jungle fastnesses of Khurdhá Proper ; nor did their infantry care to encounter on their own ground the *páiks* or local militia, who were little, if at all, inferior to them in the open. The *parganás* above mentioned became, therefore, a bone of contention, and the scene of mutual recriminations and devastations. The unfortunate inhabitants, fearful of espousing either side, suffered equally from the ravages and depredations of both. When we entered the Province in 1803, the Rájá passively espoused our cause, and tendered his allegiance to the British Government, doubtless in the hope that these *parganás*, wrung from him by the Marhattás, would be restored. The Commissioners, however, decided to retain them, as they had been taken by us from the Marhattás, who were in actual possession of them at the time of our conquest. Though this decision was at the time silently acquiesced in by the Rájá, it was a source of bitter disappointment to him. When the European troops had returned to Madras after the conquest, and the native force which remained at Cuttack had been considerably reduced in numbers by the necessity of establishing detached outposts in different parts of the country, he thought that a favourable opportunity had arrived for recovering the lost territory. As a tentative measure, he sent one of his servants in July 1804 to collect the rents of one of the villages, named Bátgáon, lying within the Mughulbandí. This messenger was summarily ejected; and the Commissioners addressed to the Rájá a strong remonstrance, with a warning against the repetition of any act of 'presumption and unprovoked aggression.' The warning appears to have had but little effect. In September of the same year (1804), the Rájá was detected in an intrigue relative to the affairs of the Purí temple. He was, therefore, forbidden to issue orders to any person whatever residing within the limits of Mughulbandí territory, without the express sanction of the Commissioners. In October, exactly one month after the issue of this order, the Rájá's troops—if a disorderly mob of *páiks* and peons can so be called—made a raid on the villages in the vicinity of Pipplí, and carried off all the cattle and other moveable property on which they could lay hands. This affair, though partaking more of the nature of a large *dakáití* or gang-robbery than of an organized and preconcerted military aggression, nevertheless occasioned considerable alarm. This was not, perhaps, under the circumstances, unnatural. The majority of our forces had returned to Madras, and what few troops remained behind were scattered over a considerable area. The nature of the country rendered speedy communication and rapid concentration impossible.

There was, moreover, a lurking suspicion that the Marhattás might be in secret league with the Rájá to harass, if not to overthrow, the British authority. The Commissioners therefore determined to be on the safe side, and to prevent, by prompt and decisive steps, these raids from growing into anything more serious. Troops were sent for from Ganjám, and a detachment marched from Cuttack as soon as the necessary supplies could be procured. The Collector was ordered, if he could not get supplies in the open market, to compel the *zamíndárs* to furnish them. The rebels, being quickly driven out of Pipplí, retreated to the fort at Khurdhá, followed by our troops. This fort, the ruins of which still remain, was situated at the foot of a hill at the east end of the valley of Khurdhá. The approaches from the south lay through a difficult pass between the Barúní hills (where the Rájá had a *put*, or place of concealment, to which he retired on the approach of our troops), and were stockaded and fortified with strong masonry barriers. It was three weeks before we were in a position to carry these works by storm. When this was at length achieved, the Rájá made good his escape south-wards with a handful of his followers, the British troops being too exhausted to pursue them. A few days afterwards, however, he surrendered, and was placed under close confinement in the fort of Cuttack. His territory was confiscated and placed in charge of Major Fletcher, who erected the first civil buildings at Khurdhá. The Rájá was released in 1807, and allowed to reside in Purí. His subsequent history is given in the following section. The estate has since been managed as a Government *khás mahál*, the Rájá receiving an allowance as *nánkár* or *málikáná*.

'THE SECOND KHURDHA REBELLION.—In 1817-18 we had to encounter a storm, which burst with such sudden fury as to threaten our expulsion, if not from the whole of Orissa, at least from the territory of Khurdhá. This was the rebellion of the *páiks*, a kind of local militia, to whom the English conquest had brought little but ruin and oppression. The causes of the rebellion will be indicated below. Rude and contemptible as this new foe undoubtedly was in comparison with our native troops, the nature of the country and their intimate knowledge of it gave them an advantage which rendered the contest more equal than it would otherwise have been. Stirling says, at page 38 of his *Historical Account of Cuttack:*—

"The *páiks*, or landed militia of the Rájwárá, combine with the most profound barbarism and the blindest devotion to the will of their chiefs, a ferocity and unquietness of disposition which have ever rendered them an important and formidable class of the population of the Province. They comprehend all castes and classes, chiefly, perhaps, the Chásá or cultivating tribe. Occasionally individuals of the lowest caste are found among them, as Kandárás, Páns, and Baurís; and the fashion has often prevailed among them of adopting into their own order some of the more savage inhabitants of remote hills, called Kandhs, as also even Musalmáns and Telingás. They are paid by service lands, which they cultivate with their own hands in time of peace, subject to the performance of certain military and police duties whenever called on by their chiefs.

' " The *páiks* of Orissa are divided into three ranks, distinguished by names taken from their occupation, or the weapons which they chiefly use, viz. :—(1) The *paháris*, who carry a large shield made of wood, covered with hide and strengthened by knobs and circles of iron, and the long straight national sword of Orissa, called the *khandá*. They are stationed chiefly as guards. (2) The *banuás*, who now principally use the matchlock (in lieu of their old missile weapons), but have besides a small shield and sword. It was their duty to take the field and go on distant expeditions. (3) The *dhenkiyás*, who are armed with bows and arrows and a sword, and perform all sorts of duties. The war dress of the *páiks* consists, or did consist, of a cap and vest made of the skin of the tiger or leopard, a sort of chain armour for the body and thighs, and a girdle formed of the tail of some wild animal. Besides the terror inspired by these unusual habiliments, they further heightened the ferocity of their appearance by staining their limbs with yellow clay and their countenances with vermilion, thus exhibiting altogether as savage and fantastic an air as one can well conceive to invest the national army of any country or people. However wild and motley their appearance and composition, they certainly did not fight badly, at least when encouraged by the proximity of their jungles, since we find them sustaining the most bloody battles with the Mughuls; and it may be doubted whether they were not superior to any infantry which the Berar Marhattás ever brought into the field during their government of the Province."

' It is clear that a body of local landed militia of this kind might have been made a tower of strength to the British Government, had liberal and conciliatory measures been adopted from the first;

but by a fatal and short-sighted policy, Major Fletcher had been allowed to resume their service lands shortly after the confiscation of the Khurdhá estate. Nor was this all. Deprived thus of the lands which they had enjoyed from time immemorial, they were subjected to the grossest extortion and oppression at the hands of the farmers, *sarbaráhkárs*, and other underlings to whom our Government entrusted the collection of the revenue, and also to the tyrannies of a corrupt and venal police.

'In this state of affairs a leader was all that was required to fan the lurking embers of rebellion into open flame. The opportunity produced the man in the person of one Jagabandhu Bidyadhar Mahápátra Bhawánbir Rái, an officer who had inherited from his ancestors the post of *bakhshí* or commander of the forces of the Rájá in Khurdhá, being second only to the Rájá himself in rank. Besides *jágírs*, and other perquisites appertaining to his station, the family of Jagabandhu had held for several generations the valuable estate of *kilá* Rorang at a low quit-rent.

'This estate was in Jagabandhu's possession at the time of the British conquest; but there was some doubt as to whether the better right was vested in Jagabandhu or in a cousin of his, who also claimed it. Jagabandhu was one of the first to proffer submission to Colonel Harcourt in 1803, and the Settlement of *kilá* Rorang was made with him for the first year of the British administration of the Province. In the following year he was allowed to enter into engagements for the triennial Settlement. At this time a Bengalí named Krishna Chandra Sinh was the *díwán* of the Collector; but he resigned his office in 1805-6, still, however, continuing to reside in Orissa. This man's brother, one Gaur Harí Sinh, was *tahsíldár* in charge of certain *khás mahóls*, which had been wrested by the Marhattás from the Rájá of Khurdhá, and which our revenue authorities were anxious to get rid of by selling them to some man of substance. The ex-*díwán*, Krishna Chandra Sinh, appears to have meditated the acquisition of the *zamíndárí* rights in these *parganás*, and the dispossession of Jagabandhu from his estate of Rorang. At his suggestion, Jagabandhu commenced to pay his revenues into the hands of Gaur Harí Sinh, the *tahsíldár* of *parganá* Ráháng, one of the *khás mahóls* which adjoined Jagabandhu's estate of *kilá* Rorang. Jagabandhu having paid his revenues to the *tahsíldár* instead of to the Collector, as formerly, it was easy for the *tahsíldár* to represent in his accounts the collections of *kilá* Rorang as belonging to

pargand Ráháng. In the Amli year 1215, *pargand* Ráháng, described as "Ráháng *oghdíra*," was farmed nominally to one Lakshmi
Náráyan, the real farmer being Krishna Chandra Sinh.   At the end
of the following year the *pargand*, described as before, was advertised
for sale and purchased by Krishna Chandra Sinh.   The *jamd* of
Rorang was added to that of Ráháng; and under the artful and
significant description "*oghdíra*," *kild* Rorang and some other *mahdls*
were formally included in *pargand* Ráháng.   Jagabandhu resisted
the attempt of the people of Krishna Chandra Sinh to take possession of his estate; a riot ensued, and petitions from both sides were
brought before the Commissioner, and matters remained in abeyance
for a long time.   The new purchasers being unable to obtain
possession, Jagabandhu let his estate in farm for the remaining
period of his Settlement.   Just at this time a suit between Jagabandhu and his cousin was decided by an amicable arrangement, to
divide the *samíndárí* of *kild* Rorang in the proportion of 10 and 6
dnnds.   In 1813 the agents of Krishna Chandra Sinh boldly stood
forward to enter into engagements for *kild* Rorang as part of their
purchase.   Jagabandhu then presented a petition, which occasioned
an investigation into his case.   It was proved beyond a question
that the annexation of Rorang to Ráháng was a fraudulent one, and
a separation of the two estates was ordered.   Bnt before this could be
carried out, it was represented that the original rights of Jagabandhu
were questionable; and the Government in June 1814 passed an
order forbidding any engagements to be taken from him, until he
should have established a title to the lands in the regular course of
law.   When these orders were communicated, Jagabandhu's complaints were loud and vehement.   He was reduced to beggary; and
for nearly two years derived his maintenance from the voluntary
contributions made by the people of Khurdhá for his support,
spending his time in wandering over the scenes of his former
consequence.   He was constantly attended by a ragged tribe of
followers, bearing the usual insignia of state pertaining to his former
condition.   When advised to institute a suit for the recovery of his
estate, he ever evinced the greatest repugnance to do so, pleading
his want of means, the degradation of sueing as a pauper, and the
inutility of any reference to the Court from an Uriyá when a rich
Bengalí was to be the defendant.

'This was the position of Jagabandhu in March 1817, when a
body of Kandhs, four hundred strong, from the Hill State of Gumsar,

in the Madras Presidency, crossed over into the Khurdhá territory
and openly unfurled the banner of revolt. The *dálbehards* and *páiks*,
under their former leader, Jagabandhu, rose as one man and joined
them. They proceeded to attack the police station (*tháná*) and
other Government buildings at Bánpur, where they killed upwards
of a hundred men, and carried off some £1500 of treasure. The
rebels then marched on Khurdhá itself, increasing in numbers as
they proceeded. Their success at Bánpur had set the whole country
in arms against us ; and, seeing the hopelessness of resistance, the
whole of the Government officers stationed at Khurdhá sought
safety in flight. All the civil buildings were burnt to the ground by
the rebels, and the treasury sacked. Another body of the rebels
advanced into *parganá* Lembái, and murdered one of our native
officials, who had rendered himself obnoxious.

'On the intelligence of these events reaching Cuttack, the authorities at once despatched such a force as they thought would be
sufficient to quell the disturbance and restore order. One detachment marched direct to Khurdhá, and another proceeded to Pipplí
to protect *parganá* Lembái.

'The Magistrate, thinking that his presence would help to restore
order, determined to proceed at once to the scene of disturbance.
He set out on April 1st, accompanied by a detachment of sixty
sepoys, with the intention of joining the force which had proceeded
to Khurdhá. On the evening of the following day he arrived at
Gangpárá, a village only about two miles distant from Khurdhá.
A barricade had been erected here, which was defended by a
considerable body of rebels. The British troops were fired upon ; and,
as it was now growing dark, it was resolved to halt for the night
and attempt to force the stockade early the next morning. A letter
was sent off to the officer who had proceeded to Khurdhá, begging
him to march out with his force from Khurdhá, so as to place the
enemy between two fires. Early next morning the messenger returned with the intelligence that the village of Khurdhá had been
totally destroyed, and that the troops were nowhere in the neighbourhood. There was nothing for it under the circumstances but
to beat a speedy retreat. No provisions had been brought from
Cuttack, and none were to be procured on the spot. The sepoys
were worn out with hunger and fatigue, and the numbers of the
rebels gradually swelled to about 3000 men. As soon as the retreat
was commenced, the enemy opened a brisk fire. The English

troops kept as much as possible to the open ; the *páiks*, on the other hand, kept well under cover of the jungle, from which they suddenly emerged now and again to fire on us, or to secure whatever of our baggage had been dropped or abandoned in the confusion. The situation was a very critical one, but no loss of life was sustained ; and after marching without a halt from 5.30 A.M. until 3.30 P.M. of the 3d April, the troops safely reached Balkatí, on the Purí road, and there halted to rest and refresh themselves. While preparing to resume their march at 9.30 P.M., they were again attacked under cover of the darkness by a large body of insurgents ; but a well-directed volley soon scattered the rebels, and our troops continued their retreat without further molestation. They reached Cuttack on the forenoon of the 4th April, *sans* tents, elephants, and every article of heavy baggage which they had taken with them. The Magistrate wrote to Government as follows :—" This instant returned, after a most fatiguing march of a day and a night, from Khurdhá ; I can only write for the information of his Lordship in Council that my retreat was forced, and that the whole of the Khurdhá territory is in a complete state of insurrection. The insurgents call upon the Rájá of Khurdhá, and Jagabandhu issues orders in his name. Their avowed intention is to proceed to Purí and reconduct him in triumph to his territory." The Magistrate also recommended that the Rájá, who had been released from the fort in 1807 and allowed to reside at Purí, should be removed to Cuttack, that a reward should be offered for the capture of each of his *sardárs*, and that martial law should be proclaimed. The detachments of sepoys which had proceeded to Khurdhá and Pipplí were not more fortunate than the Magistrate's party. The officer in command of the Pipplí detachment, in attempting to force the rebel position at Gangpárá and effect a junction with the Khurdhá force, was killed at the head of his men, as also was a native officer. Both detachments were compelled to retreat, with the loss of all their baggage, to Cuttack, *viâ* Pipplí. The latter place fell into the hands of the *páiks*, who sacked it and burnt the *tháná*.

'An officer who had been despatched with a force for the protection of Purí, reached that town on April 2d, and found all quiet there. His progress had not been molested in any way ; and he wrote to recommend that a force should be detached for the special duty of following up the rebels and bringing on a decisive action with them. Accordingly, on the 9th April, an officer with 550 men and a few guns marched on Khurdhá.

' On the 12th April martial law was proclaimed in the Khurdhá territory. On the morning of the same day a large body of the insurgents assembled at Sukal, a small village near Purí, to the south-west. In the evening they entered the town by the Loknáth *ghát*, and burnt the Government court-house and several other public and private buildings. The houses of the European residents were situated then, as now, on the sea shore, about half a mile from the native town. In these the native officers of Government took refuge. The troops were located in the bungalow of the Salt Agent. On the morning of the 13th April, the rebels emerged from the jungle which skirted the town on the east, and opened a desultory fire on our position. The sepoys returned it, and the contest was continued thus for about two hours. At length the sepoys charged the enemy and drove them back into the town, killing fifteen and wounding many more. This success was, however, only temporary. The insurgents returned in greater numbers, having been reinforced by others of their own party, and being joined by many of the rabble belonging to the temple and to the Rájá's private establishment. Some of the inhabitants of the town also joined the rebels. The priests of the temple openly proclaimed the fall of the English rule, and the restoration of the authority of the ancient line of sacred kings. Being thus hemmed in on three sides by the insurgents and the sea, it was deemed advisable to beat a speedy retreat to Cuttack by the only road still left open. Provisions were beginning to run short, and it was found impossible to procure a fresh supply. It was important, too, to prevent the Government treasure from falling into the hands of the rebels. Purí was therefore abandoned; and the fugitives, among whom were the Salt Agents and the Collector of the Pilgrim tax, reached Cuttack on the 18th April. Martial law was at once extended to the towns and neighbourhood of Purí and Pipplí, and to the *pargands* of Lembái and Kotdes. All communication between Cuttack and the southern portion of the Province was completely cut off; consequently nothing had been heard of the force despatched to Khurdhá on the 9th April, and the greatest apprehensions were entertained for its safety.

' The detachment, however, reached Khurdhá without encountering any opposition; and the officer in command, on learning that the insurgents had gone in great force in the direction of Purí, proceeded against them by forced marches. On the second day after leaving Khurdhá he came upon the rebels, about a thousand strong, drawn up behind a line of embankments. The insurgents, who had never before encountered any large body of disciplined troops, fled in the wildest dismay and confusion as soon as fire was opened. The force resumed its march on Purí, entered the town, and captured the Rájá, who was on the point of taking flight. He was taken to Calcutta and placed in confinement in Fort William, where he died in November of the same year. Several other encounters took place between our troops and the insurgent *páiks ;* and the rising spread to the neighbouring District of Cuttack, where it was stamped out without much difficulty. British authority soon re-established itself everywhere, although the country did not at once recover its accustomed tranquillity and security. Bands of *páiks*, most of them proclaimed offenders and fugitives, continued to infest the jungles of Khurdhá for some time after the pacification of the rest of the country. They committed, chiefly by night, the direst excesses. The police were equally powerless to punish or prevent. It was necessary, therefore, in the early part of the year 1818, again to have recourse to military force.'

The Commissioners appointed to investigate the causes of this outbreak reported that we ourselves were to a large extent to blame, and that the peasantry had many and real grievances to complain of. The resumption of a large tract of service land, our currency regulations, which compelled the people to pay their land tax in silver instead of in cowries as heretofore, the heavy salt duty, the extortions and chicanery of our underling Bengalí officials, were all bitter grounds of discontent. At the present day, the Khurdhá estate is a profitable and well managed Government property, and the cultivators are a contented and generally prosperous class.

STATISTICAL ACCOUNT

OF THE

ORISSA TRIBUTARY STATES.

.

STATISTICAL ACCOUNT

OF THE

ORISSA TRIBUTARY STATES.[1]

———◆———

THE TRIBUTARY STATES form the mountainous background of the Orissa Commissionership or Division. They lie between the Mahánadí delta and the interior table-land known as the Central Provinces, or between 19° 52′ 45″ and 22° 33′ 45″ north latitude, and 83° 36′ 45″ and 78° 13′ 55″ east longitude. They contain an area, as returned by the Surveyor-General in January 1876, of 16,218 square miles; and a population, as ascertained by the Census of 1872, of 1,283,309 souls. These States are nineteen in number, viz. (1) Angul, (2) Athgarh, (3) Athmallik, (4) Bánkí, (5) Barambá, (6) Bod, (7) Daspallá, (8) Dhenkánal, (9) Hindol, (10) Keunjhar, (11) Khandpárá, (12) Morbhanj, (13) Narsinhpur, (14) Nayágarh, (15) Nílgirí, (16) Pál Lahárá, (17) Ranpur, (18) Tálcher, and (19) Tigariá. States Nos. 1 (Angul) and 4 (Bánkí) are now under British administration, having been confiscated owing to misconduct on the part of the rulers. The remaining seventeen are all under the administration of their own native Chiefs.

BOUNDARIES.—The Orissa Tributary States are bounded on the

[1] This Statistical Account has been mainly compiled from my work on Orissa (2 vols. London 1872 ; Smith, Elder, and Co.), supplemented by the following other materials :—(1) Returns and Geographical Data furnished by the Surveyor-General ; (2) Bengal Census Report for 1872, with subsequent District Compilation by Mr. C. F. Magrath, C.S.; (3) *Ethnology of Bengal*, by Colonel Dalton, (Calcutta 1872) ; (4) Account of the Keunjhar Insurrection, extracted from the official *Summary of Affairs in the Foreign Department of the Government of India*, 1864 to 1869, pp. 416-430 ; (5) Report of the Inspector-General of Police for 1872 ; (6) Report of the Director of Public Instruction for 1872-73 ; (7) Report on the Charitable Dispensaries for 1872 ; (8) Geological Account of Orissa, drawn up by the Geological Survey of India:

north by the Districts of Singbhúm, Mánbhum, and Midnapur; on the east by the Districts of Balasor, Cuttack, and Purí; on the south by the Madras petty States of Gumsar and Kimidi; and on the west by the Tributary States of Patná, Sónpur, Rádhákol, Bamrá, and Sárandá in the Central Provinces, and Bonái in Chutiá Nágpur.

JURISDICTION.—The Tributary States came into our hands on the conquest of Orissa from the Marhattás in 1803; but as they had never been regular Districts of the Native Governments, we exempted them from the operation of our general Regulation system, by sections 36, 13, and 11 respectively of Regulations xii., xiii., and xiv. of 1805. This exemption was recognised on the ground of expediency only; and it was held that there was nothing in the nature of the connection of Government with the proprietors that would preclude their being brought under the ordinary jurisdiction, if it should ever be thought advisable. In 1804 the Judge and Magistrate of Cuttack had certain jurisdiction in these States; but in 1814 he was superseded by a Superintendent, 'appointed and directed to endeavour to establish such a control over the conduct of the Rájás, as would prevent the commission of crimes and outrages.'

The Chiefs administer civil and criminal justice under the control of the Commissioner of the Orissa Division, who also now exercises the political functions of Superintendent of the Tributary States. Heinous offences which require more than two years' imprisonment, and all capital cases, are sent to this officer, who also decides political causes and disputed successions. An appeal from his decision lies to the Government of Bengal. The Magistrates of Purí, Cuttack, and Balasor are *ex officio* Assistants to the Superintendent; but, with the exception of the Magistrate of Balasor, they do not ordinarily exercise criminal jurisdiction. The Superintendent has also a native Assistant, who exercises the full powers of a Magistrate, and who tries such cases as the Superintendent makes over to him. The States, during the minority of the Rájás or Chiefs, or when for political reasons they are placed under attachment, are managed by the Superintendent through a Government receiver (*tahsíldár*). The jurisdiction of the Superintendent is defined by Regulation xi. of 1816 and Act xxi. of 1850.

In 1821 the Government ruled that the interference of the Superintendent should be chiefly confined to matters of a political nature: to the suppression of feuds and animosities prevailing between the Rájás of adjoining States, or between the Rájás and their subordinate feudatories; to the correction of systematic oppression and cruelty practised by any of the Rájás or by their officers towards the inhabitants; to the cognisance of any apparent gross violation by them of their duties of allegiance and subordination; and generally, to important points, which, if not attended to, might lead to violent and general outrage and confusion, or to contempt of the paramount authority of the British Government.

In 1839 Mr. Ricketts suggested the introduction of a regular system of management, but the rules proposed by him and by his successor, Mr. Mills, were not approved. Instructions were, however, given to draw up some short, clear, and well-defined regulations, making the Rájás responsible to the Superintendent in all cases of murder, homicide, and heinous offences, without, however, interfering so far as to make them amenable to the Civil Court of the Superintendent in cases between the Rájás and their creditors. In accordance with the above instructions, Mr. Mills prepared revised rules, and submitted them for approval. These revised rules proposed that the Rájás should be prohibited from exercising the powers of life and death; from subjecting any offender to torture, mutilation, or other punishment opposed to the principles of British rule; and from allowing the practice of widow-burning and human sacrifices within their territories; that they should be made liable to punishment for murder, or other heinous offences committed by them, and should be held responsible for the amount of property robbed from travellers, if the commission of the crime and the non-recovery of the property were due to their imperfect police or want of care; that the Superintendent's power of interference should be increased, so as to take cognizance of offences committed by foreigners in the Tributary States, to hold preliminary inquiries in heinous offences committed by the Rájás, and to sentence all offenders except the Rájás to imprisonment for a term not exceeding seven years; that the punishment of the Rájás, and all punishments exceeding seven years, should be awarded by the Government of Bengal. The Bengal Government, however, thought it better not to pass any permanent or defined rules upon the subject; but directed that the spirit of the proposed rules should be acted up to in all future cases, with certain limitations, and that the Rájás should be informed that they are ordinarily amenable to the Superintendent's

Court, subject to such instructions as may from time to time be furnished by the Government. These orders are now in force; and all sentences of more than seven years' imprisonment, although passed by the Superintendent, have to be reported to Government for confirmation.

The other principal Government Rules, Legislative Acts, etc., affecting the Tributary States, are the following:—

Under Government order No. 3364, of September 1858, the system of trying petty criminal cases *vivâ voce* was extended to the Tributary States.

Act xx. of 1850 was enacted for settling the boundaries of the Tributary States, and is still in force.

Acts viii. and xiv. of 1859 were extended to the Tributary States of Bánkí and Angul, from the 1st January 1862. As regards the States under the Rájás, the proviso contained in section 11, Regulation xiv. of 1805, is still in force.

The Penal Code was declared applicable to the Tributary States by an order of the Government of India, No. 2425, dated the 18th December 1860.

Under orders of the Government of Bengal, No. 1875, dated the 11th March 1863, the criminal authorities were directed to be guided in their proceedings as closely as possible by the spirit of the Criminal Procedure Code. Section 13 of Regulation xiii. of 1805 is still in force.

In the States under the direct management of Government, viz. Bánkí and Angul, the Civil and Criminal Procedure Codes, as well as Act v. of 1861, are in force. They are in fact virtually treated as Regulation Districts. This is the case also in the Kandh-máls.

GENERAL ASPECT OF THE COUNTRY.—The Tributary States of Orissa are a succession of ranges rolling backwards towards Central India. They form, however, three watersheds from south to north, with fine valleys between, down which pour the three great rivers of the interior table-land. The southernmost is the valley of the Mahánadí, at some places closely hemmed in by peaks on either side, and forming picturesque passes; at others spreading out into fertile plains, laden with rice, and watered by a thousand mountain streams. At the Bármúl Pass, the river winds round magnificently wooded hills, from 1500 to 2500 feet high. Crags and peaks of a wild beauty overhang its channel, which at one part is so narrow that it rises seventy feet in time of flood. From the north bank of the Mahánadí, the ranges tower into a fine watershed, from 2000 to 2500 feet high, running north-west and south-east, and forming the boundary of the States of Narsinhpur and Barambá. On the other side, they slope down upon the States of Hindol and Dhenkánal, supplying countless little feeders to the Bráhmaní, which occupies the second of the three valleys. From the north bank of this river, the hills again roll back into magnificent ranges, running in the same general direction as before, but more confused and wilder, till they rise into the Keunjhar watershed, with peaks from 2500 to 3500 feet high, culminating in Maláyagirí, 3895 feet high, in the State of Pál Lahárá. This watershed, in turn, slopes down into the third valley, that of the Baitaraní, from whose eastern or left bank rise the hitherto almost unexplored mountains of Morbhanj, heaped upon each other in noble masses of rock, from 3000 to nearly 4000 feet high, sending countless tributaries to the Baitaraní on the south, and pouring down the Burábalang, with the feeders of the Subarnarekhá, on the north. The peaks are densely wooded to the summit, and, except at the regular passes, are inaccessible to beasts of burden. The intermediate valleys yield rich crops in return for negligent cultivation ; and a vast quantity of land might be reclaimed on their outskirts and lower slopes.

MOUNTAIN PEAKS.—The principal mountain peaks are fifteen in number, as follows :—(1) Maláyagirí, in the State of Pál Lahárá, in latitude 21° 22' 20", longitude 85° 18' 41" ; height, 3895 feet. (2) Meghásaní, literally, the Seat of Clouds, in Morbhanj, in lat. 21° 37' 58", long. 86° 23' 30" ; height, 3824 feet. (3) Gandha Mádan, in Keunjhar, in lat. 21° 38' 12", long. 85° 32' 56" ; height, 3479 feet. (4) Thákuráni, in Keunjhar, in lat. 22° 6' 5", long. 85° 28' 30" ; height, 3003 feet. (5) Pánch Dhar, at Athmallik, in lat. 20° 41' 28", long. 84° 43' 36" ; height, 2948 feet. (6) Tomák, on the boundary of Keunjhar and Sukindá, in lat. 21° 5' 35", long. 85° 57' 38"; height, 2577 feet. (7) Goáldeo, in Daspallá, in lat. 20° 31' 5", long. 84° 52' 43" ; height, 2546 feet. (8) Suliyá, in Nayágarh, in lat. 20° 6' 23", long. 85° 4' 0"; height, 2239 feet. (9) Kopilás, on the boundary of Athgarh and Dhenkánal, in lat. 20° 40' 40", long. 85° 48' 53" ; height, 2098 feet. This hill takes its name from that of a temple situated near the summit, which, in February, is visited by about 10,000 pilgrims, when a large fair is held, and trade to a considerable extent is carried on. At the top of the hill there is a table-land, which might be made a very pleasant place of residence during the hot months. (10) Bánkomundí, in Bod, in lat. 20° 42' 24", long. 84° 20' 18"; height, 2080 feet. (11) The Kanaká range, on the boundary of Narsinhpur and Hindol. The highest peak is in the latter State, in lat. 20° 36' 45", long. 85° 11' 7"; height, 2038 feet. (12) Bághmárí, on the boundary of Morbhanj and Singbhúm, in lat. 22° 29' 3", long. 26° 9' 27"; height, 1997 feet. (13) Tangárí, in Angul, in lat. 20° 52' 48", long. 84° 52' 50"; height, 1952 feet. (14) Siánangá, in Bod, in lat. 20° 26' 16", long. 83° 51' 28"; height, 1917 feet. (15) Sápuámundí, in Khandpárá, in lat. 20° 19' 28", long. 85° 5' 21"; height, 1769 feet.

RIVERS.—The principal rivers are the Mahánadí, the Bráhmaní, the Baitaraní, and the Burábalang. The Mahánadí enters the Tributary States of Orissa in Bod, forming the boundary between that State on the south, and Athmallik and Angul on the north, for forty-nine miles. It then divides Khandpárá and Bánkí on the south, from Narsinhpur, Barambá, and Athgarh on the north. In the last State, it debouches through a narrow gorge upon the Cuttack delta. It is everywhere navigable throughout the Tributary States, and up to Sambalpur, by flat-bottomed boats of about twenty-five tons burden, and a considerable trade is carried on. Precious stones of different kinds are found in its bed. The river would afford valuable facilities for navigation, but for the numerous sand-banks in its channel. The boatmen carry rakes and hoes, with which they clear a narrow passage just sufficient to let their craft pass. Where rocks impede the navigation, there is plenty of depth on either side; and a little blasting would enlarge the water-way, and thus lessen the force of the rapids. When full, it is a magnificent river, varying from one to two miles in breadth, and of great depth. It is liable to heavy floods, which have been described in the Statistical Account of Cuttack District (vol. xviii.), where a comprehensive account of the Mahánadí will also be found. Its chief feeders in the Tributary States are—on its north or left bank, the Sápuá in Athgarh, and the Dandátapá and Máno in Athmallik; on its south or right bank, the Kusumí and Kamáí in Khandpárá, with the Jorámu, Hinámandá Gánduni, Bolát, Sálkí Bágh, Maríní, and Tel. This last stream divides the Orissa Tributary States from those of the Central Provinces, and forms the boundary between the States of Bod and Sónpur.

THE BRAHMANI enters the Tributary States in the State of Tálcher, and passes through, it and Dhenkánal into Cuttack District. It is navigable for a few months of the year as far up as four miles below Tálcher, where there are some dangerous rocks, which might, however, be easily blasted. Common jasper abounds, along with other precious stones, in the bed of the river.

THE BAITARANI RIVER rises in the State of Keunjhar, and forms the boundary between that State and Morbhanj for forty miles. In the dry season it is navigable by small boats, but with difficulty, as far as Anandapur, a large village in Keunjhar on its south or right bank, in lat. 21° 13′ 0″ and long. 86° 11′ 0″. A considerable trade is carried on at this place, the rural and forest produce brought by land from the south-west being bartered for salt, carried by boats from the coast.

THE BURABALANG rises in the State of Morbhanj, and has been fully described in the Statistical Account of Balasor (vol. xviii.); which also see for an account of the Sálandí and Subarnarekhá.

No important instances of alluvion or diluvion are known, nor of any changes in the courses of the above rivers. The banks are generally abrupt, occasionally rising into fine heights, and the beds sandy, with the exception of that of the Baitaraní, which is rocky. Nor have any important islands been formed by the rivers within the Tributary States, but rocks and wooded cliffs have here and there been thrown up in the middle of the Baitaraní and the Mahánadí. The banks are generally buried in jungle, but in many places they might be turned into fertile fields. The Baitaraní is popularly rumoured to have a subterraneous passage, but in reality merely flows through two rocky clefts, called the Cow's Nostrils. The rivers form no lakes, and are far beyond tidal range. None of them are fordable during the rainy season, but in the dry-season they are all so at certain parts of their course.

RIVER TRAFFIC.—Three towns on the Mahánadí subsist by river traffic, namely, Baideswar in Bánkí, and Padmábatí and Kantilo in Khandpárá. These communities carry salt, spices, cocoa-nuts, and brass utensils up to Sambalpur, in the Central Provinces, bringing thence in exchange, cotton, wheat, oil-seeds, clarified butter, oil, molasses, iron, turmeric, *tasar* cloth, rice, etc. There are also several smaller towns on both sides of the Mahánadí which carry on an extensive trade in timber, bamboos, oil-seeds, and other local produce. On the Bráhmaní, the only large villages are Báulpur and Bhuvan, in the State of Dhenkánal, with a thriving river traffic in resin, lac, oil-seeds, etc. There is but a single large village within the Tributary States on the Baitaraní, viz. Anandapur in Keunjhar, the trade of which is the same as that of the villages on the Bráhmaní.

IRRIGATION.—None of the non-navigable rivers or streams are applied as a motive power for turning mills, etc.; nor is the water of the larger rivers utilized for the purpose of irrigation, although the smaller streams are often dammed and embanked for this purpose. There is no regular system of storing water at an elevation from which it can be conducted to a distance; but it is often ladled on to the fields by the ordinary native methods described in the Statistical Account of Purí District (*ante*, p. 138).

FISHERIES.—All the villages on the rivers are partly inhabited by fishermen, who form about five per cent. of the entire population along the banks, and one per cent. in the interior. The fisheries are of no great value.

EMBANKMENTS.—With the exception of Bánkí, which is directly under Government management, embankments on an extended scale are unknown within the Tributary States; nor do the Rájás possess sufficient capital for their construction.

MINERALS.—A coal-field exists in Tálcher. In 1841 an exploring party found coal in several places, extending over a tract of upwards of thirty miles. Further investigations were also made in 1855, and the results published in the *Memoirs of the Geological Survey of India*, vol. i. part i. Coal is also believed to exist in Angul, and along the banks of the Mahánadí. In 1875, a thorough examination of the Tálcher field was made by an officer of the Geological Survey, but his report is unfavourable to the prospects of Orissa coal. He considers that no coal-seam of a workable thickness and fairly good quality exists in this field; that a final and thorough exploration could only be effected at considerable expense; that there is no probability of there being a sufficient local consumption to support a proper mining establishment; and that, with the present expensive long land carriage, there is no prospect of a class of coal equal to Ráníganj competing successfully at the Orissa ports with Ráníganj coal sent from Calcutta by sea. The project for utilizing the Tálcher coal beds has therefore been compelled, for the present at least, to be abandoned. Limestone and building stone are procurable in almost all the States. Iron is found in Morbhanj, Keunjhar, Dhenkánal, Angul, Athmallik, Tálcher, and Pál Lahárá, and a considerable trade in the metal is carried on. Gold dust is washed, but to a very small extent, in the sands of a few streams in Keunjhar, Dhenkánal, and Pál Lahárá. A black stone called *mungi* is extensively quarried in Nílgirí, and manufactured into native plates and cups. Dhenkánal produces talc, and hot springs are found in Athmallik.

JUNGLE PRODUCTS. — The chief marketable timber of the Tributary States is *sál*, the forest revenue of the single State of Angul being £35. The jungle yields an annual supply of resin, lac, *tasar*, bees-wax, dyes, fibres, such as *sidrí*, the fibre of a gigantic vine used for cordage, and *murgá* (Sanseviera Zeylanica). The following classes subsist by collecting and trading in jungle products :—(1) The Kharriás, who collect and deal in catechu ; (2) the Lohárs or iron-smelters ; (3) the Kandhs ; (4) the Gonds ; (5) the Kols, who sell resin, lac, wax, etc.; (6) and (7) Juángs and Malhárs, who deal in honey and other jungle products, and who live chiefly on roots and leaves ; (8) Bhumijs ; and (9) Kostiás, dealers in *tasar*.

WILD BEASTS.—Among the larger wild animals are the elephant, tiger, panther, hyena, bear, deer of several sorts, antelope, hog, bison, etc. Wild elephants infest the jungles of Morbhanj and Keunjhar, and in lesser numbers Athmallik, Angul, and Dhenkánal. They do great damage to the crops, and occasionally trample down a barn, but very seldom destroy human life. Tigers exist everywhere, and annually carry away numbers of men and cattle. At the Mangarhghátí Pass, they killed upwards of 300 persons in three years. In the State of Bod, 86 persons were devoured in 1869, and the Rájá was obliged to engage a huntsman from Sambalpur. In some States, the tigers watch the villages and seize any one who strays beyond their limits ; but the Rájás seldom give rewards for their destruction. Some tribes, particularly the Kandhs, regard them with superstitious reverence, and will not kill them. Hundreds of people die every year from snake-bite, but payments for serpent killing are unknown. Among the smaller game, are hares, various sorts of wild fowl, wild geese, peacocks, partridges, etc. Wild-beast skins form an important article of traffic.

POPULATION.—Prior to 1872, no attempt had been made at a census of the population of the Tributary States. An estimate prepared by the Topographical Survey in 1860-62 returned the number of towns and villages at 6965, containing an estimated population of 961,355 souls, calculated at the rate of five and a half inhabitants to each house.

THE CENSUS OF 1872.—A regular Census of the Tributary States was effected in 1872 by the authority of Government, and under the direct supervision of the Commissioner of the Orissa Division. That officer reports as follows on the manner in which the work was carried out :—' As regards the Tributary States, I have as Superintendent kept the work entirely in my own hands. The whole has been done by and through the Tributary Rájás and their agents ; and in Bánkí, Angul, and the Kandh-máls by the local *tahsíldárs* and their staff, assisted by the police and by village *sarbaráhkárs*. The procedure observed in the Tributary States has varied very little from that in Regulation Districts. The only difference has been that there was no division of villages into blocks, or groups of villages into supervisors' circles. The Rájás have been their own supervisors, and each State a separate circle. During two previous seasons' cold weather tours, I visited nearly every Tributary State, and personally explained the procedure to the Rájás and enlisted their co-operation. I knew well that agency was scarce, and I did not desire that Rájás should enlist outsiders, which would not only have been a dangerous, but a costly arrangement. In fact, I scrupulously enjoined the utilization by Rájás of their own personal staff, and such of the Bráhmans and head-men as were able to read and write. In some few instances I know Rájás have incurred some expense by engaging extra hands, but it has been my policy to throw the whole responsibility and supervision as far as possible on them personally. I have now been sufficiently long in charge of the Orissa Tributary States to obtain considerable personal influence with the chiefs, and I have reason to be satisfied with the intelligence and alacrity shown by them in responding to every call, and carrying out minutely and honestly every instruction I have issued. The whole returns for the Tributary States were submitted and ready for tabulation simultaneously with those of the Regulation Districts.'

The results of the Census disclosed a total population of 1,283,309 persons, dwelling in 10,178 villages, and inhabiting 253,284 houses ; average density of the population, 79 per square mile ; average number of persons per village, 126 ; average number of persons per house, 5·1. As regards the distribution of the population in the different States, I extract the following from Mr. H.

Beverley's General Census Report of 1872 :—'The largest State is Morbhanj, which comprises 4243 square miles, with a population of a quarter of a million. A large portion of this State, called Bámangháti, is now managed under the supervision of the Deputy-Commissioner of Singbhúm, in consequence of disturbances arising out of the oppression of the aboriginal inhabitants by the Rájá's officials. Next in importance comes Keunjhar, with an area of 3096 square miles, and a population of 181,871 souls. Pál Lahárá formerly belonged to this State, and its tribute is still credited as part of that due from the Keunjhar Rájá; but for all practical purposes it is otherwise independent. Dhenkánal has an area of 1463 square miles, and a population of 178,072. Angul was confiscated in 1847, and is now managed by a *tahsíldár* under the orders of the Superintendent. Tigariá is the smallest State of all, comprising no more than 46 square miles; but it is one of the most populous for its size, having an average of 357 souls to the square mile. Bánkí was confiscated in 1840, and is under the direct management of Government. Its area is 116 square miles, with a population of 49,426 souls, making it the most densely populated of all the estates. Khandpárá, another small State of 244 square miles in extent, has an average of 249 persons to the square mile. Bod, including the Kandh-máls, measures 2064 square miles, with a population of 108,868 souls. The Kandh-máls comprise the hilly country to the south of this State, which was ceded to us in 1840 on account of the Rájá's inability to put down the practice of human sacrifice among the aboriginal inhabitants. The population of this tract numbers 51,810 souls.'

The following table (p. 206), exhibiting the area, population, villages, houses, etc. of the Tributary States, is reproduced *verbatim* from the Census Report of 1872.

POPULATION CLASSIFIED ACCORDING TO SEX, RELIGION, AND AGE.—The total population of the Tributary States of Orissa consisted in 1872 of 1,283,309 persons, viz. 646,205 males and 637,104 females. The proportion of males in the total population amounted to 50·4 per cent., and the average density of the population is 79 persons per square mile. Classifying the population according to religion and age, the Census gives the following results:—Hindus— under twelve years of age, males 174,709, and females 156,746; total, 331,455: above twelve years, males 267,002, and females

[*Sentence continued on page* 207.

ABSTRACT OF THE AREA, POPULATION, ETC. OF EACH OF THE ORISSA TRIBUTARY STATES, 1872.

Name of State	Area in Square Miles	Number of Villages or Mauzás	Number of Houses	Total Population	Averages calculated by the Census Officers.				
					Persons per Square Mile.	Villages or Mauzás per Square Mile.	Persons per Village or Mauzá or Township.	Houses per Square Mile.	Persons per House.
Bámanghátí,	4,243	1,941	33,768	164,154	61	·60	85	12	4·9
Morbhanj,	647	647	18,595	94,526	61	·60	146	12	5·1
Nílgirí,	278	264	6,319	33,944	122	·94	129	23	5·4
Keunjhar,	3,096	1,469	35,073	181,871	59	·47	124	11	5·2
Pál Laháṛá,	452	175	2,941	15,450	34	·38	88	7	5·3
Dhenkánal,	1,463	763	34,903	178,072	122	·52	233	24	5·1
Tálcher,	399	242	7,192	38,021	95	·60	157	18	5·2
Angul,	881	352	13,892	78,374	89	·39	223	16	5·3
Athmallik,	730	209	2,897	14,536	20	·28	70	4	5·6
Hindol,	312	180	5,849	28,025	90	·57	156	19	5·0
Narsinhpur,	199	181	5,500	24,758	124	·90	137	28	4·8
Barambá,	134	137	4,950	24,261	181	1·02	177	37	4·5
Tigariá,	46	75	2,927	16,420	357	1·63	219	64	4·9
Áthgarh,	168	191	4,699	26,366	157	1·13	138	28	5·6
Bánkí,	116*	140	8,432	49,426	426	1·20	353	73	5·9
Khandpárá,	244	321	12,109	60,877	249	1·31	190	50	5·0
Nayágarh,	588	637	18,271	83,249	142	1·08	131	31	4·6
Ranpur,	203	280	5,310	27,306	135	1·37	98	26	5·1
Daspallá,	568	432	7,577	34,805	61	·76	81	13	4·6
Bod,	2,064	716	11,269	57,058	53	·76	80	11	5·1
Khand-mals,		826	10,811	51,810	53	·76	63	11	4·8
Total,	16,184*	10,178	253,284	1,283,309	79	·62	126	16	5·1

* This is the area returned in the Census. The Surveyor-General, however, in a return dated January 1876, returns the area of Bánkí at 150 square miles, which would bring the total area of the Tributary States up to 16,218 square miles. For the other States, the Surveyor-General's area and that returned in the Census are precisely the same.

Sentence continued from page 205.]
281,198; total, 548,200. Total Hindus of all ages—males 441,711, and females 437,944; grand total, 879,655, or 68·5 per cent. of the total population. . Proportion of males in total Hindu population, 50·2 per cent. Muhammadans—under twelve years of age, males 769, and females 580 ; total, 1349 : above twelve years, males 1361, and females 1285; total, 2646. Total Musalmáns of all ages—males 2130, and females 1865; grand total, 3995, or ·3 per cent. of the total population. Proportion of males in total Musalmáns, 53·3 per cent. Buddhists—under twelve years of age, *nil;* above twelve years of age, males 1, and females *nil.* Christians—under twelve years of age, males 78, and females 57 ; total, 135 : above twelve years, males 85, and females 83; total, 168. Total Christians of all ages—males 163, and females 140; grand total, 303. Proportion of males in Christian population, 53·8 per cent. Other denominations not separately classified, consisting of aboriginal tribes and races—under twelve years of age, males 81,464, and females 70,427 ; total, 151,891 : above twelve years, males 120,737, and females 126,728 ; total, 247,465. Total 'others' of all ages—males 202,201, and females 197,155; grand total, 399,356, or 31·2 per cent. of the total population of the Tributary States. Proportion of males in total 'others,' 50·6 per cent. Population of all denominations—under twelve years of age, males 257,020, and females 227,810; total, 484,830: above twelve years, males 389,185, and females 409,294; total, 798,479. Total population of all ages—males 646,205 and females 637,104 ; grand total, 1,283,309. Proportion of males in total population, 50·4 per cent.

The percentage of children not exceeding twelve years of age in the population of different religions, is returned in the Census Report as follows :—Hindus—proportion of male children 19·9, and of female children 17·8 per cent. ; proportion of children of both sexes, 37·7 per cent. of the total Hindu population. Muhammadans —male children 19·2, and female children 14·5 per cent.; proportion of children of both sexes, 33·7 per cent. of the total Musalmán population. Christians—male children 25·7, and female children 18·8 per cent.; proportion of children of both sexes, 44·5 per cent. of the total Christian population. Other denominations—male children 20·4, and female children 17·7 per cent; proportion of children of both sexes, 38·1 per cent. of the total 'other' population. Population of all religions—male children 20·0, and female children

17·8 per cent.; proportion of children of both sexes, 37·8 per cent. of the total population. In the Tributary States, as elsewhere throughout Bengal, the small proportion of girls to boys, and the excessive proportion of females above twelve years of age to males of the same class, is probably due to the fact that natives consider that girls have attained womanhood at a much earlier period than boys reach manhood. The proportion of the sexes of all ages, viz. 50·4 males and 49·6 females, is probably correct.

INFIRMITIES.—The number and proportion of insanes and of persons afflicted with certain other infirmities in the Orissa Tributary States is thus returned in the Census Report :—Insanes—males 136, and females 39; total, 175, or ·0136 per cent. of the population. Idiots—males 115, and females 39; total, 154, or ·0120 per cent. of the population. Deaf and dumb—males 296, and females 101; total, 397, or ·0309 per cent. of the population. Blind—males 737, and females 523; total, 1260, or ·0982 per cent. of the population. Lepers—males 160, and females 21; total, 181, or ·0141 per cent. of the population. The total number of male infirms in the Tributary States amounts to 1444, or ·2234 per cent. of the total male population; number of female infirms, 723, or ·1134 per cent. of the total female population. The total number of infirms of both sexes amounts to 2167, or ·1688 per cent. of the total population.

ETHNICAL DIVISION OF THE PEOPLE.—The population of the Tributary States of Orissa consists almost solely of (1) Hindu Uriyás, who inhabit the valleys, and who form the largest and most import-ant section of the population; and (2) aboriginal and semi-aboriginal hill tribes, such as Savars, Kandhs, Gonds, Bhumijs, Santáls, Kols, Páns, Bhuiyás, Bathudis, Khairás, etc. The Muhammadans, who comprise the remaining section of the population, only form ·3 per cent. of the entire inhabitants of the Tributary States. The Census Report ethnically divides the population as follows :—European, 1 ; aboriginal tribes, 327,652; semi-Hinduized aborigines, 213,490 ; Hindu castes and people of Hindu origin, 738,171 ; Muhammadans, 3995 : total, 1,283,309. I take the following details (table, pp. 210-217) from Mr. C. F. Magrath's separate Census Compilation for the Orissa Tributary States. The list of Hindu castes will be reproduced on a subsequent page, but arranged in a different order to that given here, and as far as possible according to the rank in which they are held in local public esteem.

ABORIGINAL TRIBES.—The following is a brief description of the principal aboriginal tribes met with in the Orissa Tributary States. These tribes number altogether 327,652, or 25·53 per cent. of the whole population of the States. They are most numerous in the mountainous jungle tracts of Morbhanj, Keunjhar, and Bod.

KANDHS.—The most important, and nearly the most numerous, of these tribes are the Kandhs. The Census Report returns the number of these people in the Orissa Tributary States at 75,531, of whom 46,024 are found in Bod (including 34,005 belonging to the Kandh-máls—a tract now under a mild system of British administration). The other States in which the Kandhs are numerous are Daspallá (8382), Angul (5423), and Nayágarh (3928). They are also scattered through nearly all the other States, and are met with in the British Districts of Orissa and Northern Madras. The following account of the Kandhs is reprinted almost *verbatim* from a description of this people given in my *Orissa* (vol. ii. pp. 69-100), and is principally based upon the admirable Report of Lieutenant (afterwards Major) Macpherson, dated 21st June 1841 (folio ed., Calcutta 1842). Wherever sentences or paragraphs appear in inverted commas, the quotation is a direct one from Lieutenant Macpherson's Report:—

The Kandhs, who appear on the rich Orissa delta as a class of landless day-labourers,—the hewers of wood and clearers of jungle for the superior Hindu race,—survive in the mountainous background as a distinct nationality, with a history, a religion, and a system of law and landed property of their own. When questioned as to their origin, some of the tribes declare that they were driven westwards from the lower Orissa country, others that they have been pushed eastwards from Central India. In both cases they found refuge in the intermediate highlands which now form the Orissa Tributary States, and the two legends alike point to advancing waves of Hindu colonization—the one from Central India, the other from the Orissa delta. The race long enjoyed as its headquarters the State of Bod, which extends for sixty-five miles along the southern or right bank of the Mahánadí, and is divided into two parts, the more open and fertile of which is ruled by a Hindu Rájá, and occupied by Hindu husbandmen. The Kandh settlements, known as the Kandh-máls, lie deeper among the hills, scattered over a broken plateau intersected by low ridges, the last refuge of the race. Their villages are divided from each other by rugged peaks and dense forests; but a regular system

[*Sentence continued on page* 218.

RETURN OF NATIONALITIES, RACES, ETC.

NAME OF NATIONALITY, TRIBE, OR CASTE.	Total	Bamanghati	Morbhanj	Nilgiri	Keunjhar	Pal Lahara	
I.—NON-ASIATICS.							
English, . . .	I	...	...	...	I	...	
II.—MIXED RACES.							
None.	...	...	...	...	...	...	
III.—ASIATICS.							
1. *Aboriginal Tribes.*							
Gond, . . .	22,275	219	1,968	...	10,407	1,133	4,134	961
Kandh, . . .	75,531	...	4	...	271	681	2,333	632
Savar, . . .	36,280	11	1,775	258	5,125	1,387	15,934	1,442
Saurí, . . .	326	...	...	...	...	...	...	...
Uráon, . . .	325	313	...	...	12	...	...	...
Bhumíj, . . .	29,596	6,958	18,219	1,012	1,843	122	1,442	...
Juáng, . . .	9,398	...	...	...	4,592	367	4,120	...
Kharriá, . . .	3,942	1,086	2,423	25	65	330	...	...
Purán, . . .	7,634	1,693	5,941	...	...	...	...	...
Sáont, . . .	9,683	24	2,289	80	7,172	118	...	...
Santál, . . .	76,548	44,445	31,586	467	50	...	...	...
Taŝlá, . . .	18,131	8	...	...	2,905	296	2,224	901
Ghási, . . .	2,014	773	451	...	475	...	...	...
Kol, . . .	34,637	14,021	7,876	505	10,990	418	546	4
Mal, . . .	1,082	...	269	...	308	43	462	...
Bendkár, . . .	239	...	...	...	223	16	...	...
Dhángar, . . .	11	...	...	...	...	...	...	...
Total, .	327,652	69,551	72,801	2,347	44,438	4,911		
2. *Semi-Hinduized Aborigines.*							
Pán, . . .	112,628	5,100	5,900	1,001	19,827	2,145	24,099	4,616
Bhuiyá, . . .	30,724	1,102	8,690	152	18,481	1,464	345	3
Báthudí, . . .	23,564	258	13,999	1,404	7,808	2	3	...
Kháirá, . . .	11,104	...	2	...	180	...	3,928	615
Kándárá, . . .	5,028	...	289	437	76	...	I	18
Báuri, . . .	2,396	...	143	49	16	...	383	...
Kadal, . . .	1,825	...	49	410	254	...	...	...
Máhili, . . .	732	544	182	...	...	...	...	...
Ghusuriyá, . . .	69	...	...	...	67	...	...	...
Kaorá, . . .	643	...	386	...	257	...	...	...
Bágdí, . . .	653	77	121	...	273	...	...	...
Karangá, . . .	125	8	117	...	...	...	...	...
Chandál, . . .	121	...	...	...	...	...	120	...
Baghuá, . . .	21	...	8	...	13	...	...	...
Bind, . . .	42	...	7	...	14	...	...	...
Bediyá, . . .	52	...	50	...	...	...	...	...
Dháli, . . .	317	...	...	...	...	...	...	...
Dosádh, . . .	30	28	...	...	2	...		
Dom, . . .	4,853	493	635	244	615	24		
Chámár, . . .	3,201	...	32	34	970	184		
Mihtár, . . .	15,075	...	1,062	123	349	117		
Shiuli, . . .	206	...	...	...	2	...		
Yadiká, . . .	46	...	...	...	...	...		
Labaná, . . .	35	...	...	...	...	...		
Total, .	213,490	7,610	31,672	3,854	49,294	3,936		
3. *Hindus.*							
(i.) SUPERIOR CASTES.							
Bráhman, . . .	60,177	268	4,635	3,734	8,583	188		
Ganak, . . .	3,069	52	174	116	601	19		
Mostáni Bráhman, .	3,234	...	107	39	2,006	...		
Rájput, . . .	6,510	35	861	208	720	292		

IN EACH OF THE ORISSA TRIBUTARY STATES.

OF NATIONALITY, BE, OR CASTE.	Narsinhpur.	Baramba.	Tigaria.	Athgarh.	Banki.	Khandpara.	Nayagarh.	Ranpur.	Daspalla.	Bod.	Kandh-Mals.
N-ASIATICS.											
· · ·	...	...	...	...	...	...	...	...	...	...	...
IXED RACES.											
· · ·	...	...	...	...	...	...	...	...	...	...	
—ASIATICS.											
original Tribes.											
· · · ·	171	...	...	...	...	95	...	...	50	435	96
, · · · ·	1,039	1,086	152	...	...	1,596	3,928	1,257	8,382	12,019	34,005
· · · ·	...	1,016	759	3,555	2,174	1,126	52	555	109	340	62
· · · ·	...	...	...	...	...	...	...	...	...	...	326
, · · ~ ·	...	...	...	...	...	...	...	...	...	...	...
· · · ·	...	...	...	...	29	...	...	...	...	...	...
, · · ·	...	...	...	...	...	...	...	...	...	...	11
· · · ·	...	...	...	...	...	...	...	...	...	...	...
· · · ·	...	...	...	...	...	...	...	...	...	...	...
· · · ·	739	922	392	780	252	744	451	75	761	337	1,211
· · · ·	...	...	...	...	...	...	...	...	...	228	87
· · · ·	...	...	...	1	...	...	...	...	...	123	...
, · ~ ·	...	...	...	...	...	...	...	...	...	...	...
, · · ·	...	...	...	...	...	...	...	...	...	...	...
Total, ·	1,949	3,024	1,303	4,336	2,455	3,561	4,431	1,887	9,302	13,482	
'-Hinduized borigines.											
· · · ·	1,863	1,956	883	2,321	1,178	3,577	6,627	619	4,343	5,273	6,204
i · · ~ ·	...	...	...	...	...	...	...	...	61	2	...
i, · ~ ·	...	...	...	...	...	...	...	...	...	...	...
· ~ · ·	...	5	...	...	...	38	105	274	2,088	311	17
á, · · ·	378	331	...	325	298	1,064	1,672	49	56	20	5
· · · ·	...	80	12	115	1,038	...	305	250	3	...	...
· · · ·	...	...	...	...	...	...	573	...	40	425	47
yá, · · ·	...	...	...	...	...	...	...	...	...	6	...
· · · ·	...	...	...	30	152	...	...	...	...	...	...
, · ~ ·	...	...	...	...	...	...	...	...	...	...	...
, · · ·	...	...	...	...	...	...	...	...	...	...	...
· · · ·	...	...	...	...	3	...	...	...	...	18	...
· · · ·	...	...	...	...	...	...	2	...	...	...	...
· · · ·	...	43	13	4	96	...	112	...	15	34	...
	49	106	66	41	87	204	53	103	83	29	
	42	...	...	...	17	65	...	...	6	...	
	546	252	146	984	1,547	1,692	478	623	728	529	
	...	...	2	26	108	63	...	5	...	...	
	...	...	...	...	...	46	...	...	...	...	
· ~ ·	...	...	...	...	...	...	...	...	...	...	
Total, ·	3,052	1,266	3,009	3,816	6,438	11,466	1,723	7,337	6,906		
. *Hindus.*											
PERIOR CASTES.											
· · ·	1,928	901	1,513	5,424	5,842	5,824	2,504	1,161	770	125	
· ·	147	76	142	186	216	211	42	49	18	3	
Bráhman,	77	172	4	43	27	492	...	1	...	...	
· ·	113	147	134	217	90	222	352	80	98	...	

RETURN OF NATIONALITIES, RACES, ETC.

NAME OF NATIONALITY, TRIBE, OR CASTE.	Total.	Bamanghati.	Morbhanj.	Nilgiri.	Keunjhar.	Pal Lahara.	Dhenkanal.	Talcher.	Angul.	Athmallik.	Hindol.
(i.) SUPERIOR CASTES— *continued.*											
Khandáit, . . .	49,487	441	7,355	5,030	22,225	9	6,304	256	1,386	...	1,5
Khandwál, . . .	4,867	346	815	15	3,152	41	130	5	8	...	...
Mahánáik, . . .	20	...	2	...	...	...	10	...	5	...	...
Total, .	127,364	1,142	13,949	9,142	37,287	549	16,215	2,620	5,003	428	4,2
(ii.) INTERMEDIATE CASTES.											
Káyasth—											
(1) Bengali, . .	370	12	200	26	48	...	15	...	43	1	...
(2) Karan, . .	15,170	74	967	473	1,754	13	1,449	985	734	29	4
(3) Others, . .	16	...	3	...	...	...	...	...	...	...	...
Mahanti, . . .	3,372	...	...	...	1	10	103	...	71	...	9
Bhát, . . .	351	...	57	4	111	...	52	6	8	1	...
Shagirdpeshá, . .	1,996	...	168	...	55	4	133	42	14	...	2
Total, .	21,275	86	1,395	503	1,969	27	1,752	1,033	870	31	6
(iii.) TRADING CASTES.											
Agarwálá, . . .	15	...	...	...	...	...	...	...	...	...	...
Bais Baniyá, . .	2,721	...	16	18	724	...	609	211	11	2	3
Baniyá, . . .	733	2	61	15	51	...	67	...	1	...	...
Gandhabaniyá, . .	129	...	15	...	...	...	...	...	...	...	...
Kapariyá, . .	1,734	...	23	218	182	...	1,174	...	...	...	1
Kumti, . . .	973	...	...	...	...	...	...	4	...	...	...
Putlí, . . .	813	...	59	...	...	...	180	...	...	...	...
Total, .	7,118	2	174	251	957	...	2,030	215	12	2	4
(iv.) PASTORAL CASTES.											
Goálá (Ahir), . .	1,679	...	...	5	1,360	...	7	93	33	...	
Goálá (Gaur), . .	70,117	3,766	9,116	2,153	6,743	1,497	11,626	1,871	5,177	74	1,0
Goálá (Damal), . .	10,274	...	...	...	3	...	...	...	486	1,707	...
Goálá (Magadhá), .	15,995	981	190	13	4,818	...	32	108	404	656	...
Total, .	98,065	4,747	9,306	2,171	12,924	1,497	11,665	2,072	6,100	2,437	1,0
(v.) CASTES ENGAGED IN THE PREPARATION OF COOKED FOOD.											
Halwái, . . .	7	...	7	...	...	...	...	...	...	...	...
Gánrár, . . .	19,295	54	544	222	1,630	22	3,917	616	725	6	3
Rarhi, . . .	3,398	...	731	849	1,806	...	...	...	12	...	...
Total, .	22,700	54	1,282	1,071	3,436	22	3,917	616	737	6	3
(v.) AGRICULTURAL CASTES.											
Chásá, . . .	172,471	2	752	4,428	3,231	2,836	38,400	10,729	25,761	2,332	7,6
Kurmí, . . .	11,051	3,724	4,598	239	1,180	...	...	...	...	...	...
Golá, . . .	9,815	...	3,404	672	1,553	...	313	...	8	...	...
Máli, . . .	10,506	15	98	10	389	23	1,329	350	529	348	5
Sud, . . .	16,026	...	...	...	212	86	111	766	2,136	2,264	6
Or, . . .	3,570	31	...	...	...	...	...	...	3	14	...
Páik, . . .	3,643	...	...	...	...	...	31	7	...	...	...
Ráju, . . .	2,326	156	1,245	351	...	...	34	...	...	...	...
Benátiá, . . .	2,506	...	...	...	...	...	...	...	...	...	...
Kultá, . . .	2,212	...	...	...	19	...	...	...	...	3	...
Samul, . . .	1,546	...	...	...	...	11	7	1,528	...	...	...
Támbuli, . . .	1,593	168	245	28	349	...	30	...	...	...	...
Rául, . . .	101	...	...	...	...	...	18	14	...	...	...
Pandáriyá, . . .	224	...	...	...	...	...	...	...	...	...	...
Sahan, . . .	214	...	...	...	...	...	...	7	1	...	...
Paridá, . . .	162	...	...	...	...	...	22	57	9	...	...

IN EACH OF THE ORISSA TRIBUTARY STATES—*continued.*

NAME OF NATIONALITY, TRIBE, OR CASTE.	Narsinhpur.	Baramba.	Tigaria.	Athgarh.	Banki.	Khandpara.	Nayagarh.	Ranpur.	Daspalla.	Bod.
(i.) SUPERIOR CASTES— *continued.*										
Khandáit,	8	...	...	2,911	1,359	53	13	345	79	38
Khandwal,	...	...	...	...	...	5	29	36	285	...
Mahánáik,	...	...	...	...	...	...	...	...	...	3
Total,	2,202	2,265	1,296	4,704	7,229	6,233	6,791	3,279	1,655	927
(ii.) INTERMEDIATE CASTES.										
Káyasth—										
(1) Bengali,	...	...	...	4	9	1	1	...	...	9
(2) Karan,	253	322	270	448	968	1,644	2,516	984	291	362
(3) Others,	...	...	...	...	2	...	...	11	...	...
Mahanti,	1,439	825	39	1	267	66	334	47	77	...
Bhát,	30	9	...	...	6	13	13	...	...	17
Shagirdpeshá,	37	4	147	214	41	111	627	99	121	104
Total,	1,759	1,160	456	667	1,293	1,835	3,491	1,141	489	492
(iii.) TRADING CASTES.										
Agarwálá,	...	...	...	...	...	6	...	...	9	...
Bais Baniyá,	183	...	8	123	...	114	87	...	134	111
Baniyá,	...	39	37	...	1	18	372	...	8	61
Gandhabaniyá,	...	...	...	...	6	3	...	105	...	...
Kapariyá,	...	...	...	...	...	...	...	...	...	...
Kumtí,	...	...	...	...	...	...	641	213	113	...
Putlí,	...	...	95	...	318	75	...	54	32	...
Total,	183	39	140	123	325	216	1,100	372	296	172
(iv.) PASTORAL CASTES.										
Goálá (Ahir),	...	...	...	...	...	...	15	...	29	135
Goálá (Gaur),	1,858	1,712	641	1,805	2,976	3,771	6,556	2,161	2,789	2,760
Goálá (Damal),	208	...	...	...	...	...	...	...	265	6,787
Goálá (Magadhá),	...	...	...	...	...	...	...	...	108	6,635
Total,	2,066	1,712	641	1,805	2,976	3,771	6,571	2,161	3,191	16,317
(v.) CASTES ENGAGED IN THE PREPARATION OF COOKED FOOD.										
Halwái,	...	...	...	...	...	...	...	...	...	...
Gánrár,	772	640	560	813	1,711	1,949	3,255	901	544	71
Rarhi,	...	...	...	...	...	...	...	...	...	...
Total,	772	640	560	813	1,711	1,949	3,255	901	544	71
(vi.) AGRICULTURAL CASTES.										
Chásá,	3,831	4,769	4,519	5,235	10,469	11,360	23,028	8,458	4,076	1,178
Kurmí,	...	...	...	...	...	...	1,310	...	...	...
Golá,	148	12	...	...	12	173	2,716	154	46	...
Málí,	593	451	204	205	1,268	1,110	1,300	674	437	940
Sud,	1,744	273	...	171	33	66	352	10	906	4,356
Or,	...	417	...	...	6	2,182	...	278	83	520
Páik,	...	8	...	42	2,463	957	24	100	...	...
Ráju,	...	187	...	2	207	45	76	...	...	22
Benátiá,	...	...	...	...	...	2,499	...	...	...	7
Kultá,	...	...	...	...	...	...	...	...	406	1,714
Samul,	...	...	...	...	...	...	...	...	...	...
Támbulí,	11	36	27	...	70	511	53	43	2	20
Rául,	...	...	...	...	28	...	...	...	...	41
Pandáriyá,	...	...	...	...	...	34	190	...	...	...
Sahan,	78	...	...	...	...	28	2	...	93	...
Paridá,	...	...	15	...	...	...	59	...	...	...

RETURN OF NATIONALITIES, RACES, ETC.

NAME OF NATIONALITY, TRIBE, OR CASTE.	Total.	Bamanghati.	Morbhanj.	Nilgiri.
(vi.) AGRICULTURAL CASTES—*continued*.				
Dográ,	141	...	...	141
Bhopá,	51	...	...	...
Sadgop,	51	7	30	...
Agurí,	3	...	...	...
Koerí,	7	...	...	...
Total,	237,619	4,103	10,372	5,869
(vii.) CASTES ENGAGED CHIEFLY IN PERSONAL SERVICE.				
Dhobí,	16,975	550	1,911	524
Bhandárí,	14,372	223	1,128	428
Amanth,	1,548	...	1,074	183
Lodhá,	540	...	179	...
Total,	33,435	773	4,292	1,135
(viii.) ARTISAN CASTES.				
Kámár,	17,162	2,054	2,660	449
Kánsárí,	5,130	69	25	6
Rosora,	85	...	...	...
Sikalgir,	19	...	...	...
Sonár,	4,670	35	504	39
Barhái	4,945	1	58	157
Chitrakár,	194	11	16	...
Pathariá,	221	...	...	...
Kumbhar,	16,559	1,619	2,316	646
Láherí,	45	...	...	...
Kachuá,	914	...	...	...
Sankhárí,	57	...	1	10
Darzí,	225	...	...	...
Chhipí,	6	...	...	...
Telí,	38,794	290	2,437	997
Thuria,	3,682	...	...	17
Sunri,	8,465	653	693	318
Total,	101,173	4,732	8,710	2,639
(ix.) WEAVER CASTES.				
Tantí,	13,706	58	1,894	1,081
Patuá,	5,483	509	673	159
Rángí,	3,212	...	154	...
Koshtá,	2,314	13	...	...
Tulabhiná,	1,369	...	...	52
Sukli, etc.,	1,762	9	26	34
Matibansi,	459	...	4	122
Hángsí,	1,888		327	236	140
Total,	30,193		3,078	1,562	2,877
(x.) LABOURING CASTES.				
Nuniyá,	7		...	...
Korá,	1,033		...	18
Matiyál,	3,949		1,937	224
Total,	4,989		1,937	242
(xi.) CASTES ENGAGED IN SELLING FISH AND VEGETABLES.				
Nikárí,	215		3	..

IN EACH OF THE ORISSA TRIBUTARY STATES—*continued.*

NAME OF NATIONALITY, TRIBE, OR CASTE.	Narsinhpur.	Baramba.	Tigaria.	Athgarh.	Banki.	Khandpara.	Nayagarh.	Ranpur.	Despalla.	Bod.	Kandh-Mals.
(vi.) AGRICULTURAL CASTES—*continued.*											
Dográ, . . .	...	...	...	...	...	...	...	...	...	...	...
Bhopá, . . .	...	...	...	3	...	...	...	16	...	...	...
Sadgop, . . .	...	...	...	...	...	...	...	...	...	...	...
Aguri, . . .	...	...	...	...	1	...	...	...	...	...	...
Koerí, . . .	...	...	...	...	...	...	...	...	...	...	...
Total, .	6,405	6,153	4,765	5,658	14,557	18,965	29,110	9,733	6,049	8,798	1,881
(vii.) CASTES ENGAGED CHIEFLY IN PERSONAL SERVICE.											
Dhobí, . . .	319	309	211	332	736	731	1,607	301	392	765	257
Bhandárí, . .	485	548	450	391	1,008	1,469	1,448	506	406	442	105
Amanth, . .	...	...	...	...	...	...	272	...	11	5	3
Lodhá, . . .	50	110	...	57	88	...	...	29	10	3	...
Total, .	854	967	661	780	1,832	2,200	3,327	836	819	1,215	365
(viii.) ARTISAN CASTES.											
Kámár, . . .	198	69	143	330	400	564	534	151	186	377	660
Kánsárí, . .	112	72	150	27	167	926	580	278	200	155	...
Rosora, . . .	...	...	...	...	...	85	...	...	...	...	...
Sikalgir, . .	...	...	...	...	...	...	19	...	...	...	...
Sonár, . . .	95	223	209	11	281	544	299	247	128	101	7
Barhái, . . .	253	168	138	150	340	575	609	367	143	3	...
Chitrakár, . .	...	6	10	...	18	20	...	6	...	...	...
Pathariá, . .	...	...	...	4	46	...	53	13	...	...	...
Kumbhar, . .	272	319	258	191	584	690	901	320	565	1,285	598
Láheri, . . .	...	...	...	23	...	...	16	...	...	5	...
Kachuá, . . .	...	...	...	2	...	65	...	...	...	...	...
Sankhárí, . .	...	...	17	...	14	15	...	...	...	...	...
Darzi, . . .	...	22	14	3	14	9	85	28	16	...	...
Chhipí, . . .	...	...	...	...	...	...	...	...	...	6	...
Teli, . . .	1,602	1,350	1,048	1,141	3,330	3,076	3,847	1,326	1,170	958	252
Thuria, . . .	61	62	...	...	452	2,257	...	...	131	1	3
Sunri, . . .	110	48	53	250	350	506	920	315	320	377	1,629
Total, .	2,703	2,339	2,040	2,132	5,996	9,332	7,863	3,051	2,859	3,268	3,149
(ix.) WEAVER CASTES.											
Tanti, . . .	575	325	312	497	1,105	920	1,112	444	373	1	...
Patuá, . . .	24	231	1,142	26	242	232	448	306	91	44	...
Rángí, . . .	297	246	80	...	913	431	888	186	...	...	...
Koshtá, . . .	...	...	...	...	...	...	4	7	28	377	...
Tulabhiná, . .	2	53	63	71	192	162	200	45	17	22	...
Sukli, etc., .	...	394	262	...	...	252	240	25	...	...	...
Matibansi, . .	...	2	29	...	2	130	29	26	...	2	...
Hángsi, . . .	...	...	...	...	...	...	...	34	211	...	...
Total, .	898	1,251	1,888	594	2,454	2,127	2,921	1,073	720	446	...
(x.) LABOURING CASTES.											
Nuniyá, . . .	1	...	...	...	...	3	...	...	...	...	...
Korá, . . .	...	...	...	...	...	...	...	...	...	17	...
Matiyál, . . .	...	...	...	12	68	...	6	...	...	108	...
Total, .	1	...	...	12	68	3	6	...	...	125	...
(xi.) CASTES ENGAGED IN SELLING FISH AND VEGETABLES.											
Nikárí, . . .	...	...	...	...	...	167	...	...	...	...	...

RETURN OF NATIONALITIES, RACES, ETC.

NAME OF NATIONALITY, TRIBE, OR CASTE.	Total.	Bamanghati.	Morbhanj.	Nilgiri.	Keunjhar.	Pal Lahara.	Dhenkanal.	Talcher.
(xii.) BOATING AND FISHING CASTES.								
Keut,	31,384	24	1,199	220	1,267	173	7,466	993
Girgiriyá,	3,270	...	...	...	...	...	1,382	747
Tior,	1,613	...	...	...	...	...	174	...
Gokhá,	1,522	...	10	603	264	...	...	...
Dandáchatrá,	1,518	3	1,438	58	19	...	...	...
Ujiyá,	496	...	457	24	...	...	...	...
Málá,	308	49	...	53	67	...	...	...
Ghuni,	243	...	30	...	213	...	...	...
Machuá, etc.,	148	...	...	...	...	...	...	...
Dhibar,	105	...	...	...	91	...	...	...
Chalak,	93	43	50	...	...	...	...	...
Total,	40,700	119	3,184	958	1,921	173	9,022	1,740
(xiii.) DANCER, MUSICIAN, BEGGAR, AND VAGABOND CASTES.								
Kasbi,	290	...	54	16	24	3	30	...
Chokár,	216	...	106	17	1	...	...	5
Kheltá,	443	1	15	6	106	...	148	25
Kahaliá,	34	...	...	...	...	...	1	...
Total,	983	1	175	39	131	3	179	30
(xiv.) PERSONS ENUMERATED BY NATIONALITY ONLY.								
Telingá,	1,164	...	3	...	95	...	49	1
Marhattá,	6	...	...	...	...	...	...	...
Sikh,	9	...	...	...	2	...	2	...
Total,	1,179	...	3	...	97	...	51	1
(xv.) PERSONS OF UNKNOWN OR UNSPECIFIED CASTES,	3,574	6	1,255	2	183	...	817	35
GRAND TOTAL OF HINDUS,	730,582	16,387	57,275	27,282	87,029	6,440	112,696	27,107
4. Persons of Hindu origin not recognising Caste.								
Vaishnav,	5,410	392	1,496	361	412	128	516	172
Sanyási,	233	...	39	10	...	...	22	...
Jogi,	1,471	104	123	36	210	...	400	72
Mahájáti,	172	3	...	...	...	...	...	...
Buddhist,	1	...	...	...	...	...	...	...
Native Christians,	302	...	...	35	...	...	...	...
Total,	7,589	499	1,658	442	622	128	938	244
5. Muhammadans.								
Mughul,	42	...	8	...	...	...	...	...
Pathán,	2,284	14	391	18	255	35	222	...
Sayyid,	109	...	14	...	14	...	56	97
Shaikh,	1,548	462	335	1	218	...	129	3
Fakír,	12	3	...	...	...	...	9	...
Total,	3,995	479	748	19	487	35	416	100
TOTAL OF NATIVES OF INDIA,	1,283,308	94,526	164,154	33,944	181,870	15,450	178,072	38,021
GRAND TOTAL,	1,283,309	94,526	164,154	33,944	181,871	15,450	178,072	38,021

. IN EACH OF THE ORISSA TRIBUTARY STATES—*continued.*

NAME OF NATIONALITY, TRIBE, OR CASTE.	Narsinhpur.	Baramba.	Tigaria.	Athgarh.	Banki.	Khandpara.	Nayagarh.	Raupur.	Daspalla.	Bod.	Kandh-Mals.
(xii.) BOATING AND FISHING CASTES.											
Keut,	1,315	1,319	865	1,019	3,332	2,928	1,288	537	1,188	3,151	279
Girgiriyá,	157	123	20	...	136	56	...	...	38	573	...
Tior,	124	...	115	...	220	180	253	43	76	66	...
Gokhá,	...	41	...	42	511	...	22	...	...	29	...
Dandáchatrá,	...	...	...	...	...	...	...	...	...	...	...
Ujiyá,	...	15	...	...	...	...	...	...	...	...	...
Málá,	...	...	...	...	...	...	...	...	57	...	...
Ghuni,	...	...	...	...	...	...	...	...	...	...	...
Machuá, etc.,	...	...	...	35	...	...	3	109	...	1	...
Dhibar,	...	...	...	...	...	...	...	...	...	14	...
Chalak,	...	...	...	...	...	...	...	...	...	...	...
Total,	1,596	1,498	1,000	1,096	4,199	3,164	1,566	689	1,359	3,834	279
(xiii.) DANCER, MUSICIAN, BEGGAR, AND VAGABOND CASTES.											
Kasbí,	31	15	3	2	...	33	49	26	2	...	...
Chokár,	...	...	4	...	...	14	61	...	8	...	...
Kheltá,	13	...	9	13	...	16	...	9	11	...	...
Kahaliá,	...	3	...	...	20	...	...	10	...	...	...
Total,	44	18	16	15	20	63	110	45	21	...	...
(xiv.) PERSONS ENUMERATED BY NATIONALITY ONLY.											
Telingá,	6	2	...	...	2	...	640	134	2	29	17
Marhattá,	...	...	...	...	1	...	...	...	5	...	...
Sikh,	...	...	...	...	...	...	...	...	...	...	...
Total,	6	2	...	...	3	...	640	134	7	29	17
(xv.) PERSONS OF UNKNOWN OR UNSPECIFIED CASTES,	155	11	4	35	1	28	150	33	15	765	51
GRAND TOTAL OF HINDUS,	19,644	18,055	13,467	18,434	42,664	50,053	66,901	23,448	18,024	36,459	9,077
4. Persons of Hindu Origin not recognising Caste.											
Vaishnav,	108	46	137	177	147	338	221	100	136	120	93
Sanyásí,	48	17	...	8	...	88	...	...	1	...	...
Jogi,	...	...	...	2	85	192	4	...	...	...	...
Mahájáti,	...	...	...	...	...	169	...	...	...	...	...
Buddhist,	...	...	1	...	...	...	...	...	...	...	...
Native Christians,	...	...	...	257	10	...	...	...	...	...	...
Total,	156	63	138	444	242	787	225	100	137	120	93
5. Muhammadans.											
Mughul,	...	...	...	...	18	...	...	...	...	7	3
Pathán,	109	56	140	93	207	28	169	107	1	84	3
Sayyid,	...	...	...	...	10	5	3	...	...	...	2
Shaikh,	2	11	106	50	14	5	54	41	4	...	3
Fakír,	...	...	...	...	...	...	...	...	...	...	...
Total,	111	67	246	143	249	38	226	148	5	91	11
TOTAL OF NATIVES OF INDIA,	24,758	24,261	16,420	26,366	49,426	60,877	83,249	27,306	34,805	57,058	51,810
GRAND TOTAL,	24,758	24,261	16,420	26,366	49,426	60,877	83,249	27,306	34,805	57,058	51,810

Sentence continued from page 209.]
of government on the aboriginal plan is still maintained, the hamlets being distributed into *mutas* or counties, each *muta* under the supervision of its own chief. Throughout this wild tract they claim an indefeasible right in the soil. They assert that the whole State of Bod was once theirs, and that they have been pushed back into the recesses of the hills by unscrupulous invaders.

Thirty years ago this people formed one of the most difficult problems with which a Christian Government was ever called upon to deal. Up to that time we had not come into contact with them, nor were we in any way responsible for their conduct. We knew that they and the Savars inhabited the mountainous background down the coast, 'three hundred miles in length, and from fifty to a hundred in breadth, between the Mahánadí and the Godávarí.' The officer best acquainted with it (Lieutenant Macpherson) described it as a tract 'of forest, swamp, and mountain fastnesses, interspersed with open and productive valleys, and from its climate habitable with safety by strangers only during a few months of the year.' The great Hindu Principalities of Gumsar and Bod lay between us and the wild tribes beyond, and shut us out from any communication with them. But in 1835 the Gumsar Rájá fell into arrears of tribute, and our measures to enforce our just claims were followed by his rebellion and flight into the Kandh country. The insurrection ended in our attaching his territory, and this territory made us the feudal suzerain of the Kandh highlands beyond. We found that our new subjects, whose fidelity to their late Chief, even while involving severe measures, had won our respect, practised the abomination of human sacrifice both in their public and their private rites. The measures by which we suppressed this custom I shall afterwards detail. But before attempting coercive measures, Lieutenant Macpherson was deputed to ascertain the character of the people, and the real facts of the case ; and this officer's Report forms one of the most admirable and most interesting official documents to be found in the archives of any Government.

Lieutenant Macpherson's Report still remains the great storehouse of facts with regard to the Kandhs in their primitive state. The following brief description is chiefly taken from it, with such new light as the District Accounts of Vizagapatam and of the Central Provinces have within the last few years shed upon the race. In the interior table-land the Kandhs appear as a restless,

wandering caste, who seldom remain long in the same spot, and
'the greater part of whom pay nothing to Government, and have
but little intercourse with its officers.' But in the headquarters of
their race, Lieutenant Macpherson, when he visited them thirty-five
years ago, found a free and spirited people, living under a semi-
patriarchal, semi-feudal government, with a strongly developed
nationality of their own. The word 'Kandh,' like 'Máli,' and the
tribal names of other hill tribes, means in the aboriginal languages
'mountaineer.' As the Hindu Rájás drove them deeper into the
recesses of the hills, the tribe split up into three sections. The
weaker of them remained as a landless low caste in the new Hindu
Principalities; another class obtained military tenures from the
conquerors, and formed a peasant militia such as that which again
and again beat back the wave of Musalmán conquest from Orissa;
the third wrung from their Hindu neighbours the position and
the privileges of free allies. A system of military aids, homage,
investiture, and other feudal incidents, well described in Lieutenant
Macpherson's Report, sprang up, as the superior civilisation of the
Hindu Prince more and more exerted its influence on the wild
tribes. There is at least this to be said for the Hindus throughout
India, that everywhere they appear as bringing in a more humane
government and a more enlightened religion than that of the people
who preceded them, and whom they ousted from the plains.

KANDH SOCIAL ORGANIZATION.—Among the Kandhs the principle
of Family remains supreme. Hamlets certainly exist; but the social
nexus is not that of the village, as among the Hindus, but that of
the household. The three links in their organization are the family,
the sept, and the tribe. Theoretically, each tribe has sprung from
a common father, and it is governed by a patriarch who represents
the common ancestor. Each sept or branch of a tribe consists of a
number of families claiming the same progenitor, while in each
family the absolute authority rests with the house-father. Thus, the
sons have no property during their father's lifetime; and all the
male children, with their wives and descendants, continue to share
the father's meal, prepared by the common mother. As the tribes
form a federal group under a federal patriarch, and as the septs or
tribal branches form a tribe-cluster under a tribal patriarch, so the
individual families unite into little village communities under a
village father or head. Each of these three stages of organization
has its own representative assembly; the federal council being

chosen from the tribal patriarchs, the tribe-assembly from the branch or sept patriarchs, and the village elders from the house-fathers. In short, to use the words of Lieutenant Macpherson, 'the outward order of Kandh society, all its conditions, its texture, and its colouring, necessarily derive their distinctive character chiefly from the ideas which produce, or which spring from, this remarkable system of family life.'

Side by side with this principle of family, we discern another motive power at work in the social structure of the Kandhs. The patriarchal authority forms the basis of the whole, but it is modified by an elective or representative element. If a people could make sure that its natural hereditary head should be always the man best fitted for the office of leader, the hereditary principle would reign supreme among mankind. But unhappily, the natural chief of a family or tribe has often none of the qualifications required for a ruler. The Kandhs get rid of the difficulty by an ingenious compromise, which makes the patriarchal office hereditary as to family, but elective as to person. The eldest son of the patriarchal family has a prior title to the post; but if his character should unfit him for its duties, he makes way for a younger brother or an uncle. The two essentials for the patriarchal office, therefore, are personal fitness and birth within the prescribed family. Nothing like a formal election takes place. If the eldest son be deemed unsuitable, he is silently passed over as if by family arrangement, and the business managed rather by exclusion than by selection.

The Kandh social organization is therefore regulated by the harmonious action of two principles, which in other parts of the world we are accustomed to see widely dissevered. The principle of Family, modified and corrected by the Elective Principle,—that is to say, hereditary title strengthened by ascertained personal fitness for the work, gives a force to the patriarchal authority such as few civilised Governments possess. The Kandh patriarch (*abáya*, literally, father), whether of a tribe, a sept, or a village, is the Father, the Magistrate, and the High Priest of his people. The principle of Family and the principle of Election combine with religious feeling to render his office sacred. He receives no pay, nor any official privileges other than the respect and veneration which belong to him as leader, father, and priest. He 'is simply the head of a family in which every member is of equal rank—the first amongst equals. He is in no respect raised above the community, whose interests, associations, traditions, and manner of life he shares. No one ministers to his wants. He has no trace of state, however rude; no separate residence or stronghold; no retainers; no property save his ancestral fields, by the cultivation of which he lives. He receives neither tribute nor aid, save perhaps an occasional harvest-offering of goodwill. The enjoyment of the place of dignity at every public and private festival may be reckoned, as in the case of the Homeric kings, the most valuable, as it is amongst the most agreeable incidents of his situation.

'The patriarch of a tribe, whatever may be the degree of his personal authority, undertakes no measures except in emergency, and transacts no affairs without the assistance and sanction of the *abáyas* (heads of septs or branches of the tribe), or of the assembled society. He has charge of the relations of his tribe with the neighbouring tribes and principalities. He leads in war, and always accompanies the military aids rendered to the Hindu chiefs. At home he is the protector of public order, and the arbiter of private wrongs; conciliating feuds and dispensing justice, but depending for obedience to his decisions entirely upon his personal influence and the authority of his assessors. He convenes a council of the *abáyas*, or of the whole tribe, as usage may prescribe, either for deliberative or judicial purposes. He, moreover, discharges the local duties of patriarch of his family subdivision (sept), and head of his village.'

PUBLIC LAW.—The Kandh patriarch, whether of a tribe, a sept, or a village, administered a well-defined system of public and domestic law. The Kandh theory of existence was, that a state of war may be lawfully presumed against all tribes and nations with whom no express agreement to the contrary existed. Even between tribes of the same federal cluster, peace was a matter of stipulation or contract; and 'hence, while within each tribe order and security prevail, beyond it all is discord and confusion. In a word, the practical spirit of their intercourse is the result of a conflict between the anti-social spirit of independence which universally characterizes a rude people, and the love of security and enjoyment which necessarily attends the hereditary possession of competence and freedom; while, upon the whole, the latter influence predominates.'

PRIVATE BLOOD-REVENGE.—This aggressive system of public law had its counterpart in the private judicial procedure of blood-revenge. In case of murder, the duty fell upon the male kindred within certain degrees of propinquity, not very strictly determined. The custom of blood-revenge was, however, modified by the principle of money compensation, a practice that enables the friends on both sides to step in and to put a limit to hereditary retaliation. Offences against the person, such as wounding or grievous hurt, might be made amends for by compensation in property; and the sufferer, whether his injuries were severe or not, had a right to live daintily at the cost of his assailant until perfectly recovered from his hurts. No payment could wipe out the stain of adultery. The injured husband was bound to put to death an adulterer caught in the act, and to send back his wife to her father's house.

IN OFFENCES AGAINST PROPERTY, the principle of restitution reigned supreme. A stolen article must be returned, or its equivalent must be paid; the injured party could inflict no further penalty. So mild a punishment might seem to be a direct encouragement of theft. But this leniency extended only to the first offence. A repetition of the crime was dealt with not as an offence against property, or against the individual sufferer, but as a wrong perpetrated upon the whole society. No compensation could expiate it, and the criminal was expelled without mercy from his tribe. Generally speaking, offences against property among the Kandhs take one of two forms: either the theft of agricultural produce, or wrongful occupation of the soil. Questions of civil right often mingle with such cases, a claimant merely anticipating the decision of the village head by seizing the disputed land or appropriating its produce. It is this consideration which probably led the Kandhs to regard the crime of theft and ouster as so venial. The offender had to restore stolen agricultural produce at once; and when it could not be recovered, his land was made over to the injured party until its produce made good the theft. The Kandhs, however, did not leave the offender's family to starve, but yearly set aside one-half of the crop on the attached fields for their subsistence. The abundance of waste land rendered wrongful ouster, or forcible occupation of the soil, a venial offence. It involved no further punishment than its simple restoration to the party to whom it might be adjudged due.

ORIGIN OF RIGHTS.—Priority of occupation forms the sole origin of right. No complicated tenures exist, every man tilling his own field and acknowledging no landlord. But even so simple a system requires general principles to regulate it, and gives rise to conflicting claims. In the Kandh land-law, as in their political organization, we see the principle of family as the basis of the structure, but that principle modified by personal considerations. The right to the soil arises from priority of occupation by the family or tribe, and within the tribe from priority of cultivation by the individual. Kandh tillage still retains some of the migratory features common to the nomadic husbandry of most aboriginal tribes. When a piece of land shows signs of exhaustion, they abandon it, and in their native settlements they change their villages once in about fourteen years. The question of waste land therefore forms an important one. Where the population begins to press rather heavily on the territory of the tribe, they parcel out the waste lands for pasturage among the various hamlets, and thus exhibit the first model of the Hindu village of the plains. But as 'not an eighth part' of the Kandh territory 'was appropriated by individuals' in 1841, the waste lands had scarcely any value, and mostly remained unappropriated among the hamlets and common to the tribe. Generally speaking, a Kandh might take possession of any waste lands within his tribal territory, by bringing it under tillage.

TRANSFER OF RIGHTS.—If the origin of rights among the Kandhs is simple, the transfer is easy. The seller makes known his purpose to the patriarch of the sept or tribal branch, 'not to obtain his sanction, but to give publicity to his intentions.' He then leads the buyer to the hamlet where the field lies, and calling together five husbandmen of the village, delivers a handful of the earth to the purchaser, and publicly receives part of the price. At the same moment he invokes the village god as a witness that he has parted for ever with the field, and so the transaction ends. Landed disputes are adjudicated by a council of elders, who hear both parties and examine witnesses. The favourite mode of decision, however, is by judicial ordeal. The Kandhs believe that rice steeped in the blood of a sheep killed in the name of the earth-god will, if swallowed by the litigants, slay the perjured party on the spot. A lump of the disputed soil, when kneaded into clay, will produce the same desirable effect. The old chivalrous custom of the defendant purging himself upon oath still flourishes among the Kandhs. The commonest form is to take the oath upon the skin of a tiger, from which animal sure destruction will inevitably befall the false swearer. When a tiger wounds or kills a Kandh, his whole family becomes outcast; but the *domnd*, or aboriginal priest, can restore them to their status, by taking away all the property in the house of the unfortunate man who has thus visibly incurred the wrath of the Kandh deities. If the oath be taken upon a lizard's skin, scaliness will be the perjured party's lot; if upon an ant-hill, he will fall away into a heap of dust. Boiling water, hot oil, and heated iron also form favourite ordeals. The litigants pay no court fees, but the losing party has to liberally entertain the members of the tribunal with rice, flesh, and liquor.

THE LAW OF INHERITANCE assumes that no person ought to possess land who cannot with his own right hand defend it. Agricultural stock and landed property descend exclusively in the male line, the eldest son generally receiving the largest share, but among some tribes dividing equally with his brethren. On failure of sons, the land and homestead stock go to the father's brothers, as the Kandh Salic Law deems women incapable of holding real property or aught pertaining to it. On failure of heirs-male, the land passes to the village, and is parcelled out among its families. The daughters divide equally among themselves the personal ornaments, household furniture, money, and all moveable property of their deceased father, and have a right to a liberal maintenance from their brothers while they remain single, together with the expenses of the marriage ceremony when they enter on that state.

CHARACTER.—The people who live under this simple law and patriarchal Government exhibit primitive virtues which more civilised nations may well envy. 'They have the easy bearing of men unconscious of inferiority, and rarely employ expressions of courtesy. In salutation they raise the hand perpendicularly above the head; in meeting on the road, the younger person says, "I am on my way;" the elder replies, "Go on."' While willingly copying the nobler features of the Hindu civilisation and religion, they assert their superiority as a people to the more advanced race. 'Their most common boasts are, that they reverence their fathers and mothers; that they are men of one word; and that the Kandhs are one as a race, while the Hindus are endlessly subdivided.' Our officers who had to conquer them bear witness to their virtues. 'In superiority to physical pain the Kandhs are surpassed by no people. In a period of suffering rarely paralleled, during which the population wasted for two months beneath famine, disease, and the sword, no single Kandh was found to falter in his devotion to the common cause; and when at length the fathers of the tribe were betrayed and condemned to die, with what admirable courage, with what affecting resignation and simple dignity, did they meet an igno-minious fate on the sites of their ruined homesteads !' One of our prisoners tore out his tongue by the roots, and died, rather than say anything that might involve his clan. Another 'sternly refused food, and perished on the fourth day.' Here is the picture of a careworn but still vigorous Kandh patriarch in his fifty-seventh year : ' In person he is somewhat below the middle size, according to the Hindu standard; of spare habit, and by no means robustly formed. His physiognomy is spirited, and, when excited, intellectual, but with a predominating expression of benevolence. His features are regular, sufficiently bold for expression, but by no means striking, and not strongly marked by the peculiarities of his race. His manner is animated, perfectly self-possessed, and very pleasing. He might pass for a well-bred Bráhman of Orissa.'

DOMESTIC CEREMONIES.—The three great incidents of human life—birth, marriage, and death—the Kandh delights to surround with ceremonies and solemnities all his own. The expectant mother invokes the village deity for her future offspring; and should any delay in her delivery take place, the priest leads her out to the meeting of two springs, sprinkles her with water, and makes an offering to the God of Births. The choice of a name engrosses the anxious thoughts of the parents. The priest drops grains of rice into water, uttering, as each grain falls, the name of one of the family ancestors. The motions of the various seeds as they sink to the bottom of the vessel enable him to declare which forefather has reappeared upon earth in the new-born babe. On the seventh day after the birth the parents give a great dinner to the priest and the whole village, with unlimited liquor; and so the birth ceremonies end. In marriage, the necessity for maintaining the manliness of the race makes the Kandhs religiously observe the restrictions of consanguinity. No union can take place between kinsmen, or even between members of the same tribe. Intermarriage goes on independently of peace and war, the belligerent clans suspending their conflict in order to partake together of the wedding feast, and renewing the fight next day with perfect ferocity and good temper. A Kandh boy marries when he reaches his tenth or twelfth year. His wife is usually about four years older, or about fifteen. The bridegroom's father pays a price for the bride; and she remains almost as a servant in her father-in-law's house until her boy-husband reaches a fit age for the consummation of the marriage, and for bearing his own part in the world.

The betrothal consists of a procession, a libation to the gods, and a feast. The bridegroom's father assembles his family and friends, and carries a supply of rice and liquor to the girl's house. The priest stands in readiness to receive him, tastes the bowl, and pours out an offering to the gods. The parents then join hands, and the espousals are complete. The wedding itself is simply an abduction in the middle of a feast. All the kinsmen assemble at the dwelling of the bride, or, if she dwells at a distance, in some place near the bridegroom's house, and after an ample supper drink and dance the night away. The priest binds a yellow thread round the necks of the parties, and sprinkles their faces with turmeric water in the shed in which the family beats out its rice. The Hindus of the plains have adopted these aboriginal ceremonies into their own marriage rite, the yellow thread being tied round the waists of the boy and girl, and turmeric paste rubbed into their skin. Towards morning the girl's uncle lifts her on his shoulders, while one of the boy's uncles does the same thing with him. After the bride and bridegroom have thus been carried aloft among the dancers, their bearers suddenly exchange burdens, and the boy's uncle makes off with the bride. In a moment the festivities cease. The kinsmen range themselves into two hostile tribes, the girl's friends trying to recapture the bride, the boy's to cover her flight. The two clans carry the fight to great lengths ; and the conflict exhibits, in its rude original form, a custom which the Hindu conquerors of India admitted as one of their eight recognised forms of marriage. In their law-books it still bears the name of *Rákshasa*, the generic appellation in Sanskrit for the aboriginal tribes, such as the Kandhs. Among the latter, after the struggle is over, the priest attends the bride and bridegroom home, in order to avert by a charm the evil which would threaten their married life, in case their path should cross a running brook.

' In the superior age of the bride,' writes Macpherson, ' is seen a proof of the supremacy of the paternal authority amongst this singular people. The parents retain the wives of their sons during their boyhood as very valuable domestic servants, and their selections are avowedly made with a view to utility in this character.'

Women hold a high position among the Kandhs. The wife naturally exercises a considerable influence from the first upon her boy-husband; and notwithstanding the payment made by the father of the bridegroom, the girl does not in any sense become the property of the husband, or pass *in manu,* as among the Romans. Even if pregnant, she can return to her father's house within six months after the marriage, on the articles which had been paid for her being restored. If childless, she can at any time quit her husband and re-enter her own family. In no case can the husband forcibly reclaim her, but a wife separated on any grounds whatsoever from her husband cannot marry again. Adultery operates *ipso facto* as a divorce of the faithless wife. But so long as a wife remains true to her husband, he cannot contract a second marriage, or even keep a concubine, without his wife's consent. When such permission is obtained, the children of the concubine receive among some tribes an equal treatment with the legitimate sons; among others, they only inherit a half-share of the paternal property. The Kandhs faithfully observe the marriage tie; adultery is seldom heard of: the wife serves her husband while he eats; helps him in the homestead; and when out-door labour presses, she binds her baby around her waist and goes forth with him to the field.

The last incident of human life remains. On the death of a common Kandh, his kinsmen quickly burn the body, and on the tenth day give a drinking feast to the hamlet. But when a patriarch dies, his bereaved people spread over the country with gongs and drums, and summon all village and tribal heads. They place the body on a lofty timber pile, with a flagstaff and banner rising from its midst. The clothes, arms, and household vessels of the dead patriarch are laid out on a rice bag near the structure. The chief mourner with averted face applies the torch, and all the kinsmen gyrate in a funeral dance around the pyre until the flagstaff falls wholly burned. They then parcel out among the sept patriarchs the dead man's goods which had been exposed upon the rice bag, and during the next nine days the family meet together at intervals and renew their solemn dance around the ashes. On the tenth day the whole tribe with its families and septs assemble, and choose or acknowledge a new patriarch, who is generally the eldest son of the late chief.

CHARACTER.—The two great virtues of the Kandhs are their fidelity and their valour. From the first springs an excessive hospitality, which knows no bounds, and which leads them into drunkenness and feuds. 'For the safety of a guest,' runs the Kandh proverb, 'life and honour are pledged; he is to be considered before a child.' 'Every stranger is an invited guest.' As soon as a traveller enters a village, the heads of families respectfully solicit him to share their meal. He may remain as long as he chooses; 'a guest can never be turned away.' Fugitives from the field of battle, and even escaped criminals, must be hospitably received. 'If a man can make his way by any means into the house of his enemy, it is a case of refuge, and he cannot be touched, even although his life has been forfeited to his involuntary host by the law of blood-revenge.' A man belonging to one of the miserable low castes who are attached to the Kandh hamlets, killed the son of the village patriarch, and fled. Two years afterwards he suddenly rushed one night into the house of the bereaved father. The indignant patriarch with difficulty held his hand from the trembling wretch, and convened a council of the tribe to know how he might lawfully take revenge. But the assembly decided that, however grievously the refugee had wronged his host, he was now his guest, and must be kept by him in comfort and unharmed. Among some tribes, however, an enemy who thus tries to evade the law of blood-revenge does not escape. The family quit the house; and although they will not hurt him so long as he remains under what was once their roof, yet they send him no food, and the moment he crosses the threshold in quest of it, they fall upon him and slay him. But a case of this sort seldom occurs, and the Kandhs regard it, even when put in force against the murderer of a son, as unjustifiable. Sometimes a whole tribe forces itself upon the hospitality of another, and in one well-known case a fugitive clan was thus maintained by another for an entire year. A feast had given rise to a bloody feud, which ended in the tribe being driven out from their lands, and for twelve months they depended entirely upon the hospitality of their involuntary hosts. At the end of that time the clan which had seized their territory took pity upon them, and relaxed their cordon of outposts, so that the expelled tribe found re-entrance into one of their old villages. Here they immediately claimed the rights of hospitality; their enemies, who a year before had ousted them, were forced to admit the claim, and either to support them as guests, or to restore to them the lands which they had seized. In the end they adopted the latter course; and in this way the laws of hospitality act as a check alike upon the custom of blood-revenge, and upon the Kandh theory of chronic war. One creature alone among the human race could claim no shelter—the unhappy *meriah*, or victim set apart for human sacrifice.

Their fidelity to their chiefs and to their allies knows no limit. It was this virtue which first brought us into collision with them. The Gumsar Rájá, when he rebelled against us in 1835, fell back upon the Kandh settlements, and on his deathbed the clans pledged their word for the safety of his family. At first they showed rather a friendly disposition to our advancing troops; but when they learned our terms, they preferred devastation and death to perfidy. They refused 'with the most admirable constancy' to give up their guests. 'The country was laid utterly desolate. The population was unceasingly pursued by our troops;' and it was only the treachery of the Hindu borderers that, by betraying them into our hands, brought the sickening struggle to a close.

Their bravery in battle well supports this fidelity to their chiefs. The two honourable professions among the Kandhs—indeed, the sole occupation of a freeborn hill-man—are husbandry and war. Each man has his own little estate, and his heart beats with the independence which, all over the world, characterises the freeholder and the land-owning yeoman. Every Kandh tills his own land, and heartily despises all who engage in any occupation save agriculture and war. As among the earlier Hindus, whose village system, there can be little doubt, was to a large extent based upon the previous aboriginal model, each Kandh hamlet has certain servile castes belonging to it. A few families of hereditary weavers (Páns), of hereditary ironsmiths (Lohárs), of hereditary potters (Kumbhárs), of hereditary herdsmen (Gaurs), and of hereditary distillers (Sunrís), hang about the outskirts of the village, or live in a separate row of huts assigned to them by the Kandh ruling caste. The despised classes have from time immemorial formed an essential element in the aboriginal village community. No Kandh could engage in the work which they perform without degradation. Nor can a Kandh eat food prepared by their hands. The most important of them, the Pán or weaver caste, carry the summons to the council or to war, supply the music at ceremonies, and act in many matters as hereditary village servants. One of their duties points to their connection with that very ancient form of worship, which enters in different degrees alike into the Kandh and into the Hindu religion, and which both of these races seem to have adopted from a still more primitive people. On certain families of the weaver caste falls the hereditary duty of providing human victims for the Earth-God. None of the servile classes can hold land, nor can any industry raise them to an equality with the superior race. On the other hand, the Kandhs treat them with kindness, never forgetting a portion for them at a feast, and resenting any injury done to them as if it had been inflicted upon their own property. They generally maintain their blood pure, and appear to be distinct ethnical remnants of peoples whom the Kandhs subdued in very ancient times, and whom they have used ever since as servile castes. Living as they do as landless day-labourers or artisans on the outskirts alike of the Kandh and of the Hindu communities, they keep up a communication between the two superior races, and generally speak both the Kandh and the Uriyá tongues.

From his earliest boyhood, the Kandh learns to regard himself as a freeman sprung from a dominant race, with a serf population below him to do all ignoble work. His business is agriculture; his pastime, war. During seed-time and harvest he rises at daybreak, and eats a hearty meal of a sort of pulse porridge, boiled up with herbs and goat's or swine's flesh. Before the dew has risen from the land, he drives his oxen a-field, and toils without a pause till three in the afternoon. If engaged in the severer sorts of work, such as clearing jungle, he rests at mid-day and eats his dinner. But when following the plough he works right on till the afternoon, when he bathes in the nearest stream, and at evening returns home to another hearty mess of thick rich soup, with the addition of the liquor of tobacco. In choosing the site of his habitation, the Kandh displays great taste. His village lies embedded in a leafy grove, or at the foot of finely-wooded hills, or crowns some little green knoll in the valleys, well raised above the flood-level. The hamlet generally consists of two rows of houses, forming a broad curved street, and closed at both ends by a strong wooden barrier. The northern Kandh settlements, however, do not adhere to this plan. But almost everywhere the patriarch has his house in the very centre of the hamlet, close to the cotton tree which the priest plants and dedicates to the village god, as the first necessary act in building a hamlet. The low castes properly live at the extremity of the street, but in some cases erect their miserable clusters of sheds outside it. In Lieutenant Macpherson's time, a true Kandh husbandman knew nothing about money, and detested trade of every sort. Even the primitive shell currency had not reached his village;

and instead of a metal coinage, he reckoned the value of articles in
lives. As these *lives* might be either sheep or oxen, or even inanimate articles, such as rice or pease, any traffic except by actual
barter involved very complicated calculations among the Kandhs.

The Kandh intermits his field-labour by frequent predatory incur-
sions and wars. About the average height of the Hindus, his clean
and boldly-developed muscles, fleet foot, expanded forehead, and
full but not thick lips, present a type of strength, intelligence, and
determination, blended with good humour, which make him an
agreeable companion in peace, and a formidable enemy in war. He
never asks for quarter, and adorns himself for battle as for a feast,
plaiting his hair into a flat circle on the right side of the head, and
fixing into it a towering plume of feathers. The patriarch or the
tribal assembly sends out swift messengers from glen to glen, bearing
an arrow as the summons to war. Before engaging, each side records
a vow of a human victim to the Earth-deity (Berá-penu) if he gives
victory, and implores the aid of the God of War (Lohá-penu) by the
blood of goats and fowls poured out in his sacred grove and on the
field of battle. A Kandh fight resembles in many respects the listed
combats of mediæval chivalry, such as Sir Walter Scott has described
in the thirty-fourth chapter of the *Fair Maid of Perth.* The most
approved form is to go on fighting day after day, till one party or the
other is absolutely exterminated.

An eye-witness has described a conflict which lasted three days, the
challenge being renewed every morning by throwing down a piece
of bloody cloth upon the battle-field. Such a fight yields a pleasur-
able excitement not only to the warriors themselves, but to both
their villages. The women and old men past bearing arms stood
close behind the combatants during the conflict, handing them pots
of water and cooked food, with much good advice as to the conduct
of the fight. When the first man fell, all rushed to dip their axes
in his blood, and hacked the body in pieces; while the first man
who slew his enemy without getting a wound himself, hewed off the
right arm from the corpse, and ran with it to the priest among the
non-combatants in the rear, as an offering to the God of War. Before
evening a great heap of right arms had thus accumulated on each
rear,—one side having lost sixty men, and the other thirty, besides
at least as many more mortally wounded, as the result of the first
day's pastime. The Kandh uses a curiously curved sword with
singular effect and dexterity, besides the two-handed axe, a bow and

arrows, and a sling. He disdains any shield, but guards with the handle of his axe. His favourite bowshot is a sort of ricochet, the arrow touching the ground with its heel 'at a short distance from its object, which it strikes in rising, below the line of vision.' The Kandh never claims the victory as the reward of his personal valour, but invariably and with perfect good faith ascribes it to the favour of his god.

The single vice of the Kandhs is drunkenness. Their cheap liquor, made from the *mahud* flower, plays a conspicuous part at every feast, and, as among the hillmen of old Thessaly, often turns good fellowship into deadly war. But the Orissa mountaineer pays small heed to the lesson which the brawls of the Centaurs and Lapithæ, *super mero debellata*, were supposed to teach. No event of his life, no public ceremony in his village, is complete without intoxication. The women alone refrain from the cup, merely tasting it as a compliment to the company; and while drunkenness is held to be a laudable custom among the men, in a woman it is uncommon, and would be deemed disgraceful. A traveller, in passing through the Kandh country at a season of periodical intoxication, when the *mahud* flower blows, found the valleys 'covered with frantic or senseless groups of men, but no women appeared in the least intoxicated.' The same eye-witness thus sums up the character of the Kandh race :—'A passionate love of liberty, devotion to chiefs, and unconquerable resolution. They are, besides, faithful to friends, brave, hospitable, and laborious. Their vices, upon the other hand, are the indulgence of revenge, and occasionally of brutal passion. Drunkenness is universal; the habit of plunder exists in one or two small tracts alone.'

THE RELIGION of the Kandhs is essentially one of blood. Gods many and terrible dwell upon the earth and under the earth, in the waters and in the sky, each and all of whom must be propitiated by victims. As the Kandh theory of human existence is a normal state of war, broken at intervals by expressly stipulated truces, so their conception of the nature of God is one of chronic hostility to mankind, mitigated at intervals by the outpouring of blood. Their religion exhibits the transition stage between the rude worship of the primitive races of India, and that composite structure of Aryan beliefs and aboriginal rites of which modern Hinduism is made up. Their pantheon embraces one set of deities unmistakeably aboriginal, a second class of mixed or doubtful origin, and a third which in its present form they have unquestionably derived from the Hindus. The first class, or Race-Gods, consist of fourteen great deities, who dwell in the Kandh country, and preside over the fortunes of the tribes. Of these the three chief are the Earth-God (Berá-penu), the Iron-God or God of War (Lohá-penu), and the Village Deity (Nadzu-penu). Next to them rank the Sun-God (Beyelá-penu), the God of Boundaries (Sande-penu), the Deities of Streams (Jorí-penu), Forests (Gassá-penu), Tanks (Mundá-penu), Fountains (Sugu-penu), and Rain (Pidzu-penu). The God of Hunting (Pilámu-penu) has also a place, with the God of Births (Garí-penu), and the terrible Deity of the Small-pox (Jugá-penu). Eleven local or minor divinities follow, some of whom seem to represent the worship of those still earlier races whom the Kandhs reduced to servile castes. The chief of these, literally the Great Father God (Pitá-baldí), has as his sole symbol a stone smeared with turmeric under some lofty forest tree. The jungle people declare that these rude blocks mark the place where the deity has from time to time issued from or returned into the earth. Another (Bandri-penu) is represented by a mysterious piece of some unknown substance, neither gold, nor silver, nor wood, nor iron, nor stone, nor any other material named upon earth. Un-happily, when one of our officers reached the temple and wanted to see it, the priest was away at a distance, and had carried with him the key. A third (Dungárí-penu) of the Dii Minores seems to represent what may be called the worship of the *status quo*. Once a year the clans assemble, and with copious outpouring of blood upon a lofty mountain, implore the god that they may remain exactly in the state of their forefathers, and that their children after them may live exactly as themselves. Another (Singá-penu) of these lesser deities presents the ancient type of the God of Destruction, whose worship formed the first national creed of the Hindu monarchs of Orissa, on the expulsion of the strictly Buddhist dynasty. The remaining seven of these lesser deities are styled—Báhman-penu, Báhmundi-penu, Damosinghiání, Patarghar, Pinjái, Kankálí, and Balindá-silendá. The purer Aryan conception of the Godhead enables the Hindu to ennoble any aboriginal belief which he may borrow; and the God of Destruction in Bráhmanical hands stands forth also as the God of Reconstruction, death and life being but alternate forms of existence. Among the Kandhs he is simply the Tiger-God who kills and wastes. He rose from the earth in the form of a piece of iron, the metal of war among the Kandhs. The tree under which his rude symbol is placed inevitably dies. If it is laid in a stream, the water dries up. His priest can hope but for four years more of life after he enters his service, but dare not, under still more awful penalties, decline the fatal office. One of our Musalmán sepoys scornfully pricked the nose of this Tiger-God with a bayonet. 'Blood,' say the Kandhs, 'flowed from the wounds, and a pestilence wasted the English camp.' It may readily be supposed that a race accustomed to the terrors of such a deity would with trembling eagerness adopt the Hindu Goddess of Destruction (Káli) with her appalling rites. She, in fact, was long the sole representative of the third class of deities among the Kandhs, namely, those imported from the Hindu pantheon. On the other hand, there can be little doubt that the ancient Bráhmans borrowed her worship from the aboriginal tribes; and we thus see the races of Orissa mutually encouraging each other in a worship of terror during at least 1400 years, or from the accession of the Kesárí or Sivaite dynasty in 474 A.D.

As the Kandh pantheon consists of native and of imported deities, so their priesthood is composed partly of aboriginal and partly of Hindu priests. In primitive times, each god had certain families in every tribe set apart for his worship; but now-a-days, with the exception of the ministers of the chief god, no hereditary priesthood exists among the Kandhs. The result is an absolutely free trade in magical arts and incantations. Any man who can succeed in winning the belief of his neighbours, may set up on the strength of a dream or a vision as a priest; but although his calling yields him an easy subsistence, he is debarred from the enjoyments of battle, and may not eat with laymen, nor partake of food prepared by their hands. He may, however, quit the priesthood at pleasure. As a rule, the ancient Kandh deities have Kandh or aboriginal priests, while the unmistakeably Hindu Goddess of Destruction chooses her attendants from among the Hindus. The national Kandh divinities all dwell upon or under the earth, 'emerging and retiring by chinks which are occasionally discovered to their worshippers.'

HUMAN SACRIFICE. — One great ceremony united the whole Kandh race in the worship of the Earth-God. Several other deities, such as the God of Boundaries, from time to time received human victims; but the great Earth-God claimed these offerings, not only in all seasons of private calamity, but as an indispensable part of the public worship of the Kandhs. He is the supreme god of the race, the solemn symbol of the productive energy of nature; and his worship united the whole Kandh tribes (otherwise so split up and severed) by a bond of blood into a nation. 'The earth,' they say, 'was originally a crude and unstable mass, unfit for cultivation and for the convenient habitation of man. The Earth-God said, "Let human blood be spilt before me," and a child was sacrificed. The soil became forthwith firm and productive, and the deity ordained that man should repeat the rite and live.'

Association in human sacrifice formed the one indispensable nexus of tribal union among the Kandhs. The Earth-God enjoys both a public and a private worship, the former from a tribe or a village as an entity, the latter from individuals who may wish to propitiate his wrathful nature. His worship is essentially a religion of deprecation, an unceasing struggle to get him to lay aside his chronic hostility to man, and to purchase his favour by the most costly and precious victim which man can offer to God. As regards his public or tribal worship, the whole community contributed to the sacrifice, and each farm sprinkled itself with the blood of the public victim twice a year. The stated periods were at the spring sowing and after the harvest; but a human victim became equally necessary when the terrible Earth-God sent pestilence upon the people, or domestic calamity into the house of the patriarch, as their representative. Besides these public ceremonials, he received private sacrifices from families whenever sickness or great distress entered their dwelling. Thus, when a tiger carried off a child while watching the flocks, no uncommon incident in Kandh life, the father received his bereavement as a sure sign that the Earth-God demanded a human victim. If the family had none to offer on the moment, it led out a goat, whose ear was chopped off and fell to the ground as a pledge to the Earth-God, to be redeemed by a human victim within the year. Among certain tribes, the father pricked the ear of one of his surviving children, and the blood which trickled to the earth served as a pledge instead of a goat's ear. If the family could not buy a human victim before the end of the twelve months, the wretched parents had to offer up their own child, whose blood spilt upon the ground remained a witness of their vow to the Earth-God.

The victims were of either sex, and generally of tender age. The detestable office of providing them formed a hereditary privilege of the Páns, one of the alien low castes attached to the Kandh villages. Procurers of this class yearly sallied forth into the plains, and bought up a herd of promising boys and girls from the poorer Hindus. Sometimes they kidnapped their prey; and each Kandh district kept a stock of victims in reserve, 'to meet sudden demands for atonement.' Bráhmans and Kandhs were the only races whose purity exempted them from sacrifice, and a rule came down from remote antiquity that the victim *must be bought with a price.* After a village had purchased a victim, it treated him with much kindness, regarding him as a consecrated being, 'eagerly welcomed at every threshold.' If a child, he enjoyed perfect liberty; but if an adult, the patriarch kept him in his own house, and fed him well, but fettered him so that he could not escape. When the time of atonement had come, the Kandhs spent two days in feasting and lascivious riot; on the third they offered up the victim, shouting as the first blood fell to the ground, 'We bought you with a price; no sin rests with us.'

SUPPRESSION OF THE RITE.—As soon as the Kandh tribes passed under our care, it became necessary that this practice should cease. Accordingly, in 1836 we called upon the Rájá of the Tributary State of Bod to put down human sacrifice. Tribal councils and agitations followed; but in the end the patriarchs agreed to give up to us their stock of victims, not as a pledge that they would discontinue the rite, but as a peace-offering of valuable property to their new suzerain. They stipulated, however, that their honour must be saved, and this could only be done by our forcing all the other tribes to enter into a similar agreement. Such an agreement we at that time failed to effect, and the negotiations broke through. To Lieutenant S. C. Macpherson belongs the credit of extirpating the rite. He clearly discerned that if we were to deal with a people so sensitive and jealous of its honour, we must deal with it as a whole, and thus leave no ground for tribal heart-burnings. He next discovered a really effective basis for such an authority as he designed to impose. Each tribe had its internal government complete, but our suppression of the Gumsar Rájá left the nation without any central rallying point. He proposed, therefore, that we should leave the tribal administration untouched, but establish our power as a federal nexus, which all the separate clans might acknowledge and obey. They would thus lose nothing of their personal freedom, but at the same time they would be loosely bound together into a nation. In short, Lieutenant Macpherson formed the design of advancing the Kandhs from the tribal into the federal stage of society, and he executed what he had conceived.

But he did more than this. He laid it down as his fundamental principle of action, that we could only exercise rule over the people by supplying among them certain *bona fide* functions of government, the want of which they themselves had clearly felt. ' The voluntary and permanent acknowledgment of our sovereignty by these rude societies must depend upon our ability to discharge beneficially and acceptably towards them some portions of the duty of sovereignty. They will spontaneously yield allegiance to us, only in return for advantages which are suited in form and in spirit to their leading ideas and to their social wants.' The patriarchal authority within each Kandh tribe was perfect, but centuries of clan feuds had taught them the evils caused by the want of any power able to arbitrate between different tribes. 'Justice betwixt the independent societies is, in a word, the great want felt by all.' Setting out with this idea of Government having a right to exist only if it could discharge certain specific functions really required by the people, Lieutenant Macpherson gradually gained over the priesthood and the village heads. He appealed to their passionate desire to own land, and obtained for them settlements in jungle tracts of no value to us, but a perfect paradise to them. He also urged that little presents of money, cattle, and honorific dresses and titles should be given in return for their yearly homage. Above all, he insisted on employing the Kandhs as irregular police ; and even advocated the raising of a Kandh battalion as a means of civilising them, and 'as an invaluable instrument in our future dealings with the other mountain races of Orissa.' But while he thus laboured by gentle and politic devices to win the affections of the race, he made it distinctly understood that such measures of conciliation would, if required, be enforced by the British power.

Having thus established our authority on a basis of mutual goodwill, his acts convincing them that he sought their benefit, not our gain, he developed his plan for putting a stop to human sacrifices. He did not hold the Kandhs or the patriarchs to be morally guilty, but he arranged for the effective punishment of the procurers, and in a few years rendered the kidnapping or purchase of victims impossible. At the same time, he improved the material condition of the tribes, established fairs and commercial gatherings, ' to draw them from their fastnesses into friendly and familiar contact with other men;' made roads, and converted the isolated and mutually hostile tribes into a prosperous and peaceful people. The British Government, by Act xxi. of 1845, established a special Agency for dealing with the Kandhs, effectively suppressed their bloody rites, and wisely refrained from interfering further with them. To the present day they pay no rent, nor do we take any revenue whatever from them, but merely keep order by means of a local Agent, known as the *tahsíldár* of the Kandh-máls, supported by a strong force of police. This officer confines himself to putting a stop to blood-feuds, adjusting dangerous disputes likely to lead to them, and taking cognisance of any heinous crimes. He is subject to the English Commissioner of the Province at Cuttack, the Bod Rájá no longer exercising jurisdiction over the tribes. Their chief pro-duct is turmeric, of an unusually fine quality. Hindu traders now penetrate with their pack bullocks into the innermost recesses of the hills, and barter salt, cutlery, and cloth for this dye and other highland produce.

SAVARS.—In the southern Tributary States, another remnant of an ancient people still preserves a national existence. The Savars or Saurás—for the name is written and pronounced both ways—are identified as the Suari of Pliny and the Sabaræ of Ptolemy. Their principal settlements now lie among the mountainous background which rises from the Madras coast, and run down from the Chilká lake to the Godávarí river, a region two hundred miles in length. But from the notices of classical geographers at the beginning of our era, from the road books of the Chinese pilgrims (Fa Hian and Hiouen Thsang) in the mediæval centuries, and from the researches of British officers in our own time, it is clear that these Savars or Saurás form only a single branch of a widely extended tribe. Ac-cording to General Cunningham, in his *Ancient Geography of India* (vol. i. p. 509), the same people are found in Central India, in Gwálior, Márwár, and even as far as Southern Rájputáná. The Census Report returns the number of Savars in the Orissa Tributary States as 36,280, of whom 15,934, or nearly one-half, are found in Dhenkánal, 5125 in Keunjhar, and the remainder scattered through the other States. The Bendkárs are a tribe described by Colonel Dalton as 'a somewhat isolated fragment of the Savars.' They only number 239 in the Tributary States, of whom 223 are found in Keunjhar, and 16 in Pál Lahárá. The Sauris, who are in all probability also allied with the Savars, number 326 in the Tributary

States, all found in the Kandh-máls of Bod. The following description of the Bendkár branch of Savars is extracted from Colonel Dalton's *Ethnology of Bengal*, pp. 149-150 (Calcutta 1872) :—

'The largest settlement of independent Bendkárs that I have heard of is at a village called Dulukrí, under the Thákurání hill in Northern Keunjhar. It consists of eleven houses, three of Kols, the rest of Bendkárs. I have questioned the inhabitants of this village, and also several Bendkárs living as dependants in other villages; and from the answers I received, and the customs I have observed, it is difficult to regard them otherwise than as members of the great Bhuiyá family, thus connecting the Bhuiyás with the Savars. The Savars, who occupy the country between the Kandh-máls and the Godávarí, retain a primitive form of speech; but the Bendkár Savars that I have fallen in with have no language of their own, and no tradition that they ever possessed one. The form of speech used by them is Uriyá, and those living in mixed villages conform to many customs followed by Hindu Uriyás of inferior castes. The points of difference are, however, very noticeable; for on these points they follow exactly the customs of the hill Bhuiyás, and the independent Bendkárs have all the Bhuiyá characteristics.

'RELIGION.—They worship a female divinity whom they call Bánsurí and Thákuráni, no doubt the same as the bloodthirsty she-devil revered by the Bhuiyás, the prototype of the Hindu goddess Kálí. Every year, offerings are made to her of goats and fowls; but every ten years, each community of Bendkárs offers a buffalo, a boar, a sheep, and twelve fowls. The necessary victims are provided with difficulty, for it is not the custom of the Bendkárs to keep cattle of any kind. They buy what they require for sacrifice.

'FESTIVALS.—It is in their feasts, festivals, amusements, and methods of bringing about marriages, that the points of resemblance between them and the Bhuiyás are most marked. I once saw a dance by Bendkár boys and girls. The girls dance with their heads covered, bodies much inclined, and faces looking to the ground, or to their feet, which have to perform a somewhat intricate step; the right hand holds down at arm's length the portion of the dress that is thrown over the head. The men play on tambourines or half drums, and sing as they dance. The girls appear too intent on their steps to respond to them; but their peculiar attitude in the dance, the steps, and the melody are the same for all Bhuiyás, and are unmistakeable characteristics of the race, from the Ganges to the Mahánadí.

'THE MARRIAGE CEREMONIES are very simple. The formal preliminaries are arranged by mutual friends; but this generally follows a private understanding, which the parties most interested have come to without intervention. After the bridegroom has made his election, the following gifts are bestowed in his behalf: To the girl's father, a bullock; to the maternal uncle, a bullock; to the mother, a rupee in money and a cloth.

'DEATH CEREMONIES.—The Bendkárs burn the dead, following the practice of the Hindus in regard to the position of the body on the pyre, that is, with the head to the north. In this they vary from the Kols, who affect the south; and the hill Bhuiyás, who honour the quarter of the setting sun as most appropriate.

'AGRICULTURE.—When I first saw the Bendkár hand-plough, it was of wood, and consisted simply of a branch cut with a large piece of the stem from which it sprung attached to it; the whole shaped so as to give it the appearance of a miniature native plough. They have since improved on this, and now insert a piece of iron as a ploughshare. The implement answers well enough in preparing for seed the light vegetable mould of the forest, to which they confine their cultivation; but in a stiff clay it would be inoperative. The hill Bendkárs cultivate *kangni* (Panicum Italicum); *kherí; kodo* or *marud* (Eleusine corocana); *makai* or maize (Zea mays); a species of coxcomb, the seeds of which they eat; a cereal called *siko;* and a large bean, which is intoxicating or acts as an emetic when eaten raw, but is pleasant and wholesome when cooked; also *urid.* They have ordinarily no rice cultivation. They know well, and use, all the spontaneous edible productions of the forests, and showed me some wild yams which they largely consume.'

SANTALS.—The Santáls are the most numerous of the aboriginal tribes of the Orissa Tributary States. The Census Report returns their number at 76,548, of whom no less than 76,031 belong to Morbhanj. The balance is made up of 467 residing in Nilgirí and 50 in Keunjhar. The Santál Parganás in Western Bengal may now be regarded as the nucleus of the tribe; but, according to Colonel Dalton, this does not appear to have been one of their original seats. Colonel Dalton is of opinion that modern Santália has been colonized chiefly from migrations from remote Santál settlements in Hazáribágh and Bírbhúm Districts. A detailed account of the Santáls will be found in the Statistical Account of the Santál Parganás (vol. xv.).

KOLS.—The Kols number 34,637 in the Tributary States, of whom 21,897 are found in Morbhanj, and 10,990 in Keunjhar. An account of the Kol tribes will be found in the Statistical Accounts of Singbhúm and Lohárdagá (vols. xvi. and xvii.), to which Districts they more properly belong.

GONDS.—The original habitat of this tribe is the Central Provinces. The tract marked in old maps of India as Gondwáná extends from the Vindhyá Mountains to the Godávarí. In Bengal, Gond colonies are met with only in the Chutiá Nágpur and the Orissa Tributary States. In the Orissa States, the Gonds number 22,275, of whom 10,407 are found in Keunjhar, 4134 in Dhenkánal, and 2187 in Morbhanj, the remainder being scattered in small numbers through most of the other States. The Gonds form a more important section of the population of the Chutiá Nágpur than of the Orissa Tributary States, and a reference to them will be found in the Statistical Account of the Chutiá Nágpur States (vol. xvii. pp. 231, 232). The Gonds of the Tributary States are much fairer than their tribesmen of the Central Provinces, and seem to have a strong mixture of Aryan blood; they have lost their original language, and now speak Uriyá.

THE BHUMIJS, a tribe closely allied to the Kols, number 29,596 in the Orissa Tributary States, of whom 25,177 are found in Morbhanj, 1843 in Keunjhar, 1442 in Dhenkánal, 1012 in Nílgirí, and 122 in Pál Lahárá. For an account of this tribe, *vide* the Statistical Account of Mánbhúm District (vol. xvii. pp. 278-284).

THE JUANGS are described as probably the most primitive people in existence on the east side of India. They number 9398 in the Tributary States, of whom 4592 are found in Keunjhar, 4120 in Dhenkánal, 367 in Pál Lahárá, 290 in Hindol, and 290 in Bánkí. The following interesting description of this tribe is quoted from Colonel Dalton's *Ethnology of Bengal* (pp. 152-158):—

'I am informed there are thirty-two settlements of the Juáng tribe in Keunjhar, occupying the hill country to the south of Keunjhar fort as far as Handah, or between 21° 20′ and 21° 40′ of north latitude, and 85° 30′ and 85° 45′ of east longitude. They have not, however, got all this tract to themselves, the hill Bhuiyá villages and many colonies of Goálás occupying the larger portion of it. It is probable that they have been ousted by the Bhuiyás from the fertile valleys, and are thus compelled to restrict their cultivation to the steep hill-sides. The Juángs have no traditions which affiliate them with any other race; and notwithstanding a similarity in their languages (of which they knew nothing till I pointed it out to them), they repudiate all connection with Hos or Santáls. They aver very positively that they are autochthones in Keunjhar, the direct descendants of the first human beings that appeared or were produced in that country, or indeed in the world. For they assert a claim to be the first produced of the human race, though they make no pretensions to be the fathers of mankind. The head-quarters of the tribe, or cradle of the race, they consider to have been at Gonásiká, in 21° 30′ north latitude, and 85° 37′ east longitude, where issues from two holes in a rock, supposed to bear a resemblance to the nostrils of a cow, a stream which is the source of the Baitaraní. They assert that the Baitaraní, on whose banks they were created, is older than the Ganges; and that the present Juáng inhabitants of the village of Gonásiká, and other villages in the vicinity, occupy the very soil from which the parents of their race were produced. They have no traditions to record, except that very long ago nine hundred Juángs left the country of their birth and moved to Dhenkánal, and that then the Bhuiyás came and took up the land of the brethren who had left them; but it is more probable that they were driven out by the Bhuiyás, who are now the dominant race in those hills. The Bhuiyás, however, deny this, asserting that they are the true autochthones, and that the Juángs are interlopers. There is a tradition of a Borá Rájá (probably some allusion to the Baráha *avatár*, or Boar Incarnation of Vishnu) having had a fort in the heart of the country now occupied by Juángs, the remains of which are still in existence; and it is said that the Juángs are the remnant of his people.

'IN HABITS AND CUSTOMS, the Juángs are the most primitive people I have met with or read of. They occupy a hill country in which stone implements, the earliest specimens of human ingenuity that we possess, are occasionally found; and though they have now abandoned the use of such implements, and have lost the art of making them, it is not improbable that they are the direct descendants of those ancient stone-cutters, and that we have in the Juángs representatives of the stone age *in situ*. Until foreigners came amongst them, they must have used such weapons, or none at all, for they had no knowledge whatever of metals. They have no ironsmiths nor smelters of iron. They have no word in their own language for iron or other metals. They neither spin nor weave, nor have they ever attained to the simplest knowledge of pottery. In the hills of Keunjhar, they are still semi-nomadic in their habits, living together in villages during a portion of the year, but often changing the sites, and occupying isolated huts in the midst of their patches of cultivation whilst the crops are on the ground.

'DWELLINGS.—Gonásiká, one of the largest of their villages, I found to contain twenty-five houses of Juángs. The huts are amongst the smallest that human beings ever deliberately constructed as dwellings. They measure about six feet by eight, and are very low, with doors so small as to preclude the idea of a corpulent householder. Scanty as are the above dimensions for a family dwelling, the interior is divided into two compartments, one of which is the storeroom, the other being used for all domestic arrangements. The head of the family and all his belongings of the female sex huddle together in this one stall, not much larger than a dog-kennel. For the boys there is a separate dormitory. This latter is a building of some pretensions, situated at the entrance of the village. It is constructed with a solid plinth of earth raised about four feet, and has two apartments. One of these is an inner and closed one, in which the musical instruments of the village are kept, and in which most of the boys sleep; the other is open on three sides,—that is, it has no walls,—but the eaves spread far beyond the plinth, and the inmates are effectually protected. This is where all guests are lodged, and it makes a convenient travellers' rest.

'CULTIVATION.—The Juángs cultivate in the rudest way, destroying the forest trees by the process of girdling them, burning all they can of the timber when it dries, and spreading the ashes over the land. They thus raise a little early rice, Indian corn, pulses, pumpkins, sweet potatoes, ginger, and red pepper, the seed being all thrown into the ground at once, to come up as it can.

'FOOD.—They declare that they subsist every year more on wild roots and fruits than on what they rear, but I doubt if they are so badly off as they pretend to be. The area of their cultivation appeared proportionate to their numbers. They pay no rent, being under an obligation to render personal service to the Rájá, by repairing his house and carrying his burdens when required; neither do they spend money in clothes. It is difficult to understand, therefore, their not having a sufficiency of wholesome food, unless it be that they spend all their substance in drink. They are, no doubt, addicted to ardent spirits; and they are obliged to buy what they consume, as they have not acquired the art of distilling, or even of brewing rice beer, which every Kol understands. In regard to food, they are not in the least particular, eating all kinds of flesh, including mice, rats, monkeys, tigers, bears, snakes, frogs, and even offal. The jungles abound in spontaneously-produced vegetables. In the quest of such food they possess all the instinct of the animal, discerning at a glance what is nutritive, and never mistaking a noxious for an edible fungus or root.

'WEAPONS.—The Juángs do not look a warlike people; but when urged by the Bhuiyás, whose lead they invariably follow, they are sometimes troublesome. They use the bow and arrow, but their favourite weapon is the primitive sling, made entirely of cord. For missiles, they take pebbles or stones as they find them; they have no idea of fashioning them so as to produce more efficient projectiles.

'DRESS.—My first introduction to the Juángs was in 1866, whilst engaged, in company with the Superintendent of the Orissa Tributary States, in settling a boundary dispute between Keunjhar and Bonái. We were far away from any Juáng village, but my companion sent for some specimens of this interesting people; and a well-selected party, consisting of a matron, half a dozen comely maidens, and as many men, responded to the call. The females of the group had not amongst them a particle of clothing; their sole covering for purposes of decency consisted of a girdle composed of several strings of beads, from which small curtains of leaves depended before and behind. The Juángs take young shoots of the *ásán* (Terminalia tomentosa), or any tree with long soft leaves, and arrange them so as to form a flat and scale-like surface of the required size; the sprigs are simply stuck in the girdle, and the costume is complete. The beads that form the girdle are small tubes of burnt earthenware made by the wearers. The women wear also a profusion of necklaces of glass beads, and brass ornaments in their ears and on their wrists; and it was not till they saw that I had a considerable stock of such articles to dispose of, that they got over their shyness and ventured to approach us.

'DANCES. — They made their first appearance by night, and danced by torch-light. The men sang as they danced, accompanying themselves on deep-sounding tambourines, the girls holding together and circling round them ·in a solemnly grotesque manner.

There was a want of spirit in the performance, for they were shy and timid creatures, and the dancing by torch-light before so many strange spectators was evidently no pleasure to them. They executed the movements under the orders of the men with an unimpassioned obedience, as if they were so many dancing dogs or monkeys. The disarrangement of their leaves in the movements of the dance was a source of great anxiety to them, compelling them frequently to fall out of their places and retreat into the darkness to adjust their plumage.

'Next day they came to my tent at noon; and we induced them to give us not only the solemn measure of the evening before, but to perform a variety of sportive dances, some quite dramatic in effect, and it was altogether a most interesting "ballet." In one figure, the girls moved round in single file, keeping the right hand on the right shoulder of the girl in front; in another, with bodies inclined, they wreathed their arms and advanced and retreated in line. Then we had the bear dance. The girls, acting independently, advance with bodies so much inclined that their hands touch the ground; thus they move not unlike bears. The pigeon dance followed; the action of a love-making pigeon, when he struts, pouts, sticks out his breast, and scrapes the ground with his wings, was well imitated, the hands of the girls doing duty as wings. Then came a pig and tortoise dance, in which the motions of those animals were less felicitously rendered; and the quail dance, in which they squatted and pecked at the ground after the manner of those birds. They concluded with the vulture dance, a highly dramatic finale. One of the men was made to lie on the ground and represent a dead body. The girls in approaching him imitated the hopping, sidling advance of the bird of prey; and using their hands as beaks, nipped and pinched the pseudo-corpse in a manner that made him occasionally forget his character and yell with pain. This caused great amusement to his tormentors.

'The males of the community have abandoned the leaves, and use in lieu the smallest quantity of cotton cloth that can be made to serve the purposes of decency. The women were long deterred by superstition from following their example. Several traditions exist to account for this, apparently of Bráhmanical concoction. The simplest and prettiest of these is connected with the origin of the Baitaraní. The river goddess, emerging for the first time from the Gonásiká rock, came suddenly on a rollicking party of Juángs dancing naked; and, ordering them to adopt leaves on the moment as a covering, laid on them the curse that they must adhere to that costume for ever or die. Within the last few years, however, the British officer in charge of the elephant-*khedd* operations in Keunjhar, has at length induced the Juáng females to clothe themselves, he supplying the first robes. If no misfortune follow the innovation, it will probably be permanent.

'PHYSICAL CHARACTERISTICS.—The predominating physical characteristics of the Juángs, as I saw them massed in their village, appeared to be the great lateral projection of the cheek bones, or zygomatic arches and general flatness of features; forehead upright, but narrow and low, and projecting over a very depressed nasal bone; nose of the pug species; alæ spreading; mouth large, and lips very thick, but upper jaw rarely prognathous, though the lower jaw and chin are receding; hair coarse and frizzly, prevailing colour of a reddish brown. I observed that some of them had oblique eyes of the Indo-Chinese type, but in this feature there was considerable variety. It is noticeable that the Juáng women tattoo their faces with the same marks that are used by the Mundás, Kharriás, and Uráons: namely, three strokes on the forehead just over the nose, and three on each of the temples. They attach no meaning to the marks, have no ceremony in adopting them, and are ignorant of their origin.

'The Juángs are a small race, like the Uráons, the males averaging less than five feet in height, the women not more than four feet eight inches. The Ho girls of Singbhúm look like giantesses beside the Juáng females; and the Juáng males in stature and carriage are equally inferior to the Ho men. The Juáng males have round shoulders and walk with a slouching pace; while the Hos are upright in carriage, and have a stately, manly stride. Many of the latter tribe have emigrated from Singbhúm, and taken up their abode with the Juángs and Bhuiyás in the Keunjhar hills; and though in an inferior position working as farm labourers, the Hos retain their superiority of physique. The Juángs appear to bend under their burden-bearing lot. The Hos never, if they can help it, carry burdens, the use of the block-wheeled carts being almost universal amongst them.

'RELIGION.—The Juángs appear to be free from the belief in witchcraft, which is the bane of the Kols, and perniciously influences nearly all other classes in the Jungle Maháls and Tributary States. They have not, like the Kharriás, the reputation of being deeply skilled in sorcery. Their language has no words for "God," for "heaven" or "hell;" and, so far as I can learn, they have no idea of a future state. They offer fowls to the sun when in distress, and to the earth to give them its fruits in due season. On these occasions an old man officiates as priest; he is called Nagám. The even tenor of their lives is unbroken by any obligatory religious ceremonies.

'MARRIAGES.—Marriage is recognised, but is brought about in the simplest manner. If a young man fancies a girl, he sends a party of his friends to propose for her; and if the offer is accepted, a day is fixed, and a load of rice in husk is presented on his behalf. The bridegroom does not go himself to the bride's house; his friends go, and return with her and her friends. Then they make merry, eating and dancing, and all stay and make a night of it. In the morning, the bridegroom dismisses the bride's friends with a present of three measures of husked and three of unhusked rice; and this is a full and sufficient solemnization. A man may have more wives than one if he can afford it, but no Juáng has ever ventured on more than two at a time. They are divided into tribes, and are exogamous.

'FUNERAL CEREMONIES.—They burn their dead, and throw the ashes into any running stream; their mourning is an abstinence for three days from flesh and salt. They erect no monuments, and have no notion of the worship of ancestors. The dead are burned with their heads to the south; in this they agree with the Hos and their cognates, and differ from the Hindus.'

THE KHARRIAS are a tribe closely allied linguistically to the Juángs. The Census Report returns their number in the Orissa Tributary States at 3942, of whom 3509 are in Morbhanj, 330 in Pál Lahárá, 65 in Keunjhar, 25 in Nílgiri, 11 in the Bod Kandh-máls, and 2 in Angul. Tradition has it that the Kharriás, with another tribe called Puráns (described below), are aborigines of Morbhanj; and they aver that they and the family of the Rájá (Bhanj) were all produced from a pea-fowl's egg, the Bhanjs or family of the Rájás from the yolk, the Puráns from the white, and the Kharriás from the shell. A further account of the Kharriás will be found in the Statistical Account of Mánbhum (vol. xvii. pp. 285-287).

PURANS, a cognate tribe to the foregoing; number in the Orissa Tributary States, 7634—all within the State of Morbhanj.

BHUIYAS.—The Census Report returns the number of this tribe at

30,724 in the Orissa Tributary States, of whom 18,481 are found in Keunjhar, 9792 in Morbhanj, 1464 in Pál Lahárá, 345 in Dhenkánal, 329 in Athmallik, 152 in Nílgirí, 95 in Angul, 61 in Daspallá, 3 in Tálcher, and 2 in Bod. The following paragraphs respecting this tribe are quoted from Colonel Dalton's *Ethnology of Bengal*, (pp. 144-147) :—

'Keunjhar has long been one of the chief seats of the Bhuiyás. There we find them as an aboriginal race still dominant ; for, if not the most numerous, they are certainly the most influential section of the population. The Bhuiyás of the plains, including the Sáonts, a thoroughly Hinduized portion of the clan, are the organized militia of the State. They all hold their lands on conditions of service, and maintain themselves in a state of preparation for taking the field at a moment's notice, to oppose their Rájá, or to fight for him, according to their humour. Some clans of the hill Bhuiyás are similarly organized ; but the most powerful body among them, the Paurí (or Paháriá), the true hill Bhuiyás, are on a different footing. They are not bound to fight for the Rájá, though they occasionally take up arms against him. Their duty is to attend on him and carry his loads when he travels about ; and so long as they are satisfied with his person or his rule, no more willing servants or devoted subjects could be found. They are in Keunjhar, as in Bonái, a race whom one cannot help liking and taking an interest in, from the primitive simplicity of their customs, their amenability, and their anxiety to oblige ; but unsophisticated as they are, they wield an extraordinary power in Keunjhar, and when they take it into their heads to use that power, the country may be said to be governed by an oligarchy composed of the sixty chiefs of the Paurí Des or Bhuiyá highlands. A knotted string passed from village to village, in the name of the sixty chiefs, throws the entire country into commotion ; and the order, which is verbally communicated in connection with this symbol, is as implicitly obeyed as if it emanated from the most potent despot. It is not because they are stronger, braver, or better armed, that they exercise this supremacy ; it arises from two causes, prestige and position. The Paurís dispute with the Juángs the claim to be the first settlers in Keunjhar, and boldly aver that the country belongs to them. They assert that the Rájá is of their creation, and that the prerogative of installing every new Rájá on his accession is theirs, and theirs alone. The Hindu population of Keunjhar is largely in excess of the Bhuiyá, and it comprises

Gonds and Kols; but the claim of the Pauris to the dominion they arrogate is admitted by all. Even Bráhmans and Rájputs respectfully acknowledge it; and the former, by the addition of Bráhmanical rites to the wild ceremonies of the Bhuiyás, affirm and sanctify the installation. The *ganthi*, or knotted string of the sixty chiefs, has been during the recent (1868) disturbances in Keunjhar (*vide* pp. 291-298) in active operation. The last one I heard of was a forgery. An adherent of the Rájá, captured by the Pauris, ingeniously fabricated a *ganthi;* and having effected his escape from his guard, its possession passed him unquestioned through the remainder of the Bhuiyá country into our camp.

'THE SETTLEMENTS of the hill Bhuiyás are in valleys, some long and winding, some circular. Each village, or cluster of two or three villages, is snugly screened and protected by its own lofty barrier of hills, and accessible only by steep, tortuous passes, or by paths winding through ravines. Thus secured, the Pauris are beyond the reach of retaliation when they choose to make a swoop on the lowlands; and are therefore as formidable to the people of the plains, as were the highlanders to the lowlanders in Scotland a century ago. Some of the settlements are permanent; but many villages have two or more sites within the boundaries allotted to them, on one of which alternately they form a new village every ten years. The houses are nevertheless tolerably substantial and comfortable. Every village has its *darbár* or town-hall, resting-place for travellers, and sleeping-place for the young men, with its dancing-place in front for the recreations of the maidens and youths after their day's toil. The hills rise to a height of 3200 feet above the sea level, and amongst them are the sources of the Baitaraní river. The valleys are fertile, irrigated by numerous streams and sundry rills, the waters of which may with facility be economized, though the inhabitants of this hill tract rarely suffer from drought.

'TRIBAL DIVISIONS.—The Bhuiyás in Keunjhar are divided into four clans,—the Mál or Des Bhuiyás (they call themselves and are called the *des-lok*, or the people of the country), the Dandsená, the Khattí, and the Rájkulí Bhuiyás. The latter, as being connected with the royal line, I should have placed first, but I give the list the order assigned by my informants. It is said that the Bhuiyás some twenty-seven generations ago stole a child of the Morbhanj Rájá's family, brought him up, and ultimately made him their Rájá. He was freely admitted to intercourse with Bhuiyá girls, and the children of this intercourse are the progenitors of the Ráj-kulí. But they are not considered first among Bhuiyás, as they are not of pure Bhuiyá descent.

'INSTALLATION OF A RAJA BY THE BHUIYAS.—Having witnessed the installation of a Rájá of Keunjhar by the Bhuiyás, I proceed to describe the ceremony: A large shed attached to the Rájá's palace, and ordinarily used as a lumber room, was cleared out, swept and garnished, spread with carpets, and otherwise prepared for the occasion. A number of Bráhmans were in attendance in sacerdotal costume, seated amidst the sacred vessels and implements, and articles for offerings used in the consecration of Rájás, according to the ceremonies prescribed in the Vedas. Beyond the circle of the Bráhmanical preparations, a group of the principal Bhuiyás were seated, cleanly robed for the occasion and garlanded.

'When the company were all seated, and these arrangements complete, the young Rájá, Dhanurjái Bhanj, entered the apartment and distributed *pán*, confections, spices, and garlands, and retired. Then, after a pause, there was heard a great crash of the discordant but wild and deep-toned wind instruments and drums of the Bhuiyás and other tribes, and the Rájá entered, mounted on the back of a strongly built Bhuiyá chief, who plunged and pawed and snorted under him like a fiery steed. Moving to the opposite side of the Bráhmanical sacred circle, followed by a host of the tribe, one of them placed himself on a low platform covered with red cloth, and with his body and limbs formed the back and arms of the throne on which the Rájá, dismounting from his biped steed, was placed. Then the attendant Bhuiyás each received from the Rájá's usual servants extemporized imitations of the insignia of royalty—banners, standards, *pankhás, chauras, chhatras,* canopies; and thirty-six of the tribe as hereditary office-bearers, each with his symbol, ranged themselves round their chief.

'There was a temporary hitch in consequence of the unexpected absence of the hereditary sword-bearer, but after a slight delay a deputy was found, and the ceremony proceeded; not, however, until the Bhuiyás had protested against the irregularity of such a precedent. Then one of the principal Bhuiyá chiefs, taking a light flexible jungle creeper of considerable length, binds it round the Rájá's turban, as the *siropá* or honorary head-dress conferred by them. The bands strike up whilst this is done. Bards chant hymns of praise, and Bráhmans recite from the Sámá Veda; and a leading chief of the clan, dipping his finger into the saucer of sandal-wood essence, makes on the forehead of the Rájá the mark called *tiká*. The Bráhman priest, the Prime Minister or *bewartha*, and others, then repeat the ceremony of giving the *tiká*, so that a considerable amount of such sealing is required to constitute a Rájá of Keunjhar. The Bráhmanical ceremony of consecration had been duly solemnized on a previous occasion by the Bráhmans; but a portion of this ceremony, omitting the anointing with clarified butter, etc., was now again performed by the priests, ratifying and rendering sacred the act of the Bhuiyás.

'Then the sword, a very rusty old weapon, is placed in the Rájá's hands; and one of the Bhuiyá chiefs comes before him, and, kneeling sideways, the Rájá touches him on the neck with the weapon, as if about to strike off his head. It is said that in former days there was no fiction in this part of the ceremony, and the family of this chief hold their lands on the condition that a victim shall be produced when required. The man, however, hurriedly arose after the accolade, and disappeared. He must not be seen for three days; then he presents himself again to the Rájá as miraculously restored to life.

' The Bhuiyá chiefs next make offerings to the Rájá of rice, pulse, pots of *ghi*, milk, honey, and other things—each article being touched by all the *sardárs* or chiefs before it is presented. The principal *sardárs* now solemnly address him, and telling him that they have, under the authority exercised by them and their ancestors from time immemorial, made over to him the realm and the people therein, enjoin him to rule with justice and mercy. It was a long speech, of which I could catch but little. The ceremony was then concluded with a salute of guns. The Rájá arose, and, again mounted on his curvetting and frisky biped steed, left the assembly, surrounded and followed by all the Bhuiyá office-bearers with their insignia, and was thus escorted to his own apartment in the palace. Soon after—it may be on a subsequent date—the Bhuiyás do homage to the Rájá elect. They come in a body, bringing with them as gifts, rice, fruits, gourds, Indian corn, etc., and laying them at the Rájá's feet they ask after his health, his establishment, his horses, and his elephants; and in return the Rájá inquires after their crops, cows, fowls, and children. This over, each *sardár* prostrates himself, and taking the Rájá's foot in his hand, places the royal toe first on his right and then on his left ear, and then on his forehead.

'PHYSICAL TRAITS.—The Keunjhar hill Bhuiyás are of rather an exaggerated Turanian type : very large mouths, thick and somewhat projecting lips; foreheads narrow and low, but not receding; eyes dark, but well shaped; hair plentiful on the head, though rather frizzly and generally scanty on face, though to this there are notable exceptions. They are short of stature, averaging only about five feet two inches; round shouldered; and many of them with the lump that is produced by the displacement of the muscles in carrying loads *banghy* fashion. The colour of the skin varies from a deep chocolate—the predominating tint—to tawny.

'RELIGION.—Their religion appears to be the same as that of the Chutiá Nágpur Bhuiyás. They worship the sun as Dharm, and pay great attention to Borám, who is also called Bír or Mahábír Hánumán; but their private and most frequent devotions are paid to a bloodthirsty tutelary goddess called Thákuráni Mái, in all probability the origin of the Hindu Káli; for I firmly believe that goddess, with her bloody sacrifices, especially human sacrifices, was borrowed by the Hindus from the aboriginals. In three of the Bhuiyá States of Chutiá Nágpur, viz. Bámrá, Bonái, and Gángpur, human sacrifices were in former times offered to Káli at certain shrines, the priests of which were Bhuiyás, not Bráhmans. That the same custom prevailed in Keunjhar is likely enough, and that the Pauris if left to themselves would take to it again is probable. During the Keunjhar insurrection of 1868 they carried off and murdered the Rájá's Prime Minister; and on his head being taken to the rebel leader, it was treated as a sacrificial offering to the Thákuráni.

'DOMESTIC CUSTOMS.—The mother of a child remains unclean for seven days after its birth; the child's head is then shaved, and it is named, the ceremony of naming it being precisely the same as that followed by the Mundás and the Hos (*vide* Statistical Account of Lohárdagá District, vol. xvi. pp. 265–278). The name of the grandfather is given to the eldest son (except where, in consequence of the failure of the test, it is found necessary to change it), the great-grandfather's to the second son, and then the names of collateral branches are given, according to seniority. There are no religious ceremonies after this till marriage, which does not take place till the parties are of adult age. The parents have very little to do with the selection of partners. I was told by people who knew the tribes well, but did not belong to them, that the proposal of marriage came in the first place from the girl, as with the Gáros. This was not confirmed by the Bhuiyás themselves; they, however, may have had a delicacy in speaking of a custom which, they could not fail to see, astonished and amused all the natives in our camp. At the marriage there is much dancing and singing, and that is all I could find out concerning it.

'DANCES, ETC.—In each village there is, as with the Uráons, an open space for a dancing ground, called by the Bhuiyás the *darbár;* and near it the "bachelors' hall," or separate house for the young men, which is called the *dhángar-bássa* or *mandar-ghar*, as here the young men (*dhángar*) must all sleep at night, and here the drums (*mandar*) are kept. Some villages have a *dhángarín-bássa* or house for maidens, which, strange to say, they are allowed to occupy without any one to look after them. They appear to have very great liberty, and slips in morality, so long as they are confined to the tribe, are not much heeded. Whenever the young men of the village go to the *darbár* and beat the drums, the young girls join them there; and they spend the evenings dancing and enjoying themselves without any interference on the part of the elders. The Bhuiyá dances have their peculiar features, but, compared with the lively and graceful movements of the Kols, they are very tame performances. The men have each a rude kind of tambourine; they march round in a circle, beating these, and singing a very simple melody in a minor key on four notes. The women dance opposite to them, with their heads covered, and bodies much inclined, touching each other like soldiers in line, but not holding hands or wreathing arms like the Kols. The dances, when confined to the people of the village, are regarded as mere rehearsals. The more exciting and exhilarating occasions are when the young men of one village proceed to visit the maidens of another village, or when the maidens return the call. The young men provide themselves with presents for the girls, generally consisting of combs for the hair and sweetmeats, and going straight to the *darbár* of the village they visit, they proclaim their arrival loudly by beating their drums or tambourines. The girls of that village immediately join them. Their male relations and neighbours must keep entirely out of view, leaving the field clear for the guests. The offerings of the visitors are now gallantly presented and graciously accepted, and the girls at once set to work to prepare dinner for their beaux. After the meal they dance and sing and flirt all night together, and the morning dawns on more than one pair of pledged lovers. Then the girls, if the young men have conducted themselves to their satisfaction, make ready the morning meal for themselves and their guests; after which the latter rise to depart, and, still dancing and playing on the drums, move out of the village followed by the girls, who escort them to the boundary. This is generally a rock-broken stream with wooded banks; here they halt, the girls on one side, the lads on the other, and, to the accompaniment of the babbling brook, sing to each other in true bucolic style. The song ended, the girls go down on their knees, and bowing to the ground, respectfully salute the young men, who gravely and formally return the compliment, and they part. The visit is soon returned by the girls. They are received by the young men in their *darbár*, and entertained; and the girls of the receiving village must not be seen.'

SAONT.—The Census Report returns the number of this tribe in the Orissa Tributary States at 9683, of whom 7172 belong to Keunjhar, 2313 to Morbhanj, 181 to Pál Lahárá, and 80 to Nílgirí. The Orissa Sáonts are described by Colonel Dalton as 'a thoroughly Hinduized portion of the Bhuiyá clan.' A community of the same name is found in the Chutiá Nágpur Tributary States of Sargujá and Udáipur, where they form the only permanent residents of the Mainpát plateau. These, however, Colonel Dalton appears to regard as an entirely distinct people. He thinks they may possibly be an offshoot of the Santál tribe, who have completely lost their own language and speak a bastard dialect of Hindi.

TAALA.—A numerous tribe, who appear to be closely allied to the Savars, but regarding whom very little is known. They number 18,131 in the Orissa Tributary States, of whom 3358 belong to Angul, 2905 to Keunjhar, 2224 to Dhenkánal, 1622 to Hindol, and 1548 to Bod and the Khand-máls. The remainder are scattered through the other Tributary States, except Nílgirí. Like many other of the aboriginal or semi-aboriginal races, the Taálas are said to be weavers by occupation, but they are usually found as labourers and agriculturists. In Keunjhar they call themselves Taála Goálás, and assert that they are the offspring by Savar fathers of girls of the Gaur or Goálá caste.

GHASI.—A degraded tribe, whose main home is in Central India. In the Orissa States they number 2014, of whom 1224 are found in Morbhanj, 475 in Keunjhar, and 315 in Bod and the Khandmáls. The Ghásis are not represented in the other Orissa States.

Their occupation is that of scavengers and musicians to the rest of the aboriginal tribes.

HINDU CASTES.—The Hindu castes number 115. The following is the list :—

HIGH CASTES.—(1) Bráhman; members of the priesthood, and also following the same occupations as the Bráhmans elsewhere in Bengal; 60,177 in number, met with in all the Tributary States, but most numerous in Dhenkánal, Keunjhar, Khandpárá, Nayágarh, and Bánkí. For details of the number of this and of all the following castes in each State, *vide* the table at pp. 210-217 of this Statistical Account. Mastání or cultivating Bráhmans are returned separately in the Census Report as numbering 3234, most numerous in Keunjhar. (2) Kshattriya or Rájput. The Kshattriyas formed the second or warrior caste in the ancient four-fold social organization of Sanskrit times. Strictly speaking, there is not a single Kshattriya of pure descent in Orissa, but nearly all the Rájás claim this rank, or that of Rájput, for themselves and their chief connections and dependants. The Census returns the number of Rájputs at 6510, most numerous in Angul and Morbhanj. (3) Karan; the Orissa counterpart of the Káyasth or writer caste of Bengal; 15,170 in number, most numerous in Nayágarh, Keunjhar, and Khandpárá. The Bengalí and other Káyasths found in the Tributary States are returned at 386; most numerous in Morbhanj. (4) Khandáit; formerly the armed militia of the Chiefs, now principally agriculturists; 49,487 in number, most numerous in Keunjhar, Morbhanj, and Dhenkánal. (5) Khandwál; a class of Khandáits; 4867 in number, most numerous in Keunjhar and Morbhanj. (6) Mahánáik; a class of Khandáits; 20 in number. (7) Ganak; astrologers and fortune-tellers. These are a class of lapsed Bráhman; 3069 in number, most numerous in Keunjhar, but met with in every State. (8) Bhát; heralds and genealogists. These also claim to be lapsed Bráhmans, and wear the sacred thread, but their right to the rank of Bráhman is generally denied; 351 in number, principally in Keunjhar. (9) Mahantí; these belong to the same generic class as the Karans or Káyasths, but are not acknowledged as such by the orthodox Káyasths; 3372 in number, principally in Narsinhpur and Barambá. (10) Shagirdpeshá; an intermediate caste, said to be the offspring of low-caste women by Karan, Bhát, and sometimes (though rarely) by Bráhman fathers; 1996 in number, most numerous in Nayágarh and Athgarh.

RESPECTABLE CASTES.—(11) Agarwálá; traders and merchants; 15 in number, confined to Daspallá and Khandpárá. (12) Bhandárí; barbers; 14,372 in number, distributed over all the Tributary States, but most numerous in Dhenkánal and Keunjhar. (13) Kámár; blacksmiths; 17,162 in number, distributed over all the States, but most numerous in Morbhanj, Keunjhar, and Dhenkánal. (14) Kumbhar; potters; 16,559 in number, met with in every State, but most numerous in Morbhanj, Keunjhar, and Dhenkánal. (15) Sadgop; cultivators; 51 in number. (16) Támbulí; betel growers and sellers; 1593 in number, most numerous in Khandpárá. (17) Bais-baniyá; traders and merchants; 2721 in number, most numerous in Keunjhar, Dhenkánal, and Hindol. (18) Baniyá; merchants and traders; 733 in number, most numerous in Nayágarh. (19) Gandha-baniyá; grocers and spice dealers; 129 in number, almost confined to Ranpur. (20) Putlí-baniyá; spice sellers, etc.; 813 in number, most numerous in Bánkí. (21) Kapáriyá; cotton traders; 1734 in number, most numerous in Dhenkánal. (22) Kumtí; a caste of Madras traders; 973 in number, almost confined to Nayágarh, Ranpur, and Daspallá. (23) Chásá; the great cultivating caste; 172,471 in number, most numerous in Dhenkánal, Angul, and Nayágarh. (24) Súd, a corruption of Súdr⌐. The caste is a subdivision of the Chásá, but its members appear to keep themselves distinct, and refuse to intermarry with the other cultivating castes; 16,026 in number, most numerous in Bod, Athmallik, and Angul. (25) Or, a subdivision of Chásás; 3570 in number, principally in Khandpárá. (26) Páik, a subdivision of Chásás; 3643 in number, principally in Bánkí. (27) Ráju, a subdivision of Chásás; 2326 in number, principally in Morbhanj. (28) Golá, a subdivision of Chásás; 9215 in number, most numerous in Morbhanj, Nayágarh, and Keunjhar. (29) Málí; gardeners and flower sellers; 10,506 in number, distributed throughout the Tributary States, but most numerous in Dhenkánal, Nayágarh, and Bánkí. (30) Gaur; the pastoral caste of Orissa, corresponding to the Goálás of Bengal; herdsmen, etc.; 70,117 in number, distributed throughout the Tributary States, but most numerous in Morbhanj, Dhenkánal, Keunjhar, Nayágarh, and Angul. (31) Damál; a subdivision of the Gaurs or Orissa pastoral caste; 10,274 in number, principally in Bod. (32) Magadhá Goálá; the pastoral or herdsmen caste of Behar; 15,995 in number, most numerous in Bod and Keunjhar. (33) Ahír Goálá; the pastoral caste of Bengal; 1679 in number, mainly confined to

Keunjhar. (34) Barhái; carpenters; 4945 in number, most numerous in Dhenkánal. (35) Chitrakár; painters; 194 in number. (36) Kánsárí; braziers and coppersmiths; 5130 in number, most numerous in Dhenkánal and Khandpárá. (36½) Rosorá; pewterers; 85 in number, confined to Khandpárá. (37) Pathariá; stone-cutters; 221 in number. (38) Sikalgir; cutlers; 19 in number, confined to Nayágarh. (39) Sonár; goldsmiths and jewellers; 4670 in number, most numerous in Dhenkánal, Keunjhar, and Khandpárá. (40) Sankhárí; shell-cutters; 57 in number. (41) Láherí; lac-worker; 45 in number. (42) Kachuá; glass-makers; 914 in number, almost confined to Dhenkánal and Keunjhar. (43) Halwái; sweetmeat makers; 7 in number. (44) Gánrár; grain parchers; 19,295 in number, most numerous in Nayágarh and Dhenkánal. (45) Kurmí; cultivators; 11,051 in number, principally in Morbhanj. (46) Agurí; cultivators; 3 in number. (47) Koerí; cultivators; 7 in number. (48) Patuá; weavers by caste occupation, but many have taken to trade and become rich; 5483 in number, most numerous in Morbhanj and Tigariá. (49) Teli; oil pressers and sellers; 38,794 in number, most numerous in Dhenkánal, Keunjhar, Nayágarh, Bánkí, and Khandpárá. (50) Thuria; a subdivision of the foregoing caste; they deal in oil seeds, which they carry about on pack-bullocks, their caste name being derived from a bullock's pack; 3682 in number, principally in Khandpárá.

Low Castes.—The following are low castes and are despised :— (51) Dhobá; washermen; 16,975 in number, distributed throughout the States, but most numerous in Keunjhar and Dhenkánal. (52) Surí; wine sellers and distillers; 8465 in number, most numerous in Morbhanj and Dhenkánal. (53) Benatiá; cultivators; 2506 in number, almost wholly confined to Khandpárá. (54) Kultá; cultivators; 2212 in number, mainly confined to Bod. (55) Sámul; cultivators; 1546 in number, mainly confined to Tálcher. (56) Rául; cultivators; 101 in number. (57) Pandariyá; cultivators; 224 in number, confined to Nayágarh and Khandpárá. (58) Sahan; cultivators; 214 in number. (59) Paridá; cultivators; 162 in number. (60) Dográ; cultivators; 141 in number, confined to Nílgiri. (61) Bhopá; cultivators; 51 in number. (62) Darzí; tailors; 225 in number, most numerous in Nayágarh. (63) Chhipí; cotton printers; 6 in number. (64) Rarhi; a sept of the Keut or fishing caste, who have given up their own proper calling and taken to the preparation and sale of parched grain; 3398 in number, confined to Keunjhar, Nílgirí, and Morbhanj. (65) Amanth; domestic servants; 1548 in number, chiefly in Morbhanj. (66) Tántí; weavers; 13,706 in number, most numerous in Dhenkánal and Morbhanj. (67) Rangí; weavers; 3212 in number, most numerous in Bánkí and Nayágarh. (68) Koshtá; weavers of jute; 2314 in number, most numerous in Angul and Dhenkánal. (69) Tulábhiná; cotton carders; 1369 in number, most numerous in Dhenkánal and Nayágarh. (70) Suklí; weavers; 1762 in number, most numerous in Barambá and Keunjhar. (71) Matibangsí; weavers by caste, but said to be principally employed as writers and teachers; 459 in number, most numerous in Keunjhar and Khandpárá. (72) Hangsí; weavers; 1888 in number, most numerous in Dhenkánal and Morbhanj. (73) Nuniyá; salt makers; 7 in number. (74) Korá; diggers and earth workers; 1033 in number, chiefly in Angul and Athmallik. (75) Matiyál; labourers; 3949 in number, most numerous in Nílgirí and Dhenkánal. (76) Nikárí; sellers of fish and vegetables; 215 in number, chiefly in Khandpárá. (77) Keut; fishermen and boatmen; 31,384 in number, distributed throughout the Tributary States, but most numerous in Dhenkánal, Bánkí, and Khandpárá. (78) Tior; fishermen; 1613 in number, most numerous in Nayágarh and Angul. (79) Dandáchhatrá; fishermen by caste, but named from their duty of carrying the Rájá's umbrella; 1518 in number, mainly confined to Morbhanj. (80) Gokhá; fishermen; 1522 in number, mainly confined to Nílgirí and Bánkí. (81) Girgiriyá; a low caste of fishermen, who are said to have derived their name from having fallen in the social scale; 3270 in number, most numerous in Dhenkánal and Bod. (82) Ujjyá, 496; (83) Málá, 308; (84) Ghoni, 243; (85) Machuá, 148; (86) Dhibár, 105; and (87) Chalák, 93 in number—all fishing castes. (88) Kasbí; prostitutes; 290 in number. (89) Chokár; offspring of prostitutes; the males are generally procurers or musicians, while the females are usually brought up to the trade of their mothers; 216 in number. (90) Kheltá; musicians and jugglers; 443 in number, most numerous in Dhenkánal and · Keunjhar. (91) Kahaliá; musicians; 34 in number.

SEMI-ABORIGINAL CASTES.—The following are all semi-aboriginal castes, and form the very lowest sections of Hindus. Except where otherwise mentioned, their occupation is that of labourers and cultivators:—(92) Pán; the most numerous caste in the Tributary

States, numbering, according to the Census, 112,628; most numerous in Dhenkánal, Keunjhar, Morbhanj, and Angul. It has been already mentioned (p. 229) that nearly every Kandh village has a colony of this degraded caste attached to it in a servile capacity; and up to the time of the suppression of human sacrifice among the Kandhs, it was one of the duties of these Páns to obtain the necessary victims, whom they sold to the Kandhs. (93) Bhuiyá; 30,724 in number, most numerous in Keunjhar and Morbhanj. This tribe has been already described (pp. 247-254). (94) Bathudí; 23,564 in number, mainly confined to Morbhanj and Keunjhar. (95) Khairá; 11,104 in number, most numerous in Dhenkánal, Angul, and Daspallá. (96) Kandárá; 5028 in number, most numerous in Nayágarh and Khandpárá. (97) Baurí; wood-cutters and labourers; 2396 in number, most numerous in Bánkí. (98) Kadal; a subdivision of the foregoing; 1825 in number, most numerous in Nayágarh and Nílgirí. (99) Máhilí; 732 in number, confined to Morbhanj. (100) Ghusuriyá; 69 in number. (101) Kaorá; swineherds and sweepers; 643 in number, confined to Morbhanj and Keunjhar. (102) Bagdí; 653 in number, most numerous in Keunjhar and Morbhanj. (103) Karangá; 125 in number, confined to Morbhanj. (104) Chandál; 121 in number, confined to Dhenkánal. (105) Bághuá; 21 in number. (106) Bind; 42 in number. (107) Bediyá; jugglers and fortune-tellers; 52 in number. (108) Dhálí; 317 in number, most numerous in Nayágarh. (109) Dosádh; 30 in number. (110) Dom; labourers, fishermen, and basket makers; 4853 in number, most numerous in Morbhanj and Dhenkánal. (111) Chámár; shoemakers and leather dealers; 3201 in number, most numerous in Keunjhar, Tálcher, and Dhenkánal. (112) Mihtár; sweepers; 15,075 in number, most numerous in Dhenkánal, Nayágarh, and Angul. (113) Shiulí; 206 in number, most numerous in Khándpárá. (114) Yadhiká; 46 in number, confined to Nayágarh. (115) Labaná; 35 in number, confined to Athmallik.

IMMIGRATION, ETC.—No immigration nor emigration to any extent goes on in the Tributary States.

RELIGION.—As in other parts of Orissa, the great mass of the inhabitants of the Tributary States are Hindus, with the aboriginal fetish superstitions, more or less distinctly preserved. The number of Musalmáns is very small, and consists of the descendants of those who took service as soldiers under the Rájás in the time of the

Marhattás, when there was constant fighting between the various rival States. The Muhammadan religion does not make any progress among the people. In Athgarh there is a village called Chhagán Gobrá, and in Nílgirí one called Mitrapur, entirely inhabited by agricultural communities of native Christians. The principal places of pilgrimage are Kopilás in Dhenkánal, Kusaleswar and Jotipur in Keunjhar, Mántir in Morbhanj, and Sámakul in Nayágarh — all of which attract annual crowds of devotees. Some aboriginal tribes preserve their ancient rites intact. The details of the population of different religions, as returned in the Census Report, are shown in the table on the opposite page.

DISTRIBUTION OF THE PEOPLE INTO TOWN AND COUNTRY.— Nothing like town life exists anywhere throughout the Tributary States. The cultivating classes cling to their hereditary fields, enjoying them either as their own property, as in the Kandh territory, or at a rent practically fixed by custom, as in the other and more advanced States. The lower landless castes wander about the forests, and know no more permanent habitation than a leaf hut. Amid this primitive population of woodmen and cultivators, we see husbandry in a transition stage. In the rich valleys, and wherever a supply of water can be commanded, the peasants gather together into permanent homesteads : each cluster of homesteads forming a village surrounded by its communal lands. But besides settled tillage of this sort, a curious form of nomadic husbandry still survives. The intermediate classes, between the prosperous villagers and the wandering forest tribes, form temporary settlements for the purposes of cultivation. They encamp on some hill-side or jungle-covered valley, burn down the scrub and forest, and with scarcely any labour in tillage obtain rich crops of rice or cotton for three or four years, after which they abandon the locality and set up villages anew on the site of their fresh cultivation.

Throughout the whole nineteen States, covering an area of 16,218 square miles, and containing a population of 1,283,309 souls, there is only one town containing as many as between five and six thousand inhabitants, and only ten with upwards of two thousand. A large village generally gathers around the house or fortress (*garh*) of the Chief; permanent collections of huts grow up at convenient sites for trade along the rivers or roads ; but, with these exceptions, a village in the Tributary States simply means the communal home-

[*Sentence.continued on page* 262.

POPULATION OF THE ORISSA TRIBUTARY STATES, CLASSIFIED ACCORDING TO RELIGION.

Name of State.	Hindus.			Muhammadans.			Christians.			Others.			Grand Total.
	Males.	Females.	Total.	Males.	Females.	Total.	Males.	Females.	Total.	Males.	Females.	Total.	
Bámanghátí,	11,938	11,562	23,500	235	244	479	...	...	...	35,078	35,469	70,547	94,526
Morbhanj,	32,402	32,312	64,714	409	339	748	...	...	...	49,481	49,211	98,692	164,154
Nílgiri,	14,393	13,657	28,050	14	5	19	15	20	35	2,967	2,873	5,840	33,944
Keunjhar,	55,191	58,016	113,207	284	203	487	1	...	1	35,403	32,773	68,176	181,871
Pál Lahárá,	4,686	4,380	9,066	20	15	35	...	...	...	3,257	3,092	6,349	15,450
Dhenkánal,	69,857	71,564	141,421	206	210	416	...	...	...	17,978	18,257	36,235	178,072
Tálcher,	16,973	16,082	33,055	49	51	100	...	...	...	2,447	2,419	4,866	38,021
Angul,	32,199	31,306	63,505	96	93	189	...	...	...	7,482	7,198	14,680	78,374
Athmallik,	5,583	5,150	10,733	32	33	65	...	...	...	1,952	1,786	3,738	14,536
Hindol,	11,709	11,636	23,345	71	51	122	...	...	...	2,242	2,316	4,558	28,025
Narsinhpur,	11,624	10,869	22,493	52	59	111	...	...	...	1,069	1,085	2,154	24,758
Baramba,	10,508	10,547	21,055	40	27	67	...	...	...	1,562	1,577	3,139	24,261
Tigariá,	7,458	7,412	14,870	121	125	246	141	116	257	667	637	1,304	16,420
Athgarh,	10,696	10,838	21,534	73	70	143	6	4	10	2,218	2,214	4,432	26,366
Bánki,	23,514	23,039	46,553	132	117	249	...	...	...	1,318	1,296	2,614	49,426
Khandpárá,	28,302	28,705	57,007	26	12	38	...	...	...	1,906	1,926	3,832	60,877
Nayágarh,	39,976	38,052	78,028	126	100	226	...	...	...	2,666	2,389	4,995	83,249
Ranpur,	12,765	12,230	24,995	81	67	148	...	...	...	1,128	1,035	2,163	27,306
Daspallá,	11,657	11,841	23,478	5	...	5	...	...	...	5,725	5,597	11,322	34,805
Bod,	21,973	20,600	42,573	49	42	91	...	...	...	7,495	6,899	14,394	57,058
Kandh-máls,	8,327	8,146	16,473	9	2	11	...	...	...	18,220	17,106	35,326	51,810
Total,	441,711	437,944	879,655	2130	1865	3995	163	140	303	202,201	197,155	399,356	1,283,309

Sentence continued from page 260.]
stead of a cultivated valley. Such common homesteads, however, generally contain a larger outside population than the more simple Kandh village. For, besides the landless low castes, they require a small body of shopkeepers and tradesmen, suited to the more advanced state of social existence which they have reached.

The one town with a population exceeding 5000 souls is Kantilo in Khandpárá, situated on the south or right bank of the Mahánadí, in 20° 21′ 46″ north latitude, and 85° 14′ 20″ east longitude. The details of its population, according to the Census of 1872, are as follow :— Hindus—males 2605, and females 2781 ; total, 5386. Muhammadans—males 6, and females 2; total, 8. 'Others'—males 64, and females 76 ; total, 140. Total of all denominations — males 2675, and females 2859 ; grand total, 5534. This town is a considerable seat of trade, to which merchants from Cuttack bring salt, spices, etc., to exchange for cotton, wheat, clarified butter, etc., from Sambalpur.

CONDITION OF THE PEOPLE.—The peasants' food consists of boiled rice, pulse, vegetables, fish, and occasionally flesh. A prosperous cultivator lives on about seven rupees or fourteen shillings a month. His household expenses are eight shillings for rice, two for vegetables, one for salt, and three for firewood, oil, spices, and occasionally a little fish.

The dress of a well-to-do shopkeeper consists of a white cloth round the loins hanging down to the ankle (*dhutí*), and a white sheet or cloth thrown over the shoulders (*chádar*), worth altogether about four shillings. That of a peasant is a simple waistcloth, worth eighteenpence. A shopkeeper's furniture consists of a few blankets, carpets, mattresses, mats, and pillows, a wooden seat or two, and an instrument for husking rice (*dhenki*).

AGRICULTURE.—Tillage is conducted in two methods, common to the whole Tributary States : — (1) Rice cultivation in hollows and on low lands, with a command of moisture. In the valleys, where the mountain rivulets can be utilized, the peasants throw a dam across the stream and store up the water. The lower levels thus secure a supply of moisture the whole year round, and wet rice cultivation goes on throughout the twelve months. (2) Upland or *tailá* cultivation, upon newly cleared patches of land, which depends entirely on the local rainfall. The forest is cut down and burnt upon the spot; and the soil, thus enriched with salts, yields abundant crops of early rice, oil seeds, and cotton. At the end of four or five years such clearings are abandoned for new ones, and the land relapses into jungle. After years of rest, when a fresh growth of forest has sprung up, the trees and shrubs are again cut down and burnt on the spot, the whole process of clearing and cultivating for another period of five years being repeated *de novo.*

MEANS OF COMMUNICATION, TRADE, ETC.—The rivers form the great highways of the Tributary States; and these arteries of trade are now fed by a hundred rude roads and mountain tracks, suited for pack-bullocks. Wandering merchants pass secure through the deepest recesses of the mountains. The export trade of the Tributary States consists of rice, sugar-cane, oil seeds, clarified butter, cotton, coarse cereals, timber, lac, turmeric, bees-wax, and other jungle products. No permanent markets have yet developed, but each State has from three to ten villages at which weekly fairs are held. Business is conducted almost entirely by barter, a silver currency being scarcely known, and even the ancient shell money (cowries) of Orissa being sparingly used. Mention has already been made (p. 231) of the ingenious and highly artificial system by which the Kandhs facilitate trade by barter. They have invented a currency of 'lives;' the said 'lives' representing sheep or bullocks, or even inanimate objects, in different localities.

ADMINISTRATION.—The Chiefs rule their territories pretty much according to their own ideas of what is right. We leave each State under its hereditary Rájá, and allow him jurisdiction in civil disputes, and in all crimes not of a heinous character. A detailed sketch of the legislative history of our dealings with them has been given in a previous page. The Chiefs are amenable to the British Commissioner of the Province, in his character as Superintendent of the Tributary States; this officer has jurisdiction in all serious offences, and may imprison criminals for a term not exceeding seven years. Sentences for a longer period, although passed by the Commissioner, must be reported to the Bengal Government for confirmation; and it is the Government alone that can imprison or punish a Chief. The treaty engagements entered into by the Rájás are generally of the following nature:—Besides holding themselves in submission and loyal obedience to the British Government, they are bound on demand to surrender any residents of Orissa who may have fled into their territories, also any of their own subjects who may have committed offences in British territory; to furnish supplies to British troops when passing through their territories; and in case of any neighbouring Rájá or other person offering opposition to the British Government, they are on demand to depute a contingent force of their own troops to assist the forces of Government. Each Rájá pays a small tribute, now fixed in perpetuity, and bearing a very small ratio to his total income. The whole tribute derived from the seventeen States still ruled by their own princes (excluding Angul and Bánkí, confiscated and under British supervision), with a population of 1,155,509 souls, amounts to £3338, or at the rate of about three farthings per head of the population. The estimated revenue of these Chiefs is returned at £59,406, but this estimate is probably considerably under the mark. In return for their tribute, we assure them absolute security from foreign enemies, domestic rebellions, and inter-tribal feuds. In one case, that of Angul, we have had to dispossess a Chief for waging war; but his family enjoy pensions from Government. In another, that of Bánkí, the Rájá was convicted of flagrant murder and his estate confiscated. Both these States are now under direct Government management, the revenues being collected and the affairs of the State generally managed by a receiver (*tahsíldár*). The other seventeen States still remain under their native Chiefs; and the only cases of English interference have been to prevent the aggression of the strong upon the weak, or to support the authority of the hereditary Chiefs against their domestic enemies.

POLICE, ETC.—The Rájás do not maintain regular police stations, police duties being performed by the *páiks*, or cultivators holding on a tenure of military service. A regular police force, however, has been organized in the two States under Government management. Angul has one head-station at Puraná-garh, and four outposts at Tikarpárá, Máicharpur, Balarám-prasád, and Chhindipádá. In Bánkí there is a head-station at Chárchiká, with three outposts at Báideswar, Kalápathar, and Subarnapur. A police force is also maintained in the Khand-máls, consisting of one head-station at Bisipárá, and four out-stations at Khejurpárá, Kalábágh, Nayápárá, and Argirkiá, to preserve order in that wild region. The total force thus maintained in the tracts under British supervision in 1872 is returned as follows:—1 Superintendent, 2 first-class and 28 second-class subordinate officers, and 180 foot police constables; the whole maintained at a total cost of £3199. The total area thus protected is 1740 square miles, with a population of 179,610, giving an average of one policeman to every 8·2 square miles of area, or one to every 851 of the population. Besides the regular police, there is a rural force or village watch, consisting of 440 men, maintained by grants of rent-free service land from Government. The average number of houses in each village watchman's charge is 75; and the average annual emoluments from the rent-free land which he holds as remuneration for his police duties is Rs. 16 or £1, 12s. od. Including the regular police and village watch, the total strength of the force maintained for protecting life and property in the tracts under British supervision is 651 men, equal to an average of one policeman to every 2·6 square miles, or one to every 276 of the population. Three Stipendiary Magistrate's Courts have also been established.

EDUCATION.—In 1872-73 there were 19 schools in the Tributary States under the inspection of the Education Department, viz. 8 middle-class Government vernacular schools, 8 improved *páthsálás* in Dhenkánal aided by the Chief of the State, 2 unaided middle-class vernacular schools, and 1 unaided lower-class school. These 19 schools were distributed as follows:—Bánkí, 2 with 100 pupils; Angul, 6 with 167 pupils; Dhenkánal, 10 with 324 pupils; and Athgarh, 1 with 41 pupils. Besides these inspected schools, there are also schools of more or less efficiency in each of the States, maintained by the Rájás. The Commissioner reports that the Mahárájá of Dhenkánal and the Rájá of Keunjhar are conspicuous for their support of education. The future prospect of education in these tracts is promising, but a chief want is that of better masters. 'A remarkable move,' says the Commissioner, 'in relation to education has been made among the wild tribes of the Kandh hills. These people have submitted of their own wish, and indeed of their own motion, to a tax on liquor shops, the proceeds of which are devoted to the establishment of schools. The tax has been realized without difficulty, and a number of schools have been established. The schoolhouses have been built and are maintained by the people themselves.' At the time of the Census, a return was obtained of the number of schools in the Tributary States. It showed that there were altogether 9 Government schools, attended by a total of 352 pupils; 52 schools maintained or aided by the different Chiefs, of which 35 were attended by 1086 pupils; and 282 *páthsálás*, for which the number of pupils is not returned.

Details of the schools in each State will be found in the following pages, giving a brief account of each of the States.

CHARITABLE DISPENSARIES.—Three dispensaries for affording medical relief to the sick are maintained in the Tributary States. (1) The Dhenkánal dispensary, established in 1866, is entirely supported by the Mahárájá, with the exception of a supply of medicines and surgical instruments received from Government free of charge. In 1872 a total of 2626 patients were treated at the dispensary, the daily average attendance being 23. There were no in-door patients, but uncooked rations are distributed by the Mahárájá's orders to certain sick poor attending the dispensary. The total expenditure by the Mahárájá in 1872 amounted to £158, 6s. od.; the cost to Government for the supply of European medicines amounted to £37, 2s. od. (2) The Angul branch dispensary was established in March 1861, and is maintained entirely by Government. The attendance is poor, and is said to be decreasing. In 1872, 157 patients received out-door treatment, the average daily attendance being 8·11. There were no in-door patients. The total cost of the dispensary in 1872 amounted to £57, 12s. od. (3) There is also a dispensary at Bispárá in the Kandh-máls, established in 1865. The building is situated at an altitude of nearly three thousand feet, on a dry, porous, rocky soil, presenting, one would suppose, all the conditions likely to secure immunity from malarious fever; but natives from the plains seem almost invariably to contract fever of a severe and persistent form: the police especially suffer. Fever, rheumatism, dysentery and diarrhœa, and ulcers are the most common diseases. Ophthalmia appears also to be a common complaint. The number of in-door patients treated in 1872 amounted to 302, the average daily attendance being 9·36. The cost of the dispensary to Government amounted to £57, 12s. od.

SEPARATE ACCOUNT OF THE DIFFERENT STATES.

The following is a brief account, in alphabetical order, of each of the different States, their area, revenue, population, crops, history, etc. As stated previously, each State has its own Rájá or Chief, except the two which are under direct Government control.

ANGUL STATE lies between 21° 10′ 55″ and 20° 32′ 5″ north

latitude, and between 84° 18' 10" and 85° 42' 45" east longitude. It is bounded on the north by the States of Rádhákol and Bámrá in the Central Provinces; on the east by Tálcher and Hindol; on the south by Narsinhpur, Daspallá, and the Mahánadí river; and on the west by Athmallik. Area, 881 square miles; villages or *mauzás*, 352; and houses, 13,892. The Census returned the population at 78,374 souls, classified as follows:—Hindus—males, men 17,650, and boys 14,549; total, 32,199: females, women 18,301, and girls 13,005; total, 31,306. Grand total of Hindus, 63,505, or 81·0 per cent. of the population·of the State; proportion of males in total Hindu population, 50·7 per cent. Muhammadans—males, men 74, and boys 22; total, 96: females, women 64, and girls 29; total, 93. Grand total of Muhammadans, 189, or ·2 per cent. of the population; proportion of males in total Musálmans, 50·8 per cent. Christians—*nil*. Other denominations, consisting of aboriginal tribes and peoples who still retain their primitive forms of faith—males, men 4621, and boys 2861; total, 7482: females, women 4698, and girls 2500; total, 7198. Total 'others,' 14,680, or 18·8 per cent. of the total population; proportion of males in total 'other' population, 50·9 per cent. Population of all denominations—males, men 22,345, and boys 17,432; total, 39,777: females, women 23,063, and girls 15,534; total, 38,597. Total population, 78,374; proportion of males in total population, 50·7 per cent. Average density of the population, 89 per square mile; villages or *mauzás* per square mile, ·39; persons per village or *mauzá*, 223; houses per square mile, 16; persons per house, 5·6. The Census Report ethnically divides the population as follows:—Aboriginal tribes, 10,220, or 13·1 per cent. of the total population, mainly consisting of Kandhs (5423) and Taálas (3358). Semi-Hinduized aborigines, 15,910, or 20·3 per cent. of the population, almost entirely composed of Páns (10,341) and Khairás (2743). Hindu castes and persons of Hindu origin, 52,055, or 66·5 per cent. of the population, the most numerous caste being the Chásá (25,761). Muhammadans, 189, or ·2 per cent. of the population. Details of the different tribes, castes, etc. will be found in the table on pp. 210-217.

The State was confiscated in 1847, owing to the Rájá's continued disobedience of the orders of Government, and his attempt to wage war against the English. Since that time it has been under direct Government management, the revenues being collected, and the State generally managed, by a receiver (*tahsíldár*). The members of the ex-Rájá's family enjoy pensions from Government. The State was originally in the possession of a Kandh named Ano; but the ancestors of the ex-Rájá having gained a footing in the country as traders, plotted against the Kandh prince and seized his territory. The area is for the most part jungle. Rice, sugar-cane, oil seeds, cotton, and coarse cereals form the staple crops of the small portion under cultivation. Droughts frequently destroy the crops, but there is scarcely any part of the State in danger of flood.

Prior to its confiscation there was no trade in Angul, and its tribute to the British Government amounted to only £165; but since then fairs have been established at several places, which are attended by traders from Cuttack and the neighbouring Districts. The population lives almost entirely by agriculture. With the exception of the southern portion, which is hilly, the country is level, and only needs an increase of population in order to extend agriculture. The Bráhmaní river runs within a mile of the north-eastern boundary, and might form a valuable trade route for the products of the State. The high road from Cuttack to Sambalpur, which passes through the State, also forms a means of communication and transport. Coal and iron are found. The capital of the State and residence of the ex-Rájá's family is Angul village, situated in the centre of the State, 20° 47' 50" north latitude, and 85° 1' 26" east longitude; but the largest and most important village is Chhindipádá, in the north of the State, in 21° 5' 0" north latitude, and 84° 55' 0" east longitude. Neither of these villages contains upwards of 5000 inhabitants, and their population is therefore not returned separately in the Census Report. At the time of the Topographical Survey in 1860-62, Chhindipádá village contained 149 houses, and nine other villages were returned as containing upwards of 100 houses each. In the Census Report of 1872, the number of villages in the State was returned at 352, classified as follows:—211 with less than two hundred inhabitants, 104 with from two to five hundred, 31 with from five hundred to a thousand, and 6 with from one to two thousand inhabitants. For the education of the people, the Census Report returns 6 schools maintained by Government, containing 196 pupils; and 43 *páthsálás* or indigenous village schools, the number of pupils not being given.

ATHGARH STATE lies between 20° 41' 35" and 20° 25' 35" north latitude, and between 84° 34' 25" and 85° 54' 0" east longitude. It is bounded on the north by Dhenkánal; on the east by the Regulation District of Cuttack; on the south by the Mahánadí river, separating it from Cuttack District on this side also; and on the west by Tigariá and Dhenkánal. The State comprises an area of 168 square miles, containing 191 villages or *mauzás*, and 4699 houses. The Census Report returned the population in 1872 at 26,366 souls, classified as follows :—Hindus—males, men 6436, and boys 4260; total, 10,696 : females, women 6854, and girls 3984; total, 10,838. Grand total of Hindus, 21,534, or 81·6 per cent. of the total population of the State; proportion of males in total Hindu population, 49·7 per cent. Muhammadans—males, men 46, and boys 27; total, 73 : females, women 48, and girls 22; total, 70. Grand total of Muhammadans, 143, or 0·6 per cent. of the population; proportion of males in total Musalmáns, 51·0 per cent. Christians—males, men 71, and boys 70; total, 141 : females, women 72, and girls 44; total, 116. Grand total of Christians, 257, or 1·0 per cent. of the population. Other denominations—males, men 1338, and boys 880; total, 2218 : females, women 1388, and girls 826; total, 2214. Grand total of 'others,' 4432, or 16·8 per cent. of the population; proportion of males in total 'others,' 50·1 per cent. Population of all denominations—males, men 7891, and boys 5237; total, 13,128 : females, women 8362, and girls 4876; total, 13,238; total population of the State, 26,366. Proportion of males in total population, 49·8 per cent. Average density of the population, 157 per square mile; villages per square mile, 1·13; persons per village, 138; houses per square mile, 28; persons per house, 5·6. The Census Report ethnically divides the population as follows :—Aboriginal tribes, 4336, or 16·4 per cent of the population, almost entirely composed of Savars (3555). Semi-Hinduized aborigines, 3009, or 11·4 per cent. of the population, consisting chiefly of Páns (2321), Hindu castes and people of Hindu origin, 18,878, or 71·6 per cent. of the population, the most numerous being the Chásá or principal cultivating caste (5235). Muhammadans, 143, or ·6 per cent. of the population. Details of the different tribes, castes, etc. will be found in the table on pp. 210-217.

Athgarh is a low, level country, and very subject to inundation. The cultivation consists of rice, with an occasional crop of sugarcane. The Rájá's residence is buried in bamboo thickets, originally planted as a defence against the Marhattá horse. The high road from Cuttack to Sambalpur passes through the State; the Mahánadí river, which forms the southern boundary, also affords a means of communication and a trade route. The capital of the State and residence of the Rájá is Athgarh village, situated on the Cuttack and Sambalpur road, in 20° 31′ 30″ north latitude, and 85° 40′ 31″ east longitude. The principal village, and indeed the only one containing upwards of 100 houses, is Gobrá, near the eastern border of the State, in 20° 35′ 2″ north latitude, and 85° 22′ 28″ east longitude. At the village of Chhagán, situated between Gobrá and Athgarh, in 20° 34′ 14″ north latitude, and 85° 52′ 30″ east longitude, there is a peasant colony of native Christians under the charge of the Baptist Mission at Cuttack. The village has a small chapel, and is prettily situated on a slight eminence, surrounded by well-cultivated rice fields. Its population is exclusively Christian, who are employed as agriculturists. Two other Christian hamlets adjoin the village. In the Census Report of 1872, the total number of villages in the State is returned at 191, classified as follows:—145 with less than two hundred inhabitants, 43 with between two and five hundred, and 3 with between five hundred and a thousand.

Athgarh State yields to its Rájá an income estimated at £1493 a year, the tribute annually paid to the British Government being £280. In ancient times it belonged to the kings of Orissa, one of whom married the sister of his prime minister, and presented the State of Athgarh to his brother-in-law, together with the title of Rájá. The present (1876) ruler, Rájá Srí Karan Bhágirathí Bawártá Patnáik, who is about thirty-one years old, is the tenth in descent, and belongs to the writer caste (Kayásth). His militia or military force consists of 262 men, and the rural police force of 115 men. For the education of his people the Rájá maintains one school, and the Census Report returns another village school or *páthsálá*.

ATHMALLIK STATE lies between 21° 5′ 30″ and 20° 36′ 55″ north latitude, and between 84° 18′ 20″ and 84° 50′ 30″ east longitude. It is bounded on the north by the State of Rádhákol in the Central Provinces; on the east by Angul; on the south by the Mahánadí river, separating it from Bod; and on the west by the Central Provinces' States of Sónpur and Rádhákol. It comprises an area of 730 square miles, containing 209 villages and *mauzás*, and 2897 houses. The Census Report returned the population in 1872 at 14,536 souls, classified as follows:—Hindus—males, men 3274, and boys 2309; total, 5583: females, women 3125, and girls 2025; total, 5150. Grand total of Hindus, 10,733, or 73·8 per cent. of the population; proportion of males in total Hindus, 52·0 per cent. Muhammadans—males, men 22, and boys 10; total, 32 : females, women 19, and girls 14; total, 33. Grand total of Musalmáns, 65, or ·4 per cent of the population; proportion of males in total Muhammadans, 49·2 per cent. Christians—*nil*. Other denominations—males, men 1132, and boys 820; total, 1952: females, women 1085, and girls 701; total, 1786. Grand total of 'others,' 3738, or 25·7 per cent. of the population; proportion of males in total 'others,' 52·2 per cent. Total population of all denominations—males, men 4428, and boys 3139; total, 7567: females, women 4229, and girls 2740; total, 6969. Total popula·:on of the State, 14,536; proportion of males in total population, 52·0 per cent. Average density of population, 20 per square mile (being the most sparsely populated of all the Tributary States); villages per square mile, ·28; persons per village, 70; houses per square mile, 4; persons per house, 5·0. The Census Report ethnically divides the population as follows :—Aboriginal tribes, 2840, or 19·5 per cent. of the population, almost exclusively composed of Gonds (1427) and Kandhs (1112). Semi-Hinduized aborigines, 1847, or 12·8 per cent. of the population, the Páns here, as elsewhere, forming the majority (1075). Hindu castes and people of Hindu origin, 9784, or 67·3 per cent. of the population, the most numerous castes being the Chásás (2332), Suds (2264), and Damal Goálás (1707). Muhammadans, 65, or ·4 per cent. of the population. Details of the different tribes, castes, etc. will be found in the table on pp. 210-217.

Athmallik State is a dense jungle with little cultivation and no trade. A long range of hills covered with wood runs along its southern side, parallel with the Mahánadí. The crops consist of coarse rice and other inferior grains, with a few oil seeds. The residence of the Rájá is at Handápá, situated in the centre of the State, in N. latitude 20° 56' 40", and E. longitude 84° 43' 41"; but the principal village, and indeed the only one containing upwards of 100 houses, is Káintá, situated on the left or north bank of the Mahánadí. The Census Report returns the total number of villages in the State at 209, classified as follows :—195 with less than two hundred inhabitants, 13 with between two and five hundred, and only 1 with between five hundred and a thousand. .

The State yields its Chief, Jagendra Sáont (who has no legal claim to the title of Rájá, which, however, is usually accorded him in courtesy), an estimated income of £710, the annual tribute payable to the British Government being £48. The Chief's emblem of signature is a *kadamba* flower, and his family is called the Kadamba-bansá. The total militia and police force of the State is returned in the Census Report as amounting to only 18 men. A school is maintained at the expense of the Rájá.

BANKI STATE lies between 20° 30′ 0″ and 20° 15′ 30″ north latitude, and between 85° 23′ 0″ and 85° 40′ 0″ east longitude. It is bounded on the north by the Mahánadí river, separating it from Barambá and Tigariá (a small portion of the State lies north of the Mahánadí); on the east by the Regulation District of Cuttack; on the south by Purí District; and on the west by Khandpárá. It comprises an area, as returned by the Surveyor-General, of 150 square miles (the Census Report returns the area at 116 square miles), containing 140 villages and 8432 houses. The population in 1872 was returned at 49,426 souls, classified as follows :— Hindus—males, men 14,745, and boys 8769; total, 23,514: females, women 15,077, and girls 7962; total, 23,039. Grand total of Hindus, 46,553, or 94·2 per cent. of the total population of the State; proportion of males in total Hindus, 50·5 per cent. Muhammadans—males, men 93, and boys 39; total, 132: females, women 83, and girls 34; total, 117. Grand total of Musalmáns, 249, or ·5 per cent. of the population; proportion of males in total Muhammadans, 53·8 per cent. Christians—males, men 3, and boys 3; total, 6: females, women 3, and girls 1; total, 4. Total Christians, 10. Other denominations (aboriginal tribes, etc.)—males, men 843, and boys 475; total, 1318: females, women 814, and girls 482; total, 1296. Total ' others,' 2614, or 5·3 per cent. of the population; proportion of males in total ' others,' 50·4 per cent. Total of all denominations —males, men 15,684, and boys 9286; total, 24,970: females, women 15,977, and girls 8479; total, 24,456. Total population of the State, 49,426; proportion of males in total population, 54·5 per cent. The proportion of Hindus is much greater, and that of the aboriginal tribes much less, in Bánkí than in any other of the States. Average density of population (according to the Census return of area), 426 per square mile, making it the most densely populated of all the States; villages per square mile, 1·20; persons per village, 353; houses per square mile, 73; persons per house, 5·9. The population is ethnically divided as follows :—Aboriginal tribes, 2455, or 5·3 per cent. of the population, almost entirely consisting of Savars (2174). Semi-Hinduized aborigines, 3816, or 7·7 per cent. of the population, consisting principally of Páns (1178) and Baurís (1038). Hindu castes and people of Hindu origin, 42,906, or 86·5 per cent. of the population, the most numerous castes being the Chásá (10,469) and Keut (3332). Muhammadans, 249, or ·5 per cent. of the population. Details of the different tribes, castes, etc. will be found in the table on pp. 210–217. The principal village in the State is Bánkí, situated on the south or right bank of the Mahánadí, in 20° 21′ 30″ north latitude, and 85° 33′ 11″ east longitude. The total number of villages is returned in the Census Report at 140, classified as follows:—62 with less than two hundred inhabitants, 52 with between two and five hundred, 13 with between five hundred and a thousand, and 13 with between one and two thousand.

Bánkí paid an annual tribute of £443 to Government from 1805 till 1840, when it was confiscated, owing to the Rájá having been convicted of murder and sentenced to imprisonment for life. Since that time the State has been under direct Government management. In 1860-61 it yielded a revenue of £1333, which ten years later (1870-71) had increased to £1996. The Census Report returns the strength of the regular police at 33 men, and the village watch or rural constabulary at 161 men. For the education of the people, Government maintains 2 schools, attended in 1872 by 116 pupils; in the same year 31 *páthsálás* or indigenous village schools were also returned, but the number of pupils attending them is not stated.

BARAMBA STATE lies between 20° 31′ 40″ and 20° 22′ 15″ north latitude, and between 85° 15′ 0″ and 85° 31′ 30″ east longitude. It is bounded on the north by Hindol; on the east by Tigariá; on the south by the Mahánadí river, separating it from Bánkí and Khandpárá; and on the west by Narsinhpur. It comprises an area of 134 square miles, containing 137 villages and 4950 houses. The Census Report of 1872 returns the population at 24,261 souls, classified as follows:—Hindus—males, men 6530, and boys 3978; total, 10,508: females, women 6966, and girls 3581; total, 10,547. Grand total of Hindus, 21,055, or 86·8 per cent. of the population; proportion of males in total Hindus, 49·9 per cent. Muhammadans—males, men 26, and boys 14; total, 40: females, women 18, and girls 9; total, 27. Grand total of Muhammadans, 67, or ·3 per cent. of the population; proportion of males in total Musalmáns, 59·7 per cent. Christians—*nil.* Other denominations (aboriginal tribes, etc.)— males, men 963, and boys 599; total, 1562: females, women 1000,

and girls 577; total, 1577. Grand total of 'others,' 3139, or 12·9 per cent. of the population; proportion of males in total 'others,' 49·8 per cent. Population of all denominations—males, men 7519, and boys 4591; total, 12,110 : females, women 7984, and girls 4167; total, 12,151. Total population of the State, 24,261; proportion of males in total population, 49·9 per cent. Average density of the population, 181 per square mile; villages per square mile, 1·02; persons per village, 177; houses per square mile, 37; persons per house, 4·9. The population is ethnically divided as follows :—
Aboriginal tribes, 3024, or 12·5 per cent. of the population, consist-
ing of Kandhs (1086), Savars (1016), and Taálas (922); semi-
Hinduized aboriginals, 3052, or 12·5 per cent. of the District population, consisting principally of Páns (1956), and Mihtárs (546); Hindu castes and people of Hindu origin, 18,118, or 74·7 per cent. of the population, the most numerous castes being Chásás (4769), Bráhmans (1928), and Gaurs (1712); Muhammadans, 67, or ·3 per cent. of the population. Details of the different tribes, castes, etc. will be found in the table on pp. 210–217.

The Mahánadí, on the southern boundary of the State, affords excellent water carriage for its products, and logs of timber and bamboos are floated down the river to Cuttack and Purí Districts. Bi-weekly trading fairs are held at Máinábád, a small village on the Mahánadí, situated in 20° 26′ 30″ north latitude, and 85° 20′ 28″ east longitude; and at Banálipur, also on the Mahánadí, in 20° 24′ 9″ north latitude, and 85° 20′ 28″ east longitude. The principal village and residence of the Rájá is Barambá, in the centre of the State, in 20° 25′ 15″ north latitude, and 82° 22′ 41″ east longitude. The only other village of importance is Gobirátpur, on the Mahánadí, in 20° 22′ 59″ north latitude, and 85° 24′ 31″ east longitude. The total number of villages is returned in the Census Report at 137, classified as follows:—100 with less than two hundred inhabitants, 29 with from two to five hundred, 6 with from five hundred to a thousand, and 2 with from one to two thousand. The Kanaká peak, 2038 feet in height, is situated on the northern border of the State.

Barambá State yields an estimated revenue of £2606 to its Chief, the tribute to the British Government being £140. The present ruler, Rájá Dásrathí Bírbar Mangráj Mahápatra, is 24 years of age, and claims to be a Kshattriya by caste. He is the nineteenth Rájá in descent from the original chief. His emblem of signature is a dog metamorphosed into a lion—a heraldic monster that took its

is
50
five
.rom
ne of
es are
i peaks
border,
iánángá,

·ear to its
£80. The
age, and is
y claims an
stranger, who
ars ago. The
rful neighbours
In Bod Proper,
22 men, and his
·h are now under
men, and a village
·hool is maintained
iools are returned as
l, attended by about
14 other indigenous
. The growing inclina-
.on, and their voluntary
of additional schools in

10,811 houses, and a total population of 51,810, classified as follows:
—Hindus—males, men 4774, and boys 3553; total, 8327 : females,
women 4974, and girls 3172; total, 8146. Grand total of Hindus,
16,473, or 31·8 per cent. of the total population of the tract; proportion of males in total Hindus, 50·5 per cent. Muhammadans—
males, men 8, and boys 1; total 9: females, women 2, girls *nil.* Total
Musalmáns, 11. Christians—*nil.* Other denominations (aboriginal
tribes, etc.)—males, men 10,886, and boys 7334; total, 18,220 :
females, women 10,980, and girls 6126; total, 17,106. Grand total
of 'others,' 35,326, or 68·2 per cent. of the total population; proportion of males in total 'others,' 51·6 per cent. Population of all
denominations—males, men 15,668, and boys 10,888; total, 26,556:
females, women 15,956, and girls 9298; total, 25,254. Grand total,
51,810; proportion of males in total population, 51·3 per cent.

Including Bod Proper and the Kandh-máls, the State contains
1542 villages, with 22,080 houses, and a total population of 108,868,
classified as follows :—Hindus—males 30,300, and females 28,746;
total, 59,046, or 54·2 per cent. of the population. Muhammadans—
males 58, and females 44; total, 102, or ·1 per cent. of the population. Other denominations—males 25,715, and females 24,005;
total, 49,720, or 45·7 per cent. of the population. Population of all
denominations—males 56,073, and females 51,795; total, 108,868.
Average density of the population, 53 per square mile; villages per
square mile, ·74; persons per village, 70; houses per square mile,
11 ; persons per house, 4·9. The population is ethnically divided
as follows :—Bod Proper—Aboriginal tribes, 13,482, or 23·8 per
cent. of the population, nearly solely comprised of Kandhs (12,019);
semi-aboriginal castes, 6906, or 12·1 per cent. of the population,
comprised almost solely of Páns (5273) ; Hindus and people of
Hindu origin, 36,579, or 64·1 per cent. of the population, the most
numerous castes being the Damál and Magadhá Goálás, numbering
13,422, Súds (4356), and Keuts (3151); Muhammadans, 91. Kandh-
máls—Aboriginal tribes, 35,798, or 68·9 per cent. of the population,
almost entirely composed of Kandhs (34,005); semi-Hinduized
aboriginals, 6831, or 13·2 per cent., of whom 6204 are Páns; Hindu
castes and people of Hindu origin, 9170, or 17·7 per cent., the
most numerous castes being Magadhá Goálás (2045), Súds (1733),
and Surís (1629); Muhammadans, 11. In Bod Proper it will be
seen that the Hindus form the bulk of the population, while in the
Kandh-máls the aboriginal element is largely in the majority. De-

tails of the different tribes, races, etc. will be found in the table on pp. 210–217.

The Mahánadí river, which forms the northern, and the Tel river, which forms the western, boundary of the State, offer excellent facilities for water carriage; but with the exception of a small trade in *sál* timber, none of the produce of the country is exported. Weekly markets are held at eight villages for traffic in the usual simple commodities, such as coarse rice, oil seeds, and jungle products. The largest and most important town, which is also the residence of the Rájá, is Bod, situated in the north of the State, on the right bank of the Mahánadí, in 20° 50′ 20″ north latitude, and 84° 21′ 41″ east longitude. The only other village of any size is Jagatigarh. The total number of villages in Bod (including the Kandh-máls) is returned in the Census Report at 1542, classified as follows :—1450 with less than two hundred inhabitants, 82 with from two to five hundred, 8 with from five hundred to a thousand, and 1 with from one to two thousand inhabitants. Bod Proper is said to be one of the most neglected of the Tributary States, and many villages are reported to be without inhabitants. The principal mountain peaks in the State are the following :—Bondigárá, on the southern border, 3308 feet; Bankomundí, in the north, 2080 feet; and Siánángá, in the west, 1917 feet.

Bod State yields an estimated revenue of £700 a year to its Chief, the tribute to the British Government being £80. The present ruler, Rájá Pitambhar Deo, is about 54 years of age, and is a Kshattriya of the Solar race. The reigning family claims an uninterrupted descent of seventy generations from a stranger, who founded the petty Principality about a thousand years ago. The State was once much larger than at present, but powerful neighbours have from time to time wrested parts of it away. In Bod Proper, the Rájá's militia is returned as consisting only of 22 men, and his police force at 20 men. In the Kandh-máls, which are now under British management, a regular police force of 55 men, and a village watch of 119 men, are maintained. In Bod, 1 school is maintained by the Rájá, and 8 other *páthsálás* or village schools are returned as within the State. In the Kandh-máls, 1 school, attended by about 40 pupils, is maintained by Government, and 14 other indigenous village schools are reported to be in existence. The growing inclination evinced by the Kandhs towards education, and their voluntary taxation of themselves for the establishment of additional schools in their hills, has been alluded to in the general paragraph on education (*ante*, p. 265).

THE KANDH-MALS OF BOD.—These tracts are now under a mild form of British administration. The population amounts to 51,810, details of which are given in the foregoing account of Bod State. The tract comprising the Kandh-máls consists of a broken plateau intersected by ridges of low hills, the last refuge of the Kandh race. The villages are few in number, and divided from each other by rugged peaks and dense forests; but a regular system of government on the aboriginal plan is maintained, the hamlets being distributed into *mutas*, and each *muta* being under the supervision of a clan chief. Throughout this wild tract the Kandhs claim an indefeasible right in the soil. They assert that the whole of Bod and all the neighbouring country was once theirs, and that they have been gradually pushed back into the recesses of the hills by unscrupulous invaders. They deny that they ever acknowledged the rule of their oppressors, and consider themselves as wrongfully ousted, so that no length of time can bar their inalienable right to the soil. Mr. Ravenshaw, the Commissioner of Orissa, whose minute acquaintance with the people makes him the highest living authority, writes that these Kandh legends of having been driven out from more fertile territories are probably true. The Kandhs say that they were pushed eastwards from Sableiá, in Sambalpur, the ancient home of their race. The Kandh-máls, at any rate, were never more than nominally subject to the Bod Rájá, who was totally unable to control or coerce them. After the British Government discovered the frequency of human sacrifice among the Kandhs in 1836, it established an Agency to put a stop to the practice (Act xxi. of 1845); and the Bod Rájá gladly ceded the Kandh-máls to us for the better suppression of these inhuman rites. The people are a wild, impulsive race, but the Commissioner of Orissa reports that for years they have lived peaceably under our rule. They pay no rent, and we take no revenue whatever from them, but merely keep order and prevent oppression by means of a *tahsíldár*, supported by a strong force of police. This officer's principal duties are to prevent or put a stop to blood-feuds, to adjust dangerous disputes, and to take cognisance of any serious crime. The Bod Rájá exercises no authority whatever in the Kandh-máls. The chief product is turmeric, which is grown in large quantities. It is of an unusually fine quality, and is eagerly bought up by traders from the open country, who penetrate with their pack-bullocks into the innermost recesses of the hills. For further particulars regarding the Kandhs, see *ante*, p. 209, also pp. 211–238; also the *Central Provinces Gazetteer*, pp. 25, 124, 196, 239, 251, 286, 393; and the *Manual of Vizagapatam District in Madras*, pp. 323-349.

DASPALLA STATE lies between 20° 35′ 0″ and 20° 10′ 50″ north latitude, and between 84° 31′ 45″ and 85° 8′ 0″ east longitude. It is bounded on the north by Angul and Narsinhpur, the Mahánadí river marking the boundary-line, except for a short distance, where the State extends to the north of the river; on the east by Khandpárá and Nayágarh; on the south by the Madras State of Gumsar; and on the west by Bod. It comprises a total area of 568 square miles, and contains 432 villages and 7577 houses. . The Census Report of 1872 returns the population at 34,805, classified as follows:— Hindus—males, men 7386, and boys 4251; total, 11,637: females, women 7867, and girls 3974; total, 11,841. Grand total of Hindus, 23,478, or 67·5 per cent. of the population of the State; proportion of males in total Hindus, 49·6 per cent. Muhammadans—males, men 5, females *nil*. Christians—*nil*. Other denominations (aboriginal tribes, etc.)—males, men 3732, and boys 1993; total, 5725: females, women 3776, and girls 1821; total, 5597. Grand total of 'others,' 11,322, or 32·5 per cent. of the population; proportion of males in total 'others,' 50·6 per cent. Population of all denominations—males, men 11,123, and boys 6244; total, 17,367: females, women 11,643, and girls 5795; total, 17,438. Total population of the State, 34,805; proportion of males in total population, 49·9 per cent. Average density of the population, 61 per square mile; villages per square mile, ·76; persons per village, 81; persons per house, 4·6. The population is ethnically divided as follows:—Aboriginal tribes, 9302, or 26·7 per cent. of the population, the great majority (8382) being Kandhs, who are only nominally subject to the Rájá; semi-Hinduized aboriginals, 7337, or 21·1 per cent. of the population, the great majority being Páns (4343) and Kháirás (2088); Hindu tribes and persons of Hindu origin, 18,161, or 52·2 per cent. of the population, the principle castes being Chásás (4076), Gaurs (2789), and Bráhmans (1161); Muhammadans, 5. Details of the different tribes, castes, etc. will be found in the table on pp. 210–217.

. The Mahánadí, which forms the northern boundary of the State, flows through the magnificent Bármúl gorge in Daspallá territory, in a channel of great depth, with special facilities for water carriage.

The principal mountain peak in the State is Goáldes, in the north, on the right bank of the Mahánadí, 2506 feet. The principal village is Daspallá, near the eastern boundary of the State, in 20° 18' 40" N. lat., and 84° 56' 21" E. long. The other six principal villages are the following:—Kunjabaná, the Rájá's place of residence, in the centre of the State, in 20° 20' 45" N. lat., and 84° 53' 27" E. long.; Julindá, on the right bank of the Mahánadí, in 20° 31' 28" N. lat., and 84° 59' 23" E. long.; Belpádá, on the right bank of the Mahánadí, 20° 24' 59" N. lat., and 85° 6' 3" E. long.; Judum, on the left bank of the Mahánadí, 20° 31' 28" N. lat., and 85° 0' 14" E. long.; Kamaládhar, on the left bank of the Mahánadí, 20° 30' 32" N. lat., and 84° 56' 30" E. long.; Modiá Khand-patná, 20° 20' 25" N. lat., and 84° 58' 24" E. long. The total number of villages is returned in the Census Report at 432, classified as follows:—395 with less than two hundred inhabitants, 31 with from two to five hundred, 5 with from five hundred to a thousand, and 1 with from one to two thousand.

Daspallá State yields an estimated annual revenue of £1349 to its Rájá, the tribute payable to the British Government being £66. The present ruler, Rájá Cháitan Deo Bhanj, is a youth 22 years of age, claiming to belong to the Kshattriya caste. The family name of the Chiefs is Bhanj (literally, broken; also, forest), and their emblem of signature a peacock, from a legend that the founder of the family sprang from a peacock's egg (*vide* the account of Mor-bhanj State, *post*, p. 303). Daspallá is said to have been founded about five hundred years ago by a son of the Rájá of Bod, the present Chief being the sixteenth in descent. The State is divided into two parts,—Daspallá Proper, to the south of the Mahánadí, which composed the original Principality; and Judum, a small tract to the north of the Mahánadí, which was formerly a part of Angul, but subsequently annexed to Daspallá by conquest. The Rájá's military force is returned as consisting of 521 men, and his police force at 269 men. A school is maintained by the Rájá, and 5 other village schools are returned in the Census Report as being in existence in the State.

DHENKANAL STATE lies between 21° 11' 30" and 20° 31' 0" north latitude, and between 85° 3' 0" and 86° 5' 0" east longitude. It is bounded on the north by Pal Lahárá and Keunjhar; on the east by Cuttack District and Athgarh; on the south by Tigariá and Hindol; and on the west by Tálcher and Pál Lahárá, the Brahmaní river forming the boundary for a considerable distance. The State comprises a total area of 1463 square miles, and contains 763 villages and 34,903 houses. The Census Report returns the population at 178,072 souls, classified as follows:—Hindus—males, men 42,769, and boys 27,088; total, 69,857: females, women 45,366, and girls 26,198; total, 71,564. Grand total of Hindus, 141,421, or 79·4 per cent. of the population of the State; proportion of males in total Hindus, 49·4 per cent. Muhammadans—males, men 138, and boys ·68; total, 206: females, women 147, and girls 63; total, 210. Grand total of Muhammadans 416, or ·2 per cent of the population; proportion of males in total Musalmáns, 49·9 per cent. Christians— *nil.* Other denominations (aboriginal tribes, etc.)—males, men 10,836, and boys 7142; total, 17,978: females, women 11,613, and girls 6644; total, 18,257. Grand total of 'others,' 36,235, or 20·4 per cent. of the population; proportion of males in total 'others,' 49·6 per cent. Population of all denominations—males, men 53,743, and boys, 34,298; total, 88,041: females, women 57,126, and girls 32,905; total, 90,031. Total population of the State, 178,072; proportion of males in total population, 49·4 per cent. Averages— Density of the population, 122 per square mile; villages per square mile, ·52; persons per village, 233; houses per square mile, 24; persons per house, 5·1. The population is ethnically divided as follows:—Aboriginal tribes, 31,195, or 17·7 per cent. of the population, of whom the Savars are by far the most numerous (15,934); semi-Hinduized aboriginals, 32,827, or 18·3 per cent. of the population, the Páns forming here, as elsewhere, the great majority (24,099); Hindu castes and people of Hindu origin, 113,634, or 63·8 per cent. of the population, the most numerous castes being Chásás (38,400), Gaurs (11,626), Bráhmans (8587), Keuts (7466), Telís (6714), and Khandáits (6304); Muhammadans, 416, or ·2 per cent. of the population. Details of the different tribes, castes, etc. will be found in the table on pp. 210–217.

Dhenkánal is a very valuable property, and is certainly the best managed of the Orissa Tributary States, being under the personal supervision of an enlightened ruler, on whom the British Government conferred the title of Mahárájá in 1869, in recognition of his moderation and justice towards his people, and of his liberality in the Orissa famine of 1866. The Bráhmaní river runs through the State from west to east, and forms a richly cultivated valley, besides affording facilities as a trade route. There is, however, a great deal of waste land which might be brought under tillage. Iron abounds, but is only worked on a small scale. A petty trade in cochineal is also carried on. The largest and most important village, which is also the residence of the Rájá, is Dhenkánal, in the south of the State, situated in 20° 39′ 45″ N. lat., and 85° 38′ 16″ E. long. The other large villages are—Kanthio, on the left bank of the Bráhmaní, 26° 46′ 24″ N. lat., and 85° 32′ 30″ E. long.; Komár, on the left bank of the Bráhmaní, 20° 50′ 0″ N. lat., and 85° 21′ 48″ E. long.; and Sandá, situated between the last two named villages, but at a short distance from the river side, 20° 50′ 6″ N. lat., and 85° 27′ 9″ E. long. Weekly markets are also held at Hodipur and Sadáipur, two small villages on the banks of the Bráhmaní, at which the usual country produce is sold. The total number of villages in the State is returned in the Census Report at 763, classified as follows :—468 with less than two hundred inhabitants, 207 with from two to five hundred, 70 with from five hundred to a thousand, 16 with from one to two thousand, and 2 with from three to four thousand.

The State yields an estimated annual revenue of £7010 a year to its ruler, the tribute payable to the British Government being £509. The present Chief, Mahárájá Bhagirathí Mahendra Bahádur,[1] is a Kshattriya, and about 52 years of age. The name Dhenkánal is said to owe its origin to the fact of the founder of the family having killed the original owner, Dhenká, in a stream (*nálá*), about five hundred years ago; since which time twenty-three Chiefs have ruled, and constantly enlarged their territory by annexations from neighbouring States. In 1812 the British Government had to settle a dispute, which would otherwise have ended in an internecine war. During the first half of the century, family feuds and follies reduced the Principality to a miserable state; from which, however, the present Chief retrieved it, and it is now certainly the most prosperous of all the Tributary States. The Mahárájá's militia consists of a force of 286 men, besides a rural police of 742 men. Eight schools are maintained by the Mahárájá, which in 1872 were attended by 235 pupils; 17 *páthsálás* or village schools are also returned.

It may be as well here to reproduce the following description of the State and its mode of Government, as it presented itself to my view on an official visit which I paid to Dhenkánal in 1870. The sketch was originally printed in my *Orissa*, vol. ii. pp. 104-111. The

---

[1] He died in February 1877, while these sheets were in the press.

description well illustrates the modes of life and forms of human existence met with in these primitive tracts. As before stated, however, Dhenkánal is by far the most advanced of any of the Tributary States :—

'Dhenkánal village, the capital of the Mahárájá, clusters on the slope of a hill to the number of 650 houses, surmounted by a large and strongly built mansion, half fort half villa, the residence of the Chief. I found tents pitched for me under a noble grove of tamarind trees inside the outer wall of the fort. A temple, with its flag flying, rose on my right ; and an artificial lake, ornamented with a masonry islet, stretched in front. From the opposite shore of this little piece of water, a forest-laden peak rose precipitously, and the great hills stood all around the peaceful nook. The Mahárájá soon arrived in state, with sumptuously caparisoned elephants and gilded umbrella. He is a middle-aged man of courteous and intelligent demeanour, speaks Hindustání fluently, and knows a little Sanskrit. He suited his conversation to the supposed taste of the British ·Officer, and talked at great length of the 297 tigers which he had shot during his long and prosperous reign. He wore a fine silk tunic interwoven with gold spots, and had a gold-embroidered hat, shaped like a crown, on his head. His little adopted son accompanied him, and burrowed among my baggage like a ferret. He spoke with pride of his system of dealing directly with the husbandmen, and gave me a detailed account of his villages and his twenty-eight Bráhman settlements on rent-free or cheap lands. No middle-man is allowed to stand between him and the peasant, except in a few instances where grants of land have been assigned to his officers of state.

'I afterwards paid a visit to his fort, one part of which has the look of a very strongly built Italian villa, and contains a suite of rooms fitted up in the European style. It towers above the surrounding jungle, a little way up the slope of a precipitous, densely wooded hill. Irregular clusters and lines of mud huts still bear witness to the primitive dwellings in which the Rájás formerly resided. I found the courtyards, which lead one into another, filled with carts, timber, and building materials for the completion of a temple of fine white masonry to Lord Raghunáth on the right of the principal gateway. Farther in, a family shrine rises to Vishnu ; and beyond is a pretty little court planted with lemon trees, oranges, and pomegranates, giving a green, cool look to the whole place. In the

European suite of rooms, which are laid out in halls something like those of a Neapolitan nobleman, I was called on to admire a curious medley of the costliest objects of art mingled with the pettiest gimcracks. The drawing-room tables of white marble and polished fossiliferous slabs were loaded with musical boxes, three or four of which the Mahárájá set agoing at once, microscopes with beetles fixed in them, chiming timepieces, wax dolls, massive gold Albert chains, and little stucco sheep with black faces and yellow wool. Nor were books of photographs and costly engravings wanting, side by side with cheap German prints of nymphs combing their hair on the surface of a lake, and pirouetting *danseuses*. But the object of art on which he chiefly prided himself was a microscopic opera-glass, which, when you looked into it, discovered a picture of the Queen with the Prince of Wales climbing on her shoulders, and an infant slumbering in her arms.

'After examining his really interesting armoury, which includes every weapon, from the old brass-bound firelock to the latest breech-loading rifle, the Mahárájá conducted me to the roof of the house, puffing asthmatically up the steep narrow stairs. We sat and looked forth on a landscape of lofty isolated peaks and high receding ranges. The dense forest gave its dark tinge to the whole, interspersed, however, with bright azure patches of tillage, and valleys of yellow crops, which looked like streaks of gold on a carpet of sombre green velvet. The early morning tint was over all, and spiral columns of grey smoke curled upwards from a hundred hearths in the jungle. The Mahárájá pointed out the different ranges through which the rivers of Orissa rushed down from the highlands. From amid a lofty cluster of peaks, dimly visible in the cloud horizon on the south, issued the Mahánadí, emphatically The Great River. The sacred Bráhmaní wound round a nearer range of hills, swelled by a hundred highland streams, each with its river deity and legend. Throughout the vast world of forest and mountain which stretches between these two great rivers, every hamlet has its own village god, and every little division of the country its colony of priests dwelling rent-free, or at an easy rate, upon ancient grants of land. The Mahárájá told me that although he personally preferred the mild and gentlemanly forms of worship represented by Vishnu or Jagannáth, yet that he supported with an equal hand the priests of the Goddess of Destruction, and encouraged his people to worship the Great Creator under whatever form their imaginations might figure Him. He said that the wild jungle people for the most part selected the terrible aspects of the Divinity, but that human sacrifice had long ceased, and indeed the question never arose now-a-days within his territory. He himself had visited indifferently the shrines of all the great Indian deities—at Purí, at Benáres, at Allahábád, at Gayá, and at Brindában. The idea of resuming or interfering with religious grants struck the Mahárájá as peculiarly impious. It seemed to him quite natural that the land, which is the free gift of the gods, should pay something towards the worship of the gods, and a matter of profound indifference what special form of the Deity the people and the priests might prefer to recognise.

'So far as I could gather, the Mahárájá gives a fine interpretation to his position as a semi-independent Prince. On my turning our talk to the administration of justice, he had out his law books, particularly the latest commentary on the Indian Penal Code in Uriyá and Bengalí; and I found that he really understood the legal points which the annotator discussed. He does justice in public session to his people, and keeps his prisoners hard at work upon the roads. In the afternoon we went together to the jail. It consisted of a courtyard, with low thatched sheds running round three sides, and the guard-house on the fourth. The shed roofs came so low that a child might have jumped on to them, and thus got over the wall. When the guard turned out, moreover, we found it to consist of two very old men; and the Mahárájá was rather displeased to find that one of them had his matchlock under repair at the blacksmith's, while the other had left his weapon in his own village ten miles off, to protect his family during his period of service at court. Inside were sixty-nine prisoners, and I asked how it came that they did not, under the circumstances, all jump over the wall? The question seemed to strike the Mahárájá as a particularly foolish one. "Where could they go to?" he said. "On the rare occasion that a prisoner breaks jail, it is only to pay a visit to his family; and the villagers, as in duty bound, return him within a few days."

'The truth is, that the family instinct is still so strong in the Tributary States, that imprisonment, or even death itself, seems infinitely preferable to running away from kindred and home. There were no female prisoners, and the Mahárájá stated that crime among women has not yet penetrated into his country. I found the gang divided into two sections, each of which had a shed to itself on the opposite sides of the court; the shed on the third side being set apart for cooking. The one shed was monopolized by ten men, whose light complexion declared them to belong to the trading class, and who lolled at great ease and in good clothes in their prison-house. In the other shed were crowded the remaining fifty-nine, packed as close as sardines, and with no other clothing except a narrow strip round their waist. On expressing my surprise at this unequal treatment, and asking whether the ten gentlemen who took their ease were confined for lighter crimes, the Mahárájá explained : " On the contrary, these ten men are the plagues of the State. They consist of fraudulent shopkeepers, who receive stolen goods, and notorious bad characters who organize robberies. The other fifty-nine are poor Páns and other jungle people, imprisoned for petty theft, or as the tools of the ten prisoners on the opposite side. *But then the ten are respectable men, and of good caste, while the fifty-nine are mere woodmen ; and it is only proper to maintain God's distinction of caste.*" All the prisoners were in irons except one, a lame man, whose fetters had been struck off on the report of the native doctor. They looked very fat and comfortable, as indeed they well might, considering that the sixty-nine prisoners have an allowance of a hundred pounds of rice per diem, with goat's flesh once a fortnight, fish twice a month, besides a little daily allowance of split peas and spices to season their food. It did not seem to have cccurred to any of them to feel in the least ashamed on account of being in jail. One of them had been imprisoned twice before ; and, on my asking him what his trade was, he explained that "the younger brothers of his family were husbandmen, but that, for his part, he *nourished his stomach by thieving*."

'Next day the Mahárájá took me over his school and his charitable dispensary, both framed on the model of our own Bengal institutions of the same sort, especially in the number of registers kept, and the multitudinous returns regarding the pupils and patients. About noon arrived a band of jungle people, whose national dance the Mahárájá wished to show me. The men wore a single cotton cloth. The women had not even this, but simply a string round their waists, with a bunch of leaves before and behind. Two or three of the men beat with their fingers on little drums, while the women formed a semicircle and moved backwards and forwards in a rather tedious dance. They dwell apart from the agricultural population, and speak a language of their own, of which the Mahárájá afterwards gave me a vocabulary. The life they love best is to wander about the woods collecting the wild products, which they barter for food. Occasionally they hire themselves out in gangs to clear the forest for the more settled husbandmen; but even while thus engaged they hold no intercourse with the agriculturists, and receive the stipulated amount of rice through the hands of one or two representatives.

'The Mahárájá told me that, as he is anxious to extend cultivation, he asks no rent from any jungle tribe that will settle down. They may cut down as much forest as they choose, and cultivate the clearing as long as they please. But all his efforts have failed to induce the nomadic tribes to submit to the toil of permanent husbandry. They willingly burn a patch of jungle, but avoid the chance of any question of rent arising, by deserting their clearing every third year. This practice simply means, that where land is to be had for the clearing, it pays better to take a rapid succession of exhausting crops off the virgin soil, than to adopt the laborious processes of regular cultivation. The forest tribes show great talent in making a livelihood with the minimum of labour, and this is one of the ways in which they solve the problem. Several of the hill Chiefs try to levy a rent the second year on such clearings; but such efforts only result in the nomadic husbandmen deserting their settlements a year sooner, and having to burn new jungle every third year instead of every fourth. The Chiefs find themselves no richer, and the attempt to levy rent only makes their jungle subjects the poorer and more restless. In Dhenkánal, where the Mahárájá looks on the whole subject of jungle clearings with good-natured indifference, and indeed is anxious to encourage them as opening new ground for permanent tillage, the forest tribes seem to lead a contented, well-fed existence. They raise just as much grain or cotton as they require from the virgin soil without the labour of ploughing, and spend their days in hunting, feasting, dancing, sleeping, and sunning themselves at the door of their leaf huts. If they want a little money, or any article that they must buy with money, is there not the *sál* forest around them waiting to be cut, and sharp lowland traders in the *bázár* a day's journey off? These latter will only cheat them to the orthodox amount of one-half, both in what they buy and in what they sell, and in the result give them a full one-fourth of the value of their timber.'

HINDOL STATE lies between 20° 49′ 30″ and 20° 29′ 30″ north

148, and girls 55; total, 203. Grand total of Muhammadans, 487, or ·3 per cent. of the population; proportion of males in total Muhammadans, 58·3 per cent. Christians—1. Other denominations (aboriginal tribes, etc.)—males, men 20,294, and boys 15,109; total, 35,403: females, women 20,407, and girls 12,366; total, 32,773. Grand total of 'others,' 68,176, or 37·5 per cent. of the population; proportion of males in total 'others,' 51·9 per cent. Population of all denominations—males, men 53,189, and boys 37,690; total, 90,879: females, women 57,875, and girls 33,117; total, 90,992. Total population of the State, 181,871; proportion of males in total population, 50·0 per cent. Averages—Density of the population, 59 per square mile; villages per square mile, ·47; persons per village, 124; houses per square mile, 11; persons per house, 5·2. The population is ethnically divided as follows :—Aboriginal tribes, 44,438, or 24·3 per cent. of the population, principally composed of Kols (10,990), Gonds (10,407), Sáonts (7172), and Savars (5125); semi-Hinduized aboriginals, 49,294, or 27·2 per cent. of the population, mainly composed of Páns (19,827), Bhuiyás (18,481), and Báthudis (7898); Hindu castes and people of Hindu origin, 87,651, or 48·2 per cent. of the population, the most numerous castes being Khandáits (22,225), Bráhmans (8583), and Gaurs, (6743); Muhammadans, 487, or ·3 per cent. of the population. Details of the different tribes, castes, etc. will be found in the table on pp. 210–217.

Keunjhar is divided into two wild tracts,—Lower Keunjhar, including the valleys; and Upper Keunjhar, embracing the mountainous highlands. The latter consists of great clusters of rugged crags, which afford almost inaccessible retreats to their inhabitants; and which, although from the plains they appear to be sharply ridged or peaked, have extensive table-lands on their summits, equally fit for pasture and for tillage.

The Baitaraní river takes its rise among the ranges of the north-west division of this State. The principal mountain peaks are— Thákwání, 3003 feet; Gandhá-Madán, 3479 feet; Tomák, 2577 feet; Bolat, 1818 feet. The Sambalpur and Midnapur road crosses the State. The principal village and capital of the State is Keunjhar, situated on the Midnapur road, in 21° 37′ 25″ N. lat., and 85° 37′ 31″ E. long. The total number of villages returned in the Census Report is 1469, classified as follows:—1231 with less than two hundred inhabitants, 198 with from two to five hundred, 36 with from five hundred to a thousand, 3 with from one to two thousand, and 1 with from two to three thousand.

Keunjhar yields an estimated annual revenue of £6339 to its Chief, the tribute payable to the British Government being £197. The present Ruler, Mahárájá Dhanurjái Náráyan Bhanj Deo, is 27 years of age, and is by caste a Rájput of the Solar race. His emblem of signature is a pea-fowl. The Chief's militia consists of a force of 1758 men and 318 village police. A Government elephant (*khedá*) establishment is maintained at Keunjhar, under the superintendence of an English officer, and a number of valuable elephants are captured annually. The Mahárájá is a great promoter of education, and maintains twenty schools in the State, which are attended by about 700 scholars; 19 other unaided village schools (*páthsálás*) are returned in the Census Report. Keunjhar originally formed part of Morbhanj; but about two hundred years ago, the tribes of this part, finding it a great hardship to travel through the perilous forests of Morbhanj to obtain justice from their prince, separated themselves, and set up the brother of the Morbhanj Rájá as their independent Chief. Since then, twenty-seven Rájás have ruled. The last Prince rendered good service during the Kol rebellion in 1857, and was rewarded by Government with the title of Mahárájá. He died in 1861 without legitimate issue. On our nominating his natural son, the present Mahárájá, to succeed him, a dispute arose as to the succession, which ultimately culminated in an insurrection of the Bhuiyá and Juáng tribes in favour of an alleged adopted son, which called for the intervention of regular troops before it was suppressed.

The following account of the disputed claim to the succession, and of the insurrection which followed the installation of the present Chief, is quoted as affording a good illustration of the peculiar relations which exist between the Bhuiyá and other aboriginal tribes of Keunjhar, and the Rájás of the country. The extract is taken from the official *Summary of Affairs in the Foreign Department of the Government of India*, 1864 to 1869, pp. 416-430:—

'On the 22d March 1861, the Rájá of Keunjhar died at Tribení, near Calcutta, leaving a widow who was childless, and two illegitimate sons by a Phulbhái concubine, who were named Dhanurjái and Chandra Sikhar. On the 3d April the minister of Keunjhar reported that Dhanurjái had been placed on the throne with the consent of the Rání. On the 9th April, the Rájá of Morbhanj represented that a grandson of his, named Brindában, had been adopted by the late Rájá of Keunjhar, and that he was going to Keunjhar to instal the boy. The Superintendent of the Tributary States directed that the Morbhanj Rájá should take no action in the matter; but the Rájá sent his grandson to Keunjhar, where the latter was secretly installed by the Rání and some of the principal Chiefs of the State. The story of the adoption of Brindában subsequently proved to be altogether untrue. The Rání, however, abandoned the cause of Dhanurjái, if she had ever countenanced it, and supported the claim of the so-called adopted son Brindában. She asserted that Dhanurjái was not the son of a Phulbhái ór respectable concubine, but only the son of a slave-girl.

'The respective claims of Dhanurjái the illegitimate and Brindában the adopted were closely investigated by the Superintendent, in accordance with the established rule under which all claims to succession in these States are decided, laid down by Regulation xi. of 1816. The Superintendent decided in favour of Dhanurjái. The party in favour of Brindában then appealed to the High Court at Calcutta; but the decision of the Superintendent was upheld by the Court, and the case dismissed. Finally, they appealed to the Privy Council in England, but with the same result.

'Meantime the decision in favour of Dhanurjái was confirmed by the Bengal Government, and the Rání was informed that Dhanurjái was recognised as Rájá of Keunjhar. An establishment out of the State funds was sanctioned for Dhanurjái, who was still a minor; and the management of the State was left to a *tahsíldár* and the prime minister. Dhanurjái pursued his studies during his minority at Cuttack, whilst the Rání continued to reside at the family house at Keunjhar.

'Thus matters stood till January 1867, when Mr. Ravenshaw, the Superintendent of the States, reported to the Bengal Government that Dhanurjái would attain his majority in the following September, when the State might be made over to his charge; and the Lieutenant-Governor, Sir Cecil Beadon, ruled that the young Rájá should not be debarred his rights because the appeal before the Privy Council was still pending. In September, the Commissioner reported that he had made over charge of the State to Dhanurjái at Cuttack, and proposed proceeding with him to Keunjhar, in order to instal him formally upon the throne. Meantime, the Rání petitioned that the installation might be postponed until the appeal before the Privy Council should be finally settled, or that, if he should be put into possession, security might be taken from him. In October, the Honourable Mr. Grey, who had succeeded Sir Cecil Beadon as Lieutenant-Governor, called on the Superintendent to report if it was possible to comply with the wishes of the Ráni. Meantime, the Superintendent reported that the refractory Keunjhar dependants, who had hitherto opposed the succession of Dhanurjái, had tendered their unqualified submission to the young Rájá at Cuttack, and promised to be loyal and obedient to him. He therefore considered that this reconciliation would render it unnecessary for him to accompany the young Rájá to Keunjhar; and that it would suffice to send his Assistant with him as far as Anandpur, where Dhanurjái wished to remain before going to the family house at Keunjhar, in order to ascertain if the Ráni would accept him as the successor to the Ráj. The Superintendent expected that the Ráni would acquiesce; and when the reconciliation had been effected, he proposed joining the Rájá at Anandpur, and marching with him to Keunjhar, and there summoning the hill tribes to give in their adherence to Dhanurjái. It was also expected that the reconciliation of the Ráni with Dhanurjái would probably lead to the withdrawal of the appeal to the Privy Council. Subsequently seven or eight hundred heads of villages and office holders arrived of their own accord at Cuttack, and escorted the Rájá to Anandpur, accompanied by the Superintendent's Assistant. The Superintendent retained one refractory *sardár* at Cuttack, and considered that there was only one other individual who was openly hostile to the installation of Dhanurjái, a *sardár* of the hill tribes named Ratná Náik, who was said to have declared in favour of Brindában. The Bengal Government telegraphed in reply that the installation of Dhanurjái might proceed.

'On the 1st November, it was evident that the Ráni was carrying on secret communications with the hill tribes. These people occupy a tract to the westward of Keunjhar, and mainly consist of two tribes, the Juángs and the Bhuiyás. The latter are the more numerous, and moreover claimed a right to instal each Keunjhar Rájá separately after their own fashion. The principal leader of the Bhuiyás was Ratná Náik, already mentioned; and it appeared that, ever since the death of the late Rájá in 1861, this man had supported the Ráni in her efforts to set up Brindában. The Ráni now threatened to leave Keunjhar if the young Rájá Dhanurjái came there; and it was expected that the Bhuiyás and Juángs would raise a disturbance if the Rání quitted the family house. The Superintendent, therefore, directed his Assistant to proceed to Keunjhar and deliver a letter to the Rání, and also to explain to the hill Chiefs that the Rájá was desirous that the Rání should reside in the family house, but that, if she was determined to leave, she would be properly escorted wherever she pleased to go. On arriving at Keunjhar, the Assistant found that the agents of the Rání were fomenting disaffection. A large body of people, who were proceeding to Anandpur to tender fealty to the Rájá, were led away by one of the Rání's servants into Morbhanj. Meantime a large deputation of hill-men proceeded to Calcutta, and in December the Lieutenant-Governor granted an interview to a select number who were chosen by themselves. The men said that they only wished to know what were the real orders of Government. In reply, they were told that Government intended to support Dhanurjái, unless the Privy Council decreed in favour of Brindában. The deputation then declared that they would acknowledge Dhanurjái, and that they would make no disturbance; and they asked that the Rání might receive her allowance through the Superintendent, and that the prime minister of the State might not be allowed to do them any ill turn. They were promised the first point, and assured the protection of Government if they only kept peaceable. Strict orders were then sent to the Superintendent to warn the Rájá and his minister to avoid giving any cause of complaint. The Superintendent, when he proceeded to Anandpur, found no traces of disaffection there. The Rájá was popular, and had been accepted by the village head-men; revenue collections were going on as usual, and all seemed fair. He heard, however, that there were large gatherings of hill-men in the neighbouring jungles, and that deputations were passing between them and the Rání.

'On the 5th December, the Superintendent arrived at Keunjhar with the Rájá, and reported that his journey had not been satisfactory. The people on the road were in alarm; no provisions had been supplied to his camp; and there were constant rumours of opposition. The head-men of the villages had gone off, either to the assemblages on the hills · or with the deputation to Calcutta. On reaching Keunjhar he found the town nearly deserted, and the Rání preparing for flight; and on remonstrating with the Rání, she had removed into another set of rooms, which is equivalent in native ideas to beginning a journey. He obtained an interview with a party from the two hill tribes, the Bhuiyás and Juángs, at which the Juángs promised to accept Dhanurjái; but the general result of the meeting was that no definite answer could be given, until both tribes had held a conference together. Meantime the Superintendent found that the Rání was perfectly implacable and impracticable. All the connections of the late Rájá accepted Dhanurjái, but the Rání utterly refused to recognise him; and her influence was so considerable, that Dhanurjái, who had previously begged that she would remain at the family house, was now willing that she should leave Keunjhar.

'In December, however, Mr. Ravenshaw formally installed Dhanurjái, amidst the abuse of the Rání and her women. The ceremony was attended by many of the Juángs, but not by the Bhuiyás, and was quite distinct from that of recognition by the hill tribes. The Superintendent had twenty constables with him, and he sent for twenty more to remain at Keunjhar with the Rájá after he left. He reported, however, that the people of Keunjhar had no grievance, save the objection, fomented by the Rání, to the succession of the son of a concubine; and yet such a succession was in accordance with the custom of the Tributary States, and had occurred several times before.

'In the same month, namely, December 1867, the Superintendent proceeded on a journey through the hills, and for some days found that the people were warmly espousing the cause of the Rání and expressing their opposition to Dhanurjái. After a short while, he found that there was a manifest change in public opinion. Colonel Dalton, Commissioner of the neighbouring Province of Chutiá Nágpur, joined Mr. Ravenshaw; and the chiefs who accompanied Colonel Dalton at once recognised Dhanurjái. An important section of the community, known as the Sáonts, also declared for Dhanurjái; the Juángs followed, and ultimately the bulk of the Keunjhar tribes gave in their adhesion. The Bhuiyás, however, held out stoutly, being strongly under the influence of Ratná Náik, who was said to have been bound by an oath not to desert the cause of the Rání. This opposition was of some importance, in consequence of the prescriptive right claimed by the Bhuiyás, of confirming the installation of a new Rájá by certain peculiar ceremonies. It was, however, expected that if the Rání could be quietly removed from Keunjhar to Purí, the Bhuiyás would accept Dhanurjái.

'On the 16th January 1868, the Ráni left Keunjhar, but halted seven miles off at the village of Basantpur, where she remained some days. Meantime the Bhuiyás assembled in the neighbourhood, and the Superintendent found that the jungle was full of Bhuiyás, armed with bows, arrows, and axes. Mr. Ravenshàw and his constables caught a hundred of them, and brought them into the presence of the Ráni, and asked her if she wished to bring all her so-called children into a similar predicament. At length the Ráni formally released the Bhuiyás from their oath, and consented to invest Dhanurjái with the usual insignia of her acquiescence in his succession, and to withdraw from all further interference. The captured Bhuiyás were released, and despatched with conciliatory messages to their fellow-tribesmen of the hills; and eventually the whole tribe, excepting Ratná Náik, renounced further opposition. Ratná Náik succeeded in making his escape, but he had created so much terror that the Bhuiyás themselves aided in pursuing him. He, however, succeeded in making his escape, but his influence seemed to have passed away. The Ráni, at the earnest entreaties of the Bhuiyás, who addressed her as their mother, returned from Basantpur to Keunjhar, and took up her abode in the palace. On the 13th February 1868 she was present at the installation of Rájá Dhanurjái by the Bhuiyás, and on the next day she conferred on the Rájá a *soropá*, or token of her acknowledgment of his succession.' [A description of the ceremonies followed at the Bhuiyá installation of this and of every new Rájá is given in the account of that tribe, quoted *ante*, pp. 250–251.]

'On the 17th February 1868, the final ceremony of "first-offering," in token of submission, was performed by the Bhuiyás and Juángs. The Rájá was seated on a low throne of cushions in the outer courtyard, and received the people, who flocked in with music playing and garlands round their necks. Each Bhuiyá head-man in succession kissed the foot of the Rájá, and then pressed it to his forehead and ears. Offerings of pumpkins, plantains, and grain were then presented, and salutations were exchanged. The Juángs followed the Bhuiyás, and separately made offerings and addresses to the Rájá. Each head-man was then presented with a *tasar* silk turban and a suit of clothes; goats and fowls were provided, and the people celebrated the occasion with a general feast.

'The succession seemed to be now finally settled. The Ráni decided upon remaining three months at Keunjhar, in order to support Rájá Dhanurjái by her presence, and then to proceed to Purí. A *panchdyat* or court of awards, consisting of her two brothers, the native Assistant to the Superintendent, the Rájá, and his prime minister, fixed her allowance at Rs. 600 per mensem (£720 per annum). She asked for Rs. 1500, which was nearly one-third of the entire revenue of the State. Ultimately she was allowed Rs. 550 in cash, and villages yielding Rs. 50 per mensem. By the end of February all the police force, excepting twenty constables, was removed, and for two months the public tranquillity remained undisturbed.

'About the end of April the Bhuiyás suddenly broke into insurrection under Ratná Náik and Nandá Náik. They plundered the Keunjhar *bázár*, and carried off the Rájá's minister with a hundred of his partizans. They also disarmed the twenty constables and dismounted the Rájá's guns. According to their statement, the minister had promised to place Brindában upon the throne within three months, if they would recognise Dhanurjái during the interval. It turned out, however, that they had a more substantial grievance; for the minister had found the partizans of Brindában in power, and had turned them out to make room for his own relations. By this rising the whole country was disorganized, and all the wild clans joined in the insurrection. Dr. Hayes, the Deputy-Commissioner of Singbhúm, with a police force and body of Kols, immediately started for Keunjhar, which he reached on the 7th May, and found that the Rájá was regularly besieged by the wild tribes, who were armed with bows and arrows, axes, and swords. He at once released the Rájá from his position, by disarming the besiegers and turning them out of the fort. He then sent a written demand to the Bhuiyás for the surrender of their captives, but without effect; and on making a detour into the hill country, the inhabitants fled at his approach. Subsequently further steps were taken to put down the rising, rescue the captives, and apprehend the two ringleaders, Ratná Náik and Nandá Náik.

'Orders were issued by the Bengal Government for the immediate advance of troops and police to Keunjhar. Colonel Dalton, the Commissioner of Chutiá Nágpur, who was known to possess great personal influence over the chiefs of his Province, was ordered to proceed to Keunjhar and take charge of affairs on the spot; while Mr. Ravenshaw was directed to devote himself to the task of throwing in supplies from the Cuttack side, and opening up communications from Anandpur. Colonel Dalton was unable to reach Keunjhar till the end of June. Active hostilities, however, were commenced in the last week of May. A party of police advancing from Anandpur were attacked on the 27th May, and had to fight their way back with the loss of their baggage. Another party of police, however, managed to force a passage *viâ* Dhenkánal; and large reinforcements from the Chutiá Nágpur side reached Dr. Hayes throughout both May and June. Dr. Hayes succeeded in securing the people of the plains from the raids of the hill-men, who looted the villages which would not join them; but though he repulsed every attack upon his posts, he was not strong enough to retaliate, and could only shut up insurrection in the hills until succour arrived.

'At the end of June, Colonel Dalton reached Keunjhar with a strong force, and at once proceeded to carry the war into the enemy's fastnesses. These lay in a wild hilly tract, covered with deadly jungle, which would have been pathless but for the water-courses, which were now filled by the heavy rains of June. It was here that the unfortunate minister and other adherents had been carried by the insurgents. Small flying columns were sent out from Keunjhar fort, and they succeeded in releasing many of the captives and burning the villages in which they had been confined. Several disaffected chiefs now submitted to Colonel Dalton; and it appeared from them that the captured minister had been cruelly murdered by the hill-men soon after his capture. On the 10th July, the Bhuiyás made overtures of submission. Meantime Mr. Ravenshaw had completed his work on the Cuttack side, and reached Keunjhar just eight days after Colonel Dalton, and was associated with him in the management of affairs. Accordingly Colonel Dalton, in conjunction with Mr. Ravenshaw, insisted upon an unreserved surrender of the ringleaders and delivery of the captives, and would not agree to a suspension of hostilities for a single day.

'About this time the neighbouring Rájás took active measures to support the British troops; and their acclimatized forces were of great assistance in beating up the inner fastnesses, and thus saving the health of our soldiers and police. The Rájá of Udáipur joined with a force of ten elephants, fifteen troopers (*sawárs*), and two hundred well-armed sepoys. The Rájás of Bonái, Pál Lahárá, Dhenkánal, and Morbhanj also furnished contingents. On the 1st August twenty-five Bhuiyá chiefs submitted to the Bonái Rájá, and twenty-five Juáng chiefs surrendered in like manner to the Rájá of

Udáipur. On the 15th August Ratná Náik was captured, with his principal coadjutor, Nandá Pradhán.'

This ended the rebellion. The trials which followed dealt leniently with men who, after all, had only acted according to their immemorial custom. Out of the mass of prisoners taken red-handed in murderous revolt, only six, who were the ringleaders or directly concerned in the cold-blooded murder of the Rájá's minister, received sentence of death. About a hundred others suffered various terms of imprisonment.

KHANDPARA STATE lies between 20° 25' 0" and 20° 11' 15" north latitude, and between 85° 1' 0" and 85° 24' 40" east longitude. It is bounded on the north by the Mahánadí, which separates it from Narsinhpur and Barambá; on the east by Bánkí and the District of Purí; on the south by Purí and Nayágarh; and on the west by Daspallá. The State covers a total area of 244 square miles, comprising 321 villages and 12,109 houses. The Census Report of 1872 returns the population at 60,877 souls, classified as follows :— Hindus—males, men 17,842, and boys 10,460; total, 28,302 : females, women 18,945, and girls 9760; total, 28,705. Grand total of Hindus, 57,007, or 93.6 per cent. of the population of the State ; proportion of males in total Hindus, 49.6 per cent. Muhammadans —males, men 19, and boys 7; total, 26 : females, women 8, and girls 4; total, 12. Grand total of Musalmáns, 38, or ·1 per cent. of the population. Christians—*nil.* Other denominations (aboriginal tribes, etc.)—males, men 1206, and boys 700; total, 1906 : females, women 1215, and girls 711 ; total, 1926. Grand total of 'others,' 3832, or 6.3 per cent. of the population; proportion of males in total 'others,' 49.7 per cent. Population of all denominations—males, men 19,067, and boys 11,167 ; total, 30,234 : females, women 20,168, and girls 10,475 ; total, 30,643. Total population of the State, 60,877 ; proportion of males in total population, 49.7 per cent. Averages—Density of the population, 249 per square mile; villages per square mile, 1.31 ; persons per village, 190 ; houses per square mile, 50; persons per house, 5.0. The Census Report ethnically classifies the population as follows :— Aboriginal tribes, 3561, or 5.9 per cent. of the population, being mainly composed of Kandhs (1596) and Savars (1126); semi-Hinduized aborigines, 6438, or 10.6 per cent. of the population, consisting principally of Páns (3577), Mihtárs (1547), and Kandárás (1064) ; Hindu castes and people of Hindu origin, 50,840, or 83.5

per cent. of the population; Muhammadans, 38. Details of the different tribes, castes, etc. will be found in the table on pp. 210–217.

Khandpárá is a very valuable territory, and one of the most highly cultivated of the Tributary States. Fine *sál* timber abounds in the hilly parts of the State, and magnificent mango and banyan trees stud the plains. No regular trading fairs are held, but merchants from Cuttack bring salt, spices, etc., to exchange for cotton, wheat, clarified butter, and oil seeds from Sambalpur. The principal seat of trade in the State is Kantilo, situated on the right or south bank of the Mahánadí, in 20° 21′ 46″ N. lat., and 85° 14′ 20″ E. long. Kantilo is the largest town in the whole Tributary States, and indeed is the only one returned in the Census Report as containing upwards of five thousand inhabitants; it contains 1113 houses, and a populalation of 5534 souls, classified as follows:—Hindus—males 2605, and females 2781; total, 5386. Muhammadans—males 6, and females 2; total, 8. Other denominations—males 64, and females 76; total, 140. Population of all denominations—males 2675, and females 2859; grand total, 5534. The only other trading town in the State is Padmavatí, situated on the Mahánadí, near the eastern border of the State, in 20° 20′ 27″ N. lat., and 85° 21′ 46″ E. long.; 282 houses. Besides the two seats of trade above mentioned, five other villages contain upwards of a hundred houses, viz. Khandpárá, the capital of the State and residence of the Rájá, situated in 20° 15′ 50″ N. lat., and 85° 12′ 51″ E. long.; 680 houses. Biengoniá, situated in 20° 15′ 8″ N. lat., and 85° 16′ 0″ E. long.; 211 houses. Fathiágarh, situated in 20° 17′ 37″ N. lat., and 85° 22′ 33″ E. long.; 158 houses. Banmálipur, situated in 20° 16′ 14″ N. lat., and 85° 15′ 12″ E. long.; 130 houses. Nemápol, situated in 20° 16′ 10″ N. lat., and 85° 16′ 14″ E. long. The total number of villages in the State is returned in the Census Report as 321, classified as follows:—248 with less than two hundred inhabitants; 57 with from two to five hundred; 9 with from five hundred to a thousand; 5 with from one to two thousand; 1 with from three to four thousand; and 1 with from five to six thousand inhabitants.

Khandpárá yields an estimated annual revenue of £2258 to its Chief, the tribute payable to the British Government being £421. The present ruler, Rájá Natabar Murdráj Bráhmabar Rái, is thirty-nine years old, and a Rájput by caste. He is the eighth chief in descent. The State originally formed a part of Nayágarh, and was separated about two hundred years ago by a brother of the Nayágarh

Chief, who set up for himself. The family emblem of signature is a tiger's head. The Rájá's militia is returned at 198 men, and the village police at 499 men. One school in the State is maintained by the Rájá, and four others are returned in the Census Report.

MORBHANJ STATE, including Bámanghátí, a tract now under British management, is at once the most northerly and the largest of the Tributary States of Orissa. It lies between 22° 33' 45" and 21° 17' 0" north latitude, and between 85° 42' 30" and 87° 13' 55" east longitude. It is bounded on the north by the Districts of Singbhúm, Mánbhúm, and Midnapur; on the east by Balasor District; on the south by Nílgirí and Purí; and on the west by Keunjhar. The total area of Morbhanj, including Bámanghátí, is 4243 square miles. The Census Report of 1872 returns the population of these tracts separately, as follows :—

Bámanghátí, which forms the northern portion of the State, is now, and has been for many years past, under British management, the controlling authority resting with the Deputy-Commissioner of Singbhúm. It contains 647 villages, 18,595 houses, and a total population of 94,526 souls, classified as follows : Hindus—males, men 7017, and boys 4921; total, 11,938 : females, women 7316, and girls 4246; total, 11,562. Grand total of Hindus, 23,500, or 24·9 per cent. of the population ; proportion of males in total Hindus, 50·8 per cent. Muhammadans—males, men 159, and boys 76; total, 235 : females, women 165, and girls 79; total, 244. Grand total of Musalmáns, 479, or ·5 per cent. of the population ; proportion of males in total Muhammadans, 49·0 per cent. Christians— *nil.* Other denominations (aboriginal tribes, etc.)—males, men 19,846, and boys 15,232; total, 35,078 : females, women 21,117, and girls 14,352; total, 35,469. Grand total of 'others,' 70,547, or 74·6 per cent. of the population ; proportion of males in total population, 49·7 per cent. Population of all denominations—males, men 27,022, and boys 20,229; total, 47,251 : females, women 28,598, and girls 18,677; total, 47,275. Grand total, 94,526; proportion of males in total population, 50·0 per cent.

Morbhanj Proper contains 1941 villages, 33,768 houses, and a total population of 164,154, classified as follows :—Hindus—males, men 19,523, and boys 12,879; total, 32,402: females, women 20,052, and girls 12,260; total, 32,312. Grand total of Hindus, 64,714, or 39·4 per cent. of the population ; proportion of males in total Hindus, 50·1 per cent. Muhammadans—males, men 212, and boys

197; total, 409: females, women 224, and girls 115; total, 339. Grand total of Musalmáns, 748; proportion of males in total Muhammadans, 54·7 per cent. Other denominations (aboriginal tribes, etc.)—males, men 30,100, and boys 19,381; total, 49,481: females, women 33,665, and girls 15,546; total, 49,211. Grand total of 'others,' 98,692, or 60·1 per cent. of the population; proportion of males in total 'others,' 50·1 per cent. Population of all denominations—males, men 49,835, and boys 32,457; total, 82,292: females, women 53,941, and girls 27,921; total, 81,862. Grand total, 164,154; proportion of males in total population, 50·1 per cent.

Including Bámanghátí and Morbhanj Proper, the State comprises a total area of 4243 square miles, containing 2588 villages, 52,363 houses, and a total population of 258,680, as follows:—Hindus, males 44,340, and females 43,874; total, 88,214, or 34·1 per cent. of the total population. Muhammadans—males 644, and females 583; total, 1227, or ·5 per cent. of the population. Christians—nil. Other denominations—males 84,559, and females 84,680; total, 169,239, or 65·4 per cent. of the population. Population of all denominations—males 129,543, and females 129,137; total population of the State, 258,680. Averages—Density of the population, 61 per square mile; villages per square mile, ·60; persons per village or township, 99; houses per square mile, 12; persons per house, 5. The population is ethnically divided as follows:— Bámanghátí— Aboriginal tribes, 69,551, or 73·4 per cent. of the population, consisting principally of Santáls (44,445) and Kols (14,021); semi-Hinduized aborigines, 7610, or 8·1 per cent. of the population, the most numerous class being the Páns (5100) and Bhuiyás (1102); Hindu castes and people of Hindu origin, 16,886, or 17·9 per cent. of the population, the most numerous castes being the Gaurs (3766) and Kurmís (3724); Muhammadans, 479, or ·5 per cent. of the population. Morbhanj Proper—Aboriginal tribes, 72,801, or 44·4 per cent. of the population, consisting principally of Santáls (31,586), Bhumijs (18,219), and Kols (7867); semi-Hinduized aborigines, 31,672, or 19·4 per cent. of the population, the most numerous classes being the Bathudís (13,999) and Bhuiyás (8690); Hindu castes and people of Hindu origin, 58,933, or 35·8 per cent. of the population, the most numerous castes being Gaurs (9116), Khandáits (7355), Bráhmans (4635), and Kurmís (4598); Muhammadans, 748, or ·4 per cent. of the population. Details of the different tribes, races, etc. will be found in the table on pp. 210-217.

Morbhanj State extends over an area of 4243 square miles, and presents every variety of soil and scenery. It abounds in rich valleys; but a vast extent still remains under primeval jungle, of which a considerable proportion, however, might be brought under tillage. The Meghásaní hill rises to the height of 3824 feet in the southern part of the State, and well merits its name—literally, the Seat of Clouds. Morbhanj State is divided into three parts—Morbhanj Proper, Upen-bágh, and Bámanghátí. The last is under British management, necessitated by a peasant rebellion brought on by the oppression of the aboriginal Kols and Bhuiyás, at the hands of the land stewards and petty officials of the Rájá. Upen-bágh is also under English surveillance, a body of our police being quartered there at the Rájá's expense. Large herds of elephants roam through the forests and mountains of Morbhanj, and very successful *khedá* operations have been carried on for the last few years. The principal villages in the State are Baripádá, situated on the left bank of the Burábalang river, in 21° 56′ 5″ north latitude, and 86° 45′ 41″ east longitude; and Daspur, on the high road from Midnapur to Sambalpur, in 21° 57′ 40″ north latitude, and 86° 7′ 11″ east longitude. The total number of villages in the State is returned in the Census Report at 2588, classified as follows:—2284 with less than two hundred inhabitants; 273 with from two to five hundred; and 31 with from five hundred to a thousand.

Morbhanj yields an estimated revenue of £20,500 to its Chief, and pays an annual tribute to the British Government of £106. The present ruler, Rájá Krishna Chandra Bhanj, is twenty-eight years old, and a Kshattriya by caste. Native chronicles relate that the Principality was founded more than two thousand years ago by a relative of the Rájá of Jáipur in Rájputáná. The Chief's emblem of signature is a pea-fowl, from a tradition of the family having originally sprung from a pea-fowl's egg, and the killing of this heraldic bird is strictly prohibited throughout the State. The Rájá's militia is returned at 972, and the police force at 483 men. Eight schools in the State are supported by the Rájá, and twenty others are returned in the Census Report.

NARSINHPUR STATE is situated between 20° 37′ 0″ and 20° 24′ 0″ north latitude, and between 85° 0′ 0″ and 85° 16′ 15″ east longitude. It is bounded on the north by a range of jungly mountains, which separate it from Angul and Hindol; on the east by Barambá; on the south and south-west by the Mahánadí river; and on the west by Angul. The State comprises a total area of 199 square miles, and contains 181 villages and 5500 houses. The Census Report of 1872 returns the population at 24,758, classified as follows :—Hindus— males, men 7041, and boys 4583; total, 11,624: females, women 7525, and girls 3344; total, 10,869. Grand total of Hindus, 22,493, or 90·8 per cent. of the population of the State; proportion of males in total Hindus, 51·6 per cent. Muhammadans—males, men 32, and boys 20; total, 52: females, women 42, and girls 17; total, 59. Grand total of Muhammadans, 111, or ·5 per cent. of the population; proportion of males in total Musalmáns, 46·8 per cent. Christians—*nil.* Other denominations (aboriginal tribes, etc.)— males, men 703, and boys 366; total, 1069: females, women 801, and girls 284; total, 1085. Grand total of ' others,' 2154, or 8·7 per cent. of the population; proportion of males in total ' others,' 49·6 per cent. Population of all denominations—males, men 7776, and boys 4969; total, 12,745: females, women 8368, and girls 3645; total, 12,013. Total population of the State, 24,758; propor- tion of males in total population, 51·0 per cent. Averages— Density of the population, 124 per square mile ; villages per square mile, ·90; persons per village, 137; houses per square mile, 28; persons per house, 4·5. The Census Report ethnically classifies the population as follows :—Aboriginal tribes, 1949, or 7·9 per cent. of the population, mainly composed of Kandhs (1039) and Taálas (739); semi-Hinduized aborigines, 2898, or 11·7 per cent. of the population, consisting principally of Páns (1863); Hindu castes and people of Hindu origin, 19,800, or 79·9 per cent. of the population, the most numerous castes being Chásás (3831), Gaurs (1858), and Bráhmans (1709); Muhammadans, 111, or ·5 per cent. of the population. Details of the tribes, castes, etc. will be found in the table on pp. 210–217.

The principal seat of trade in the State is Kánpur, a town of about 331 houses, situated on the left bank of the Mahánadí, in 20° 24' 4" N. lat., and 85° 3' 21" E. long. Bi-weekly markets are held here, at which grain, cotton, sugar-cane, and oil seeds, which form the princi- pal products of the State, are bartered for salt and cloth from Cuttack. Five other towns contain over a hundred houses, viz. Narsinhpur, the capital of the State and residence of the Rájá; 313 houses; situated in 20° 28' 0" N. lat., and 85° 7' ·1" E. long.: Adáigundí; 151 houses; situated in 20° 27' 59" N. lat., and 85° 11' 53" E. long.: Ekdál; 126 houses; situated in 20° 23' 52" N. lat., and 85° 10' 37" E.

long.: Bukdá; 122 houses; situated in 20° 27′ 35″ N. lat., and 85° 12′ 57″ E. long.: and Ságar; 101 houses; situated in 20° 27′ 49″ N. lat., and 85° 11′ 6″ E. long. The total number of villages in the State is returned in the Census Report as 181, classified as follows:—141 with less than two hundred inhabitants, 32 with from two to five hundred, 7 with from five hundred to a thousand, and 1 with from one to two thousand inhabitants.

Narsinhpur State was founded some three hundred years ago by a Rájput, who slew its former Chiefs, two Kandhs named Narsinh and Poro. The present ruler, Rájá Braja Sundra Mán Sinh Harichandan Mahápátra, is thirty-one years old, and is the twenty-third Chief in descent. The emblem of signature is a scorpion. The State yields an estimated yearly revenue of £984 to its Chief, and pays an annual tribute of £145 to the British Government. The Rájá's militia consists of a force of 583 men, and the police of 196 men. The State contains ten schools, one of which is aided by the Rájá.

NAYAGARH STATE lies between 20° 20′ 30″ and 19° 54′ 30″ north latitude, and between 84° 50′ 45″ and 85° 18′ 0″ east longitude. It is bounded on the north by Khandpárá; on the east by Ranpur; on the south by Purí District; and on the west by the Madras State of Gumsar and Daspallá. It comprises a total area of 588 square miles, and contains 637 villages, and 18,271 houses. The Census Report of 1872 returns the population at 83,249 souls, classified as follows:—Hindus—males, men 25,944, and boys 14,032; total, 39,976: females, women 26,643, and girls 11,409; total, 38,052. Grand total of Hindus, 78,028, or 93·7 per cent. of the population; proportion of males in total Hindus, 51·2 per cent. Muhammadans—males, men 86, and boys 40; total, 126: females, women 69, and girls 31; total, 100. Grand total of Musalmáns, 226, or ·3 per cent. of the population; proportion of males in total Muhammadans, 55·8 per cent. Christians—nil. Other denominations (aboriginal tribes, etc.)—males, men 1878, and boys 728; total, 2606: females, women 1789, and girls 600; total, 2389. Grand total of 'others,' 4995, or 6·0 per cent. of the population of the State; proportion of males in total 'others,' 52·1 per cent. Population of all denominations—males, men 27,908, and boys 14,800; total, 42,708: females, women 28,501, and girls 12,040; total, 40,541. Total population of the State, 83,249; proportion of males in total population, 51·3 per cent. Averages—Density of the population, 142 per square mile; villages per square mile, 1·08; persons per village, 131; houses per square mile, 31; persons per house, 4·6· The population is ethnically divided as follows :—Aboriginal tribes, 4431, or 5·3 per cent. of the population, mainly composed of Kandhs (3928); semi-Hinduized aboriginal tribes, 11,466, or 13·7 per cent. of the population, the most numerous being the Páns (6627), Mihtárs (1692), and Kandárás (1672); Hindu castes and people of Hindu origin, 67,126, or 80·7 per cent. of the population, the most numerous castes being Chásás (23,028), Gaurs (6556), Bráhmans (5824), Telís (3847), and Gáurás (3255); Muhammadans, 226, or ·3 per cent. of the population. Details of the different tribes, castes, etc. will be found in the table on pp. 210–217.

Nayágarh is a large and valuable State, with wide-spread tracts of highly cultivated land. Towards the south and south-east, however, the country is exceedingly wild, and incapable of tillage; but the jungles on the west might be profitably brought under cultivation. The State abounds in noble scenery ; and a splendid range of hills, varying from two to three thousand feet in height, runs through its centre. It sends rice, coarse grains, cotton, sugar-cane, and several kinds of oil-seeds to the neighbouring Districts of Cuttack and Ganjám. Nine villages contain upwards of 100 houses, viz. : (1) Nayágarh, 495 houses; N. latitude 20° 7′ 45″, E. longitude 85° 7′ 56″. (2) Itámáti, where bi-weekly markets are held, 360 houses; N. lat. 20° 8′ 12″, E. long. 85° 11′ 42″. (3) Nandigoro, 200 houses; N. lat. 20° 0′ 51″, E. long. 85° 9′ 9″. (4) Kurál, 217 houses; N. lat. 20° 0′ 52″, E. long. 84° 57′ 40″. (5) Godiápárá, 168 houses ; N. lat. 20° 2′ 22″, E. long. 85° 12′ 29″. (6) Nátipádá, 190 houses; N. lat. 20° 26′ 3″, E. long. 85° 11′ 50″. (7) Birudá, 135 houses ; N. lat. 20° 7′ 57″, E. long. 85° 13′ 47″. (8) Bansiápárá, 199 houses; N. lat. 20° 10′ 0″, E. long. 85° 13′ 56″. (9) Shikárpur, 160 houses ; N. lat. 20° 1′ 50″, E. long. 85° 8′ 40″. The total number of villages in the State is returned in the Census Report at 637, classified as follows :—511 with less than two hundred inhabitants, 107 with from two to five hundred, 13 with from five hundred to a thousand, 5 with from one to two thousand, and 1 with from two to three thousand inhabitants.

This State was founded about five hundred years ago by a Rájput belonging to the family of the Rájá of Rewá, twenty-one generations distant from the present chief. It originally comprised Khandpárá; but a brother of the then ruling chief separated this latter territory about two hundred years ago, and erected it into an independent State. The present ruler, Rájá Ludukisor Sinh Mandhata, is thirty-four years of age. His emblem of signature is a tiger's head. Nayágarh State yields an estimated annual revenue of £5418 to its Chief, who pays £552 a year as tribute to the British Government. The Rájá's militia consists of 62, and the police force of 495 men. Nineteen schools are scattered throughout the State.

NILGIRI STATE lies between 21° 37′ 0″ and 21° 18′ 50″ north latitude, and between 86° 29′ 0″ and 86° 51′ 30″ east longitude. It is bounded on the west and north by Morbhanj, and on the east and south by Balasor District. The State comprises a total area of 278 square miles, and contains 264 villages and 6319 houses. The Census Report of 1872 returns the total population at 33,944 souls, classified as follows :—Hindus—males, men 8615, and boys 5778; total, 14,393 : females, women 9438, and girls 4219; total, 13,657. Grand total of Hindus, 28,050, or 82·6 per cent. of the population of the State; proportion of males in total Hindus, 51·3 per cent. Muhammadans—males, men 13, and boys 1; total, 14 : females, women 4, and girls 1; total, 5. Grand total of Musalmáns, 19. Christians—males, men 10, and boys 5; total, 15 : females, women 8, and girls 12; total, 20. Grand total of Christians, 35. Other denominations (aboriginal tribes, etc.)—males, men 1709, and boys 1258; total, 2967 : females, women 1904, and girls 969; total, 2873. Grand total of 'others,' 5840, or 17·2 per cent. of the total population; proportion of males in total 'others,' 50·8 per cent. Population of all denominations—males, men 10,347, and, boys 7042; total, 17,389 : females, women 11,354, and girls 5201; total, 16,555. Total population of the State, 33,944; proportion of males in total population, 51·2 per cent. Averages — Density of the population, 122 per square mile; villages per square mile, ·94; persons per village, 129; houses per square mile, 23; persons per house, 5·4· The population is ethnically divided as follows :— Aboriginal tribes, 2347, or 6·9 per cent. of the population, mainly composed of Bhumijs (1012); semi-Hinduized aboriginal tribes, 3854, or 11·4 per cent. of the population; Hindu castes and people of Hindu origin, 27,724, or 81·7 per cent. of the population, the most numerous castes being Khandáits (5030), Chásás (4428), Bráhmans (3734), and Gaurs (2153); Muhammadans, 19. Details of the different tribes, castes, etc. will be found in the table on pp. 210–217.

The Rájá's capital is situated in 21° 27′ 20″ north latitude, and

86° 48′ 41″ east longitude. The total number of villages in the
State is returned in the Census Report at 264, classified as follows:
—210 with less than two hundred inhabitants, 45 with from two to
five hundred, 8 with from five hundred to a thousand, and 1 with
from one to two thousand inhabitants. One-third of the State consists of uncultivated mountain land, one-third of waste jungle land,
while the remaining third is under cultivation. Valuable quarries
of black stone are worked, from which are made cups, bowls,
platters, etc.

Nílgirí was founded by a kinsman of the Rájá of Chutiá Nágpur,
who married a daughter of the King of Orissa, Pratáp Rudra Deo.
The present Rájá, Krishna Chandra Murdráj Harichandan, is fifty-
four years of age, of the Kshattriya caste, and claims to be the
twenty-fourth chief in the line of descent. The State yields an
estimated annual income of £2179 to its Rájá, and pays an annual
tribute of £390 to the British Government. The Rájá's militia
consists of 28, and the police force of 76 men. The State contains
18 schools.

PAL LAHARA STATE is situated between 21° 40′ 35″ and 21° 8′ 30″
north latitude, and between 85° 3′ 0″ and 85° 21′ 30″ east longitude.
It is bounded on the north by the Chutiá Nágpur State of Bonái;
east by Keunjhar; south by Tálcher; and west by Bámrá. It comprises a total area of 452 square miles, and contains 175 villages,
and 2941 houses. The Census Report of 1872 returns the total
population at 15,450, classified as follows:—Hindus—males, men
2646, and boys 2040; total, 4686: females, women 2533, and girls
1847; total, 4380. Grand total of Hindus, 9066, or 58·7 per cent.
of the population of the State; proportion of males in total Hindus,
51·7 per cent. Muhammadans — males, men 12, and boys 8;
total, 20: females, women 11, and girls 4; total, 15. Grand total
of Musálmans, 35, or ·2 per cent. of the population; proportion of
males in total Muhammadans, 57·1 per cent. Christians—*nil.*
Other denominations (aboriginal tribes, etc.)—males, men 2073,
and boys 1184; total, 3257: females, women 2017, and girls 1075;
total, 3092. Grand total of 'others,' 6349, or 41·1 per cent. of the
population; proportion of males in total 'others,' 51·3 per cent.
Population of all denominations—males, men 4731, and boys 3232;
total, 7963: females, women 4561, and girls 2926; total, 7487.
Total population of the State, 15,450; proportion of males in total
population, 51·5 per cent. Averages—Density of the population,

34 per square mile; villages per square mile, ·38; persons per village, 88; houses per square mile, 7; persons per house, 5·3. The Census Report ethnically divides the population as follows :— Aboriginal tribes, 4911, or 31·8 per cent. of the population, the most numerous being Savars (1387) and Gonds (1133); semi-Hinduized aboriginals, 3936, or 25·5 per cent. of the population, consisting mainly of Páns (2145) and Bhuiyás (1464); Hindu castes and people of Hindu origin, 6568, or 42·5 per cent. of the population, the most numerous being the cultivating and cattle-breeding castes (2836); Muhammadans, 35, or ·2 per cent. of the total population. Details of the different tribes, castes, etc. will be found in the table on pp. 210–217.

The east and north of the State are occupied with hills. A magnificent mountain, Maláyagirí, 3895 feet high, with building space and water on its summit, towers above the lesser ranges. The State contains some of the finest *sál* forests to be found in the world. Its agricultural productions consist of the usual coarse grains and oil-seeds, but it has nothing worthy of the name of trade. Lahárá, the residence of the Rájá, situated in north latitude 21° 26′ 0″, and east longitude 85° 13′ 46″, is the only village with upwards of 100 houses. The total number of villages returned in the Census Report is 175, classified as follows :—155 with less than two hundred inhabitants, 19 with from two to five hundred, and 1 with from five hundred to a thousand. The Midnapur and Sambalpur high road passes through the State from east to west.

Pal Lahárá formerly belonged to Keunjhar, but was partially separated in consequence of family quarrels. The story of the separation is as follows :—Once upon a time, the Keunjhar Rájá compelled his feudatory of Pal Lahárá to dance before him in woman's attire. From this affront a deadly quarrel resulted; and at the end, as the price of peace, the Pal Lahárá chief was exempted from any longer paying his tribute through the Keunjhar Rájá, and now pays it to the British Government direct. The money, however, is still credited in our treasury accounts to the Keunjhar State, although, for all practical purposes, Pal Lahárá is independent of the Keunjhar Rájá and utterly disowns his authority. The present Chief, Munipál, claims to be a Kshattriya by caste, and is forty-four years old. For distinguished services rendered at the time of the Keunjhar rebellion in 1867-68, the British Government conferred upon him the title of Rájá Bahádur.

Estimated annual revenue of the Rájá, £120; tribute, £26. The Rájá's militia consists of 67, and the police force of 57 men.

RANPUR STATE is situated between 20° 12' 0" and 19° 52' 45" north latitude, and between 85° 9' 15" and 85° 29' 15" east longitude. It is bounded on the north, east, and south by Purí District; and on the west by Nayágarh. It comprises a total area of 203 square miles, and contains 280 villages, and 5310 houses. The Census Report of 1872 returns the total population of the State at 27,306, classified as follows:—Hindus—males, men 8009, and boys 4756; total, 12,765: females, women 8211, and girls 4019; total, 12,230. Grand total of Hindus, 24,995, or 91·6 per cent. of the population of the State; proportion of males in total Hindus, 51·1 per cent. Muhammadans—males, men 42, and boys 39; total, 81: females, women 48, and girls 19; total, 67. Grand total of Muhammadans, 148, or ·5 per cent. of the population; proportion of males in total Musalmáns, 54·7 per cent. Other denominations (aboriginal tribes, etc.)—males, men 782, and boys 346; total, 1128: females, women 724, and girls 311; total, 1035. Grand total of 'others,' 2163, or 7·9 per cent. of the population; proportion of males in total 'others,' 52·1 per cent. Population of all denominations—males, men 8833, and boys 5141; total, 13,974: females, women 8983, and girls 4349; total, 13,332. Total population of the State, 27,306; proportion of males in the total population, 51·2 per cent. Averages—Density of the population, 135 per square mile; villages per square mile, 1·37; persons per village, 98; houses per square mile, 26; persons per house, 5·1. The Census Report ethnically divides the population as follows:—Aboriginal tribes, 1887, or 7·0 per cent. of the population, mainly composed of Kandhs (1257); semi-Hinduized aborigines, 1723, or 6·3 per cent. of the population, principally composed of Páns (619) and Mihtárs (478); Hindu castes and people of Hindu origin, 23,548, or 86·2 per cent. of the population, the principal castes being the Chásás (8458), Gaurs (2161), and Bráhmans (2504); Muhammadans, 148, or ·5 per cent. of the population. Details of the different tribes, castes, etc. will be found in the table on pp. 210–217.

The only town in the State is the Rájá's place of residence, situated in north latitude 20° 3' 55", and east longitude 85° 23' 26", which consists of one long and wide street containing 600 houses. The country products are here bartered at bi-weekly markets, for iron, cotton, blankets, cloth, silk, wheat, and clarified butter, brought from Khandpárá; and for fish from the Chilká lake. The total number of villages returned in the Census Report is 280, classified as follows:—258 with less than two hundred inhabitants; 19 with from two to five hundred; 2 with from five hundred to a thousand; and 1 with from three to four thousand inhabitants. The south-west part of Ranpur is a region of jungly hills, almost entirely waste and uninhabited, which wall in its whole western side, except at a single point where a pass leads into the adjoining State of Nayágarh.

Tradition states that Ranpur was founded some 3600 years ago by a hunter named Básara Básuk. It was originally of small extent; but 109 generations of Chiefs had constantly annexed their neigh-bours' territories, until the accession of the British power put an end to such internecine struggles. The State is said to derive its name from a giant named Ranásur, who lived in it. The present Rájá, Benudhar Bájrudhar Narendra Mahápátra, claims to be a Kshattriya by caste, and is fifty-nine years of age. His emblem of signa-ture is a sword. Estimated annual revenue of the Rájá, £696; tribute, £140. The Rájá's militia consists of 8, and the police force of 94 men. Forty-one schools are scattered through the State.

TALCHER STATE is situated between 21° 18′ 0″ and 20 52′ 30″ north latitude, and between 84° 57′ 0″ and 85° 17′ 45″ east longi-tude. It is bounded on the north by Pal Lahárá; on the east by Dhenkánal; and on the south and west by Angul. It comprises a total area of 399 square miles, and contains 242 villages and 7192 houses. The Census Report of 1872 returns the total population of the State at 38,021 souls, classified as follows:—Hindus—males, men 9861, and boys 7112; total, 16,973: females, women 10,005, and girls 6077; total, 16,082. Grand total of Hindus, 33,055, or 86·9 per cent. of the population; proportion of males in total Hindus, 51·3 per cent. Muhammadans—males, men 32, and boys 17; total, 49: females, women 35, and girls 16; total, 51. Grand total of Muham-madans, 100, or ·2 per cent. of the population; proportion of males in total Musalmáns, 49·0 per cent. Other denominations (aboriginal tribes, etc.)—males, men 1428, and boys 1019; total, 2447: females, women 1478, and girls 941; total, 2419. Grand total of ' others,' 4866, or 12·9 per cent. of the population; proportion of males in total ' others,' 50·3 per cent. Population of all denominations—males, men 11,321, and boys 8148, total, 19,469; females, women 11,518, and girls 7034; total, 18,552. Total population of the State, 38,021; proportion of males in total population, 51·2 per cent. Averages —Density of the population, 95 per square mile; villages per square mile, ·60; persons per village, 157; houses per square mile, 18; persons per house, 5·3. The Census Report ethnically divides the population as follows:—Aboriginal tribes, 3940, or 10·4 per cent. of the population, consisting mainly of Savars (1442), Gonds (961), and Táalas (901); semi-Hinduized aborigines, 6630, or 17·7 per cent. of the population, consisting mainly of Páns (4616); Hindu castes and people of Hindu origin, 27,351, or 71·9 per cent. of the population, the most numerous castes being Chásás (10,729), Gaurs (1871), Bráhmans (1865), and Kámárs (1349); Muhammadans, 100, or ·2 per cent. of the total population. Details of the different tribes, castes, etc. will be found in the table on pp. 210–217.

Iron, lime, and coal are found near the banks of the Bráhmaní; but, as stated in a previous page (*ante*, p. 202), there does not appear at present any prospect of Tálcher coal successfully competing at the Orissa ports with Ráníganj coal sent from Calcutta by sea. Gold is obtained by washing the sand of the river, but the process is very primitive, and yields but little profit to the workers. The only town of any size in the State is Tálcher, the residence of the Rájá, situated on the right bank of the Bráhmaní, in north latitude 20° 57′ 20″, east longitude 85° 16′ 11″, and containing about 500 houses. The total number of villages in the State is returned in the Census Report at 242, classified as follows:—183 with less than two hundred inhabitants, 49 with from two to five hundred, 9 with from five hundred to a thousand, and 1 with from two to three thousand inhabitants.

The State is said to have been founded about five hundred years ago by a son of the then Rájá of Oudh, who forcibly ejected the savage tribe which had previously inhabited it. It is stated that the founder had to uproot many palm (*tál*) trees, in order to make room for his habitation, and that the name Tálcher was derived from this circumstance. The title of Mahendrá Bahádur was bestowed upon the late Rájá by the British Government, as a reward for services rendered during the Angul disturbances in 1847. The present Rájá, Rámchandra Birbar Harichandan, the nineteenth in descent from the founder, is nineteen years of age, and a Rájput by caste. His emblem of signature is a tiger's head. The State is a valuable one, yielding an estimated annual revenue of £4147 to its Rájá, who pays a yearly tribute of £103 to the British Government. The Rájá's militia consists of 615, and the police force of 267 men. Fifteen schools are scattered through the State.

TIGARIA STATE lies between 20° 32′ 20″ and 20° 25′ 0″ north latitude, and between 85° 27′ 45″ and 85° 35′ 30″ east longitude. It is bounded on the north by Dhenkánal; on the east by Athgarh; on the south by the Mahánadí; and on the west by Barambá. It is the smallest of all the Tributary States, having an area of only 46 square miles. It contains 75 villages, 2927 houses, and a total population of 16,420 souls, classified as follows :—Hindus—males, men 4721, and boys 2737; total, 7458 : females, women 4844, and girls 2568; total, 7412. Grand total of Hindus, 14,870, or 90·6 per cent. of the population; proportion of males in total Hindus, 50·2 per cent. Muhammadans—males, men 76, and boys 45; total, 121 : females, women 80, and girls 45 ; total, 125. Grand total of Muhammadans, 246, or 1·5 per cent. of the population ; proportion of males in total Musalmáns, 45·1 per cent. Christians—*nil.* Other denominations (aboriginal tribes, etc.)—males, men 384, and boys 283; total, 667 : females, women 392, and girls 245 ; total, 637. Grand total of 'others,' 1304, or 7·9 per cent. of the population ; proportion of males in total 'others,' 51·1 per cent. Population of all denominations—males, men 5181, and boys 3065 ; total, 8246 : females, women 5316, and girls 2858; total, 8174. Total population of the State, 16,420; proportion of males in total population, 50·2 per cent. Averages—Density of the population, 357 per square mile ; villages per square mile, 1·63 ; persons per village 219 ; houses per square mile, 64; persons per house, 5·6. The population is ethnically divided as follows :—Aboriginal tribes, 1303, or 7·9 per cent. of the population, principally composed of Savars (759) ; semi-Hinduized aborigines, 1266, or 7·7 per cent. of the population, chiefly Páns (883) ; Hindu castes and persons of Hindu origin, 13,605, or 82·9 per cent. of the population, the most numerous castes being Chásás (4519), Patuás (1142), and Telis (1048) ; Muhammadans, 246, or 1·5 per cent. of the population. Details of the different tribes, castes, etc. will be found in the table on pp. 210–217.

Although the smallest in point of size, Tigariá is, with the single exception of Bánkí, the most densely peopled of the Orissa Tributary States, and is well cultivated except among the hills and jungles at its northern end. It produces the usual coarse rice and grains, oil-seeds, sugar-cane, tobacco, cotton, etc., for the transport of which the Mahánadí affords ample facilities throughout its whole southern part. Only two villages, however, boast of the bi-weekly markets common in the Tributary States. Tigariá, the residence of the Rájá, is situated in north latitude 20° 28′ 15″, east longitude 84° 33′ 31″. Two towns contain upwards of 100 houses,—Gopináthpur, north latitude 20° 26′ 46″, east longitude 85° 30′ 38″, 490 houses ; and Pánchgáon, north latitude 20° 28′ 1″, east longitude 85° 34′ 4″. The total number of villages in the State is returned in the Census Report at 75, classified as follows :—54 with less than two hundred inhabitants, 14 with from two to five hundred, 5 with from five hundred to a thousand, 1 with from one to two thousand, and 1 with from two to three thousand.

This little principality dates from about four hundred years ago, when one Sur Tung Sinh, a Purí pilgrim from Northern India, halted on his way back, drove out the aborigines, seized the country, and founded the present family. Twenty-six Chiefs have reigned since then. The State was originally much larger than at present, and is said to derive its name from the fact of its having consisted of three divisions defended by forts (*tri garh*, or in Uriyá, *gara*). Extensive domains have, however, been carved out of it by neighbouring Chiefs in the time of the Marhattá Government. The present Rájá, Harihar Kshattriya Birbar Champti Sinh Mahápátra, claims to belong to the Kshattriya caste, and is forty-nine years of age. His emblem of signature is the Five Weapons (*sastra pancha*). Estimated revenue of the Rájá, £800 per annum; annual tribute, £88. The militia consists of 393, and the police force of 77 men. Twelve schools are distributed through the State.

APPENDIX.

GEOLOGICAL ACCOUNT OF ORISSA.

THE following Account has been kindly drawn up for me by the Geological Survey of India; and I take this opportunity of acknowledging the generous assistance of Dr. Oldham, the head of the Survey, in many matters connected with the Gazetteer of Bengal:—

'The Province of Orissa consists, geologically as well as geographically, of two very distinct portions: the one, a belt of nearly flat country, from fifteen to fifty miles in breadth, extending along the coast; and the other, an undulating area, broken by ranges of hills, in the interior. The former is entirely of alluvial formations, the greater portion of its surface being probably composed of deposits from the great river Mahánadí, and the smaller streams, the Bráhmaní and Baitaraní. Near its western limit alone, a few hills of gneissose rock rise from the alluvial plain, especially between the Bráhmaní and Mahánadí. The inland hill tract, on the other hand, is chiefly composed of rocks of very ancient date, so completely altered and crystallized by metamorphic action, that all traces of their original structure are lost, and any organic remains obliterated which they may originally have contained. The same rocks cover an enormous area in Eastern and Southern India, and are usually spoken of, in works on Indian geology, as the crystalline or metamorphic series.

'Further exploration in the less known Tributary States will doubtless show the existence of beds belonging to other formations; but hitherto the only instance in which any considerable area is known to be occupied by rocks of later date than the metamorphics, is in the tract known as the Tálcher coal-field, in the States of

Tálcher, Angul, Bánkí, Athmallik, and Dhenkánal; also in Rádhákol in the Central Provinces. High up the Bráhmaní valley a series of very slightly altered or unaltered rocks, comprising slates with jasper, quartzites, and schistose beds, are known to occur; but it has not been ascertained whether they extend into the district administered from Cuttack, though they are believed to occupy portions of Keunjhar and of Bonái in the Chutiá Nágpur Division.

'The greater portion of the Tributary States have never been explored geologically, and the information procurable as to their character is most imperfect. It is possible that other coal-fields may exist, though not probable. Up to 1874-75 even the Tálcher coal-field had only received, for the most part, a very hurried examination. Excluding the formations of which no accurate information has been obtained, such as the slates, quartzites, and jasper, believed to be found in Keunjhar and Bonái, the following is a list, in descending order, of the rock systems hitherto described as existing in Orissa:—(8) *Blown sands.* (7) *Alluvium.* *b.* River delta deposits. *a.* Older alluvium of coast plain. (6) *Laterite.* (5) *Cuttack or Athgarh sandstone.* (4) *Mahádeva or Pánchet sandstone and grit.* (3) *Dámodar sandstone, shale, and coal.* (2) *Tálcher sandstone, shale, silt and boulder bed.* (1) *Metamorphic or crystalline rocks.*

'The following is a brief description of the characters of each of these formations, as found in Orissa :—

'(1) METAMORPHIC OR CRYSTALLINE ROCKS.— These consist of various forms of gneiss, mica-schist, hornblende-schist, quartzite, etc. Crystalline limestone, common in many parts of India, has not been hitherto observed in Orissa. True granite is found in the form of veins traversing the gneiss, and is of various forms, the most common being a highly crystalline variety, with but little mica, and passing into pegmatite, of the kind known as graphic granite, beautiful specimens of which have been found in parts of the Tributary States. This granite is apparently, for the most part at least, of cotemporaneous age with the metamorphism of the gneiss. But besides this, the gneiss itself frequently passes into a granitoid form, perfectly undistinguishable in blocks from granite; but which, when in place, is usually found to retain, every here and there, traces of its original lamination, and to pass by insensible degrees into a distinct laminated gneiss of the usual form.

'Other prevalent forms are ordinary gneiss, composed of quartz, felspar, and mica; hornblendic gneiss, in which the mica is replaced by hornblende, the latter mineral sometimes forming a very large proportion of the rock; and quartzose gneiss, in which the felspar and mica, or hornblende, are in very small proportion, and the quartz predominates. This gradually passes into quartzite, in which felspar and mica are either wanting, or occur only in very small quantities.

'The above may be considered the prevailing forms of the crystalline rocks; but there are others of less frequent occurrence. Amongst these are diorite, amphibolite, syenite, and a magnesian rock—a kind of potstone. These may all very possibly be of later date than most of the metamorphics, though the serpentine-like potstone appears to be fairly intercalated.

'(2) TALCHER GROUP.—The lowest beds associated with the coal-bearing strata are themselves destitute of useful fuel, and well distinguished mineralogically from the Dámodar or coal-bearing rocks. They were first separated from the overlying beds in Orissa, and named after the State in which they were found. They consist, in the case of the Tálcher coal-field, of blue nodular shale, fine buff or greenish sandstone, and extremely fine silt beds, often inter-stratified with sandstone more or less coarse in texture, in thin alternating laminæ. The sandstones frequently contain felspar grains, which are usually undecomposed. In the sandstone and fine silty shale, rounded pebbles, and boulders of granite, gneiss, and other crystalline rocks abound, some of them as much as four or five feet in diameter. This remarkable formation is known as the boulder bed. It is peculiar to the Tálcher group, and has been found in India wherever that group has been examined,—in the valleys of the Dámodar, the Són, the Narbadá, and the Godávarí, as well as in that of the Bráhmaní.

'Of this singular association of large blocks of stone in a fine matrix, but few other instances are known, the most remarkable one being that of the "boulder clay" of Great Britain and other countries, which is now considered by most geologists to be of glacial origin. The boulder bed of the Tálcher group, however, differs entirely from the boulder clay. In the former the fine matrix is distinctly stratified, and the boulders are rounded, neither of which is the usual condition of the boulder clay. But the origin of such a rock is in both instances surrounded by the same difficulty, viz. that any current of water which could round and transport the boulders would sweep away, instead of depositing, the fine sand, clay, and silt in which they are embedded. Yet nothing is clearer than that the two were deposited together. Ice is rather a startling power to invoke in endeavouring to explain the phenomena of rocks found in a tropical climate; but without its agency it appears difficult, in the present state of geological knowledge, to account for the Tálcher boulder bed.

'In 1855, Mr. Blanford suggested (*Memoirs of Geological Survey of India*, i. p. 49) that these beds might have been deposited in a high table-land, and that the association of the boulders was perhaps due to ground ice. The advance of cosmical theories since that time has rather tended to increase the possibility of periods of cold having occurred in the course of the earth's history, some of which may have been sufficiently severe to affect the tropics, or portions of them. Tálchers have now been found over so extensive an area, that the probability of their having been deposited at any considerable elevation above the sea has greatly diminished, and observers are inclined to consider them marine, — a view which Mr. Blanford does not share. No other hypothesis, however, not involving ice-action, has been offered which accounts satisfactorily for their peculiarities.

'(3) DAMODAR GROUP. — Above the Tálcher, or occasionally resting upon the metamorphic rocks, without the intervention of any other sedimentary beds, is found a series of sandstone and shale, with beds of coal. The sandstone is mostly coarse grey and brown rocks passing into grits. They are usually more or less felspathic, the felspar being decomposed and converted into clay, and are often ferruginous. Blue and carbonaceous shale, often more or less micaceous, and ferruginous shaly sandstone, are characteristic of this group. Fossil plants, chiefly consisting of ferns, such as *Glossopteris, Pecopteris, Trizygia, Equisetaceæ,* and *Calamites,* and above all, peculiar stems divided into segments (*Vertebraria*), believed to be roots of unknown affinities, are frequently found. Most of the fossil species found, perhaps all, are characteristic of the Dámodar formation.

'The peculiar interest attaching to this group of rocks is, however, derived from its being the only one in which workable coal has been found in the peninsula of India. All the coals of Ráníganj and the other fields of the Dámodar valley, as well as all those of the Narbadá valley, and of other parts of the Central Provinces, are in Dámodar rocks. So far as they have hitherto been examined, the coals of

Tálcher appear to be of inferior quality to those of Ráníganj, the Narbadá, and other localities; but the field in the Tributary States has by no means been sufficiently explored.

'(4) MAHADEVA GROUP. — Above the coal-bearing series in the eastern part of the Tálcher coal-field, a considerable thickness of coarse sandstone, grits, and conglomerates is found, quite different in character from the beds of the Tálcher and Dámodar groups, and resting unconformably upon them. These rocks are usually coloured with various shades of brown, and are frequently very ferruginous. The separate beds composing them are massive, and not interrupted, as the Dámodar sandstones frequently are, by partings of shale. They form hills of considerable size in the State of Rádhákol, in the Central Provinces.

'It is by no means clear that these beds are the representatives of the group in the Narbadá valley, to which the name Mahádeva was first applied; but there is a general subdivision of the rocks through-out the greater portion of the Indian coal-fields into three principal groups. To the higher of these, the term Mahádeva has been given in the Narbadá valley, in Orissa, and Pánchet in Bengal; and until a re-examination of the Orissa beds has enabled their relations to that of other coal-fields to be more accurately made out than was possible when they were first mapped, it appears best to retain the name first applied to them.

'(5) CUTTACK OR ATHGARH GROUP.—South-west of the town of Cuttack is a considerable area, occupied by grit, sandstone, and con-glomerate, with one or more beds of white or pinkish clay. The beds are very similar in general character to those last described; but there is no evidence of any connection with them, and it appears at least as probable that the Cuttack rocks are of later date. No fossils have been found in these beds except some obscure impres-sions, apparently of vegetable origin, in the clays.

'(6) LATERITE.—The laterite of Orissa is evidently of detrital origin, and consists essentially of small pisolitic nodules, chiefly com-posed of hydrated oxide of iron (brown hæmatite) and coarse quartz sand, cemented together more or less perfectly into either a firm, though somewhat vesicular, rock, or into a less coherent mass, or at times remaining in a loose gravelly condition, and thus passing by various gradations into a sandy clay, with a few pisolitic iron nodules. As a rule, the forms containing most iron are the most coherent, and *vice versâ*. The more solid sorts are largely used as building stone, having the peculiar but important property of being softest when first cut, and of hardening greatly on exposure.

' Beneath the detrital laterite, especially when a felspathic form of the metamorphic rocks occurs, the decomposed upper portion of the latter is frequently greatly impregnated with iron, and converted into a kind of lithomarge, which closely resembles the detrital laterite in appearance, and is employed for the same purposes. The massive form of laterite which caps many of the higher hills in Central India, and which is more compact than the detrital laterite, is not known to occur in Orissa.

' (7) ALLUVIUM—a. OLDER ALLUVIUM OF COAST PLAIN.—In the neighbourhood of the hills, and frequently for many miles from their base, the alluvium of the plains consists of clay and sand, usually more or less commingled, and in most places containing calcareous concretions (*kankar* or *ghutin*) and pisolitic ferruginous nodules. This deposit passes by insensible degrees into laterite on the one hand, and into the more recent deltaic alluvium on the other; but in its typical form it is well distinguished from both, by being more sandy, and containing nodular carbonate of lime, or *kankar*.

' The age of this alluvial deposit is shown by its surface having been modified and rendered uneven by the action of rain and streams, so that the country composed of it is more or less undulating. Whether this formation, or any portion of it, is of marine origin, is a question hitherto undetermined. So far as it has been yet examined, it appears to be in Orissa unfossiliferous. The greater portion has doubtless been produced by deposits washed down by the great rivers from the higher country to the westward; and it appears likely that a portion of these have been deposited along the coast. But other deposits have been in all probability formed upon the original marine beds, by the additional accumulations brought down by streams and washed by rain from the hills, so that it is questionable whether the lower marine beds which probably exist are anywhere exposed.

' *b*. RIVER DELTA DEPOSITS.—In the neighbourhood of the great rivers, the soil is finer and the country level, the greater portion being yearly inundated by flood-waters, and receiving a fresh deposit from them, except in places where they are kept from over-flow by artificial means. The alluvium thus formed is generally highly fertile, but the country is swampy, and often malarious. As above pointed out, the only character by which this modern alluvium can be distinguished is the flatness of its surface, showing that the area occupied by it is one of deposition, and not of denudation. Usually, also, it is less sandy than the older alluvium, and *kankar* is not of frequent occurrence in it, though a thin layer of it often covers deposits of calcareous sand and clay, from which the later deposit can with difficulty be distinguished.

'(8) BLOWN SAND.—Along the coast, as at Purí, large tracts of ground are covered with sand blown inland from the beach. The nature and origin of the formation is obvious, being simply a deposit of sand carried onward from the margin of the sea by the monsoon, and sometimes rising into ridges and cliffs.

'In proceeding to give a sketch of the geological character of the different Districts and States of which Orissa is composed, I shall first describe the Districts of Balasor, Cuttack, and Purí, and subsequently those Tributary States with regard to which any definite information has been obtained.

'BALASOR.—Almost the whole District consists of alluvial deposits. Metamorphic rocks occur in the Nílgirí hills, along the western boundary; but they scarcely enter the district anywhere, and in no case are found more than a mile or two within the boundary. Laterite, frequently massive, forms in some places a narrow fringe to the mountains. A few sandhills skirt the shore in the north-eastern part of the District, which to the east of the Subarnarekhá extend from three to four miles inland. The older alluvium occupies the greater portion of the District, the flat river alluvium forming the southern part near the Baitaraní, Kharsuá, and Bráhmaní rivers, and a tract in the north-east near the Subarnarekhá. Around Balasor itself the soil is rather sandy, and contains laterite gravel. Concretionary carbonate of lime (*kankar*) is widely distributed, especially in the western part of the District.

'IN CUTTACK, as in Balasor, the largest part of the District consists of alluvium, the older form with an undulating surface occupying, however, a much smaller area proportionally, and being confined to the north-western part of the District, nearly all of the remainder being composed of the flat deltas of the Mahánadí and Bráhmaní. Along the sea-coast, blown sand is generally found, but it only forms a narrow belt.

'Between the rivers Bráhmaní and Mahánadí, in the *kilás* of Balrámpur, Madhupur, Darpan, Kalkalá, Dálijorá, and scattered over the country to the east in *pargaṅá* Altí, there are numerous hills, all more or less isolated, and all composed of gneiss. Along the Bráhmaní, near Balrámpur, and for some miles to the south-east, the rock is compact and granitoid. Farther south it is less compact, and usually soft from partial disintegration near the surface. It is marked with numerous red blotches, the remains of decomposed garnets. This soft decomposing gneiss is sometimes quarried, and used for building. The hills in this part of the country are not accurately represented on the Revenue Survey maps; but those shown in the Topographical Survey maps of the Tributary States are very correctly drawn.

'No laterite occurs around the more eastern hills, but around those in the neighbourhood of the road from Calcutta to Cuttack there is frequently a narrow fringe, often conglomeritic, as if it had been originally a beach deposit; and to the west of the high road to Cuttack, the metamorphic hills are surrounded in general by broad terrace-like flats, frequently stretching from hill to hill; and when they do not do so, affording evidence that the laterite is continued beneath the intervening alluvium. This laterite is frequently employed for building purposes.

'PURI, the southern District of Orissa, contains a much larger extent of hard rocks than either Cuttack or Balasor. All the country near the coast, and a broad tract in the north-east of the District, are alluvial; but the western part of the area is occupied by laterite, sandstone, and metamorphic rocks. There is a very small extent of the older undulating alluvium. Almost all the eastern part of the District, and the country extending from the Mahánadí to the Chilká lake, is perfectly flat, and consists of the newer or delta alluvium. Hence its liability to flooding from the Mahánadí. Hills of blown sand extend along the whole coast, and frequently are disposed in two or three principal ranges, the first close to the shore, the second from one to two miles inland; occasionally another range lies still farther from the sea.

'The greater portion of Dompárá and Dándimál, south-west of the town of Cuttack, consists of the Athgarh sandstone. To the west, these beds appear to rest on the metamorphic rocks, and they have a general dip to the east and south-east, at low angles not exceeding 5° or 6°. They are surrounded on all sides by laterite and alluvium. At their apparent base to the west is a coarse conglomerate, the pebbles chiefly of quartzite. These rocks contain one band at least of white clay, which is largely dug, and used for whitewashing houses and for other purposes. South-west of the sandstone countries, and west of Khurdhá, there is a broad undulating plain, partly covered with laterite, through which the gneiss rises at intervals. In the extreme west of the District, around Bolgarh and Goriálí, there are two very barren ranges of no great height, running east and west, and formed of compact, rather granitoid gneiss.

' From this point, where the boundary of the District turns to the eastward, as far as the Chilká lake, only detached hills occur, all of gneiss, with intervening plains of laterite and alluvium. The group of hills near Chatármá are of granitoid gneiss; most of the others are of garnetiferous gneiss, with quartzose bands. Such are Khurdhá hill, with the smaller elevations in the neighbourhood, and also the hills east of the Cuttack and Ganjám road between Rámeswar and Monglápurí.

' A precisely similar country extends to the west of the Chilká lake. The lake itself was formerly a part of the sea, first rendered shallow by deposits from the mouths of the Mahánadí. It is now entirely cut off from the sea by a spit of sand, formed by the violent winds of the southern monsoon. Near the south-western extremity of this spit there is a considerable deposit of estuarine shells, at a height of twenty to thirty feet above the present flood-level of the Chilká. The shells found—*Cythera casta* and *Area granosa*—have not been observed living in the Chilká, and both are estuarine species, not occurring in the sea itself; but the former is now abundant in the estuary connecting the lake with the sea. This deposit appears to afford evidence of a recent elevation of the land.

' There can be but little doubt that the Chilká is gradually diminishing in size and in depth; but as it receives no streams of importance, the quantity of water charged with sediment poured into it is small, and its rate of decrease is probably very slow. Its fauna is peculiar, and deserves more attention than it has hitherto received. Indeed, the whole estuarine fauna of the Indian backwaters and deltas has been but imperfectly studied; and further information is extremely desirable, above all, regarding the mollusca, for the illustration of the fossils of the many deposits which have doubtless accumulated under very similar circumstances in past times.

' TRIBUTARY STATES.—Of the geology of the States of Morbhanj, Pal Lahará, Narsinhpur, Barambá, and Tigariá, lying north of the Mahánadí, and of all the States south of the Mahánadí river, except Bánkí, viz. Bod, Daspallá, Khandpárá, Nayágarh, and

Ranpur, nothing definite is known. It is pretty certain that a large proportion of their area consists of metamorphic rocks, and it is possible that no others may be found.

'Of Keunjhar and Nílgirí, only the edges bordering on Balasor District have been examined. Hindol has been traversed; portions of Dhenkánal and Athmallik have been examined; whilst in Angul, Tálcher, and the little States of Athgarh and Bánkí, a more general survey has been made, but still far from a complete or detailed one.

'NILGIRI AND KEUNJHAR.—The hills bordering on Balasor consist entirely of metamorphic rocks of various kinds. In the northern part of the range, gneiss is found, so granitic that the direction of the foliation can scarcely be ascertained. It appears to be nearly parallel with the escarpment of the range. Granite veins are scarce; but greenstone dykes, or pseudo-dykes, many of them of great size, abound, and most of them, if not all, appear to run parallel with the gneissic foliation. These facts render it probable that the dykes in question are really beds, so altered as to be perfectly crystalline. A kind of black magnesian rock, intermediate in composition between potstone and serpentine, approaching the former in appearance, but less greasy in texture, is quarried to some extent, chiefly for the manufacture of stone dishes, plates, and bowls. The stones are roughly cut into shape in the quarry, and finished, partly with tools and partly on a lathe, in the villages. The rock employed is found interfoliated with the gneiss in several places, and is quarried at the villages of Sántrágodiá and Gujádihá, a few miles south of Nílgirí, at a spot two or three miles from Jugjuri, and in scattered localities to the north-west.

'A few miles west-south-west of Jugjuri, near Parkpádá, the granitoid rocks are replaced by a tough, hard, indistinctly crystalline hornblendic rock, resembling diorite, but exhibiting more foliation than is seen in the hills near Nílgirí. Still farther to the south-west, quartz schist appears in a well-foliated form, occasionally containing talc. A detached hill near Bákipur consists of this rock, and so does the whole south-west portion of the range as far as Rogadi, except in the immediate neighbourhood of the Sálandí river, where it leaves the hill. Here syenite occurs, which forms a detached hill near Dárápur. The southern portion of the range is free from the trap dykes which are so conspicuous to the north-east of Jugjuri. All the western portions of Keunjhar are unexplored.

'TALCHER, ANGUL, AND ATHMALLIK.—*The Tálcher coal-field.*—
These States comprise by far the most interesting geological area
in Orissa and its dependencies. The basin of sedimentary rocks
known as the Tálcher coal-field is surrounded on all sides by metamorphics. This basin extends about seventy miles from west by
north to east by south, with a general breadth of from fifteen to
twenty miles, its eastern extremity at Karakprasád on the Bráhmaní
river being nearly fifty miles north-west of Cuttack town. Its
western limit is not far from Rámpur, in the State of Rádhákol,
in the Central Provinces, and it comprises nearly the whole of
Tálcher, and a considerable portion of Angul and Rádhákol, with
smaller parts of Bánkí, Athmallik, and Dhenkánal. The western
half of this field is chiefly occupied by the rocks already described
as belonging to the Mahádeva group, conglomerate and coarse sandstone, which form hills of considerable height in a very wild, jungly,
and thinly inhabited country. At the period when the Tálcher coal-
field was first examined, nothing whatever was known of the classification of rocks which has since been demonstrated by the Geological
Survey in the various coal-fields of India. Indeed, one of the very
first and most important distinctions, that of the Tálcher group,
below the coal-bearing division, was made in this region, as already
mentioned. The boundaries of the Mahádevas and Dámodars, on
the map in the *Memoirs of the Geological Survey of India*, is merely a
rough approximation made from memory, and partly by guess, after
quitting the field. The differences of the rocks have been noted
in the field, but their area had not been mapped.

'It is by no means improbable that the Dámodar coal-bearing
rocks will hereafter be found in portions of this area. Indeed, they
have been observed at the village of Patrápádá.

'In the extreme west of the field, Tálcher beds occur in the upper
part of the valley of a stream tributary to the Tikariá, near Deinchá,
and also near the village of Rámpur, in Rádhákol. In both cases,
Mahádeva rocks appear to rest directly on them, without the intervention of any Dámodars.

'Besides occupying the western part of the field, the Mahádevas are
found in two places along the northern boundary, which is formed
by a fault of considerable dimensions. One of these places is near
the villages of Bodaharna and Dereng, where the upper beds occur
as a narrow belt, five or six miles from east to west, their presence
being marked by low hills of hard conglomerate. Farther to the west,

they recur in another isolated patch, forming the rise called Khandgirí
Hill. This hill consists of sandstone, capped by conglomerate, the
pebbles from which weather out and cover the sides of the hill,
concealing the sandstone beneath.

'The northern part of the field in which these outliers of the
Mahádevas occur is much cut up by faults, or, to speak more correctly,
by branches of one great fault. These faults are in some places
marked by a quartzose breccia, containing fragments of sandstone
and other rocks. The vein of breccia varies in breadth. At the
village of Karganj it is so largely developed that it forms a hill of
considerable height. Between the branches of the fault, Tálcher
beds and metamorphics occur; north of all the faults, metamorphics only are found.

'The eastern part of the field, from near Karganj on the Tikariá
river, and Kánkurái on the Tengrá, to the east of the Bráhmaní,
is principally composed of Dámodar rock. These may usually be
recognised by the occasional occurrence of blue and black shale,
the latter carbonaceous, and sometimes containing coal. The
general section of the beds, so far as could be made out in a
difficult country, much obscured by surface clays and jungle, is as
follows:—

' 1. Interstratifications of blue and black shale, often very micaceous, with ironstone and coarse felspathic sandstone. These are at
least 1500 feet thick.

' 2. Carbonaceous shale and coal, about 150 feet.

' 3. Shale and coarse sandstone, the latter prevailing towards the
base; thickness doubtful, but not less than 100 feet.

' If this be correct, the coal only occurs upon one horizon. It is
by no means impossible, however, that other beds may be found.
Coal is known to be exposed in three places. The most westwardly
of these is at Patrápádá, in Angul, a village on the Medúliá Jor, a
tributary of the Aulí river. Here some six feet of carbonaceous
shale and coal are seen on the banks of the stream, capped by clay,
upon which rest the coarse grits of the Mahádeva group. The area
occupied by the beds is small. The next place, which is far better
known, is at Gopálprasád, in Tálcher, on the Tengrá river. The
rocks at this spot are nearly horizontal for a long distance, and the
coal-bed extends for some miles along the banks of the stream above
the village. It also recurs lower down the stream. The thickness
of the bed is considerable, but its quality is inferior, the greater

portion being excessively shaly and impure. Selected specimens contain upwards of thirty per cent. of ash, but it by no means follows that better coal may not be found; and even the inferior fuel would be useful for many purposes, if any local demand existed; while from the horizontality of the beds, a large quantity might be procured with very little labour. The general dip in the neighbourhood is to the north; and any attempts at working the coal on a large scale, or further explorations by boring, should be made north of the Tengrá stream.

'The third locality is in a small stream running into the Bráhmaní from the west, just north of the town of Tálcher. Beds lower than the coal are seen on the bank of the Bráhmaní, at the Rájá's residence. The carbonaceous shale with coal is exposed about 400 yards from the river, in the small watercourse. Only two or three feet are visible. The dip is north-west, and the coal is covered by micaceous, sandy, and shaly beds. A boring north-west of this spot would test the bed fairly.

'There is another locality in which the section can be tested, at the village of Kankarápál, in Angul, about ten miles north-west of Gopálprasád. It is by no means certain that the Gopálprasád shale is close to the surface here; but the spot is the summit of an anticlinal, and some black shale seen in the stream resembles the uppermost portion of the rocks of Gopálprasád. It is highly probable that closer search will show other places where coal is exposed at the surface. The south-eastern part of the field consists of Tálcher beds, in which boulders are only occasionally found towards the base. They are micaceous near the village of Porongo. Above the silt-bed containing the boulders, there is a fine sandstone, frequently containing grains of undecomposed felspar. There is no chance of coal being found in this portion of the basin; that is, south of a line drawn from east by north to west by south, running about two miles south of Tálcher.

'In several places in the Tálcher field, iron is worked. The ore varies. Sometimes the ironstones of the Dámodar beds are used, but more frequently surface concretions, the supply of which is necessarily limited. Sometimes the little pisolitic nodules of the laterite are found washed from their matrix, and deposited in sufficient quantities in alluvial formations to be worth collecting. In one instance, the ore was derived from the metamorphic rocks, and brought from a distant locality. It resembled the mixture of peroxide of iron and quartz found at the outcrop of metallic lodes, and known as "gossan" in Cornwall. The method of smelting the iron in small furnaces is similar to that in use in other parts of India; but the bellows employed are worked with the foot, a peculiarity only found in the south-western dependencies of Bengal and Orissa. An account of the process, with figures, by Mr. H. F. Blanford, will be found in Dr. Percy's *Metallurgy of Iron and Steel*, p. 261.

'The arenaceous ironstones of the Dámodar group would, doubtless, yield a large supply of ore.

'DHENKANAL and HINDOL.—These regions require scarcely any notice. So far as is known, they consist of metamorphic rocks, except the western extremity of the first-named State, which comprises the eastern end of the Tálcher basin. The metamorphic rocks are of the usual descriptions.

'ATHGARH.—The northern and western parts of this State consist of metamorphic rocks. Along the Mahánadí, from near Cuttack to the boundary of the State, within three or four miles of the village of Tigariá, there is a belt four or five miles broad, of the same "Cuttack sandstones" as are seen south of the Mahánadí, in Purí District,—being, in fact, a portion of the same basin. The rocks are precisely similar—coarse sandstone and conglomerate, with one or more bands of white clay.

'BANKI.—West of the sandstone area in Purí District, there is a broad expanse of alluvium running for a considerable distance to the southward from the Mahánadí. West of this, again, metamorphic rocks occur. There is a fine semicircle of detached hills running from Bánkígarh to the village of Baideswar. The hills are partly of garnetiferous gneiss, partly of compact hornblendic gneiss—Bánkí Peak of very quartzose gneiss. The strike varies in a peculiar manner, being very irregular, but with a general tendency in all the hills to dip towards the centre of the semicircle. South of the hills is a large undulating plain, partly covered with laterite.'—W. T. B.

INDEX

TO

PURI AND THE ORISSA TRIBUTARY STATES.